SOVEREIGNTY EXPERIMENTS

Studies of the Weatherhead East Asian Institute, Columbia University

The Studies of the Weatherhead East Asian Institute of Columbia University were inaugurated in 1962 to bring to a wider public the results of significant new research on modern and contemporary East Asia.

SOVEREIGNTY EXPERIMENTS

Korean Migrants and the Building of
Borders in Northeast Asia, 1860–1945

Alyssa M. Park

CORNELL UNIVERSITY PRESS   **ITHACA AND LONDON**

Cornell University Press gratefully acknowledges receipt of a subvention from the College of Liberal Arts and Sciences at the University of Iowa, which assisted in the publication of this book.

First published 2019 by Cornell University Press

Printed in the United States of America

Library of Congress Cataloging-in-Publication Data

Names: Park, Alyssa M., author.
Title: Sovereignty experiments : Korean migrants and the building of borders in northeast Asia, 1860–1945 / Alyssa M. Park.
Description: Ithaca [New York] : Cornell University Press, 2019. | Series: Studies of the Weatherhead East Asian Institute, Columbia University | Includes bibliographical references and index.
Identifiers: LCCN 2018060436 (print) | LCCN 2019001070 (ebook) | ISBN 9781501738371 (e-book pdf) | ISBN 9781501738388 (e-book epub/mobi) | ISBN 9781501738364 (hardcover ; alk. paper)
Subjects: LCSH: Koreans—East Asia—History. | Koreans—Russia (Federation)— Russian Far East—History. | Korea—Emigration and immigration— History. | East Asia—Emigration and immigration—History. | Russian Far East (Russia)—Emigration and immigration—History. | Borderlands—East Asia—History. | Borderlands—Korea—History. | Borderlands—Russia (Federation)—Russian Far East—History.
Classification: LCC DS904.7 (ebook) | LCC DS904.7 .P37 2019 (print) | DDC 305.8957/0509041—dc23
LC record available at https://lccn.loc.gov/2018060436

For my parents

Contents

Illustrations

Maps

Figures

Tables

Acknowledgments

Growing up in New York, I found myself surrounded by people who came from elsewhere. Some arrived from a neighboring borough, others from far-off places I had not heard of. It was their stories of journeying that stirred my curiosity about connections between near and distant places and liminal spaces. A personal interest grew into a scholarly one, and this book is the product of that journey.

Many people helped me along the way. At Columbia I benefited greatly from the advising of Charles Armstrong, Jahyun Kim Haboush, Ted Hughes, Adam McKeown, Carol Gluck, and Mark von Hagen, all of whom inspired me and provided constructive criticism when I needed it. Adam wrestled with my draft chapters and chatted with me about the possibilities of doing transnational history. Stephen Kotkin, who first introduced me to Russian history at Princeton, pushed me to think broadly and helped shape the project from its inception. Columbia was also a stimulating place to work because of fellow graduate students. I especially thank Matt Augustine, Li Chen, Hwisang Cho, Adam Clulow, Colin Jaundrill, Charles Kim, Cheehyung Kim, Jisoo Kim, Joy Kim, Liz LaCouture, and Jason Petrulis.

During my research stints abroad, I received kindness from local scholars. In Vladivostok, Igor Tolstokulakov helped me navigate the intricacies of working at Far Eastern State University, Institute of History, Archaeology and Ethnography, and state archives. Aleksandr Toropov and his staff provided guidance in the Russian State Historical Archive of the Far East, and librarians at the Institute of History generously allowed me to use their collection. I give special thanks to Slava and Hŭigyŏng, who helped me transcribe documents because photocopying was not possible. During my stay in Korea, Lew Young-Ick at Yonsei University and Ban Byung Yool at the Northeast Asia History Foundation introduced me to scholars and sources related to my topic. Finally, I thank Ross King at the University of British Columbia and German Kim at Kazakh National University for opening up their homes and personal libraries to me in Vancouver and Almaty, respectively, many years ago.

At the University of Iowa, I have had the privilege of being part of a nurturing intellectual community. In particular, I thank Elizabeth Heineman and Glenn Penny for their encouragement. Jen Sessions always had her door open and provided critical feedback on the book when I needed it most. Shuang Chen is a warm-hearted colleague; I owe her special thanks for checking many of my translations of literary Chinese documents. I am grateful to Stephen Vlastos for reading a draft of most of the manuscript and for believing in the project. For conviviality and meals along the way, I thank Songmi An, Steve Choe, Melissa-Anne Curley, Kendall Heitzman, Yumiko Nishi, and Jiyeon Kang.

A number of colleagues have provided encouragement over the years: Sayaka Chatani, Eleanor Hyun, Nancy Lin, Jenny Wang Medina, and Yumi Kim. I am grateful to Yumi and Charles Steinwedel for reading several chapters of the manuscript and helping me clarify my arguments. I thank Daham Chŏng and Hanshin Kim for annotated translations of several literary Chinese sources into Korean, and Aiqi Liu for translations of two select Chinese documents. Andre Schmid was an ideal "anonymous" reader. His comments and those of another reader helped improve this work immensely.

The project has benefited from the financial support of several institutions. I gratefully acknowledge Columbia University, the International Research and Exchanges Board, Fulbright-Hays Commission, Mellon/ACLS, Korea Foundation, Korea Institute at Harvard University, Council on East Asian Studies at Yale University, University of Iowa, and Kennan Institute of the Woodrow Wilson Center in Washington, D.C. At Cornell University Press, I thank Roger Haydon for guiding the book through the publishing process. I also thank Rob Shepard at the University of Iowa's Digital Studio for making the maps. Paul Behringer helped secure permissions for the images. Any errors are, of course, my own.

Finally, I am indebted to my family and friends on the East and West Coasts and in Iowa, especially Deborah, Felice, Joyce, and Jenny. My greatest debt is to my parents, my brother, and his family. They have been with me the longest on this journey, and I could not have finished without them.

Abbreviations

AVPRI—Arkhiv vneshnei politiki Rossiiskoi imperii (Archive of Foreign Policy of the Russian Empire)

DO—Dalekaia okraina

f./o./d./—convention to denote *fond* (archival collection), *opis'* (subdivision within archival collection), *delo* (folder) for Russian archival materials

GARF—Gosudarstvennyi arkhiv Rossiiskoi Federatsii (State Archive of the Russian Federation)

GAPK—Gosudarstvennyi arkhiv Primorskogo Kraia (State Archive of Primorskii Krai)

Chuhan Ilbon kongsagwan—Kuksa P'yŏnch'an Wiwŏnhoe, ed., *Chuhan Ilbon kongsagwan kirok*

Hanin kwallyŏn charyo—Ku Sŏnhŭi and Cho Myŏnghŭi, eds., *Chungguk tongbuk chiyŏk Hanin kwallyŏn charyo*

Itogi perepisi Koreiskogo naseleniia v 1929 g.—Vladivostokskii okruzhnoi statisticheskii otdel, *Itogi perepisi Koreiskogo naseleniia Vladivostokskogo okruga v 1929 goda*

K voprosu o migratsii Koreiskogo naseleniia—Ispolnitel'nyi komitet Primorskogo kraevogo Soveta narodnykh deputatov, *K voprosu o migratsii Koreiskogo naseleniia na iuge Dal'nego Vostoka (1864–1932 gg.)*

Kangjwa yŏjigi—Kukhak Chinhŭng Yŏn'gu Saŏp Unyŏng Wiwŏnhoe, ed., *Kangbuk ilgi; Kangjwa yŏjigi; Aguk yŏjido*

Ku Han'guk oegyo munsŏ—Koryŏ Taehakkyo Asea Munje Yŏn'guso, ed., *Ku Han'guk oegyo munsŏ*

Ku Hanmal ŭi choyak—Kukhoe Tosŏgwan Ippŏp Chosaguk, ed., *Ku Hanmal ŭi choyak*

l.—*list* or *listy* (page number) for Russian archival materials

Obzor PO—Obzor Primorskoi oblasti

RGIADV—Rossiiskii gosudarstvennyi istoricheskii arkhiv Dal'nego Vostoka (Russian State Historical Archive of the Far East)

Tongmun hwigo—Pae Usŏng and Ku Pŏmjin, eds., *Kugyŏk 'Tongmun hwigo' pŏmwŏl saryo*

VEV—Vladivostokskie eparkhial'nye vedomosti

This book is a transnational history of a people and place, located at the intersection of four states and at the putative divide between East Asia and Russia. Writing about this subject has required a careful consideration of names and terms because naming itself lay at the heart of disputes between various actors in the region. I clarify terms below and explain administrative-territorial toponyms to help the reader along.

Places

The "Tumen valley" is the name I give to a region that spanned the contiguous areas of the Maritime Province in Russia, Jilin Province in China, and Hamgyŏng Province in northern Korea. It is a geographical designation for a region through which the Tumen River flowed.

More specifically, the book focuses on the Kando region in Jilin and Ussuri in the Maritime. Kando was the subject of disputes first between Chosŏn Korea and Qing China, and then Qing/Republican China and Japan. "Kando," the Korean transliteration for "island in between" (Kantō in Japanese; Jiandao in Chinese), came into use in the late nineteenth century. The toponym, however, was never agreed upon. The area was referred to in general terms, such as "area near the river," as well as "Yanji" in the Qing case and "Kando" in the Chosŏn case. The Japanese called the region "Kantō" and established a consular regime there in 1907. For discussion prior to 1907, I use topographical designations for the region ("left" or "north bank of the Tumen") and privilege the Korean transliteration of "Kando" because that is what the majority population of Koreans called it. After 1907, when the region's districts and cities were discussed with more specificity in documents, I give both Chinese and Korean transliterations, which are still in use today. My choices should not be read as acquiescence to the nationalist and imperialist views of contemporaries. The same holds for my use of "Manchuria," which refers to the region of northeast China bordering on Korea and Russia.

The territory of Kando in the book roughly corresponds to that of present-day Yanji, Tumen, Longjing, Helong, and Hunchun cities and Wangqing County in Yanbian Prefecture, which is also known as the Korean Autonomous Prefecture,

People's Republic of China. The area of Kando in the Tumen valley map, based on data from 1911, covers about 10,100 sq. mi. The boundary lines should be taken as approximate.

On the Russian side, I focus on South Ussuri, the southernmost part of the Maritime Province. Ussuri, which extended from the Korean border in the south to the Khabarovsk area in the north, became part of Russia in 1860. By 1888, Ussuri had been divided into South Ussuri and Ussuri Cossack (military) lands. They formed two of nine *okrug* in the Maritime Province. In official documents, Ussuri and South Ussuri are often used interchangeably, and there is ambiguity about whether or not military lands are included in survey data. In part, the lack of precision stems from the fact that most civilians in Ussuri and the Maritime were concentrated in the southernmost part of South Ussuri; there was little need to distinguish between administrative units when discussing the population. My own terminology follows the language in the sources. For general discussion about the region, I use Ussuri, but for analysis of population figures, I refer to the more specific South Ussuri.

South Ussuri's names and boundaries changed over time. In the early 1900s it spanned 73,000 sq. mi., roughly equivalent to the area of present-day Primor-skii Krai. By 1913 South Ussuri's area had decreased to 56,000 sq. mi. It had also ceased to exist as an administrative unit. In the 1920s, under the Soviet regime, most of former South Ussuri's territory became part of a newly established Vladi-vostok *okrug*, which appeared to extend just beyond Lake Khanka (about 33,000 sq. mi.). It consisted of 14 *raiony*. In 1930, Vladivostok *okrug* ceased to exist, but the *raiony* remained.[1] Delineations for South Ussuri in the Tumen valley map are based on 1907 data and should be taken as approximate.

I also expand discussion to include the Maritime Province (Primorskaia oblast', Primore) and the Russian Far East (Dal'nyi Vostok), which, in the book, refer to the two most populous provinces of the Maritime and Amur. Tsarist officials often spoke of their agenda in the region in general terms and used Ussuri, Maritime, Priamur, and Russian Far East interchangeably; I follow con-temporary usage. As for the Russian Far East, it is a geographical description of the region that extends from Lake Baikal to the Pacific Ocean. In adminis-trative terms, it was part of the Governor-Generalship of Eastern Siberia until 1884. It then became part of the Priamur Governor-Generalship (1884–1917), which included the Maritime, Amur, Transbaikal (until 1905), and Kamchatka (until 1909) Provinces and Sakhalin Island (after 1909). After 1917, the Maritime

---

1. *Obzor PO za 1901–2 g*, appendix 1; *Obzor PO za 1913 g.*, appendix 1; *K voprosu o migratsii Koreiskogo naseleniia*; Fridtjof Nansen, *Through Siberia*, trans. Arthur G. Chater (London, 1914), 333; A. I. Krushanova, ed., *Administrativno-territorial'noe delenie Primorskogo kraia* (Vladivostok, 1984), 10.

Province and Russian Far East underwent several boundary and name changes.[2] The term "Far East" is a common abbreviation of "Russian Far East," and not a contemporary Orientalist reference for "the East" or Asia.

Terms

Some readers may wonder why I use "migrant" to refer to Koreans in Russia and China because it does not convey their tendency to settle in these countries. They may also point out that it is not an accurate rendering of terms that were used at the time. In East Asian countries, officials employed various expressions, including "border trespassers," "wanderers," "cultivators," and "our people"; Russian administrators described them as "people who resettle," "foreign Koreans," and "yellows." I am sensitive to the ways in which these terms were used by officials— to possess, use, exclude, and punish Koreans in law and in discourse. Indeed, one of the goals of this book is precisely to place these terms in their historical context, and to show how disagreements over how to categorize Koreans emerged, changed, and were grappled with. I use "migrant" and "mobile" as general terms to describe Koreans who moved across borders and lived in a new country for a season or indefinite period. I also use Korean "settler," though it should be noted that the term (and its variants) was a contemporary expression that conveyed the respective colonizing projects of the Chosŏn, Russian, Qing, and Japanese governments in the region. The term "settler" is helpful in specific cases to distinguish those who demonstrated an intention to remain in a new place from those who intended to stay there for a season. Because Koreans moved between several countries that lay in close proximity to each other, however, the line between a "migrant" and a "settler" was frequently blurred. Finally, I use neutral terms, such as "arrivals" and "those who left."

I distinguish "migrants" from "émigrés," a privileged, cosmopolitan group of Koreans who traveled and lived in Russia, China, and other places to conduct anti-Japanese activities. Most migrants and settlers were economically and socially marginalized.

I usually refer to Korean migrants and settlers as "Koreans." The term denotes those who shared a common country of origin, Korea. Most of the "Russians" who migrated to the Russian Far East were "Little Russians" (Ukrainians). I use "Russian" when discussing these settlers to retain the language of contemporary documents. These designations should not be read as an acceptance of either the

---

2. John J. Stephan, *The Russian Far East* (Stanford, 1994).

idea of primordial ethnic identities or the ways in which identity was mobilized by Korean and Russian (Orthodox Eastern Slav) nationalists.

For readability, common English renderings for proper nouns, such as Seoul, have been used. The Library of Congress system has been used to transliterate Russian names and words, the McCune-Reischauer for Korean, and *pinyin* for Chinese. The Russian transliteration of East Asian proper nouns has been retained; when the original name can be ascertained, it is noted and transliterated according to one of the aforementioned systems. In Korean, Chinese, and Japanese personal names, the surname precedes the given name. The apostrophe for the soft sign in Pos'et district has been suppressed and the name rendered as Poset. All translations are the author's unless otherwise noted.

Weights and measures remain in their original form. Definitions can be found in the glossary.

Dates for East Asian events and sources have been converted to the Gregorian calendar. Dates for Russian events and sources follow the Julian calendar (thirteen days behind the Gregorian calendar) until January 31, 1918, when Russia adopted the Gregorian calendar.

The notes omit subtitles and publishers of cited works. Full citations can be found in the bibliography.

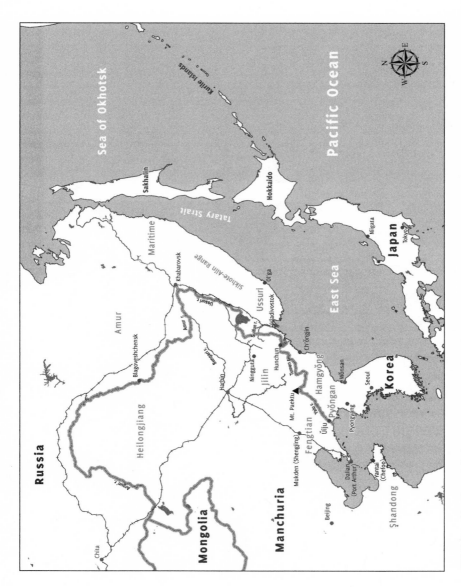

MAP 1. Northeast Asia

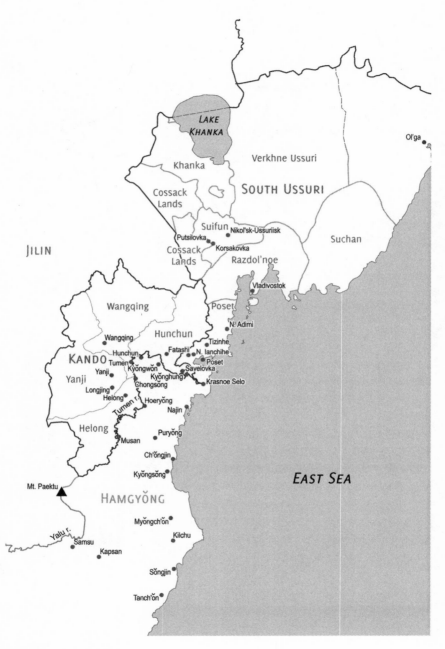

MAP 2. Tumen valley

SOVEREIGNTY
EXPERIMENTS

Introduction

This story takes place in the Tumen valley, a borderland that buffered Chosŏn Korea and Qing China for centuries and, after the redrawing of the boundary in 1860, included the Russian empire. Though located in a remote periphery, distant from centers of power in St. Petersburg, Beijing, and Seoul, the Tumen acted as a crucible in which statesmen tested a fundamental idea that came to define the modern sovereign state: the alignment of state authority with territorial borders and people. In the late nineteenth century, fissures in the East Asian realm and the arrival of Western imperialism sparked conflicts about how this conception of sovereignty could be implemented in a borderland where state authority had long been asserted but not necessarily enforced. Multiple powers angled to legitimate old and new claims to territory by conducting diplomacy and signing treaties, and, often when those methods failed, by resorting to violence. Parallel to these collisions over geography, a quieter, more complex debate unfolded over how to exercise sovereignty over people—mobile Koreans.

In the mid-nineteenth century, Koreans began to leave their native villages in Hamgyŏng Province by the thousands and plant themselves in the Russian Maritime and Chinese Jilin Province, a stone's throw across the Tumen River. They brought their families and oxen, erected thatched-roofed houses, and raised farms of vegetables, barley, and rice that fed the region's growing population. Each year, their numbers were buoyed by the arrival of families as well as seasonal laborers who came to work in the fledgling industries of agriculture, mining,

1

and construction. Entire communities also crossed back and forth between Russia and China. By the century's end, Koreans formed the largest ethnic population on all three sides of the Tumen. In the Maritime Province, they grew from approximately 20,000 in the late 1890s to 150,000 in 1929.[1] On the Chinese side, Koreans rose in number from 50,000 in 1910 to 280,000 in 1919.[2]

The dramatic rise in Korean migration had much to do with the transformation of the Tumen valley itself. In 1860 the Tumen's boundaries were abruptly remapped. The Qing empire ceded thousands of acres of historic lands in the northeast to Russia, giving the latter a border with Korea and a permanent place in East Asia. The geographical remapping of the region both integrated the Tumen into a larger world and created an intimate space where contiguous states and peoples came into close contact. Koreans, along with Russians, Han Chinese, Japanese, and others, arrived at the banks of the Tumen and intermingled with indigenous tribes who had long made it their home. Environmental and economic factors further pushed people to the region. Heavy flooding along the intricate network of rivers propelled people across borders to seek a livelihood, while state-led exploitation of the region by Russia and China swept them up in peregrine pursuits, from chasing fish along the shores of the East Sea and gold in the depths of Siberia to peddling wares to meet the needs of an increasingly itinerant workforce. From the late nineteenth century, innovations in transportation accelerated the pace of travel and thickened connections across land and sea. In tides of tens of thousands, Koreans entered and left the Russian Far East every spring and fall. Chinese arrivals reached over half a million in just five years, from 1906 to 1910, exceeding the total number of Chinese who crossed into the United States over six decades, from the early 1880s to 1940s.[3]

Yet, as migration proliferated, the impulse of states to bind people to territory intensified. The settlement and mobility of Koreans across borders drew stark attention from officials of states on all sides of the Tumen, each of which made distinct claims over the jurisdiction of Koreans and sought to restrict their movement. They clashed in their attempts. Chosŏn insisted on their belonging to Chosŏn, Russia proclaimed them as Russian subjects, and China and Japan

---

1. Figures are specifically for South Ussuri, where the vast majority of Koreans resided. P. F. Unterberger, *Primorskaia oblast'* (St. Petersburg, 1900), 31; *Itogi perepisi Koreiskogo naseleniia v 1929 g.*, IV; *K voprosu o migratsii Koreiskogo naseleniia.*

2. Figures are for the territory known as Kando. Another source estimates that the Korean population in Kando in 1910 was 109,500. Nianshen Song, "My Land, My People" (Ph.D. diss., University of Chicago, 2013), 326; C. Walter Young, *Korean Problems in Manchuria as Factors in the Sino-Japanese Dispute* (Geneva, 1932), 27.

3. There were 423,000 Chinese who entered the United States between 1882 and 1943. The U.S. Chinese population reached a peak of 107,000 in 1890. T. N. Sorokina, *Khoziaistvennaia deiatel'nost' kitaiskikh poddannykh* (Omsk, 1999), 39; Erika Lee, *At America's Gates* (Chapel Hill, 2003), 238, 273–74n17.

soon followed suit, respectively calling them subjects of the Qing in the 1880s and subjects of the Japanese empire after 1910. Statesmen also offered conflicting ideas about how to control cross-border migration, wondering whether the responsibility lay with the home state, the destination state, or perhaps an overlapping regime of authority. Which country possessed the right to exercise authority over mobile Koreans and where? Which country the right to control their movements?

This book explores the attempts of multiple states to govern Korean migrants in the Tumen valley. It contends that these processes were part of a broader push by various states to build modern sovereignty in northeast Asia in the late nineteenth and twentieth centuries. Borrowing from recent work in the field of international relations, I define modern sovereignty as a set of "institutionalized authority claims," in which the state asserts ultimate power to a range of activities within a given political space.[4] State authority is both indivisible and territorially bounded. This unitary idea of sovereignty arose with the modern interstate system and was gradually forged through conflicts and interactions at the boundary of states, where their authority was frequently challenged.[5] The mobility of Koreans across the peripheries of multiple states constituted one such challenge. At a moment of rapid transition in the late 1800s, when states in East Asia were subjected to particularly violent forms of Western imperialism, the dispersion of Koreans across borders became another cause for concern. Crossing from place to place, they transgressed long-held boundaries and deepened states' anxieties about protecting their authority over territory and people from neighbors next door. Eventually dubbed both a "problem" and a "question" in officialdom in Korea, Russia, China, and Japan, Korean migrants kindled a competition between states to claim Koreans by defining them as national subjects, incorporating them into their respective states, and creating programs and policies to regulate movement across national territories. These acts of claiming people and defining borders, I argue, were central to the production of state sovereignty in the region.

Told from the interstices of several states, the story of Koreans in the Tumen reveals that sovereignty was not, as is commonly believed, a naturally preexisting institution or unilaterally imposed from above. It was an institution that was forged through conflicts and negotiations over the boundaries of territory and political community. Migrants, who appeared to stretch the borders of one state

---

4. Janice E. Thomson, *Mercenaries, Pirates, and Sovereigns* (Princeton, 1994), 14–15.

5. Ibid.; John Ruggie, "Territoriality and Beyond," *International Organization* 47 (1992): 139–74; Lauren Benton and Adam Clulow, "Legal Encounters and the Origins of Global Law," in *The Cambridge World History*, vol. 6, *The Construction of a Global World, 1400–1800 CE, Part 2: Patterns of Change*, ed. Jerry H. Bentley et al. (Cambridge, 2015), 89–95.

into the domain of another, were essential to this process. Inside each country and across them, they prompted statesmen, diplomats, border officials, and local administrators to grapple with a host of old and new paradigms to address issues of jurisdiction and border control. With no set norms to follow, officials experimented along the way. Until the 1880s, statesmen in Korea, Russia, and China drew on idiosyncratic diplomatic protocols, including treaties about plural jurisdiction and historic tributary relations, to lodge claims on Koreans and control their movement as they saw fit. In the 1880s and 1890s, they sought to apply the terms of jurisdiction and "international" law outlined in newly signed extraterritoriality treaties to the situation on the border. By the turn of the twentieth century, conceptions of state authority over people and territory as ultimate had become naturalized. China and Russia declared sovereign prerogative to justify the inclusion of Koreans as "subjects" or exclusion as "foreigners," while Japan claimed all Koreans abroad as colonial subjects. Tracing the evolution of these governing experiments and their deployment among Koreans, this book shows that it was these parallel and intersecting efforts to govern migrants, settlers, and borders that helped cement the foundations of the modern state.

This exploration of governing practices also examines interactions between officials and migrants. For as much as bureaucrats, high and low, conjured plans to map out the jurisdiction of Koreans and guide their movements, migrants themselves helped shape the course of policy on the ground. By crossing borders and setting up homes in Russia and China, Koreans stimulated statesmen to take note of their acts, legal and illegal, and compelled them to engage in an iterative process of experimentation in which policies were refined according to how migrants received them. Koreans both abided procedures and turned them to their own uses, at once effecting policies designed to control them and subverting those same efforts. This pattern of control from above—mapping Koreans according to national borders—and subversion from below—Koreans' transnational movements and lives—constituted one of the primary tensions of implementing forms of state sovereignty in the Tumen valley. Ultimately, the complexity of the Tumen drove states, particularly the Soviet Union, to drastic measures to achieve ideal sovereignty: the sealing of borders and removal of a bordered people.

The Tumen Valley: A Borderland

The Tumen valley forms the central terrain in which to examine the coming into being of sovereignty in northeast Asia.[6] I have chosen the Tumen not only

---

6. I thank an anonymous reader for the phrasing "coming into being."

because it lay at the geographical nexus of multiple states. It exemplified a site of productive interaction between states as well as between global, regional, and local forces, all of which struggled to establish claims on its territory and people. These interactions were obscured in studies of the region, which tended to narrate its history as a story of diplomatic competition among imperialist powers and the race to carve up the resource-rich area in and around the Tumen (Manchuria, Siberia, Korea). Given that successive wars erupted out of this competition in the first half of the twentieth century, not to mention the Cold War tensions that emerged later, it is no surprise that high-level power politics remained a dominant theme in historical writing about events leading up to 1945. The focus on rivalry, however, yielded narratives that emphasized deep national divisions and portrayed historical actors solely as advocates or opponents of national agendas. Connections across countries and the people in between them, including Korean migrants, were hidden from view. Situating the book in the Tumen is a way to bring these elements to the center and enables the telling of a different story: one where sovereignty was determined in the periphery.

To center people and places in between, the book draws on several related fields of scholarship. The first is borderland studies. Though increasingly diverse in definition, borderland studies are united by a common perspective of seeing the edges of states—frontiers, peripheries, colonies—as sites where power is negotiated and identity is situational. Whereas frontiers are "spaces of narrative closure" that see national expansion as an inevitable end, borderlands are places where "stories take unpredictable turns" at various nodes of encounter.[7] This book considers the Tumen as such a borderland. At the same time, it departs from most borderlands studies in that it does not focus on the nonstate world of villages and indigenous peoples in the period before 1800.[8] Located in the middle of multiple long-standing states—a "bordered" land—at a particular historical moment when the nation spread as the predominant political unit around the world, the Tumen was transformed into an arena where local officials debated the precise terms of political sovereignty and inhabitants negotiated the boundaries of emergent nations. I approach the borderland's history as the history of the consolidation of modern states and their attempt to bring territory, people, and authority claims over them into a cohesive whole.

Such matters of state formation and sovereignty are primary concerns in the fields of international relations and history of empire, both of which focus

---

7. Pekka Hämäläinen and Samuel Truett, "On Borderlands," *Journal of American History* 98, no. 2 (2011): 338.

8. Some well-known works include Richard White, *The Middle Ground* (Cambridge, 1991); Brett L. Walker, *The Conquest of Ainu Lands* (Berkeley, 2001).

on early modern and modern Europe. The former, rooted in the critical theory that inspired the study of borderlands, explores the contingent, "socially constructed" set of relations underpinning the modern system of states. A primary claim is that nation-states were not preconstituted actors and did not possess an already-existing sovereign will to rule; neither were their boundaries permanent. Rather, scholars such as Janice Thomson demonstrate that the precise link between state authority and territorial boundaries was forged in collectivity, as states held each other accountable for acts of nonstate violence emanating in "in-between" places. Through negotiations, rulers came to recognize the territorial boundary as the line between internal and external authority claims. The proliferation of such borders around the globe eventually divided political space into mutually exclusive, territorial units.[9] While scholars of international relations offer a macro view of border making between states, historians of European law and empire focus on how this process unfolded in specific places. They show that issues of sovereignty and territorial jurisdiction became central preoccupations of administrators in colonial peripheries, where a plurality of legal practices sparked conflicts between imperial agents and indigenous peoples. The studies reveal that officials maintained, appropriated, and ultimately extinguished local practices of jurisdiction, thereby instigating a gradual shift toward a unitary conception of sovereignty as the undisputed power of the state over a bounded territory.[10] Together, the two fields show that the modern institution of sovereignty as a mutually exclusive claim over territory and everything within it was far from natural—an inevitable end—but was produced in a process of interaction and negotiation.

The book brings these perspectives of sovereignty and borderlands to bear on the Tumen valley—the meeting place of Korea's Hamgyŏng Province, Russia's Maritime Province, and China's Jilin Province (northeast Manchuria). In many ways, the Tumen stands out as a unique case of a borderland. It was a bordered, governed, state space. Prior to Russia's annexation of the Maritime in 1860, the Tumen region, named after the river that ran through it, straddled the states

---

9. Ruggie, "Territoriality and Beyond," 162; Prasenjit Duara, *Sovereignty and Authenticity* (Lanham, MD, 2003), 20–21; Thomson, *Mercenaries, Pirates, and Sovereigns*.

10. Lauren Benton states that *dominum*, the right to possess territory, and *imperium*, sovereign jurisdiction over people, territorial units, and bodies of law, remained imprecisely defined in European empires prior to the 1800s. Peter Sahlins demonstrates how such overlapping ideas of sovereignty, territorial and jurisdictional, gradually coalesced into "national territorial sovereignty" in modern France. Lauren Benton, *A Search for Sovereignty* (Cambridge, 2010), 4–5; Benton and Clulow, "Legal Encounters," 89–95; Lisa Ford, *Settler Sovereignty*, Harvard Historical Studies (Cambridge, MA, 2010); Peter Sahlins, *Boundaries* (Berkeley, 1989). For a study on East Asia that considers definitions of ethnicity as central to the process of state formation, see David Howell, "Ainu Ethnicity and the Boundaries of the Early Modern Japanese State," *Past and Present* 142 (February 1994): 69–93.

of Chosŏn Korea (1392–1910) and Qing China (1644–1912). The Chosŏn-Qing boundary was one of the only land borders in the so-called Sinocentric Confucian world as well as the most stable. The border's immovability, in part, reflected the longevity of the two states, both of which were centralized bureaucratic polities that understood their territorial realms as finite and visually depicted this understanding in administrative maps. The region also formed part of the "prohibited zone" (*ponggŭm chidae*), officially sanctioned by both governments. Stretching from Liaodong peninsula to the northeast border with Chosŏn and Russia, the "prohibited zone"—also translated as "segregation" or "closed off"— marked the grounds of Manchuria, the historic homeland of the ruling Manchu people. The zone was effectively a policy that banned movement into Manchuria and prohibited private commercial activity there. By passing such restrictions, the Qing hoped to preserve the identity of the minority Manchus and maintain a rich reserve of natural resources. Equally important was its desire to secure a military buffer at its most sensitive border with Russia and Korea, along the Tumen and Yalu Rivers, by stopping its own subjects from leaving and by deterring foreigners from entering. Chosŏn, bounded to the north by the powerful Qing and elsewhere by the sea, guarded its borders more rigorously. It observed its own policy of prohibition. Crossing the border into the "zone" and mixing with outside elements was banned, and anyone who did so was punished severely. Foreigners found to be traveling illegally were also reported and returned to their original country by each government.

Beneath such official proclamations of "prohibition," however, lay a world of encounter and fluidity. Space was made and unmade by the people who lived there. For as strong as the ban on movement was, it could not be effectively or methodically enforced due to weak state presence in and around the boundary. In pockets throughout the region, a fluid, multiethnic society developed. Manchuria beckoned Korean and Han merchants who wished to profit from its trove of resources, and formed a lifeline for runaway slaves who hoped to reinvent themselves in a place where they were unknown. It was also the home, native and adopted, of Manchus and bannermen, who functioned as a military force and manned garrisons in the border area. Together these diverse elements formed communities that depended on one another to survive in a place where the rule of law needed to be negotiated and resources diligently procured. Existing both apart from and among these inhabitants, indigenous peoples flourished in their natural milieu of the Tumen. Seminomadic tribes, including the Heje, Oroqen, and Sibe, traversed the valley according to the season, settling in one spot to farm and moving to another to hunt for snow leopards or forage for ginseng. Allied with no one state, they complied with tribute mandates and offered ginseng and furs to Beijing, but they also engaged in trade with Koreans and Russians. Tribal peoples forged their own spaces of family and government, which simultaneously transgressed and recognized the territory claimed by surrounding states.

This book explores the Tumen borderland beginning in the late nineteenth century, a critical juncture of unprecedented mobility and exchange between states and peoples. During this time, Koreans grew into the largest ethnic group in the border region. A confluence of several factors, including environmental disasters and geographical proximity, drove thousands of Koreans to leave their homes and settle in the "prohibited zone." The presence of Russia, too, pulled Koreans to the region. Having acquired a significant piece of Qing lands adjacent to Chosŏn in the 1860 Treaty of Beijing, Russia embarked on numerous projects to develop its newest territory, finding in Koreans a useful force to fulfill this purpose. Their numbers were also sustained and replenished by seasonal migration. At the same time, Russians and Han Chinese began to settle in the region, the latter largely limited to seasonal migrants. The indigenous population, meanwhile, dwindled. Over time, natives witnessed their enduring sources of livelihood cut off by people who settled their lands and by agents of the tsarist and Qing empires who exploited the territory for commercial gain.

Amid rapidly changing circumstances in the Tumen, Koreans, the largest settled group, became a source of anxiety for the surrounding states. A central argument of the book is that the mobility of Koreans catalyzed a change in how the three states understood and managed the borderland and its inhabitants. To Chosŏn and Qing officials, their presence outside of Korea was vexing not only because Koreans had moved into the banned area and committed border infractions so numerous that punishment was impossible. They also inhabited the territory of a "barbarian" power that was considered an outsider to the region. Russian officials, too, came to see migrants as a problem. On all three sides, statesmen struggled to come to terms with the phenomenon of Korean mobility and settlement, and began to craft novel governing practices out of new and old ideas about jurisdiction, distinctions between subjects and foreigners, and ideas about civilization. In a process that began in the 1860s and lasted through the 1930s, officials of Korea, China, Russia, and later Japan used a trial-and-error process to incorporate Koreans into their states and control their movement across borders. Their actions revealed a shared vision of territoriality as the indivisible realm of the state.

Convergence and Divergence

The story of Koreans in the Tumen is one of convergence and divergence. Convergence can be found in efforts to govern recently arrived and departed Koreans.

From plural concepts and practices of managing people and place emerged a gradual coming together—a standardization—in concepts of territoriality, both the border and everything within it, as the domain of the sovereign state. The book explores the attempted processes of standardization inside and across three countries of how borders and peripheries were conceived and governed, and of how Koreans inside those borders were legally constituted as subjects or foreigners. It further examines the divergence of such practices.

The project of standardizing borders and people is the core project of the modern state: to make territory and society "legible." As James Scott shows, legibility encompassed a wide range of disparate activities, including the standardization of weights and measures, language, and legal discourse, and the establishment of population data. By creating a rationalized, standard grid out of "exceptionally complex, illegible, and local social practices," the state enhanced its capacity to "see" and thus govern its realm.[11] This book argues that these practices were most vigorously pursued in the periphery because the necessity to govern at the state's territorial limit was most intense. In the Tumen, the state's attempts to make society "legible" were continuously tested, undermined, and refined by other states seeking to enforce their own authority on the other side of the border.[12] The presence of transborder Koreans who traveled from place to place also forced states to take notice of the periphery and drove their efforts to govern. By the late nineteenth century, preoccupations about contiguous states and transborder Koreans compelled officials to bring the population "into view." To do so, tsarist Russia and Qing China had to shed their existing practices of plural jurisdiction, a system which maintained "distinction and hierarchy" over a panoply of peoples and territories and paid little heed to the difference between "insiders" and "outsiders."[13] Statesmen soon came to see this distinction as central to defining political community. They began to standardize definitions of who constituted a "subject" through policies of inclusion (creating subjects, registering people, distributing passports) and, in the case of Russia, who constituted an "alien" through policies of exclusion (denying subjecthood, appropriating temporary status on migrants). Chosŏn, too, aspired to solidify the boundaries of its political community by registering

---

11. James C. Scott, *Seeing Like a State* (New Haven, 1998), 2.

12. In contrast to the stark distinction that James Scott draws between the "ungoverned periphery" and "governed" state space, this book shows that the Tumen borderland, despite being considered a periphery by Korea and China, was not ungoverned. The existence of the "prohibition" policy between the two states proves this. What shifted in the nineteenth century was the intensification of attempts to incorporate the periphery into more sharply delineated states. James C. Scott, *The Art of Not Being Governed* (New Haven, 2009).

13. Jane Burbank and Frederick Cooper, *Empires in World History* (Princeton, 2010), 8.

the Korean population abroad as "subjects" of Chosŏn and persuading them to return. Each state simultaneously undertook to institutionalize the border itself through myriad migration laws and checkpoints.

Seeing border and migrant control as a central practice of the sovereign state allows us to expand the traditional boundaries of histories of migration, immigration, and governance. North Asia and Russia are usually omitted from such histories. This is, in part, because movement was largely intracontinental and was thus recorded as internal movement within empires. But it is also because of an assumption about the character of movement itself as "forced" or state driven, a contrast to the "voluntary" migration seen in the West.[14] This view is reinforced in Russian, Korean, and Chinese documents where the ubiquity of terms such as "registration," "resettlement," and "subjecthood" seems to offer proof that the state treated immobility and deprivation of rights as norms. That their successor states North Korea, the Soviet Union, and China ostensibly took exceptional paths to statehood has further excluded them from broader histories of migration and governance. Because they ended up as so-called illiberal regimes, they are considered deviant, and any comparison to liberal regimes is assumed to be unproductive. In a similar vein, the significant body of scholarship on migration that focuses on Europe, the United States, and the New World in the nineteenth and twentieth centuries has hindered connections from being made. Here, standard accounts take liberal "rights" as an unquestionable ideal. Movement and citizenship are viewed as inalienable rights, and borders as the limits of a liberal democratic nation-state that guarantees those rights. Even studies that critique the exclusionary policy of countries, especially the United States, which historically withheld these rights from "undesirable" immigrant groups, are based in a vision of these states as protectors of the universal right of movement.[15] There is little room in these narratives for stories of migration and border regulation in North Asia and Russia.

---

14. Scholars long assumed Asian migration was propelled by European colonial projects or despotic Asian regimes, a contrast to the apparently free and capitalist-driven transatlantic migrations. In recent years, scholars have moved beyond binaries of voluntary/free and involuntary/coerced movement. Migration was rarely a free choice made by an individual, but transpired within networks of capital, family, and cultural practices. Voluntary migration itself was an outcome of government regulation. Adam McKeown, "Global Migration," *Journal of World History* 15, no. 2 (June 2004): 168–82. For works on migrant networks, see Charles Tilly, "Transplanted Networks," in *Immigration Reconsidered*, ed. Virginia Yans-McLaughlin (New York, 1990), 79–95; Jan Lucassen and Leo Lucassen, *Migration, Migration History, History* (Bern, 1999); Adam McKeown, *Chinese Migrant Networks and Cultural Change* (Chicago, 2001). This scholarship should be distinguished from histories that focus on actual coerced movement, including the slave trade and transportation of indentured laborers.

15. The trope "nation of immigrants" articulates a belief in the United States' exceptionalist role in upholding liberal democratic ideals by its ostensible welcome of immigrants. This view is powerfully influenced by nationalism, as Mae Ngai argues. Recent works put U.S. immigration history in a broader transnational and global framework, showing that policies of exclusion and border control

Analyzing mobility and border governance in a global context, as universal tools of surveillance employed by all sovereign states, fosters comparisons. Despite their varying geographical and political contexts, officials in the Tumen and their counterparts elsewhere around the world acted with a like mind to confront the phenomenon of mass mobility from the nineteenth century. In Russia, attempts to standardize definitions of "subjects" and "aliens" paralleled the actions of nation-states to define the boundaries of their citizenries by excluding unwanted immigrants. Tsarist border officials also looked to the Anglophone world to adopt legal models to exclude "Asians" from entering their territory, participating in a converging global discourse. And across the Tumen, Chosŏn, Qing, and Russian statesmen's calls to unilaterally decide the jurisdictional status of Koreans resonated with the actions of other countries in the New World, which declared immigration and border control as the prerogative of the sovereign state.[16]

For all that the story of the Tumen reveals about convergence in state practices, however, the region also witnessed significant divergence for which the book also accounts. Russia and China embarked on a similar path to simplify jurisdiction in their vast multiethnic empires and unify the definition of political community. Yet this path led them to starkly different end points in the early decades of the twentieth century. While landed empires elsewhere collapsed, Russia preserved its autonomy over territory and people. Its actions toward Koreans in the Far East (Dal'nyi Vostok) tested and reinforced this position. Though initially engaging in debates with the Qing and Chosŏn over the mobile population, tsarist officials decided the fate of Koreans unilaterally, by establishing a cutoff year that determined who would become "subjects" and who would become "foreigners." This policy was enforced at the local level in Korean villages, where officials carried out investigations to identify potential subjects, deported squatters, and conducted missions to assimilate the empire's newest subjects. The regime's policies in the Far East mirrored its actions on the western end of the empire. In 1922, following the Bolshevik Revolution and ensuing civil war, the Soviet Union resumed the project. And by the 1930s, fears of a rising Japanese power on its eastern border, coupled with the frenzy of the campaign of Great Terror from within, drove this border-building project to an apogee: the complete removal of Koreans from the Soviet Far East.

---

were part of a common endeavor of emerging nation-states to implement new forms of sovereignty. Mae Ngai, *Impossible Subjects* (Princeton, 2004), 11; Lee, *At America's Gates*; Adam McKeown, *Melancholy Order* (New York, 2008); Rachel St. John, *Line in the Sand* (Princeton, 2011); Kornel Chang, *Pacific Connections* (Berkeley, 2012).

16. Ngai, *Impossible Subjects*; Lee, *At America's Gates*; McKeown, *Melancholy Order*; St. John, *Line in the Sand*; Chang, *Pacific Connections*.

The case of China serves as a counterpoint to what unfolded in Russia. China was unable to act decisively with regard to its Korean population. Its contested status as a sovereign state left the issue of borders and jurisdiction open to ongoing interpretation and debate with other states. From the 1880s to early 1900s, Chosŏn was a formidable opponent to the Qing. The Chosŏn court not only refused to relinquish its claims over Koreans but also insisted that the territory they inhabited on the Qing side of the Tumen, called Kando, was its own rightful possession. It lodged repeated protests to the Qing, dispatched overseers to manage the expatriate population, and conducted missions to map the sources of the Tumen River on Mount Paektu. Not until the end of the Russo-Japanese War in 1905 was Chosŏn's voice in the debate silenced. Having established a protectorate over Korea, Japan assumed control of Chosŏn's foreign affairs. It concluded a treaty with the Qing to create Japanese-owned extraterritorial leaseholds in Kando and left the Qing to contend with the formation of a semicolony within its borders. Kando and its Koreans remained ambiguous legal entities, belonging fully to neither China nor Japan. The imbroglio intensified in subsequent years. In the 1930s, Japan's founding of the state of Manchukuo in northeast China added complexity to the matter and drew the attention of the international community to the region. The "question" of Koreans' legal status in Manchuria escalated into an international concern, suspended between the claims of the Japanese empire and a fractured China. The issue reached a resting point only in the early 1950s, following the defeat of Japan in the Second World War and the reemergence of China and the two Koreas as sovereign powers.

The result of these projects was uneven. Given the relatively weak state presence in the Tumen, policies were often left unenforced. When the law was implemented, it more often produced unwanted consequences, such as the illegal selling of documents or the circumvention of border checkpoints. Authorities were also prone to making mistakes. Yet it would be hasty to dismiss altogether the significance of these governing projects because of their ostensible inefficacy. Laws and policies did have clear effects on Koreans. Over time, they created structures that channeled migration, defined registration practices, and shaped institutions, penetrating down into the everyday lives of migrants. Koreans put the law to creative use as well. In Russia, where Koreans were officially designated heads of villages and counties, the highest level of peasant self-government, they not only employed the law to conduct surveillance as tsarist officials mandated but also selectively adapted the law to create a space for their own practices to flourish. The standardization of subjects as a legal category also enabled Koreans to slip in and out of a particular status; Koreans chose which one suited them best, petitioning for "Russian" subjecthood in one year and applying for

"Chinese" residence status in another. Despite officials' laments about the proliferation of such illegal activities and loopholes, these practices, in fact, were
among the best signs that the law was being acknowledged.

Between Nationalist and Imperialist Histories

In a book that tracks several strands of convergence and divergence across multiple countries, it is nevertheless Korean migrants—the conflicts and interactions they produced—that weave these narratives together into a single story.
The modern Korean "diaspora" has occupied a central place in scholarly discussion in recent years.[17] Indeed, given the diaspora's place among the largest
population movements in the region in the first half of the twentieth century,
this notice is long overdue.[18] At the end of the Pacific War, at least 12 percent
of the entire Korean population ended up outside of Korea proper: Japan and
Manchuria each had 1,500,000, while the population of 170,000 in the Russian
Far East had been moved to Central Asia.[19] Though many of these Koreans
returned to Korea after the war, those who remained in their adopted countries

---

17. I define "diaspora" broadly as a people of shared origin whose movements have taken
them outside their original country or putative homeland. I do not use it to refer to an essential-
ized "Korean" ethnicity. "Diaspora" has expanded beyond its original meaning of Jewish exile to
include transnational ties between mobile people and their "home," a perspective, a consciousness,
circulation, and subjective experiences of displacement and cultural hybridity. See William Safran,
"Diasporas in Modern Societies," *Diaspora* 1 (1991): 83–99; Adam McKeown, "Conceptualizing Chinese Diasporas, 1842–1949," *Journal of Asian Studies* 58, no. 2 (May 1999): 306–37; Sunil Amrith,
"Tamil Diasporas Across the Bay of Bengal," *American Historical Review* 114, no. 3 (2009): 547–72;
Shelly Chan, "The Case for Diaspora," *Journal of Asian Studies* 74, no. 1 (2014): 107–28. For a review
and critique of diaspora studies, see Aihwa Ong, *Flexible Citizenship* (Durham, NC, 1999), 12–16.
18. Much of the recent Anglophone work on Korean "diaspora" in northeast Asia focuses on the
postwar and contemporary periods. Contesting notions of stable identity and place, these nuanced
works explore issues of transnationalism, entrepreneurship, culture, and citizenship in present-day
communities. See John Lie, *Zainichi (Koreans in Japan)* (Berkeley, 2008); June Hee Kwon, "Mobile
Ethnicity: The Formation of the Korean Chinese Transnational Migrant Class" (Ph.D. diss., Duke University, 2013); Sharon Yoon, "Re-Conceptualizing the Enclave in an Era of Transnationalism" (Ph.D.
diss., Princeton University, 2013); Jaeeun Kim, *Contested Embrace* (Stanford, 2016); Hyun-Gwi Park,
The Displacement of Borders among Russian Koreans in Northeast Asia (Amsterdam, 2018). For historical works on the 1920s through 1945, see Hyun Ok Park, *Two Dreams in One Bed* (Durham, NC, 2005);
Ken Kawashima, *Proletarian Gamble* (Durham, NC, 2009). Work on "diasporic" migration before the
1920s, especially Russia, remains scant, and this book helps fill that gap.
19. These commonly cited figures are for 1944 and taken from Irene Taeuber, "The Population
Potential of Postwar Korea," *Far Eastern Quarterly* 5, no. 3 (May 1946): 298; Irene Taeuber and George
Barclay, "Korea and the Koreans in the Northeast Asian Region," *Population Index* 16, no. 4 (October 1950): 289, 292; Glenn Trewartha and Wilbur Zelinsky, "Population Distribution and Change in
Korea," *Geographical Review* 45, no. 1 (January 1955): 4, 14, 25. More recent studies estimate higher
figures: 1.7 million in Manchuria, 1.9 million in Japan, and at least 15 percent residing outside Korea

formed the base of some of the largest minority populations in each of those states.[20] Today, there are 1,800,000 ethnic Koreans in the People's Republic of China, 500,000 in Japan, and, until the collapse of the Soviet Union, 450,000 in its former territories.[21]

Yet it is perhaps because this mobility reached its peak at the height of international tensions in northeast Asia and came to a halt at the beginning of the Cold War that existing diaspora scholarship has effaced the interactions and dialogue that Korean migrants sparked in an earlier period. Scholars examining the history of Koreans abroad have subsumed it within separate, national histories.[22] In the Korea field, there is a tendency to portray Koreans in China or Russia—or any place abroad, for that matter—as tethered to an ethnic Korean homeland, believed to be an unchanging repository for an ancient people and state. Contending that these ties were preserved even after Korea's colonization by Japan, scholars focus on a politically active group of émigrés who waged a guerrilla war to free Korea from its colonizer and conducted campaigns to spread ideas about the nation among their compatriots in Manchuria, Russia, and the United States. That many of these émigrés became leaders of North and South Korea after 1945 seemed to validate such nationcentric stories of loyalty and purity. In the Soviet Union and People's Republic of China, the few scholars who wrote histories of diaspora, many ethnic Koreans themselves, were mostly concerned with proving the usefulness or devotion of Koreans to their adopted country, as well as their marked success in retaining an essential Korean nature.[23] Such narratives mistakenly assume the existence of discrete and stable Korean, Chinese, and Russian identities.

in 1944. See Pak Kyŏngsuk, "Singminji sigi (1910 nyŏn–1945 nyŏn) Chosŏn ŭi in'gu tongt'ae wa kujo," *Han'guk in'guhak* 32, no. 2 (August 2009): 29–58.

20. The supreme commander for the Allied powers undertook a massive repatriation program in 1945–46. It facilitated the repatriation of 1.1–1.5 million Koreans from Japan to Korea, but there was significant movement of Koreans back to Japan. Taeuber and Barclay, "Korea and the Koreans," 290; Matthew Augustine, "From Empire to Nation" (Ph.D. diss., Columbia University, 2009), 79.

21. The Japan figure is for 2015; the China figure is for 2010. There are 737,000 Koreans in Yanbian Korean Autonomous Prefecture, Jilin Province. Korean Residents Union in Japan website, https://www.mindan.org/shokai/toukei.html; China Geo-Explorer II, https://www.lib.umich.edu/database/china-geo-explorer-ii; yanbian.gov.cn; German N. Kim, *Istoriia immigratsii Koreitsev* (Almaty, Kazakhstan, 1999), 9.

22. "Nationalist" frameworks, which take the nation as a natural entity, guide much of the historical scholarship produced in South Korea and North Korea. Recent Anglophone scholarship on Koreans abroad is based in a critique of such frameworks. For a discussion of the problem of methodological nationalism in historical writing, see Manu Goswami, *Producing India* (Chicago, 2004), 13–20.

23. For examples, see Changyu Piao, "The History of Koreans in China and the Yanbian Korean Automonous Prefecture," in *Koreans in China*, ed. Dae-Sook Suh and Edward Schultz (Honolulu, 1990),

While "diasporic" studies valorized Koreans for their exceptional role in promoting national agendas and identities, Koreans rarely appeared in Russian and Soviet histories. If they were mentioned at all, they were included in broad histories of empire that counted them as one of many minority peoples in a vast multiethnic state. Such studies of empire flourished after the dissolution of the Soviet Union and the opening of archives in 1991. A primary concern of scholars was to explain the remarkable feat of the Soviet Union in consolidating power over diverse peoples and territories, and its sudden collapse into fifteen distinct states. Setting their studies in the center and the periphery, historians showed that the Soviet state had actively supported and "engineered" the making of ethnicities and "nationalities."[24] In this scholarship, Koreans, as well as other minority groups, figured as recipients of the central state's programs. Histories of pre-1917 Russia, too, focused on the actions and imaginings of the state on its borders. Notwithstanding their emphasis on the challenges that officials faced in colonizing and assimilating the "borderlands," these centrist histories were primarily interested in how the Russian empire carried out a project of incorporation, and they tended to portray minority ethnic groups on the frontier solely as objects of this imperial project.[25] The groups were significant only insofar as they shed light on the imperial self and revealed how the empire had transformed them.[26] The particular transnational circumstances of Koreans—circular movements, cross-border ties of family and work, association with Korea and the Japanese empire—were overlooked.

Integrating sources from multiple geographies and languages opens a new window to explore the transnational dimensions of Korean migration and its impact on three states. Single nation- and empire-centric histories, which limit

---

44–77; Syn Khva Kim, *Ocherki po istorii Sovetskikh Koreitsev* (Almaty, Kazakhstan, 1964); B. D. Pak, *Bor'ba Rossiiskikh Koreitsev za nezavisimost' Korei* (Moscow, 2009).

24. In the Soviet period, "nationality" (*natsional'nost'*) referred to titular (main) "national identities" that were imputed on various ethnic groups. For example, Russians officially had a Russian nationality, Koreans a Korean nationality. "Nationality" was different from "citizenship," which was Soviet. Suny argues that the "creation" of nationalities contributed to the demise of the Soviet Union. Ronald Grigor Suny, *The Revenge of the Past* (Stanford, 1993); Yuri Slezkine, "The USSR as a Communal Apartment," *Slavic Review* 53, no. 2 (Summer 1994): 414–52; Terry Martin, *The Affirmative Action Empire* (Ithaca, 2001). For an analysis of this literature, see the introduction to Francine Hirsch, *Empire of Nations* (Ithaca, 2005).

25. Michael Khodarkovsky, *Russia's Steppe Frontier* (Bloomington, IN, 2002); Willard Sunderland, *Taming the Wild Field* (Ithaca, 2004); Nicholas Breyfogle et al., eds., *Peopling the Russian Periphery* (London, 2007); Alfred Rieber, *The Struggle for the Eurasian Borderlands* (Cambridge, 2014).

26. This phrasing is from Hämäläinen and Truett. Writing about early American history, they eloquently point out that such center-driven borderlands histories remain "shadows of imperial narratives" in which indigenous peoples are seen as merely reacting to the center's policies. Hämäläinen and Truett, "On Borderlands," 345, 351.

the study of Koreans to the boundaries of would-be states, have missed their fluid position. A Korean's status was in fact malleable: one could leave Korea, enter Russia as a temporary worker, become a squatter, and move to Qing territory. A Korean migrant was not a permanent member of "our people" (*amin*) or a "settler," as the Chosŏn and tsarist governments respectively claimed. Likewise, reasons for traveling varied. Some moved to acquire land, some traveled to attend to the graves of their ancestors, and some simply went because others did. Tracking sources across borders further allows us to see the striking dissonance and overlap in ideas about political community and territory that migrants generated. Among officials there arose a consensus that Koreans were a "problem" (*vopros, munje, mondai*), a source of preoccupation. Because Koreans traveled across borders close to their native land, one country's concerns about Koreans who left became fused with another country's anxieties about Koreans who arrived. Thousands of documents capture the concerns of officials and the new ideas they generated about the people as developers of land, about claiming them as part of their community, and about excluding others. Together the records show that migrants became a common concern not only because they disrupted existing norms of mobility but also because they challenged what had become the universally accepted ideal of the modern state—strong borders and a fixed community. The diverse range of sources across states—diplomatic documents, internal correspondence, meeting memoranda, reports, travelogues, and newspapers—illuminates the evolution of such ideas and norms and how they were put into practice. The process was continuous, interactive, and experimental.

An exploration of migrants and the conflicts they produced across borders also compels us to rethink conventional definitions of the regions in which their histories have been bounded. For it is not only nation- and empire-centric frameworks that have obscured connections that occurred across borders but also long-held conceptions of Russia and East Asia. Scholarship on the late nineteenth and twentieth centuries focuses primarily on foreign policy and reduces the two regions to antagonistic "others" in which there is little possibility of productive interaction.[27] Though definitions of East Asia have expanded in recent

---

27. For an exception, see Victor Zatsepine, *Beyond the Amur* (Vancouver, 2017). Karafuto/Sakhalin, because of its shifting boundaries, is also an exception; see Svetlana Paichadze and Philip Seaton, eds., *Voices from the Shifting Russo-Japanese Border* (Abingdon, UK, 2015). There is a growing body of works that examine productive relations between Russia and Inner Asia/Eurasia, which I distinguish from "maritime East Asia." See Judd Kinzley, "Staking Claims to China's Borderland" (Ph.D. diss., University of California San Diego, 2012); David Brophy, *Uyghur Nation* (Cambridge, MA, 2016).

years, historians are still reluctant to include Russia in the region because it lay outside the so-called Sinocentric world.[28] Intellectual, social, and economic connections between Russia and Korea, Japan, and China in this period remain vastly understudied compared to relations that East Asian states forged with Europe, the United States, and the Pacific world. In the field of imperial Russian history, too, few scholars have delved into an exploration of on-the-ground encounters between the Russian Far East and maritime East Asia.[29] Recently, scholars have taken the important step of moving away from monolithic definitions of "Asia" as a vast territory from the Black Sea to the East Sea and begun to explore specific regions surrounding the Russian empire.[30] The growing body of works exploring Russia's relationship with the Muslim world and Central Asia, in particular, has done much to advance our understanding of how the tsarist state considered the milieu of its Muslim populations and interacted with those inside and outside its borders.[31] This approach suggests powerful new ways to explore Russia's place in maritime East Asia. For one, it demands that the specific dynamics of the region be taken into account. The presence of long-standing centralized bureaucratic states, Russia's relative weakness vis-à-vis its neighbors, and the frontier character of the area all deeply influenced interstate relations. No single hegemon emerged. This book shows that it was these very circumstances that emboldened various actors to lay claim to the area and the people who inhabited it. At the epicenter of East Asia and Russia—in the Tumen—where no one state or group possessed the upper hand, it became possible for officials, diplomats, explorers, and migrants each to seize the opportunity to participate in what I call the "sovereignty experiment."

The structure of the book reflects its concern in tracing the governance of Korean migrants at the international, national, and local levels, and its particular interest in what unfolded on the Russian side. Part 1, "Across the Tumen Valley," moves

Eurasian frontier zones prior to the nineteenth century are the subject of much scholarship. See, for example, Peter Perdue, *China Marches West* (Cambridge, MA, 2005).

28. Recently, historians have attempted to broaden the definition of East Asia beyond China, Japan, and Korea to include Inner Asia and Southeast Asia. Giovanni Arrighi et al., eds., *The Resurgence of East Asia* (London, 2003), 1–16.

29. My definition of "maritime East Asia" includes Korea, the northeastern provinces of China, the Russian Far East, Japan, and the islands between Russia and Japan.

30. Scholars have noted that the complexity and diversity of the Russian empire necessitate a regional approach. See Anatolyi Remnev, "Siberia and the Russian Far East in the Imperial Geography of Power," in *Russian Empire*, ed. Jane Burbank et al. (Bloomington, IN, 2007), 425–54.

31. See Robert Crews, *For Prophet and Tsar* (Cambridge, MA, 2006); Eileen Kane, *Russian Hajj* (Ithaca, 2015).

chronologically through time and covers the space of the Tumen valley as a whole, from its prehistory as a sparsely inhabited borderland between Chosŏn Korea and Qing China (chapter 1) to a sharply delineated border region that was claimed by multiple states. It focuses on the engagement between officials to institutionalize borders and define political community. Chapter 2 examines the uncertainty and tensions that arose as a result of the unprecedented migration of Koreans from 1860 to 1888. Korean, Chinese, and Russian officials struggled to reconcile Koreans' migration and settlement abroad with existing norms surrounding the "prohibited zone," Russia's newfound presence in the region, and extraterritoriality treaties. The next two chapters chart the divergent fates of Koreans on the Qing (Kando) and Russian (Maritime) sides of the Tumen valley, respectively. Chapter 3, which focuses on Kando, explores the competition between officials of China, Korea, and Japan to stake their claims on the expatriate Korean population from the late 1870s to 1930s. Set against the backdrop of a dramatic reconfiguration of interstate relations in northeast Asia, it shows how the question of "citizenship" was inextricably tied to the contested sovereignty of Kando and larger Manchuria. Chapter 4 addresses the tsarist state's efforts to govern Koreans in the Maritime Province from 1880 to the 1920s. It sees these policies as part of a broader project to eradicate a pluralistic legal regime in the border region and sharpen the divide between "subjects" and "aliens." These legal categories were subsequently appropriated by Korean migrants to advance their own agendas.

Part 2, "Across the Tumen North Bank," examines more closely the Russian case and the borderland society that Koreans formed at the county and village levels. It is thematic in structure. Chapter 5 explains the migration of Koreans into Russia as a product of environmental, economic, and personal networks and describes the rise of an economy in which Russians and Chinese likewise played an integral part. Chapters 6 and 7 explore the state's effort to bring the project of jurisdiction to the local level, into the heart of Korean settlements. The chapters illuminate the in-between role of Koreans as agents of the tsarist government in matters of administration, law, and religion, and the challenges of implementing "Russian" practices among a border population. After 1905, when nationalist émigrés from Korea began to filter into the region, the Korean expatriate community became the target of a new national project: turning the population into "Koreans."

The epilogue takes up the story of border making in the Russian Far East from the 1920s to the 1940s, when the Soviet Union and Japan competed for sovereignty in northeast Asia. At the height of domestic and international tensions, the Soviet state resettled the entire population of Koreans away from the border zone. More than a peculiar tragedy of the times, as it is often called, the resettlement was an extreme attempt by the state to achieve ideal sovereignty by asserting its power over the periphery and its people.[32] This book illuminates the conflicts and negotiations between migrants and officials that drove this process, and the indelible mark they left on the region.

---

32. I agree with Scott's view that this ideal, which he describes as the "immanent logic" of the state to bring all areas under its control, is unlikely ever to be fully realized. Scott, *Art of Not Being Governed*, 10–11.

Part I

ACROSS THE TUMEN VALLEY

BORDERLAND AND PROHIBITED ZONE

In his travelogue of exile in the late eighteenth century, Chosŏn official Yu Ŭiyang recalled legends of marauders and local heroes who had set foot in the northern region, close to the Tumen River. Every place and town he alighted conjured an episodic history. Stories of "barbarian" Jurchen pillagers,[1] wily Korean magistrates, and generals who had thrashed Toyotomi Hideyoshi and his army[2] followed descriptions about Fort Kyŏngsŏng's "magnificent wall" and Bell Mountain, the former home of Jurchen tribes. The Jurchens had left the region many years before Yu arrived, yet their presence lingered in his imaginings of this place. The northern region, which stretched along the Tumen and Yalu Rivers, seemed as desolate and distant as it had been centuries earlier. Sights such as bustling markets were scarce and the warmth of a palatable bowl of rice even rarer. Meanwhile, lonely Chosŏn officials turned to debauchery and *kisaeng* (professional female entertainers) to lift their spirits, a clear sign in Yu's eyes that this place had morally degraded them.[3]

---

1. Jurchens were a diverse seminomadic people commonly referred to as "barbarians" by Chosŏn. By the early seventeenth century, various Jurchen clans and other peoples in Manchuria were subjugated by Nurhaci, who founded the state of "Later Jin." In 1635 his son Hong Taiji officially adopted the term "Manchu" to refer to all Jurchens and changed the name of the dynasty to "Qing." Mark C. Elliott, *The Manchu Way* (Stanford, 2001), 47–65.

2. Toyotomi Hideyoshi led an invasion of Korea, called the Imjin War, from 1592 to 1598.

3. Yu Ŭiyang, *Pukkwan nojŏngnok*, ed. Ch'oi Kanghyŏn (Seoul, 1976).

Yu's portrait of the northern region aptly captured the multiple worlds that confronted one another in this place, past and present. Rulers of Chosŏn Korea (1392–1910) and Qing China (1644–1912) claimed the fertile swaths of land by the rivers as their own, while hosts of people—including Jurchen tribes, Manchu bannermen, indigenous peoples, Han Chinese, and Koreans—traveled in and out of the valleys, where military conflict and trade formed the primary currencies of exchange. Indeed, contact among various groups was often violent. In recurring cycles, Jurchens attacked Chosŏn villages along the Tumen River, wreaking havoc on the lives of inhabitants and stirring a sense of fear that was not easily dispelled. In hopes of putting a stop to such rapacious acts, the early rulers of Chosŏn erected military forts, including Kyŏngsŏng, which served as visible bulwarks of state presence on the border. They also served as occasional marketplaces, a peaceful means of meeting the everyday needs of Jurchen tribes who would otherwise plunder for farming implements and horses. In the mid-1600s, however, when large numbers of Jurchens left the region, inhabitants' apprehensions about the world beyond the Tumen began to fade. More and more, Koreans began to wander beyond the perimeters of their villages and cross to Manchuria, where a reserve of natural resources flourished under the thick canopy of trees. Koreans participated in a loosely organized economy based on foraging, hunting, and trading.

Most of the visitors to the valley, however, never made it their permanent place of dwelling. Apart from military men, native peoples, and those seeking profit or escape from their former lives, the Tumen valley remained sparsely populated. Its remote geography had much to do with it. Situated at the northernmost edges of the Chosŏn and Qing states—hundreds of miles from the capitals—and surrounded by steep mountains and wide plateaus, the region was inaccessible to all but nearby inhabitants and those capable of alpine feats. For Koreans, memories of barbarian incursions also lingered, making the place feel more distant and dangerous than it was in reality. State policy, too, reinforced the region's relative emptiness. Both the Chosŏn and Qing courts actively preserved the Tumen valley as part of the "prohibited zone" (ponggŭm chidae), a buffer area that was designed to secure peace and stability in a sensitive border area by discouraging movement in general. In the eyes of the respective courts, leaving the area free of people was the best measure to safeguard it.

The region remained a buffer area even after attempts to mark the exact boundary delineating the two states. In the early eighteenth century, Chosŏn and Qing officials followed the example of statesmen across the Eurasian continent, who in their attempt to solidify sovereign claims to territory deemed it necessary to eliminate ambiguous frontier areas between states and clarify the

MAP 3.   Chosŏn-Qing border region

border itself.[4] Chosŏn and the Qing, in fact, had long asserted sovereign authority over their respective realms and even recognized the Tumen and Yalu Rivers
as their shared boundary. Yet the two states had never surveyed the location of
the riverheads or their flows, which tended to shift over time. Court officials
reasoned that a clearly defined border would allow them to conduct stricter
surveillance over border transgressors, who seemed to grow in number every
year. Initial surveying efforts, however, yielded few concrete results. The Tumen
valley remained an in-between place, suspended between political attachment
to far-off capitals and engagement with various peoples. Due in part to a lack of

---

4. Peter C. Perdue, "Boundaries, Maps, and Movement," *International History Review* 20, no. 2
(1998): 263–86; Sahlins, *Boundaries*.

oversight by the respective governments and in part by their desire to preserve the prohibited zone, the region was left to its own. In the depths of the forests and on the banks of the rivers, Korean villagers, indigenous hunters and fishermen, and itinerant merchants continued to interact with relative impunity.

A Military Frontier in Chosŏn

By the seventeenth century, the northern territory of Chosŏn, spanning Hamgyŏng and Pyŏngan Provinces along the Tumen and Yalu Rivers, had developed into a military frontier that seemed a world apart from the rest of the country. Life necessarily revolved around military concerns. The endless cycle of Jurchen attacks, erupting from internecine fighting in Manchuria, compelled the Chosŏn government to build fortresses and border posts near the rivers and to relocate civilians to the uninhabited areas surrounding them. Even after the raids died down, the population lived in a permanent state of alert.

The northern region had functioned as Chosŏn's first line of defense ever since General Yi Sŏnggye, the founder of the Chosŏn dynasty, conquered land up to the Tumen River and declared it part of Korea in the late fourteenth century. By that time, most Mongols living in the region had left, and Jurchens who chose to remain on what was now Chosŏn territory were incorporated into the state. Yi had successfully engaged in diplomacy to subdue the population, granting court ranks to their leaders and making them subjects of Chosŏn to win their loyalty.[5] In the eyes of the court, Jurchens, by shedding their seminomadic lifestyles and adopting sedentary ones, had also left behind their "barbarian" ways. But such political accommodations failed to halt the incursions of Jurchens who had not submitted to the court. They continued to cross to Chosŏn to raid and trade for daily necessities. In response, starting in 1398 with Kyŏngwŏn on the lower Tumen, King T'aejo and his successors built a string of garrisons at Kyŏnghŭng, Onsŏng, Chongsŏng, Hoeryŏng, and Puryŏng; these collectively became known as the Six Forts (*yukchin*).[6] In addition to the garrisons, the Four Counties (*p'yesagun*) were established on the upper Yalu River to stand as visible signs of Chosŏn's power on the border.[7] Border defense also took the form of

---

5. Kenneth R. Robinson, "From Raiders to Traders," *Korean Studies* 16 (1992): 97–98.

6. Soon after Kyŏngwŏn had been established, Chosŏn's actual line of defense was pushed southward because of Jurchen invasions. Kyŏngwŏn was resurrected under King Sejong (r. 1418–50). Musan supplanted Puryŏng as one of the Six Forts in 1684. Kang Sŏkhwa, "Chosŏn hugi Hamgyŏng-do yukchin chiyŏk ŭi pangŏ ch'egye," *Han'guk munhwa* 36 (2005): 300–302.

7. In the mid-fifteenth century, the court decided to close the counties off and leave them undeveloped, giving them the name "Four Abolished Counties." Seonmin Kim, *Ginseng and Borderland* (Berkeley, 2017), 29, 72–73.

trade. In the early fifteenth century, to stop the Jurchen plundering of Korean villages, the Chosŏn court established official markets in Kyŏngwŏn and the coastal town of Kyŏngsŏng, where the outsiders could peacefully exchange horses and furs for goods, such as grain, cloth, and farming tools.[8] Trade was regularized after the Manchu invasions of Chosŏn in 1637, with markets held in Hoeryŏng every year and in Kyŏngwŏn every other year for different tribes. Both sides gained something from this arrangement: Jurchens received foodstuffs and cloth, while Chosŏn secured amicable relations with their immediate neighbors and, later, the new Manchu emperor in Beijing.[9]

To support the garrison system and its expanding role as a frontier trading market, the Chosŏn court resettled peoples from locations farther south through state-sponsored programs. Few Koreans in the early years of the dynasty dared to strike out on their own to travel to the north, which was still associated with "barbarians" and harsh environmental conditions. In the fifteenth and sixteenth centuries, resettlement programs carried a mélange of peoples northward by force or by will, including state slaves, who were promised emancipation and commoner status, and rich and poor commoner families, who were supposed to provide stability to the area. Desirable settlers were given additional incentives, such as free passage and plots of land. As many as a hundred thousand people moved to the north over the course of two centuries and at least ten thousand to the Tumen River area itself.[10]

The northern frontier also became a penal colony for criminals and political elites. Those who had committed misdemeanors and moral crimes, such as violating Confucian social norms, found themselves exiled to Hamgyŏng and Pyŏngan Provinces.[11] Likewise, officials who fell out of favor with the court were sentenced to years of duty in the north. In the early years of Chosŏn, the court permanently resettled a large number of local clerks (*hyangni*) from their hometowns to punish them for obstructing the central government's efforts to conduct land reconnaissance and army conscription in the provinces. It also relocated scholar-officials in the central bureaucracy (*sajok*) for crimes ranging from the concealment of slaves and evasion of military duty to the simple act of crossing the king's will. While officials and their families suffered the stigma of crime, the court reaped immeasurable benefits by moving them. Under this policy of

---

8. Robinson, "From Raiders to Traders," 99–100.

9. Ko Sŭnghŭi, *Chosŏn hugi Hamgyŏng-do sangŏp yŏn'gu* (Seoul, 2003), 121–24.

10. Kyung Moon Hwang, "From the Dirt to Heaven," *Harvard Journal of Asiatic Studies* 62, no. 1 (June 2002): 145–46n23.

11. Sun Joo Kim, *Marginality and Subversion in Korea* (Seattle, 2007), 20–21; Kang Sŏkhwa, "Hamgyŏng-do yukchin chiyŏk ŭi pangŏ ch'egye," 312–13.

relocation, the court was able to remove uncooperative clerks from their traditional bastions of power in the village and transplant a class of skilled administrators and hereditary elites to the north, thus extending the power of the central
government up to the north and down to the local level there.[12]

Despite the diversity of peoples who arrived, outside threats reinforced a spar-
tan culture that revolved around the military. Commoners and slaves, in particular, were directly and indirectly bound to a life of service. Their ties to the
military were strongest in the immediate border area where they were forced to
live in or near the garrisons for survival. In the winter, they huddled in the forts to
protect themselves against the harsh climate, in which icy winds from Siberia and
subzero temperatures threatened frostbite. When spring came, they broke their
plows on the hardened earth to produce food for the growing military population. Apart from farming, their duties extended to reconstruction and repair in
the forts, whose location in low-lying areas left them vulnerable to flooding from
the shallow Tumen River.[13] Inhabitants also bore a heavier burden of taxes than
did those in other provinces—hemp tax, grain tax, labor service obligations, and
military service. The most hated duty was manning the guard post (pasuch'o),
which required working around the clock. One official surmised that this service
was "the very reason the people in forts run away."[14]

Indeed, burdensome duties, natural disasters, and recurring Jurchen attacks
drove many to flee the region in early Chosŏn. While no figures on the total
number of arrivals and departures in this period exist, the fact that the government passed a law called "Runaways" in the dynastic code (Kyŏngguk taejŏn,
1471) suggests that the phenomenon was widespread. According to the law, if a
runaway was caught in flight, he would be executed and his wife and children
made slaves, but if after leaving the north he turned himself in, he would be
safely returned to his original place and his family freed.[15] Settlers frequently
fled from the harsh conditions in the north, while those who had only heard
rumors about the place feigned poverty to escape recruitment. Others took
extreme measures. Thinking that families with no household head would be
spared from relocation, men took their lives; some maimed themselves on purpose.[16] Such patterns of flight and avoidance ultimately diminished the efficacy
of resettlement programs.

---

12. Sun Joo Kim, *Marginality and Subversion in Korea*, 21.
13. Kang Sŏkhwa, "Hamgyŏng-do yukchin chiyŏk ŭi pangŏ ch'egye," 304.
14. Quoted ibid., 319.
15. Hwang, "From the Dirt to Heaven," 146.
16. Yi Sanghyŏp, "Chosŏn chŏn'gi pukpang samin kwa min ŭi tonghyang," *Kangwŏn sahak* 17–18
(2002): 179–80.

The military force itself occupied an ambiguous position in the Chosŏn bureaucracy. The central government, to be sure, honored its commanders and local gentry for their service. After the Japanese-led invasions (1592–98) and Manchu incursions (1626, 1637), soldiers were exalted to near godlike status, and scholar-officials were rewarded with honorary ranks and offices for mobilizing grassroots militia, called Righteous Armies (*ŭibyŏng*), which played a pivotal role in defeating the enemy.[17] Apart from bestowing rewards, the court created a new cavalry in Hamgyŏng, the Chin'giwi, in 1684 to provide a reliable channel for several thousands of soldiers to enter the central military bureaucracy at the lower levels.[18] It also established a supplementary defense force in the Six Forts, manned by those who passed the military examination.[19] Still, the Chosŏn court preferred men of letters, who distinguished themselves by their Confucian learning and their advancement through the rigorous civil service examinations (*munkwa*). It also favored hereditary appointments, a system that privileged families with illustrious pedigrees from the south and disadvantaged those in the north. Even local elites with military learning were unable to break into the ranks of the central military aristocracy (*muban*).[20] The capital Seoul remained the "civilized" seat of government, in which northern officials found themselves excluded.

A perception of cultural inferiority also marginalized the northern territories from the south. Elites who were native to the north were quick to admit their cultural backwardness to envoys or officials who passed through. When local scholars heard that the Seoul-based official Yu Ŭiyang had arrived in the north, they sought him out and confessed, "We are so ashamed of our dimwittedness in scholarship and the literary arts, for we were born and raised in the north."[21] Yu responded to them with encouragement, citing the commonly accepted belief that "it is Heaven that decides the destiny of people." What use was it, then, he asked, "to say that people in the south are always endowed with many blessings and northerners with few?" In a monologue he proceeded to name famous denizens of the north, including the virtuous wife Honggae of Hamhŭng, the trustworthy soldier Immyŏng, and the belletrist Pak Hŭngjong, whose poem was "recited by many people and is famous even in bustling Seoul."[22] Yet the rest of

---

17. Sun Joo Kim, *Marginality and Subversion in Korea*, 27.

18. Hwang, "From the Dirt to Heaven," 153.

19. This supplementary defense force (*pubang*) was dismantled after the Manchu invasions. Kang Sŏkhwa, "Hamgyŏng-do yukchin chiyŏk ŭi pangŏ ch'egye," 312.

20. Sun Joo Kim demonstrates that local elites in Pyŏngan Province rebelled against the central government because of their marginalized status. *Marginality and Subversion in Korea*, 27.

21. Yu Ŭiyang, *Pukkwan nojŏngnok*, 80.

22. Ibid., 81.

Yu Ŭiyang's diary was replete with references to former "barbarian" inhabitants, the customs of the people, and the unpalatable food, revealing his unequivocal prejudice against the region as a backward place.

The otherness of the Tumen valley, the northernmost part of Hamgyŏng Province, was most stark. Local Koreans bore the brunt of enemy attacks and suffered from natural disasters. Location, environment, and the lack of a stable population left its inhabitants dependent on foodstuffs and other basic necessities from the central government and from soldiers and merchants who traveled to and from the region.[23] It was only after large-scale Jurchen incursions died down in the early seventeenth century that inhabitants were finally able to profit from their geographical location and seek opportunities beyond the Tumen.

"Prohibited Zone"

The departure of the last Jurchens from the banks of the Tumen River and the Manchu conquest of China in 1644 initiated a period of relative peace between Chosŏn and its northern neighbors. For a time, it seemed that neither the court nor the local inhabitants needed to worry any longer about Jurchen attacks that had plagued the villages along the embankment. Yet the subsequent consolidation of Jurchen tribes into the single state of the Qing created a new enemy for Chosŏn. The Chosŏn court had esteemed the previous Ming dynasty as the center of the civilized world. The Ming's demise by the "barbarian" Qing was considered a calamity, and the court sought to distance itself from its new neighbor. Security concerns on both sides, as well as a desire for stability, reinforced the relative emptiness of the area.

The emptying of the valley of Jurchens removed a long-standing buffer between Chosŏn and the Manchurian interior. Although most Jurchen tribes had been driven out by General Yi Sŏnggye during battles in the late 1300s, a small number had chosen to remain in what was now Chosŏn territory. Literally called "Jurchen who live at the foot of the fortifications" because of their location in and near the Six Forts along the Tumen River, the tribes submitted to the Chosŏn government and intermarried with Korean settlers while simultaneously

---

23. Kang Sŏkhwa, "Hamgyŏng-do yukchin chiyŏk ŭi pangŏ ch'egye," 312. The Chosŏn government operated mutual relief granaries (*kyojech'ang*) on a national scale, transporting grains from the southern provinces to Hamgyŏng Province during periods of natural disaster. Ko Sŭnghŭi, "Chosŏn hugi Hamgyŏng-do ŭi kyojech'ang unyŏng kwa chinja konggŭpch'aek ŭi pyŏnhwa," *Ihwa sahak yŏn'guso* 27 (2000): 237–60.

maintaining their own kinship systems and ties to other tribes.[24] At the founding
of the Chosŏn dynasty, there were 1,712 adult male Jurchens (782 households)
on the Chosŏn side.[25] While it is unclear how this population fared over time, it
is known that they played a vital role as mediators between their newly adopted
state and "deep-dwelling Jurchens," who resided farther inland. Their trading
partnerships with such Jurchens proved invaluable to Chosŏn officials, as did
their access to information about internecine warfare in Manchuria, including
possible attacks near the state border.[26] In the late 1500s, however, the fortunes of
this population swiftly changed. The Tumen Jurchens became victims of Nurhaci's wars. Nurhaci (1559–1626), the founder of the Qing imperial family who
consolidated control over various clans of Jurchens and other peoples, forcibly
removed this group from the Tumen and resettled them farther south in Liaoning.[27] By 1609, the buffer between Chosŏn and its "barbarian" neighbors had
been wiped out. As official Yi Sugwang remarked, "When the lips are gone the
teeth grow cold—this is an unspeakable worry!"[28] Yi's anxieties about an imminent threat from across the border eventually became a reality. In 1626 forces
from Manchuria invaded Chosŏn's northern frontier; about a decade later, they
struck again. In 1644 the Jurchen tribal people, now known as the "Manchus,"
entered Beijing and declared the new dynasty of the Qing.

The rise of the Qing stirred the animosity of the Chosŏn court, which was
affronted by the idea of a barbarian-led China. During the invasions, the court
had been forced to relinquish its support of the Ming and accept Manchu suzerainty, sending the crown prince Hyojong to Jehol as a guarantee of its submis-
sion. Indelibly marked by his experience as a hostage, Hyojong returned to Seoul
more than a decade later to accede to the throne (1649–59) and plotted to avenge
Chosŏn and Ming loyalists by carrying out a "northern expedition" against the
Qing. Prodigious sums were poured into the military to this end. While the military campaign never materialized, an anti-Manchu policy dominated the court

24. They were more generally known as *pŏnho*. Adam Bohnet, "Migrant and Border Subjects"
(Ph.D. diss., University of Toronto, 2008), 51–52. See also John B. Duncan, "*Hwanghwain*," Acta Koreana 3 (2000): 99–113.

25. More than 50 percent belonged to the Wuliangha tribe; other tribes included the Odoli, Nu-
chen, and Hurhan. Phillip Woodruff, "Status and Lineage among the Jurchens of the Korean Northeast in the Mid-Fifteenth Century," *Central and Inner Asian Studies* 1 (1987): 124–25.

26. Their connections to deep-dwelling Jurchens could also be used against Chosŏn. See Bohnet,
"Migrant and Border Subjects," 51–55.

27. Nurhaci's efforts were met with resistance: various Jurchen clans and other ethnic groups
launched an offensive against Nurhaci in the Nine Tribes War of 1592. Some Jurchens escaped and
fled to the southern part of Chosŏn, in Kyŏnggi Province and the capital Seoul. Ibid., 57–59, 68;
Loretta Kim, "Marginal Constituencies" (Ph.D. diss., Harvard University, 2009), 52–53.

28. Quoted in Bohnet, "Migrant and Border Subjects," 47.

and intellectual circles for decades. The famous official Song Siyŏl, the most vehement opponent of the Manchus, exhorted the court to wait patiently for a heaven-bestowed opportunity to drive out the Qing while continuing to "reject barbarians." In the meantime, a radical idea began to spread in official circles about Chosŏn's new place in the Confucian world: it was now Chosŏn that constituted the center of civilization, not China.[29]

Anxious about the events that portended disasters in Beijing and near the Tumen, Chosŏn officials called for reinforcement on the border. Much of the territory around the Six Forts and Four Counties had remained unoccupied despite the general rise in population in Hamgyŏng and Pyŏngan Provinces. In 1672 Nam Kuman hastened to benefit from the absence of Jurchens. Noting that it had been more than fifty years since the Jurchens had left, Nam urged the government to stop dithering and acting as if the land still belonged to the barbarians. He maintained that the Chosŏn court should instead fill the land with people. This was an "opportunity that cannot be missed" lest a new wave of Jurchens return to reoccupy the land.[30] In practical terms, he proposed that the now defunct Four Counties on the Yalu River be restored and villages in the interior of Hamgyŏng Province moved to the banks of the Tumen River to resurrect the first line of defense. Within the next decade, the fortress at Musan was transported to the Tumen and three new forts were established at Huju, Much'ang, and Chasŏng. Attempts to settle more people along the border were also made.[31]

On its part, the Qing sought to secure its realm in Manchuria through the policy of the "prohibited zone." After consolidating control of China proper, Nurhaci's son Hong Taiji and his successors set out to distinguish the Manchus as a ruling class by delimiting the entire northern territory of Manchuria as the homeland of the Manchus. No one was allowed to settle permanently in the zone unless permitted by the ruler. The ban on settlement was intended to protect the purity of the historic bastion of the Manchus and their way of life, which included values of frugality, simplicity, and skills in warfare. Recent historians have noted that the prohibited zone, where there was likewise a prohibition on private commercial activity, also preserved the region's surfeit of riches—ranging from timber and ginseng to sable and freshwater pearls—as tribute items that

---

29. Andre Schmid, "Tributary Relations and the Qing-Chosŏn Frontier on Mount Paektu," in *Chinese State at the Borders*, ed. Diana Lary (Vancouver, 2008), 130; JaHyun Kim Haboush, "Constructing the Center," in *Culture and the State in Late Chosŏn Korea*, ed. JaHyun Kim Haboush and Martina Deuchler (Cambridge, MA, 1999), 46–90.

30. Quoted in Kang Sŏkhwa, *Chosŏn hugi Hamgyŏng-do wa pukpang yŏngt'o ŭisik* (Seoul, 2000), 36.

31. Ibid., 38.

were to be offered to the emperor. Perhaps most significant, however, was the desire to maintain an empty zone, a buffer, in the most sensitive border region with Russia and Korea.[32] Also translated as "segregation" or "closed off," the prohibited area extended from the Willow Palisade (*liutiaobian*) in Liaoning, the southern limit of the Manchurian homeland, to the northeastern limit on the border with Chosŏn.[33]

Chosŏn upheld its own prohibited policy on its perimeters. In the early years of the dynasty, when security concerns on its northern borderlands were paramount, the court sought to minimize contact with outside elements. In 1492 the court promulgated a law to ban private commercial activity in the Six Forts area in Hamgyŏng Province; trade was only to be held at official markets. A similar policy was upheld around Chosŏn's maritime borders. In the south, the court created an economic trading zone at the Waegwan in Pusan, where merchants from Japan were able to trade with Koreans.[34] In the same way that the court limited outside contact by preventing foreigners from entering its borders, it prohibited its own people from leaving.

Fears about the military strength of neighboring states also compelled officials to tread carefully in the area. In the Chosŏn court, initial hostility toward the Qing reinforced the idea that it was better to preserve the relative emptiness of the border area than to invite trouble from the outside by filling it with people. Thus, resettlement programs went unenforced and construction of roads unfinished; even new fortresses that had been built in the border area at the behest of Nam Kuman were dismantled.[35] Meanwhile, in the Qing, worries about the encroachment of Russians near the Amur River drove officials to deepen its administrative infrastructure. It added border guards (*karun*), created the administrative district of Heilongjiang (in northwestern Jilin), and appointed a military governor in 1683.[36] The borderland remained off-limits to all except those who were native to the region or had been granted permission.[37]

32. Jonathan Schlesinger, *A World Trimmed with Fur* (Stanford, 2017), 148.

33. The Willow Palisade was originally built by the Ming and resurrected by the Qing shortly after its conquest of China. Kim, *Ginseng and Borderland*, 80.

34. For information on the Waegwan, see James Bryant Lewis, *Frontier Contact between Chosŏn Korea and Tokugawa Japan* (London, 2003).

35. Kang Sŏkhwa, *Hamgyŏng-do wa pukpang yŏngt'o ŭisik*, 39–40.

36. Robert Lee, *The Manchurian Frontier in Ch'ing History* (Cambridge, MA, 1970), 60.

37. The Qing government did carry out numerous resettlement programs of Han Chinese and metropolitan bannermen to Manchuria. The official ban on Han migration to Manchuria, however, remained. For an example of such a resettlement, see Shuang Chen, *State-Sponsored Inequality* (Stanford, 2017).

Border Crossings

Though the valley in the northeast remained thinly inhabited, pockets of a fluid society nevertheless existed throughout the borderland. Indigenous peoples, including the Heje, Oroqen, and Sibe, continued their lifestyles of hunting, fishing, and seasonal farming, while Manchu bannermen lived and worked in garrisons and border posts scattered throughout Manchuria. The natural resources of the region also beckoned newcomers. The riches of wild ginseng and timber, in particular, attracted Koreans, Han Chinese, and others to cross into the valley and engage in legal and illegal activities, among them the collection of tribute items, private trade, and poaching of the resources of the area. Given the weak state presence in and around the boundary, native inhabitants and visitors were free to participate in a local economy, apart from the state, with relative impunity.

By the 1700s, the "wandering" (yumang) of Koreans had caught the attention of Chosŏn officials. The term largely referred to the movement of people from their original place of residence to another due to unforeseen circumstances, such as natural disaster or war. A combination of the low population density of the northern provinces and a large number of settlers who had no original ties to that place, especially former criminals and slaves, created the conditions for a mobile population. Their movements from one place to another were sometimes temporary, as seen in the area of Yŏnghŭng in Hamgyŏng Province. In the early 1790s, a bad harvest drove 570 of the approximately 2,500 households to leave their homes to seek a livelihood; over the course of two years, they eventually resettled in Yŏnghŭng.[38] Unregistered and untethered from landed society, "wanderers" (yumin) stirred the anxieties of officials, who attempted to return all to their original place. The sheer number of wanderers was daunting. In 1731 Yi Chongsŏng, a frontier guard on the Yalu River, noted that "tens of thousands" had scattered to places nestled between mountains and cultivated land as they wished. While expressing sympathy for these people, who had no means of a livelihood and no higher authority on which to lean, he nevertheless called for strict control.[39] The overall increase in the population in northern Hamgyŏng may have intensified the worries of officials. By 1759 there were 47,000 households (248,000 people); by 1828 the number of households had grown to 67,000 (390,000 people).[40]

---

38. *Chŏngjo sillok* 17/5/9 no. 2 (June 16, 1793).

39. Pyŏn Chusŭng, "Chosŏn hugi yumin ŭi pukpang pyŏn'gyŏng yuip kwa kŭ silt'ae," *Kukhak yŏn'gu* 13 (December 2008): 202.

40. Figures are for Hamgyŏng Province's "northern region" (pukkwan), which included the Six Forts, Kilchu, Myŏngch'ŏn, Kyŏngsŏng, and the "area near the river" (kangbyŏn), which included Samsu, Kapsan, Musan, Changjin, and Huju. The figures do not include the southern part of the

While natural disasters displaced groups of Koreans temporarily, natural resources pushed inhabitants abroad and back, creating lifestyles of movement. An abundance of timber and ginseng drew Koreans to Qing territory as well as Qing subjects to Chosŏn. Mutual poaching of natural resources had become endemic by the sixteenth century.[41] During his years in Hamgyŏng, Yu Ŭiyang commented on the tendency for inhabitants of the Six Forts to cross to the Qing side of the Tumen River to cut down trees for firewood and for lumber to build houses.[42] Acknowledging that timber was a necessity, the local officer had turned a blind eye to this illegal activity. Distant officials in Seoul also noted that logging on the opposite bank had become a "habit." Even Qing officials accepted the practice during market seasons in Hoeryŏng.[43] The rampant timber cutting shaved the forested mountains to near nakedness on the Hamgyŏng side and drove Koreans across the border to seek out wood in other areas.[44]

The promise of ginseng, too, drew Koreans to the borderland. Ginseng root, named for its resemblance to a human torso and legs (insam), was prized for its practical and magical powers. According to folklore, it not only healed people of ailments and stimulated the senses but also made infertile women virile and restored the dead to life.[45] Competition to obtain wild ginseng was fiercest in the Chosŏn-Qing borderland, where it flourished under the shade of forests on hills and mountains, free from the constant tread of plows and people. It was one of the main tribute items that was offered up to the Qing emperor, and licenses and permits were required to forage for it.[46] Chosŏn, too, was responsible for procuring this precious treasure as a tribute offering, and it was the inhabitants of the border region who bore the largest burden of collecting it for the Beijing-bound missions every year. Ginseng was prized not only for its inherent value as an elixir and tribute product but also for its selling power on the private market. The root became one of the most lucrative and sought-after products on the international market spanning Korea, China, and Japan. It was Chosŏn's most important export. And at a time when China and Japan had not established

---

province (namgwan). More studies need to be done to understand the extent to which natural population growth and in-migration contributed to the population increase. Kang Sŏkhwa, Hamgyŏng-do wa pukpang yŏngt'o ŭisik, 153.

41. David Bello, "The Cultured Nature of Imperial Foraging in Manchuria," Late Imperial China 31, no. 2 (December 2010): 6–7.

42. Yu Ŭiyang, Pukkwan nojŏngnok, 69.

43. Pibyŏnsa tŭngnok, Sukchong 25/6/21 (July 17, 1699).

44. Yi Uk, "17–18 segi pŏmwŏl sagŏn ŭl t'onghae pon Hamgyŏng-do chumin ŭi kyŏngje saenghwal," Han'guk kukhak chinhŭng yŏn'guwŏn (2005): 149.

45. Richard Heffern, The Complete Book of Ginseng (Millbrae, CA, 1976), 46–49.

46. The management of licenses and permits was a complex system that changed over time under the Qing. Schlesinger, World Trimmed with Fur, 79–88.

official relations, Korean merchants acted as middlemen between buyers and sellers abroad and were uniquely positioned to collect a windfall of profit. With a keen knowledge of supply and demand as well as the prices of silver, Korean merchants sold the root to Japan (which had no wild ginseng of its own), received silver as payment, and used it to trade with Qing merchants. At the peak of trade in 1694, a total of 6,542 *kŭn* (3.9 metric tons) of wild ginseng was exported from Chosŏn to Japan via Tsushima Island.[47] The sheer quantity was staggering when one considered the price of ginseng by weight: 1 *kŭn* (600 grams) fetched 192 silver *nyang* in 1663. As the reserves of wild ginseng dried up, prices shot up to 480–640 *nyang* for the same quantity in 1759; to 1,600 *nyang* in 1768; and to 6,400 *nyang* in 1798, when the root had finally become extinct in Korea.[48] While merchants in the commercial centers of Kaesŏng, Seoul, and Pyongyang reaped the most profit, it was the inhabitants in the border regions who controlled the inventory. The potential for profit pushed them to pursue ginseng wherever it grew, regardless of state boundaries.

For many borderland inhabitants, ginseng served as a currency and a lifestyle. A predictable pattern emerged every spring, when individuals and groups traveled to mountains and forests in the Chosŏn-Qing border region for weeks or months at a time.[49] They spent the days foraging and nights resting in makeshift huts left by previous diggers.[50] On their trips, ginseng was a useful commodity that could be exchanged for an array of goods, such as rice, grains, cloth, horses, and rifles from fellow Koreans and from Manchus. People could also exchange it for ready-made Manchu clothes if they needed a disguise on Qing territory.[51] Indeed, officials recognized that residents of Samsu-Kapsan in Hamgyŏng Province considered the ginseng they gathered as a kind of currency, and that crossing the border for ginseng had become a "custom" that supplemented the very basis of living.[52] These practices had become so common that Chosŏn officials

---

47. Calculated from number of "actual imports." Kim Dongchul, "The Waegwan Open Market Trade and Tongnae Merchants in the Late Chosŏn Period," trans. Han Seokyung and J. B. Lewis, *Acta Koreana* 7, no. 1 (January 2004): 19.

48. O Sŏng, "Insam sangin kwa kŭmsam chŏngch'aek," in *Chosŏn hugi sangin yŏn'gu* (Seoul, 1989), 12; Kim Dongchul, "Waegwan Open Market Trade," 18.

49. Similar patterns were seen in farming on Qing territory. See the case of Koreans spending the entire planting season, April to August, in Manchuria and returning to Korea after the harvest. Yi Uk, "17–18 segi pŏmwŏl sagŏn," 154.

50. See the case of a Qing investigation of an area near the Qing-Chosŏn border in which empty houses were discovered. Authorities guessed that the people living there were not residents of the area but periodically came by boat from Shandong to gather ginseng. *Tongmun hwigo*, 4:253–54 (1745).

51. Ibid.

52. *Pibyŏnsa tŭngnok*, Sukchong 12/6/29 (August 17, 1686).

themselves were drawn into the illegal business, participating indirectly by com-missioning individuals to forage and trade on their behalf.[53]

The widespread poaching of ginseng eventually drew the ire of Qing offi-cials, who blamed the Chosŏn court for its negligence. According to the Qing, the court had failed to control its subjects: it had neither prevented the people from entering the prohibited zone nor stopped them from stealing treasures that were the rightful possessions of the Qing emperor. The well-documented Sandaogou incident of 1685 reveals the tensions that had surfaced. That fall, the imperial envoy Le Chu traveled to the border region on the Yalu to conduct a survey for the *Comprehensive Gazetteer of the Qing Dynasty* (*Daqing yitongzhi*), a map of the entire realm. At Sandaogou, he and his companions stumbled on a large group of Koreans digging for ginseng. They immediately began to shoot arrows at the trespassers. The Koreans, shocked and scared, fired back with rifles. At the end of the skirmish, casualties on the Qing side included one dead official, two maimed, and several horses that had been killed in the crossfire.[54] The incident quickly escalated into an international debacle between Seoul and Beijing, because it involved not only the imperial grounds of the northeast but also an imperial envoy from the capital. The Kangxi emperor sent an investigator to Seoul and demanded 20,000 *nyang* to "punish the king for not paying more attention to border security and to warn him to enforce the law in the future."[55] It was a huge sum, especially considering that the Chosŏn court had paid a 10,000-*nyang* fine the previous year for a border-crossing incident over timber. Chosŏn paid the fine, executed the trespassers, and punished local officials.

Despite the reprimand, however, little changed in terms of regulation. To be sure, the severity of the Qing reaction in the Sandaogou incident compelled the Chosŏn court to pass laws regarding mobility and trade. From 1686 to 1690, new laws forbade people from crossing the border to collect and trade ginseng, stipulated punishment for all transgressors, and mandated checks for ginseng and weapon supplies every five days. Those who crossed would be beheaded and their heads hung near the river.[56] The 1686 ban on crossing the border (*pŏmwŏl*) to gather ginseng and engage in commerce, in particular, explicitly stated what had been assumed until that point—that no one should cross into the territory of another country without permission. The ban also enforced the Qing policy of prohibition, which sealed off Manchuria to outsiders. Yet two decades later, in

53. Yi Uk, "17–18 segi pŏmwŏl sagŏn," 144–46.
54. Seonmin Kim, "Borders and Crossings" (Ph.D. thesis, Duke University, 2006), 106–9.
55. Quoted ibid., 108.
56. Ibid., 108–9; Pyŏn Chusŭng, "Chosŏn hugi yumin ŭi pukpang pyŏn'gyŏng yuip," 212.

1706, the Chosŏn ban on ginseng gathering was lifted.[57] It seemed that breaking the dependence of inhabitants on the region's natural resources was too difficult. Indeed, in 1692 a group of illegal ginseng gatherers pleaded with Chosŏn officials that their livelihood was "dependent" on ginseng and that they would die without it. If forbidden from collecting it, they explained, they and others would have to abandon Samsu-Kapsan, leaving it deserted.[58] Similar reports confirmed the concerns of court officials, who noted that the strict prohibitions on border crossing and ginseng gathering had taken a toll on borderland inhabitants, because their lifeline had been cut off and their capital had disappeared.[59]

Countless incidents of border crossing and conflicts occurred in the years following the decrees.[60] Unlucky Koreans were caught by Qing soldiers and were reported to the head of the Manchurian prefectural government in Shengjing, which sent word to the Chosŏn court; likewise, Qing subjects caught on Chosŏn territory were reported to Shengjing.[61] Both governments made sure to repatriate subjects to their original country and punish them on their return.[62] Pillaging of Korean villages and violence between Manchus, indigenous peoples, Koreans, and others attracted the attention of officials. But surprising details about cooperation and adaptation among different ethnic groups also came to light. Whether a gatherer who had wandered too far from his compatriots on a hunting round or an orphan who had lost his way in the labyrinth of foothills, Koreans who ended up on Qing territory learned to acclimate to life among diverse groups. They joined Manchus and Han Chinese on ginseng-gathering expeditions as far as the Amur River, learned their languages, and wore their clothes.[63] Their skills and ambiguous identities made them suitable brokers between Manchus and Chosŏn merchants, who hoped to sidestep the law in search of profit. Such discoveries of cooperation hinted at widespread practices of poaching and border crossing, practices that persisted despite the prohibitions against them.

---

57. Kang Sŏkhwa, "1712-nyŏn ŭi Cho-Ch'ŏng chŏnggye wa 18-segi Chosŏn ŭi pukpang kyŏngyŏng," *Chŏngbo chindan hakpo* 79, no. 1 (1995): 142.

58. Quoted in Sin Kisŏk, "Kando kwisok munje," in *Chungang taehakkyo nonmunjip* (Seoul, 1955), 7.

59. *Pibyŏnsa tŭngnok*, Sukchong 12/6/29.

60. See *Tongmun hwigo* (Compendium of diplomatic documents) for a collection of border-crossing cases from the 1630s to the mid-1800s.

61. Shengjing is also known as Shenyang and Mukden.

62. The issue of repatriation is addressed in chapter 2.

63. *Tongmun hwigo*, 4:308–18 (1817).

Defining the Border

The tide of border crossing and stealing in the late seventeenth century eventually brought Chosŏn and Qing officials to conclude an agreement about their shared border on the Tumen and Yalu Rivers. Given that the two powers already recognized each other's sovereign authority over territory and implicitly understood the two rivers as the natural geographical boundary, coming to an agreement should have been a simple affair. The task of border delineation, however, posed myriad logistical challenges. Marking the exact sources of the rivers required trekking to the peak of Mount Paektu (Ch: Changbai), a treacherous journey through valleys and hills that took several weeks. The prospect of jointly assessing the geography of Mount Paektu, moreover, stirred the emotions of Chosŏn officials, who worried that making such knowledge available to their powerful neighbor would undermine a border policy that relied on preserving ambiguity and empty zones. When the time to delineate the rivers came, officials from both the Qing and Chosŏn found it difficult to part with long-standing practices of governing their shared borderland.

The first sign of difficulty arose in the late seventeenth century when the Kangxi emperor asked for the Chosŏn court's help in conducting an expedition to map the northeast. After quelling rebellions on the other side of his empire, Kangxi determined to consolidate his reign in the Amur region, where the threat of Russians had already brought the two powers to delineate their shared border in the 1689 Treaty of Nerchinsk. The creation of a map of the northeast fulfilled both Kangxi's need to monitor the area and his seemingly insatiable desire for geographical knowledge and learning. Indeed, his penchant for maps led him to commission Jesuit missionaries with producing an atlas of the entire empire (*Daqing yitongzhi*). But when the Jesuits reached the Chosŏn border, Kangxi forbade them to cross it. The emperor, understanding tributary protocol, which prohibited all unauthorized foreigners from gaining access to Chosŏn, assumed rightly that the Koreans would not allow the Jesuits in.[64] Chosŏn officials had similarly rebuffed requests for information about the border area and rejected missions that had been dispatched by Kangxi himself.[65]

Chosŏn officials' endeavors to stop the Qing from gaining access reflected a keen awareness of the correspondence between territory and the limits of state power. The two states, in fact, had already recognized in principle

---

64. Gari K. Ledyard, "Cartography in Korea," in *The History of Cartography*, ed. J. B. Harley and David Woodward (Chicago, 1994), vol. 2, bk. 2, 299.

65. Schmid, "Tributary Relations," 133.

the "finiteness of their realms," as historian Andre Schmid points out. In 1627, after the first Manchu invasion, King Injo and Hong Taiji, Nurhaci's son, signed a joint oath in which the former acknowledged the suzerainty of the ascendant Manchus. In the oath they declared, "We two *kuk* [countries] have now established peace. From today onward, let us respect this agreement, each observe our realms and refrain from disputing trifling matters."[66] Without delineating the exact border, then, the two courts understood that the Yalu and Tumen Rivers constituted the limit of their states. When the Kangxi emperor proposed to map the border in its entirety, including the location of the shifting sources of the rivers in the mountains, however, the Chosŏn court was alarmed. For although the court trusted that the Qing heeded the territorial border, it still relied primarily on an ambiguity of geography and sparsity of peoples to protect its realm against its neighbor. Qing surveys of the border area might lead to a loss of territory or autonomy in the region. Thus, when the court caught wind of Kangxi's most recent plan to conduct a reconnaissance of Mount Paektu during what was officially a murder investigation, it prepared to obstruct the mission in any way possible. In 1710 the Manchu envoy Mukedeng arrived as head of the mission. Chosŏn officials, determined to deter him, steered the envoy up impassable valleys and debated over access to specific areas. They succeeded in undermining his mission. A year later, they heard that Mukedeng would return to complete the survey of Paektu. To prepare for his arrival, officials undertook a thorough review of available maps and atlases, collecting as much evidence as possible to preempt the envoy's arguments. They consulted the *Comprehensive Gazetteer of the Ming Dynasty* (*Daming yitongzhi*) and the *Shengjing Gazetteer,* a contraband book at the time, to prove that land south of the Yalu and Tumen Rivers belonged to Chosŏn. They also conducted preliminary reconnaissance missions to find the sources of the rivers. In spite of the inconclusiveness of their research, they were determined to assert that "everything south of the rivers is 'our land' [*aji*]." Insisting on the urgency of protecting the country's territorial limits, the Chosŏn king pressed his officials to "make great efforts" in talks with Mukedeng because "territory [*kangyŏk*] is of the utmost significance."[67]

The aftermath of Mukedeng's famous 1712 mission was anticlimactic. After several months of work, which involved a joint Qing and Chosŏn entourage of envoys, servants, and mapmakers and arduous treks through grasslands and mountain ranges, the entire length of the shared border was delineated for the

66. Quoted in Andre Schmid, *Korea between Empires* (New York, 2003), 204.
67. Quoted ibid., 208–9; Schmid, "Tributary Relations," 142–43.

first time.[68] A stone stele was lodged at the top of Mount Paektu to mark the disputed spot, the watershed where the Yalu River flowed west and the Tumen River flowed east. Over the next year, at Mukedeng's request, a fence was also built along the stretch of the border where the river went underground to "make the people realize that a border exists."[69] Soon after, much ado arose in the Chosŏn court when officials discovered that the stele had been lodged in the wrong place due to the negligence of Chosŏn envoys, a mistake that had potentially cost Chosŏn three hundred *li* of land.[70] But apart from ordering more investigations of the site, little was done. Mukedeng, when asked whether he would inspect the fence, entrusted the task entirely to the Chosŏn court. Since the borderline had already been agreed upon and its significance made apparent, the two countries discussed it no further. For Chosŏn, unresolved ambiguities were acceptable— even preferable—as long as the Qing recognized its authority over the peninsula and refrained from intruding on its space.

Life and government in the region continued much as they had in the past. Illegal border crossings persisted, proving Mukedeng wrong in his assertion that marking the border would put an end to such transgressions.[71] The abundance of natural resources and sparsity of settled peoples, together with the relative lack of surveillance, encouraged movement and interaction in limited areas throughout the region. More and more, Chosŏn and Qing subjects risked execution by beheading, traveling across the Tumen valley in search of products to profit from and resources to live by. Still, the two powers were content to preserve the valley as it was: a prohibited zone that was protected by its remoteness as well as ambiguous geographical limits. The arrival of Russia in the Tumen in 1860, as well as the migration of Koreans across borders by the thousands, eventually forced the Chosŏn and Qing courts to clarify the sources of the rivers and to consider how emerging notions of jurisdiction applied to the growing population in the region. But until then, people were free to slip in and out of the forests and mountain ranges, escaping the watchful gaze of states.

---

68. The Ming and Chosŏn had come to an agreement about part of the border in 1605, but they had not discussed the border in its entirety. Kang Sŏkhwa, *Hamgyŏng-do wa pukpang yŏngt'o ŭisik*, 25.

69. Quoted in Schmid, *Korea between Empires*, 207; Schmid, "Tributary Relations," 146.

70. For more details about the names and location of the rivers, see Nianshen Song, "The Journey towards 'No Man's Land,'" *Journal of Asian Studies* 76, no. 4 (2017): 1044–46.

71. Schmid, "Tributary Relations," 146.

2

PEOPLE AND PLACE
Jurisdiction and Borders, 1860–1888

In 1867 a Jilin garrison commander spotted two hundred Koreans rushing eastward in ox-driven wagons. He raced after them and asked where they were going. A Korean who knew a bit of Chinese said, "Russia has recruited thousands of our people and is developing land in Tizinhe. . . . There have been bad years of harvest and taxes have increased to the point that we cannot pay them. We are unable to make a living. So we had no other path but to abandon our homes and escape to eke out a living."[1] The commander ordered an investigation of the matter. He was shocked at what he soon discovered. A thousand Koreans had already made a permanent home for themselves in Tizinhe and other places in Ussuri, a territory Russia had acquired only a few years earlier. They walked about in Russian, Qing, and Chosŏn clothing, rendering a picture of motley enclaves where "there was no uniformity in the clothes and hats." A local Qing official tried to persuade the Koreans to return to Chosŏn, but his efforts were frustrated by a Russian border guard. The Russian staunchly claimed that the Koreans were "under the jurisdiction of Russia." News of the incident flew up the ranks of the Qing bureaucracy to the Shengjing Board of Rites, which urged the Chosŏn king to rectify the situation on the border.

The departure of Koreans to Russia, a new neighbor, posed an unprecedented challenge to existing understandings of borders and territory. For years, Chosŏn

---

1. *Tongmun hwigo*, 4:502.

and the Qing had upheld a mutual policy of prohibition. Designed to secure peace in a region historically fraught with strife and to preserve the area's natural resources, the prohibition made crossing the border and settling in the prohibited zone a crime: offenders were reported, returned to their original country, and punished accordingly. Weak state presence in and around the boundary, to be sure, allowed most instances of border crossings and permanent settlement to slip by unnoticed; even when illegal activity was detected, it was often tolerated or ignored. Yet from officials' point of view, such border infractions did not pose a serious threat to the integrity of the prohibited zone, which remained sparsely inhabited. Neither did they imperil the sovereign authority of the two states, which mutually recognized their territorial realms as distinct and did not seek to violate the limit between them. The sheer number of Korean border transgressors arising in the mid-nineteenth century, however, was impossible to ignore. Russia's actions, too, had disrupted existing norms of governance. After annexing a significant piece of historic Qing lands—in the prohibited zone—tsarist officials embarked on various colonization projects in the region. They also accepted the permanent settlement of Chosŏn subjects on their territory and lodged claims on them. Russia had willfully flouted the policy of prohibition and disregarded the claims of Chosŏn over its own people.

Over the next two decades, the triumvirate of states undertook to resolve the issue of mobile Koreans, grappling with an array of attendant matters of diplomacy, law, jurisdiction, and meanings of sovereignty in the process. In the 1860s Qing and Chosŏn officials conducted investigations, yet it was unclear whether their protocols of diplomatic relations or prohibition could be applied to Russia. The Qing, already suspicious of Russia's imperialist ambitions in Asia, initially took upon itself the role of intermediary to protect its interests in the region as well as those of its tributary state Chosŏn, which had no formal relations with Russia. Russia, however, refused to accept the former's position as suzerain over Chosŏn. Tsarist officials, concerned about the interference of foreign countries in their affairs, pursued their own inquiry into the matter of jurisdiction. They looked to extraterritoriality treaties that had been concluded in the 1850s and 1860s. But such treaties focused only on the terms of jurisdiction of Europeans and Americans in treaty ports in East Asia; they said nothing about the mobility and settlement of Asians in Russia. Earlier Sino-Russian treaties, too, failed to shed light on the present situation. Meanwhile, Chosŏn and Russia, which had no history of interaction, could find no common ground in their initial meetings, each challenging the other's right to claim the Koreans as their own and to control their mobility. With no set of agreed-upon norms to address the departure and arrival of Koreans, the three states were left to improvise ways of negotiating, often in incommensurable ways.

This chapter traces the manifold conversations that emerged over the migration of Koreans, examining the evolving disputes and proposed solutions from multiple angles—between Chosŏn and the Qing, the Qing and Russia, and Chosŏn and Russia. It further delves into the reaction of the Chosŏn court. In the 1880s growing anxieties about instability in the countryside and the intrusion of foreign powers emboldened officials to lodge claims over Koreans abroad. King Kojong began to articulate a new vision of statehood, which concomitantly drew on Confucian concepts of the body politic and resonated with emerging notions of territorial sovereignty. In this new conception, people—including those outside Chosŏn—became central to the identity of the state. Koreans abroad were imagined as a crucial resource for upholding the sovereignty of the nation in a time of crisis. No longer denouncing the population as "criminals," Kojong dispatched a secret mission to Russia to embrace the community as loyal subjects of Chosŏn, to incorporate them into the household registers, and to entreat them to return. So firm were the court's assertions of authority over the population that it declined the insertion of a clause about subjecthood in a newly signed treaty with Russia in 1888. What the treaty accomplished, however, was momentous. It would alter the terms of movement across Chosŏn's newest border.

Unsettling People and Place

In 1860 Chosŏn's northern border was redrawn. That year, the Qing and Russian empires signed the Treaty of Beijing, which ceded a wide swath of territory called Ussuri to Russia.[2] The verdant littoral, bordering on the Ussuri River to the west, Tumen River to the south, and the East Sea, glittered among the collection of territories that Russia had amassed on continental Asia for the past two centuries. Its newest acquisition not only completed the last part of the thousand-mile-long border with the Qing but also drew Russia into the maritime world of East Asia. It gained access to Korea by land and to Japan by sea. To make visible its aspirations in East Asia, tsarist officials bestowed on the port city the name Vladivostok—"Rule the East"—and started to settle the region with soldiers and peasants. For

---

2. Under the terms of the 1858 Treaty of Aigun, the Qing ceded the left bank of the Amur River to Russia and retained the right bank as far as the Ussuri River. Ussuri, the littoral between Korea and Manchuria, was to be jointly held. Provisions to delineate the rest of the Sino-Russian border were included in the Treaty of Tianjin, which was signed one month later, but there was disagreement about the exact area of the undemarcated territory. Two years later, Russia was able to take advantage of the ambiguity and annex the Ussuri region through the Treaty of Beijing. The total territory Russia gained in 1858–60 was 281,000 sq. mi. John J. Stephan, *The Russian Far East* (Stanford, 1994), 48–49; S. C. M. Paine, *Imperial Rivals* (Armonk, NY, 1996), 94; Nansen, *Through Siberia*, 333.

China, the treaty rent another piece of land from the historic Manchu homeland. The Qing had already ceded a large section of the north bank of the Amur River to Russia in the 1858 Treaty of Aigun. To forestall the encroachment of its neighbor, the Qing began to reverse previous practices of governing the border area. Officials recruited indigenous peoples into military units instead of employing Manchu bannermen as the sole military force and contemplated lifting the long-time prohibition on settlement in Manchuria.[3] Anxieties about rapidly changing geopolitics had prompted a shift in border policies on the Qing side. This was also true for Chosŏn, which gained a new boundary with Russia.

The delineation of the tripartite border transpired without the knowledge of the Chosŏn court. Indeed, officials were surprised to learn that their country had acquired a new neighbor. The first recorded exchange between Chosŏn and Russia occurred in 1861, a year after the conclusion of the Treaty of Beijing. Captain Turbin and a group of Russian soldiers sailed to the lower reaches of the Tumen River to mark Russia's new border with China. They were met by Korean officials, who crossed to the north bank of the river to inquire "who they were and why they had come."[4] When shown a copy of the treaty in Chinese script, the Koreans said that they had not heard about it. Subsequent Russian attempts to initiate relations with Korea met with little success. In 1864 the magistrate (*pusa*) of the border town Kyŏnghŭng, Yun Hyŏp, noted that a "strange looking people," with "high nose ridges" and "bluish eyes," and wrapped in bearskins and leather, had crossed the river to present a letter asking to engage in trade.[5] Yun promptly rejected their request, claiming that he possessed no authority in such matters. He also condemned as traitors the Koreans who had allegedly helped the Russians write the letter. They were executed for their crime and their heads hung near the Tumen River bank as a warning to Russians to stay out and to Koreans to stay put.[6]

In rebuffing the request of Russian officials, Yun had acted in accordance with the norms of the tributary system, which demanded the precedence of ceremony and ritual over diplomacy and trade. Based on the belief that the cosmic world was inseparable from the human social world, states enacted their distinct roles within the Sinocentric Confucian universe through ritual: inferior tribes, states, and kingdoms conducted rites and offered tribute to the superior "Middle Kingdom," and the emperor, in turn, recognized the various domains as part of

3. Loretta Kim, "Marginal Constituencies," 170–225.
4. Quoted in B. D. Pak, *Rossiia i Koreia* (Moscow, 1979), 35.
5. *Kojong sillok* 1/2/28 no. 5 (April 4, 1864).
6. Ibid.; *Kojong sillok* 1/5/15 no. 6 (June 18, 1864); Ch'oe Ching Young, *The Rule of the Taewŏngun* (Cambridge, MA, 1972), 84.

the Sinic order by receiving their tribute.[7] The maintenance of cosmic relations ensured order and peace in the realm. As a state built on neo-Confucian ideology, Chosŏn took its role seriously, practicing *sadae* ("serving the Great") with the Qing and *kyorin* ("friendly relations") with Ryukyuan kings and Japanese shoguns, whom it regarded as rulers of equal standing.[8] Russia, and its demands for trade, had no place in this system.

It was, in fact, the breaking of these norms that provoked Chosŏn officials to act. In late December 1866 local magistrate Yun Hyŏp reported that twelve foreigners had arrived at Kyŏnghŭng's east gate to announce that Russia would soon build a house near the border stele on the Tumen River.[9] News quickly traveled from the provincial authorities to the State Council (Ŭijŏngbu), the highest governing body. King Kojong also expressed his concerns to the Board of Rites in Shengjing, saying that the coming and going of Russians had shaken the order that had lasted hundreds of years, when "there was no worry on the wide territory and people had lived at peace."[10] More precisely, he pointed out the laws that governed the border area:

> Through the generations, our dynasty has strictly enforced the boundary between the interior and exterior realms. Due to the dangers of subterfuge, intrusion, intermingling [of peoples] and border crossings, there is a prohibition against building a house and cultivating land in the border region between the Great State and this Small Country. Up and down, along the river, all the land has been made empty. This has been a circumspect plan and farsighted strategy with attention given to all areas, and its consideration extends for ten thousand generations.[11]

Given the boldness of the Russians' plans to erect a house, Kojong appealed to the Tongzhi emperor to act immediately, citing previous examples of Qing intervention in border matters. He wrote that in 1714 and 1788, when Chosŏn officials had discovered Qing subjects living in the prohibited zone, both the Kangxi and Qianlong emperors had removed their subjects as the Chosŏn king had requested.[12]

The building of the house was the latest incident in a recent spate of crimes committed at the border that month, all of which escalated worries about

---

7. See James Hevia, *Cherishing Men from Afar* (Durham, NC, 1995).

8. Kenneth R. Robinson, "Centering the King of Chosŏn," *Journal of Asian Studies* 59, no. 1 (February 2000): 109–25.

9. *Tongmun hwigo*, 4:784 (February 8, 1867).

10. Ibid., 4:785 (February 8, 1867).

11. Ibid., 4:804 (July 18, 1868).

12. Ibid., 4:798 (May 14, 1867).

occasional intruders to a grave matter deserving the attention of the central government. On the first day of December 1866, the magistrate at Kyŏngwŏn, Pak Chisu, reported that nine Koreans from Paekach'on village had run across the Tumen River. On the sixth day, hundreds of "Qing people" (*sanggukin*) sacked the village, took the wives, children, oxen, and possessions of those who had left a few days earlier, and absconded across the border with seventy-five Koreans trailing after them. In the skirmish, three villagers suffered bullet wounds and several guard posts went up in flames.[13] Two weeks later, as mentioned above, Russians arrived in Kyŏnghŭng to announce the building of a house. The close timing of the border crossings, which under normal circumstances would have been treated separately, tied the incidents together as one looming offense that needed to be examined closely.

King Kojong demanded that the Qing intervene by appealing to shared norms about the border and joint jurisdiction. Since "matters related to the border territory cannot be decided haphazardly," Kojong asked the Qing to conduct a detailed investigation and arrest the "Qing people" who had not only illegally crossed the border but committed acts of violence.[14] There were historical precedents for the joint administration of justice in the border region, as Kojong noted. Citing a case from 1727, when the Yongzheng emperor had granted permission to Chosŏn to punish Qing subjects, Kojong quoted the words of the emperor himself: "If there are bandits looting in your country, it is fine for the Chosŏn king to arrest and execute them. If people on a ship that goes adrift do not have a pass [*chǔngp'yo*], act recklessly, and cause a ruckus, the king of that country should deal with it according to his country's laws." Since the recent border crossers had escaped before Chosŏn could punish them, Kojong hoped that recalling the past would remind the Tongzhi emperor of his obligation to pass an imperial edict to punish the offenders and aid Chosŏn.[15] In addition, Kojong requested that the Qing repatriate all of the Koreans who had gone abroad.

Qing officials, from the emperor and Shengjing Board of Rites down to the Hunchun captain (*zuoling*) Song Heng, took their part in the investigation seriously and tried to piece together the truth behind the multiple cross-border affairs. Captain Song headed an entourage of officials and soldiers to the border town Kyŏnghŭng, on the Chosŏn side, to obtain a clear account of the December events. But the magistrate Pak stopped them at the city gates, saying he had not received orders from higher authorities to participate in the investigation. Song decided to return to China and from there go directly to Russia to continue his

---

13. Ibid., 4:498 (January 14, 1867), 513, 792.
14. Ibid., 4:498–99.
15. Ibid., 4:797 (May 14, 1867).

mission. Carried by ferry boat, he and his team sailed across the Tumen River toward the spot where the Russians had lodged the border stele, to the southwest of Hunchun and directly opposite Kyŏnghŭng. Their journey was interrupted again, this time by a rising tide that stranded them in the middle of the waters. Only after a rescue by a fisherman and a night spent on the Russian side were Song's efforts at last rewarded. Song discovered a thousand "Chosŏn escapees" (*tomin*) living in villages called Tizinhe and Ianchihe, a confirmation of what officials in Hamgyŏng and Jilin Provinces had suspected for the past few years: Koreans were settling permanently in Russia. Song noted that in the villages, "There was no uniformity in the clothes and hats. Some were wearing Qing [*chungguk*] clothes and hats and others Russian [*aguk*] clothes and hats. There were also many people wearing Chosŏn clothes and hats."[16] Judging from the abundance of "homes with chickens and dogs" and "Koryŏ-style ox-driven carts," it seemed safe to conclude that the people were permanent settlers, not temporary dwellers. To ascertain the identity of the people, the Qing officials personally questioned those wearing Qing, Russian, and Chosŏn clothing and found that they were, in fact, all Korean, for they all spoke the "Koryŏ language." The presence of the large population of Koreans dressed in "mixed clothing" led officials to rule out the possibility that the attackers on Paekach'on village were "Qing people," as King Kojong had assumed. Song guessed that the plunderers were Koreans who had garbed themselves in foreign dress and sheltered themselves in a foreign country.[17]

The discovery confirmed that Koreans had flouted the border prohibition, but the usual course of action did not seem to apply to the post-1860 world. In accordance with previous practice, Song understood that the Koreans belonged under the jurisdiction of their original country, Chosŏn, and thus should be repatriated. He entreated the Koreans to return to their homeland (*koguk*). The passing Russian border guard, however, stopped Song from intervening. He rejected Song's claims on the Koreans and insisted that they were, in fact, "under the jurisdiction of Russia" (*aguk kwanha*). As such, he would not repatriate the Koreans. Song tried to persuade the guard, but afraid that strife would break out, he gave up.[18] The Shengjing Board of Rites and King Kojong heard about the incident, but little was done.

Tension in the border region resurfaced in late 1869, when a mass exodus of six thousand Koreans to Ussuri and Jilin stirred the worries of officials in the three countries. Floods had devastated the autumn harvest in Hamgyŏng Province,

16. Ibid., 4:515 (July 2, 1867).
17. Ibid., 4:515–17.
18. Ibid., 4:516.

and Koreans fled across the Tumen River to beg for shelter and food, wandering about "exhausted and depleted." On the Russian side, the Koreans found haven among their compatriots in Tizinhe and Ianchihe.[19] The Russian military also provided them with foodstuffs from the state reserves.[20] Overwhelmed by the number of Koreans in need, the temporary border commissar of South Ussuri, Count Y. N. Trubetskoi, sent a letter to the Kyŏnghŭng magistrate explaining that the tsarist government "could not view with favor the steadily growing number of homeless people who cross from Korea to Russia" and had "to pass decisive measures to put a stop to this evil." He did not threaten expulsion but expressed a desire to "pass measures with the consent of Korean authorities."[21] The two parties eventually met in Kyŏnghŭng in January 1870 and agreed that the Koreans would be returned to Korea. Given the recent famine, lack of foodstuffs, and rising number of bandit attacks in South Ussuri, returning the thousands of Koreans seemed the easiest solution to Count Trubetskoi.

Conversations between Russian and Qing officials, however, revealed that Russia had decided to take matters into its own hands. The border commissar claimed that he had a right to handle the Koreans as he pleased, not according to Chosŏn-Qing norms. In response to the Hunchun captain's demand for Russia to return the Koreans, he wrote that since "there are already so many people, we cannot chase them out."[22] He added that, on the order of the governor of Eastern Siberia, he planned to send the Koreans to the region of Suifun "to work as conscripted laborers" and "cultivate the land."[23] Disturbed by the border commissar's letter, the Hunchun captain traveled to Russia to pursue the matter in person. But the Russian official rejected the Qing's interference in what he saw as a bilateral matter, saying, "I have already notified the Chosŏn king about the situation. In the future, [such matters] have nothing to do with Hunchun."[24] Minister of foreign affairs A. M. Gorchakov agreed. In his view, Russia "should not give back the [Korean] settlers because we do not have a treaty with Korea and Korea was not mentioned in our treaties with China."[25] Both Russian officials challenged the Qing's role as intermediary in Chosŏn's foreign affairs and the validity of the

19. By early October 1869, 1,850 Koreans had arrived in Poset district; in subsequent months, an additional 4,500 arrived. V. I. Vagin, "Koreitsy na Amure," *Sbornik istoriko-statisticheskikh svedenii o Sibiri i sopredel'nykh ei stranakh* 1 (1875): 3–4, 7.

20. Ibid., 8.

21. Quoted in Pak, *Rossiia i Koreia*, 39.

22. *Tongmun hwigo*, 4:545, quoted in Jilin commander report dated September 29, 1870.

23. Ibid., 4:544–45. The tsarist state had experimented with resettlement programs as early as 1865, when it sent a group of Koreans to Suchan. See chapter 5.

24. Ibid., 4:545.

25. Quoted in Pak, *Rossiia i Koreia*, 40 (November 8, 1871).

border prohibition. From their perspective, Koreans on Russian territory were no longer subject to Chosŏn-Qing border laws.

The handling of Koreans in Russia contrasted with the fate of their compatriots who ended up on the Chinese side. Korean "refugees" became a heavy burden to Qing authorities, who reported that there was "no end to the Chosŏn people" roaming banner garrisons and cities in search of food and shelter. One guard, frustrated, exclaimed, "Considering that this is a bad year of harvest for both Ningguta and Hunchun, we do not have enough aid for our own people. How can we dare help the Chosŏn refugees [*nanmin*] who are so numerous?"[26] In the end, the situation was resolved according to past practices. The Ningguta lieutenant garrison commander (*fudutong*) entreated Chosŏn border authorities to gather the Koreans and take them back to Chosŏn. In a letter, he wrote, "Please keep them from running away and crossing the border. Establishing peace in our respective border region is definitely the way for both our countries to have harmony and good relations, and to avoid conflicts. Let us not look at this as mere words, but consider it an important issue."[27] All Jilin officials were also ordered to "put a stop" to the border crossers.[28] By late 1871, Chosŏn envoy Kim Kwangu had helped repatriate more than five hundred Koreans, including some who had crossed from Russia to China.[29] The affair was concluded with another exchange of letters between the Qing and Chosŏn, the former expressing its resolve to ramp up surveillance through border guards and the latter stating its determination to punish negligent officials. What to do about the continuing cross-border movement of Koreans, however, remained an open question for the three powers. Tsarist officials on their own began to look to recently concluded treaties in search of answers.

Inadequacy of Extraterritoriality Treaties

In the mid-nineteenth century, at the conclusion of the Opium Wars (1856–60), the new treaty regime in East Asia heralded the region's entrance into the modern international system. The United States and European powers forced China and Japan to sign so-called unequal treaties, which gave the former exclusive jurisdiction over their subjects in Asia and tangible privileges, including special access to treaty ports and a favorable tariff system. What was experienced

---

26. *Tongmun hwigo*, 4:564 (March 21, 1871).
27. Ibid., 4:565.
28. Ibid., 4:563.
29. Ibid., 4:567–70 (November 3, 1871).

by Western countries as a boon, however, was seen by rulers in East Asia as an infringement of sovereignty. The treaties not only curtailed China's and Japan's sovereignty in particular treaty ports but also stripped away their ability to negotiate or refute the terms. All rights and privileges granted to Western countries were to be interpreted solely through the terms of the treaties, which, by the second half of the century, meant according to Western diplomatic and legal norms. In the eyes of Western powers, the treaties not only confirmed the political feebleness of China and Japan but also served as de facto proof of their exclusion from the "family of nations." For sovereignty, by definition, required a state to have complete political and legal control over its people and territory.[30] In the last decades of the nineteenth century, then, even as Tianjin, Shanghai, and Nagasaki thrived as cosmopolitan centers of global commerce, the enclaves of exclusive jurisdiction inside these cities came to symbolize the partial surrender of sovereignty and the unequal terms through which East Asia had entered the modern international system.

Extraterritorial regimes unequivocally declared the West's right to impose its own version of jurisdiction in East Asia, but the impact of this new regime was less clear in the distant borderland, where overlapping jurisdictions had been the norm. Similar to other empires, Russia and China had governed their vast lands through plural legal jurisdiction, in which rulers applied specific laws to distinct groups, and even allowed diplomats and foreign merchant communities to govern themselves under their own laws. A ruler interpreted this jurisdictional autonomy as a privilege he granted and a right he could revoke, not as an infringement on the sovereignty of his domain.[31] In the Sino-Russian borderland, the two empires took this flexible approach to governance a step further and codified the principle of "shared jurisdiction," or "mutual extraterritoriality," in the 1689 Treaty of Nerchinsk. In addition to delineating the exact boundary line between the two states, the treaty codified procedures for handling cross-border crimes, which had become a thorn in the side of local officials and inhabitants. It allowed for the mutual extradition and execution of *both* Qing and Russian criminals who had absconded across the border. The treaty defined jurisdiction according to the nationality of the criminal—meaning that authorities of the criminal's original country would try and execute him—and at the same time permitted

---

30. It should be noted that rulers in China and Japan did not immediately interpret the treaties as "unequal" and may have understood them as variations of earlier jurisdictional practices. Pär Cassel argues that China, a legally pluralistic empire, adapted extraterritorial regimes to its particular context. Adam McKeown, *Melancholy Order* (New York, 2008), 151–52; Pär Kristoffer Cassel, *Grounds of Judgment* (Oxford, 2012).

31. McKeown, *Melancholy Order*, 150.

joint investigations between the two states when necessary.[32] The 1768 Supplementary Treaty of Kiakhta stated explicitly the principle of shared jurisdiction; border officials would hold a *joint* trial at the site of the arrest and execute the criminal if he was found guilty. In both treaties, the idea of jurisdiction based on territory coexisted with an ambiguous legal regime in which Qing and Russian officials consulted each other in regard to border issues.[33] Later confirming what had been agreed upon, the Russian domestic penal code, published in 1832 and 1842, stated that Russian subjects who had committed crimes in China would be extradited to Russia for trial; Chinese criminals in Russia held the same privilege of extradition.[34]

This historical practice of plural jurisdiction insinuated itself into the terms of new treaties signed in the mid-nineteenth century. In 1858 Russia and China concluded the Treaty of Aigun. In addition to specifying the Amur basin lands the Qing would cede to Russia, the treaty declared that Qing subjects living on the north bank of the Amur River at the time of the signing of the treaty would be left there and remain "under the jurisdiction" (*pod vedeniem*) of the Qing.[35] One month later, the Treaty of Tianjin abrogated all previous Sino-Russian treaties and pronounced "unilateral extraterritoriality" for Russians in China. Based on the British model, the new unequal treaty confirmed the extradition of Russians who committed crimes on Chinese territory. The declaration of unilateral extraterritoriality, however, did not necessarily annul previous agreements about mutual extradition, as the subsequent Supplementary Treaty of Beijing in 1860 showed. Though this treaty stated that all the terms of Tianjin held true, it also reiterated the principle of plural jurisdiction mentioned in the earlier 1858 Aigun treaty: if "settlements of Chinese subjects" were found "in the places described above"—that is, in ceded territories—the Russian government would leave them there and allow them to continue their livelihoods as hunters and fishermen.[36]

32. Cassel, *Grounds of Judgment*, 43.

33. Ibid., 44–45. Cassel later claims that Russia abandoned the practice of mutual extraterritoriality by signing the Tianjin Treaty of 1858, a new "unequal treaty" based on the British model. But as we shall see, this was not necessarily the understanding between Russia and the Qing. The Qing, on its own part, did attempt to continue its practice of joint trials and mutual extraterritoriality. Ibid., 60, 102.

34. *Svod zakonov Rossiiskoi imperii* (St. Petersburg, 1857), t. 15, radz. I, gl. 5, odt. 2, st. 188; A. I. Petrov, *Istoriia Kitaitsev v Rossii* (St. Petersburg, 2003), 238.

35. Statute 1 of Treaty of Aigun. The treaty specifically refers to the "Manchurian Government" (*Man'chzhurskoe pravitel'stvo*). The primary purpose of the treaty was to declare the ceding of additional Qing territory on the north bank of the Amur River and south of the Outer Xingan range to Russia. Ministerstvo Torgovli i Promyshlennosti, *Sbornik torgovykh dogovorov i drugikh vytekaiushchikh iz nikh soglashenii* (Petrograd, 1915), 312–13.

36. Statute 1 of Supplementary Treaty of Beijing. Ibid., 322.

Taken as a whole, the treaties presented two coexisting, contradictory views of jurisdiction—exclusive territorial jurisdiction and plural jurisdiction. Overlapping jurisdiction in the Qing-Russia borderland remained the norm.

In the early 1880s, as international tensions flared between the two states, tsarist officials pushed the issue of jurisdiction to the fore of their agenda in the region.[37] In the capitals of Beijing and St. Petersburg, Russian dignitaries roundly rejected past practices of plural jurisdiction. In 1881, A. Koiander, Russian plenipotentiary in Beijing, expressed his desire "to terminate the exclusive rights enjoyed by Qing subjects living on Russian territory until now."[38] He also opposed the opening of a Qing consulate in the Russian Far East because he feared the "formation of a foreign [Chinese] colony, constituting a 'state within a state.'"[39] Affirming this view, State Secretary D. N. Nabokov asserted that the "question of extraterritoriality of Chinese subjects living in Russia should be decided, in my view, so that Chinese subjects are subject to the actions of Russian criminal law in cases where crimes are committed on Russian territory."[40]

Applying unilateral extraterritoriality in the border region, however, was not as easy as a simple pronouncement of a principle. In fact, according to the Russian legal code (1866 publication), it was a direct violation of a mutual extradition statute. Statute 172 stated that "Chinese who committed crimes on the Russian side of the border will be given over to their government, just as Russian subjects who commit crimes on the border territories of China will be handed over for trial to the Russian government." Even Secretary Nabokov, who hoped to subject Chinese criminals on Russian territory to Russian law, maintained that relations in the border region still operated under a separate legal regime. Indeed, he drew a distinction between law in the borderland and law in the rest of the country. Mutual extraterritoriality, as stated in the legal code, applied to Chinese "who had committed crimes on the border line"; by contrast, Russian domestic law applied to Chinese criminals in "places that do not border with China." The coexistence of such laws created confusion for local officials who had to deal with offenders firsthand. In 1882 the newly appointed military governor of the Maritime Province, I. G. Baranov, wrote to the Ministry of Foreign Affairs and asked for an explanation of the eighth and tenth statutes of the Treaty of Beijing: "Do Chinese subjects who commit crimes in Russia have the benefit of extraterritoriality or

37. In 1880–81, the Qing and Russia were embroiled in a dispute over the Ili valley in Turkestan, which was later incorporated into the Qing empire as Xinjiang Province. For the background of these disputes and their effect on the local population, see David Brophy, *Uyghur Nation* (Cambridge, MA, 2016), 53–78.

38. Quoted in Petrov, *Istoriia Kitaitsev v Rossii*, 241.

39. Quoted ibid., 240 (May 24, 1881).

40. Quoted ibid., 242 (October 22, 1881).

are they tried in our courts?" A. A. Mel'nikov, vice director of the Asia Department in the Foreign Ministry, confessed his ignorance on the matter, saying he would ask diplomats in Beijing. It turned out that neither domestic laws nor international treaties could clarify the issue of jurisdiction. Meanwhile, the Qing asserted that Chinese were "directly subject to Chinese authorities," because the treaties said nothing about the migration of additional Chinese to Russian territory after 1860.[41]

As statesmen struggled to clarify the terms of jurisdiction, border inhabitants found their own means to handle changing circumstances in the region. In many ways, seminomadic peoples lived their lives much as they had in the past. They continued their cyclical migration patterns, settling on the north bank of the Tumen for a season of farming and moving to Heilongjiang at other times of the year to hunt. Tribes who ended up on the Russian side after 1860 also continued to offer ginseng and sable pelts as tribute through the late 1890s, much to the dismay of Russian authorities, who complained about the collection of "taxes" by the Qing.[42] At the same time, Russia's presence in the area offered natives another way of life. Many fled to Russia to escape heavy tribute burdens or smuggled tribute items to sell for exorbitant sums of money on the Russian market. Such instances of border crossings grew in number as the store of natural resources in Heilongjiang and Jilin was gradually depleted.[43]

Border officials, new arrivals, and existing inhabitants in the region also took the law into their own hands, often resorting to violent means to settle cross-border crimes and rights over land. In direct violation of the 1860 Treaty of Beijing, which allowed existing Qing subjects to remain in Ussuri, the local Russian administration ordered Cossacks and soldiers to destroy the homes of Qing subjects and drive them out to clear a space for Russian settlers. During his travels in the area of Suchan, A. V. Eliseev frequently came across the "burnt-down remains of Chinese huts [kitaiskie fanzy]," which, according to local legend, were the result of a "violent eviction" campaign that was "carried out energetically and without pardon" by soldiers. In retaliation, the Qing subjects burned down the houses of Russian settlers, sometimes putting them to death.[44] Multiethnic "dens" of bandits also became infamous for their nefarious acts. Variously referred to as honghuzi ("red beards") for the color of their masks, "Manzas," or the misnomer

---

41. Ibid., 242, 247, 244.
42. Ibid., 236–37.
43. According to Robert Lee, the tributary system was in a state of decline in the 1880s. *Manchurian Frontier*, 125–27.
44. In describing the violent incident, Eliseev calls South Ussuri an "American corner of Russia," perhaps to draw similarities between indigenous-settler clashes in the two parts of the world. A. V. Eliseev, *Po belu-svetu*, vol. 4 (St. Petersburg, 1898), 75–76.

"Chinese" (*kitaitsy*), the bandits constituted a mélange of indigenous peoples, bannermen, Han Chinese, Mongols, and even Koreans. Together they wreaked havoc throughout Ussuri.[45] They plundered villages and carried out "beastly murders," particularly in Suifun valley. The spate of attacks often escalated into reprisals and counterattacks that involved multiple groups. The Shiteulin affair of 1879 was one such instance. In June of that year, a band of Manzas attacked the Korean village of Putsilovka—on the Russian side—murdering eight Koreans and wounding a dozen more. To exact justice for the Koreans, a Cossack detachment embarked on a manhunt that lasted a fortnight. The hunt led them into Qing territory, where they shot and wounded 120 people before realizing that the suspects were not bandits, but Qing bannermen.[46] The illegal border crossing and brute violence enraged the Qing government and drew the attention of the Russian chargé d'affaires in Beijing, who tried to consult recent treaties for a way out of the messy affair. He shifted the blame to the Qing, saying that it should "take the border question seriously" and stop the bandits who had "dominated over our Ussuri district for the past ten years."[47]

Strained relations between China and Russia affected jurisdictional disputes over Koreans in Russia. Under the norms of the tributary system, the Qing acted as Choson's intermediary with countries outside the system. Russia, however, refused to accept Qing involvement and instead tried to engage directly with Chosŏn. Until 1884, when Russia and Chosŏn finally established formal diplomatic relations, the tsarist government resorted to ad hoc measures to resolve jurisdictional issues. As early as 1865, it had incorporated Koreans into the state peasantry and provided them with lands, saying that "all foreigners were allowed to become Russian subjects without soliciting the permission of their governments."[48] Tsarist authorities also continued to challenge the Qing's claims on the Koreans, as the 1882 dispute over Savelovka demonstrated.[49] Savelovka, a small village nestled in a riverbed at the intersection of the three countries' borders, became the subject of a four-year altercation between Russia and the Qing,

---

45. Eventually, the gangs grew in size and discarded their masks, but they were still identified as "red beards." Their reputation as good shots drew them out of banditry and into international wars, where they worked as mercenaries for the Qing, Russians, and Japanese. Robert Lee, *Manchurian Frontier*, 93–96; Patrick Fuliang Shan, "Insecurity, Outlawry and Social Order," *Journal of Social History* 40, no. 1 (2006): 30.

46. RGIADV 1/1/502, l. 34–34ob (September 1, 1879).

47. RGIADV 1/1/697, l. 76ob, 81–82 (February 24, 1880). The question of jurisdiction over Qing subjects in Russia remained unresolved until 1885, when the Priamur governor-general passed a resolution to prohibit Chinese from crossing the Russian border without a passport. See chapter 4.

48. Military Governor of Maritime Province, Contra-Admiral P. V. Kazakevich, quoted in letter in Pak, *Rossiia i Koreia*, 36.

49. Savelovka was known as Hŭkjŏngja to Koreans.

both of which declared that the village and the five hundred Koreans who lived there belonged to their respective states. A Qing imperial official, Liu Tszin Iun, ordered the Koreans to leave or to become Qing subjects, while Border Commissar Nikolai Gavrilovich Matiunin claimed that the Russian government had bestowed Russian subjecthood on the Koreans and did not "dar[e] draw any distinction between them and other Russian subjects."[50] N. G. Matiunin, who hoped to avoid any complications in Russo-Korean relations in the future, decided that the best way to resolve the matter was to erase it. He proposed moving the Koreans farther inland, away from the disapproving Qing gaze, and repopulating the border region with Russian settlers.[51] Four years later, Russia relinquished Savelovka to the Qing, but the question of Koreans' jurisdiction was still unsettled.

Contradictory claims about jurisdiction persisted as a contentious issue between Russia and China. Russian statesmen searched extraterritoriality treaties to clarify the jurisdiction of the burgeoning population of Koreans and Chinese on their territory. Yet the treaties failed to provide satisfactory answers. Concerned primarily with key commercial centers in East Asia, the treaties only stipulated the terms of jurisdiction of Westerners in a handful of treaty ports. The meaning of the new treaty regime for the borderland, where Chosŏn and Qing subjects continually moved and settled, was unclear. While statesmen debated the terms of the treaties, inhabitants continued to resolve border disputes in their own ways.

Preserving the Body Politic

The unprecedented migration of Koreans from the southern bank of the Tumen valley spurred a wave of inward reflection in the Chosŏn court amid a time of crisis. After hearing endless news about Western "barbarians" wreaking havoc in China, the court itself faced the arrival of foreigners it had shunned until then. A series of events seized the attention of the court. In 1868 a Prussian merchant, frustrated by the court's denial of his offers to trade, attempted to unearth the grave of the regent Taewŏngun's father in protest. A few years later, in 1871, a heavily armed flotilla of American ships with twelve hundred men aboard invaded Kanghwa Island, attempting to avenge the deaths of American and British sailors in an earlier incident and to force the country to open to trade. Though the Taewŏngun successfully averted the attack and even commemorated

---

50. RGIADV 1/2/829, l. 13 (August 2, 1882), l. 207 (March 29, 1883).
51. Ibid., l. 32–32ob (August 10, 1882).

the victory by erecting steles in major cities, the peace that ensued was temporary. Meanwhile, internal woes in all corners of the country deepened the sense
of urgency in the court. Peasants everywhere protested injustices at the hands of
corrupt clerks while the court found itself mired in contradictory fiscal policies
that had sunk it near the point of bankruptcy. Threatening the stability of the
family, state, and entire realm, the continuous movement of Koreans into foreign
lands was yet another sign that internal and external calamities had befallen the
country. As officials struggled to make sense of expatriate Koreans within the
framework of Confucian ideas and past practices, a gradual transformation in
thinking about the body politic and the Koreans abroad took place. The expatriate community soon presented a possible solution to the country's problems, and
not a problem itself.

The emptying of the northern borderlands signaled dire economic prospects
for the country as a whole. Years of flooding and bad harvests drove away thousands and left "nine out of ten homes" in the Six Forts empty. For a country
that aspired to neo-Confucian ideals, in which agriculture was considered the
foundation of the economy and peasants were the foundation of the state, land
with no people to cultivate it was a real cause for concern.[52] The well-being of
peasants had long formed a major topic of debate among Confucian scholar-
officials, who understood their pivotal role in the state. Already in the eighteenth
century, reform scholars lamented that unequal distribution of land had created
an exploited class of tenant farmers who roamed from farm to farm in search of
a living. Even in Hamgyŏng Province, where an abundance of fallow land and a
shortage of people had created relative security for tenants and owner-farmers,
frequent bouts of inclement weather upset the delicate link between the health of
the economy and the health of the state by ruining crops and depriving peasants
of their ability to pay taxes.[53] The recent loss of people in the north was looked
on as yet another drain on the wealth of the country.

The departure of Koreans was also seen as a crime, one that potentially risked
the stability of the state. In Confucian cosmology, the heavens (ch'ŏnha), state
(kuk), and family (ka) operated as an organic unit. Order at the highest level,
in the heavens, depended on order in three realms, for the root of the heavenly
realm was the state, the root of the state was the family, and the root of the family
was the self-cultivation of the individual—that is, his performance of ancestral

---

52. Peter H. Lee and William Theodore De Bary, eds., *Sources of Korean Tradition*, vol. 2 (New
York, 2000), 45.

53. Permanent tenure seemed to be practiced only in a limited number of geographical areas in
Korea. Susan S. Shin, "Some Aspects of Landlord-Tenant Relations in Yi Dynasty Korea," *Occasional
Papers on Korea*, no. 3 (June 1975): 68, 72.

rites and learning.[54] Koreans who abandoned their country set off a chain reaction of disorder that rippled through all levels of society. They forsook ancestral rites, angered the spirits of their ancestors, and risked the well-being of their families, all of which portended disorder in the state. Leaving was a crime tantamount to betraying one's family as well as one's country. Indeed, in his message to the residents of Hamgyŏng Province, King Kojong cried out against the wrongs they had committed: "Ah! You have abandoned the land of your parents, become the people of another country, worn the clothes of another country, and eaten food grown in another country. What a great crime this is!"[55]

The migration of Koreans abroad could also be seen as a physical severing of the body politic. Previously, the prohibition on border crossing had bound the body politic together, symbolically and practically, by discouraging people from leaving their original place. But the mass departure of Koreans made it impossible for officials to rectify the situation through simple repatriation and punishment. The permanent existence of Koreans outside Korea threw into question the state-family (*kukka*) ideal of the Chosŏn body politic. By leaving for another country, they had broken ties with the state, and by "abandoning the graves of their ancestors," they had broken links with their living and dead family members.[56] Koreans, in fact, were aware of the importance of maintaining ties with their ancestors, and they frequently disinterred and moved ancestral graves abroad.[57] Yet this act symbolically tore the family from the state and cut off the lineage of the body politic.

To preserve the body politic, King Kojong appealed to people's sense of responsibility to the country. For the *kukka* comprised the state and the family, and the two were mutually dependent; the king needed to act out his dual role as head of state and head of family and the people their role as moral subjects and obedient children. In a letter to the people in 1876, Kojong drew on the Confucian language of remonstrance and reasoned that their respective parent and child roles had bound them to specific duties. "I consider you my children and myself as your parent," he explained. "A child should understand a parent's heart and obey them." Kojong also highlighted the sovereign-subject relationship. Staking his place as king in a long line of sagacious rulers who had "bestowed great blessings of nurturing," he proclaimed that the king had historically cast his enlightenment onto the people and thus enabled them to preserve their morality

54. Kyung Moon Hwang, "Country or State?," *Korean Studies* 24 (2000): 7.
55. *Kojong sillok* 13/8/9 no. 1 (September 26, 1876).
56. *Kojong sillok* 13/8/10 no. 1 (September 27, 1876).
57. *Kojong sillok* 14/12/12 no. 1 (January 14, 1878). Russian officials noticed that Koreans frequently changed the location of graves; officials were initially confused by this practice.

(*isŏng*) by demonstrating their filial piety toward their parents, affection for their superiors, loyalty to the country, and learnedness in the classics.[58] The havoc that had been created by the lack of morality, he believed, could be reversed only if they returned to their rightful place—to the realm of enlightenment. Kojong was incessant in his call for the people to return.

The king had reason to hope that Koreans abroad had retained their attachment to the body politic because they exhibited a modicum of ethics (*ri*). Physical proof lay in their preservation of a fundamental custom: some did still wear Korean clothes. Kojong believed that their clothes reflected not only their holding fast to the "ways of the original country" but also their adherence to one's duty to long for one's home. A case from ancient history also served as prima facie evidence of their loyalty. In an 1880 admonishment to the people in the north, Kojong wrote that if even the birds of Yue and the horses of Dai[59] who had been scattered had had the sense to pine for their old homes, how much more so would the people, who had unswervingly followed correct ways, pine for their country? If one's moral duty was inextricably bound to a longing for the homeland, then it was impossible for the people to forget any thought of returning to "our" country even for a second.[60]

Court officials tackled the question of emigrants by criticizing the local government in the north. They reasoned that since deterrents to crossing the border were high—cutting off one's head and one's family ties—it must have been the poor governance by officials that drove them away. In a meeting of the State Council, King Kojong exclaimed, "Do you think the people cross the border because they want to? If you consider it wholeheartedly, it is beyond reason that they would leave the hometowns in which their relatives live, abandon the land of their parents, and break the law by secretly running away." He concluded that the people must have done so because they had "no place to report their injustices and sufferings."[61] The court admitted that the people's list of grievances was long, extending from heavy taxes, military duties, and lack of aid during times of disaster to crimes committed by officials themselves, including usury, bribery, unjust lawsuits, and severe punishments.[62] "The local magistrates are not taking care of them," "Officials have not guided the people well," and "It must be

58. *Kojong sillok* 13/8/9 no. 1.

59. Yue and Dai were states that existed in ancient China during the Spring and Autumn period (approximately 770–481 BCE).

60. *Kojong sillok* 17/10/9 no. 1 (November 11, 1880).

61. *Kojong sillok* 13/7/13 no. 1 (August 31, 1876).

62. *Kojong sillok* 17/10/9 no. 1.

the responsibility of the local magistrates" became refrains in court discussions about the plight of people at the border.[63]

It was not only arbitrary corruption but also want of correct attitudes that had diminished just governance. Official Pak Kyusu derided the slackening of duty among northern inspectors (*pukp'yŏngsa*) who "choose what is convenient." Previously, inspectors had taken their post seriously: they inquired after the people's welfare, investigated the wrongs of the local magistrates, and personally traveled to each of the Six Forts. By contrast, current officers merely strode through the market once and then called it a day, leaving Pak to lament their lack of a sense of responsibility. Magistrates, too, languished in their posts. According to Pak, they mismanaged affairs because of an inherent handicap. As military men (*muin*), they lacked the learning of men of letters (*munin*) and the ability to care for and love the people. But such a disadvantage could not justify their impatience in "eagerly wait[ing] for their tenure to be over."[64] The halt of inspection tours by provincial governors (*kamsa*) in the 1840s removed another layer of accountability.

As news spread about the settled population of Koreans abroad, King Kojong did what was in his power to correct existing wrongs in the north. In 1876 he appointed Hamgyŏng provincial governor Kim Yuyŏn to the new post of royal commissioner (*anmusa*) to examine the situation in the Six Forts and surrounding areas, duties that had been neglected due to the abolition of inspection tours.[65] Having served as governor for a decade, Kim understood the ins and outs of local politics and proved himself capable of investigating the population drain from the Six Forts to Russia. But five years into his new post, he remained doubtful about his ability to stop the departure of Koreans. He noted that a valuable "source of profit" in Russia continued to pull people across the border, making their departure "difficult to strictly prohibit." When the king suggested fixing the "evils of the grain-loan system" in the Six Forts to appease disgruntled residents, Kim graciously agreed that he would try. Yet he acknowledged the challenges of estimating how much capital was required to "correct the vices" of the system.[66] Renovating the grain-loan system was indeed a herculean task. Originally designed to provide relief and to stabilize commodity prices by selling grain in times of scarcity when the market price shot up and using the proceeds to buy grain after a bumper crop when the price fell, the system had become saddled

63. *Kojong sillok* 3/12/4 no. 3 (January 9, 1867), 4/3/15 no. 5 (April 19, 1867).
64. *Kojong sillok* 13/7/13 no. 1.
65. *Kojong sillok* 13/8/9 no. 1. Kim Yuyŏn served both as royal commissioner and governor of Hamgyŏng Province until his resignation in 1886.
66. *Kojong sillok* 18/01/17 no. 1 (February 17, 1881).

with corruption and internal contradictions and eventually bankrupted the most vulnerable of peasants.[67]

While questions about how to stem the loss of people continued in court discussions, pivotal changes inside Chosŏn eventually prompted Kojong to take unprecedented measures in regard to its newest neighbor. In autumn 1882 he initiated attempts to look outward for a solution. He dispatched a secret mission to investigate the military capabilities of Russia and the situation of Koreans who had settled there. The mission was highly unusual. In the past, Chosŏn officials had routinely made visits to longtime neighbor China, and more recently they had traveled to Japan on fact-finding missions to examine the modernizing efforts of the Meiji state (1868–1912). But the visit to Russia was the first time that officials had been sent to a country outside the tributary system to investigate an expatriate community. Extenuating circumstances had made it necessary. The 1880s marked the beginning of "high imperial" politics in Chosŏn. Western powers made inroads into the country, and Japan, the first to conclude a modern treaty with Chosŏn, deepened its involvement in court intrigues, in which the regent Taewŏngun and Queen Min plotted against each other and King Kojong sought to appease both progressive and conservative scholar-officials. Events came to a head in 1882, when a group of disgruntled soldiers staged a riot in protest of recent modernization efforts that had diverted funds from their own salaries. They not only destroyed the property of court officials but also incinerated the building of the Japanese legation. The incident did not stop there. In an unparalleled move, the Qing, worried that Japan would retaliate and attempt a takeover of the capital, dispatched troops from China to restore order in Seoul. It later stationed a "chief commissioner of diplomatic and commercial affairs" there to manage the foreign affairs of the country. Its actions marked the commencement of a new period in Qing-Chosŏn relations. The Qing had reinvented its role in Korea from a distant, ceremonial superior and occasional advisor to active intermediary in Chosŏn's affairs, akin to a modern imperial power.[68] The secret mission to Russia was part of Kojong's efforts to look to the outside world for possible allies and threats.[69]

---

67. The system was sustained by "ever-normal granaries," named for their function in normalizing prices. Grain was usually purchased and sold in the fall and spring, respectively. For more information on the system in Pyŏngan Province, see Sun Joo Kim, *Marginality and Subversion in Korea*, 71–76. On attempts to reform the system, see James B. Palais, *Politics and Policy in Traditional Korea* (Cambridge, MA, 1975), 132–59.

68. For more on the transformation of the Qing's position from noninterference to military intervention, see Key-Hiuk Kim, *Last Phase of the East Asian World Order* (Berkeley, 1980).

69. The 1882 mission, led by Kim Kwanghun and Sin Sŏnuk, was followed by another mission in 1884, after the Kapsin coup. In addition to Kim and Sin, two other officials participated in the

In 1882 Kim Kwanghun and Sin Sŏnuk traveled to the Russian Maritime Province on the mission charged by the king. In the record of their journey, *Diary on the Left Bank of the River*, the envoys poetically described the Maritime as a region tinged with melancholy reminders of "barbarians" and the warriors who fought them. They also expressed wonder at its dramatic transformation. They drew a vivid picture of a land that was brimming with new structures, including telegraph lines, military posts, and a buildup of defenses along the border and inside Ussuri. Russian soldiers moved in perfect lockstep according to spoken commands, and the telegraph swiftly carried messages, making a *zzzz* sound, similar to what one would hear on "entering a beehive."[70] Telegraphs were already in use in Korea, Japan, and China, but the sheer distance that messages had to travel from the capital of St. Petersburg to Vladivostok—five thousand miles—left a deep impression.

Apart from the changes in the land, Kim and Sin's account illuminated a shift in thinking about the expatriate community itself. In the familiar Confucian language of remonstrance, the envoys echoed laments about the departure of "children" to a foreign land and censure of local officials who had driven the people away.[71] Yet rather than seeing the Koreans in Russia as traitors who had abandoned their country, Kim and Sin reconceived the people as loyal subjects who had retained the culture of their homeland.[72] Offering myriad examples, the envoys celebrated what they saw as evidence of cultural preservation. The people still married according to the "rituals of our country," even secretly holding wedding ceremonies in the pitch dark of night so that disapproving Russian authorities would not find out; they educated their children in the Confucian classics and the works of the sages; and they held a poetry contest to memorialize the visit of the envoys in the tradition of scholar-officials. Village leaders, moreover, proved exemplary in their morals, for they were able to distinguish the "public from the private" and imbued the people with virtue even though they lived in Russia. The emissaries concluded that everything they bore

---

second mission, Kwŏn Tongsu and Kim Yongwŏn. They supposedly delivered a secret "friendly letter" from King Kojong. Russia and Korea established official relations soon thereafter in the 1884 Treaty of Friendship. There has been scholarly debate over the timing of the first secret mission, but I have settled on 1882, based on the editor's commentary in the diary. *Kangjwa yŏjigi*, 39. For discussion about the timing of another publication produced by these missions, in particular maps, see Sergey Yu. Vradiy, "Primorskii Borderland on the 'Map of Russia' *Aguk-yeojido*," *Eurasia Border Review* 3, no. 2 (Fall 2012): 103–18.

70. *Kangjwa yŏjigi*, 141, 134.

71. Ibid., 166.

72. A similar shift occurred in Qing attitudes toward overseas Chinese in the late nineteenth century. Gungwu Wang, "A Note on the Origins of Hua-Ch'iao," in *Community and Nation*, ed. Gungwu Wang and Anthony Reid (Singapore, 1981), 118–27.

witness to constituted "strong signs that the [people] cannot forget their roots." It did not matter that the Koreans were physically located outside the boundaries of Korea because, according to Kim and Sin, they maintained a desire to return home. Everywhere they traveled, the envoys remarked that Koreans professed this desire: "Even though we live here and are here in body, our hearts are over there. We are but the distance of a bridge crossing from there. How can we forget our desire to return to our homeland?" Portraying the Koreans as holding steadfast to Chosŏn, the envoys assumed that it was either the Russian government or fears of punishment at the hands of corrupt clerks in Chosŏn that had deterred the people from returning.[73]

In addition to extolling Koreans for preserving their original culture, Kim and Sin praised them for acquiring new knowledge in a new country. The envoys noted that all the Russian translators were Korean and familiar with Western ways: they had knowledge of Western learning, Western weaponry, and Western military strategy and secret code. The Koreans who stepped beyond the boundaries of Korea had also become worldly and were able to give their perspective on rapidly changing international politics. One villager freely offered his views on Russia, Korea, and the world beyond, saying that "the situation in the world is very different from before. If you look at the ships, locomotives, and weapons of the Western countries, it seems that it is necessary to possess these things. All the more so because Russia is only a river crossing away. It can easily take our land if it wants to." Such knowledge was of material benefit to Chosŏn's security. Since they "already knew the strengths of the Russians," the people said, if Russia ever attacked Chosŏn, they would know how to stop it. The envoys exulted in the promise made by more than one hundred people to "gallop on our horses in a day's time" and fight with a "cheerful and willing heart" should anything happen to their homeland.[74] The people's loyalty and skills provided hope.

The emissaries also undertook to claim the people by institutionally binding them to the body politic. They declared that one of their objectives was to register the expatriates in the household registers and store their information in the capital. As the administrative mechanism of the state, the household registration system (hojŏk) represented the body politic in the most literal sense: by the names of its people. It was a record of all family members within a household: a compendium of data about the household head, his clan seat, year of birth, ancestors, and children, and parallel information for the wife. Threading the generations of the present and past together into a book, the hojŏk read like a continuous

73. Ibid., 157, 163, 135, 161, 156, 164.
74. Ibid., 165, 158, 161.

history that reached back for centuries. It was also a practical instrument for the state to keep track of people and to calculate taxes.[75] Though it was unlikely that the state would be able to use the record to levy taxes on the Koreans in Russia, the *hojŏk* would nevertheless act as a symbol of their connection to Chosŏn and a reminder to the people that they should not forget their "original country" (*pont'o*). Contemplating more ways to solidify the community's position within the body politic, the envoys believed that bestowing a special rank on elders would be "an effective way to govern the people's hearts and have them receive the rule of the king."[76] The elders, in turn, might serve as a resource to whom the king could turn in the event of a crisis.

The imagining of Koreans as loyal subjects suggests that new ideas about sovereignty and nationhood were taking form even as preexisting ideas about place held true. Since early Chosŏn, the relationship between state authority and territory had been precisely defined. The Qing and Chosŏn mutually recognized the limit of their realms and sought to repatriate and punish those who crossed that limit. In urging the people to return, Chosŏn officials operated according to a familiar logic: the best way to maintain peace on the border was to discourage people from transgressing it. Yet their assessment of the people as a resource to the nation—exemplified by their loyalty, knowledge, and skills—also reflected the emergence of a nationalist strain of thinking that imagined the state as not only a delimited territory but also a collective body to which individuals must belong.[77] People had become central to the state. And their permanent loss portended a disintegration of the state. Officials' attempts to register people abroad and recall their ties to Chosŏn represented nascent efforts to claim the people and to refashion them into a political community that underpinned an emergent

---

75. Surveys were conducted every three years by local officials, who collected taxes and compiled lists of people for military and labor service. Because it was a tool for taxation, commoners did all they could to avoid being included. Kyung Moon Hwang, "Citizenship, Social Equality and Government Reform," *Modern Asian Studies* 38, no. 2 (2004): 356–57.

76. *Kangjwa yŏjigi*, 162, 163.

77. Winichakul Thongchai, *Siam Mapped* (Honolulu, 1994), 1. Late nineteenth-century Korea witnessed the rise of revisionist thinking about the concept of the state. Kyung Moon Hwang shows that some enlightenment thinkers formulated a collectivist idea of the state (*kukka*). This conception drew on Confucian ideas of the collective, familial character of country, while simultaneously embracing new liberal ideas about popular sovereignty, which placed people at the center. Historian Yi T'aejin offers a similar view, saying that there was a shift from a sovereign-centered *kukka* to a more modern people-centered view of the state. He also argues the concept of *kunmin ilch'ae* (the "sovereign and people are one body")—a resurrection of former rulers' idea of "protecting the people" (*sŏmin poho*)—arose in the 1880s and 1890s. Still other thinkers emphasized state authority in concepts of the state. Hwang, "Country or State"; Yi T'aejin, *Kojong sidae ŭi chae chomyŏng* (Seoul, 2000), 231–78.

nation. It remained to be seen, though, how Chosŏn officials would frame these ideas in dialogue with other countries.

Jurisdiction and Incommensurability

While the Chosŏn court fretted over the departure of its people in the north, Russian officials worried about the influx of Koreans into its newest territory. They had provided aid to the first waves of migrants, but as Koreans continued to arrive, officials wondered how they could support them. Koreans also risked complicating Russia's foreign relations with the Qing and Chosŏn, for they did not stay in Russia but frequently traveled back and forth across the border and purportedly engaged in nefarious acts while abroad, stealing and even kidnapping women. Russian soldiers complained that they had to cross the border illegally to rescue "our" Koreans and bring them back to Russia as well as protect them from bandits who roved the borderland.[78] Despite tsarist officials' attempts to establish relations with Chosŏn to discuss such matters, they had been unsuccessful. Negotiations thus far had been conducted through the Qing, in accordance with tributary practice. When officials of the two countries finally met, they had no international treaties, no historical model of foreign relations, and no universal standards on which to draw. Each side spoke out according to its own view of what an "international" norm constituted, citing laws and rules about engagement and jurisdiction whose terms were often incommensurable.

Tensions over Chosŏn's adherence to tributary practices arose in a February 1880 meeting between the two states. Discussions were held in the border town Kyŏnghŭng, more than a decade after their first meeting and four years before the conclusion of official diplomatic relations.[79] Border commissar N. G. Matiunin crossed the frozen Tumen River with a convoy of nineteen people, which included Korean and Manchu translators.[80] They were greeted by a retinue of a dozen Koreans, who serenaded them with a marching tune during the three-kilometer

---

78. While no detailed information is given about the stealing or kidnapping, these types of cross-border crimes were a frequent topic of discussion among local Russian officials, who complained that Chinese, "bandits," and many Koreans were wreaking havoc in the border area. RGIADV 1/1/769 (*otpusk telegrammy*, January 26, 1880, no. 44), 119–119ob (March 1, 1880).

79. The negotiations are recorded in *Kojong sillok* 17/02/27 no. 2 (April 6, 1880). For the Russian border commissar's report of the talks, see RGIADV 1/1/769, l. 119ob–120. By the Julian calendar, the meeting took place at the end of February 1880.

80. The Russian source mentions that a convoy of 815 Cossack cavalrymen crossed the river with them.

walk from the border to the government office. Matiunin hoped that the talks would lead to the establishment of "good relations" between the two countries so that they could "put a stop" to the "evils" on the border.[81] But after sitting through what seemed like painstaking formalities, meals, and entertainment, he realized that there would be no serious talks during his visit. The Kyŏnghŭng magistrate Sin Yŏnghan, the highest-ranking authority there, arrived at the meeting with a script of questions and hardly deviated from it. Matiunin tried to dispel any suspicion that Russia was trying to militarily seize Korea, saying, "Our land is wide in territory and rich in resources. We do not seek to snatch other countries. We merely want to have good relations with them." In response, Sin firmly declared that no laws existed to formally engage with Russia. "Our country only protects our own territory," he said. "We do not have a law to establish relations with foreign countries."

The two sides also disagreed about how to control the mobility of the people. Matiunin reported that Koreans formed gangs, violated widows, and plundered their compatriots in the border region. Koreans on the Russian side, moreover, added to the disorder by traveling back and forth to Korea. He proposed the creation of a "pass system" (*kongmun*), reasoning that "if there are no established regulations, then we will not be able to stop these evil people." Under the new system, Russian authorities would issue documents to travelers and restrict transit to the border towns of Hunchun and Kyŏngwŏn. But Sin refused. The proposal flew in the face of two long-held practices in Chosŏn. The first was the prohibition on border crossing. Travel passes (*kongmun*) had been issued to people with special status or reason to travel, such as envoys and merchants. Commoners were not allowed to go abroad. Chosŏn officials had already expressed their surprise at the "Russian custom" of allowing migrants to stay in Russia, even feeding them, instead of forcing them to return to their original country.[82] Matiunin's proposal to issue a pass to anyone who desired to cross the border was tantamount to abolishing this ban. Indeed, when Matiunin asked whether occasionally crossing the border was a violation of the law, Sin flatly responded that the border prohibition "already exists and is not subject to discussion." Second, the proposal challenged Chosŏn's authority over the people. In Sin's thinking, only a person's original country had the right to issue a pass, and that country was Chosŏn. As such, he said, "it is not for your [Russian] authorities to issue and receive documents as they please." His

81. *Kojong sillok* 17/02/27 no. 2.
82. *Kojong sillok* 14/12/12 no. 1 (January 14, 1878).

rejection of Matiunin's proposal was a rejection of Russia's authority to govern the movement of Koreans in and out of Chosŏn.

Apart from the issue of mobility, Matiunin and Sin challenged each other's authority to adjudicate cross-border crimes. To control the outbreak of violence on the border, Matiunin suggested that if naturalized Korean-Russians committed a crime on Chosŏn territory, they should be extradited to Russia and punished according to Russian law. He reasoned that "the people who ran away from your country and live here are now our people [amin]."[83] Thus, "if they come [to Chosŏn] and commit evils here, we will take care of it with severity as long as you inform our officials." By his statement, Matiunin made known the tsarist government's claim on Koreans and its intent to exercise joint jurisdiction in cross-border affairs. Sin, again, challenged him, albeit in a roundabout manner. He responded, "Severe punishment of those who commit a crime is an administrative matter for your authorities alone. It would be good if you informed our border people about this [policy]. However, it is not for you to do as you please before receiving a response from the higher authorities." When Matiunin further suggested that written communication between the two states was necessary to rectify the situation on the border, Sin rejected the idea. Sin most likely believed that Chosŏn's lack of formal relations with Russia made this impossible. Matiunin tried to press the issue by pointing to Chosŏn's new relations with Japan after 1876.[84] But the magistrate Sin said, "We have conducted neighborly relations [kyorin] with Japan since the year of Imjin (1592). It has already been three hundred years." In Sin's view, the two countries merely "relate as we did before." Matiunin did not pursue the matter any further because any misstep might prevent Russia from establishing diplomatic relations with Chosŏn in the future.[85]

If Sin Yŏnghan viewed the Russian government's proposals as a challenge to Chosŏn border practices, N. G. Matiunin took Chosŏn's own actions in the Maritime as a direct affront to Russian authority over its territory and people. In 1882 Matiunin learned that a secret Chosŏn envoy, "Kuan San Ni-gai," had arrived

---

83. According to the dialogue recorded in *Kojong sillok*, Matiunin refers to Koreans who fled to Russia as "our people" (*amin*). Based on other documents at the time and tsarist Russian practices of conferring subjecthood on its various peoples, I assume that Matiunin uses the Russian word for "subject" (*poddanyi*) and that the Koreans he mentions had naturalized as Russian subjects.

84. Japan and Korea concluded the Treaty of Kanghwa in 1876. Historians consider it Korea's first modern treaty and interpret it as Japan's attempt to sever Korea's tributary relations with China. The Chosŏn court at the time, however, did not view the treaty in these terms; it was a way to avoid an immediate Japanese invasion. Kirk W. Larsen, *Tradition, Treaties, and Trade* (Cambridge, MA, 2008), 62–67.

85. RGIADV 1/1/769, l. 119 (March 1, 1880).

on the Russian side. He was immediately suspicious and ordered the police to detain him.[86] When questioned, Ni-gai said that he was a retired official and had merely come to visit old acquaintances who had moved to Russia. Matiunin released Ni-gai on the condition that he stop visiting Korean villages. But suspicions mounted when Ni-gai disobeyed the order and traveled to Korsakovka and Tizinhe where large numbers of Koreans "treat[ed] him with respect." The Russian police arrested him at Tizinhe and seized all his documents. His papers revealed that he had come at the order of the Chosŏn king himself "to observe the way of life of our Koreans [*nashi koreitsy*] and compose a detailed family register." Ni-gai also confessed that the "king intended, by concluding a treaty with us [Russia], to pronounce our Koreans as subjects of the Korean Kingdom though they remain on our territory."[87] Disturbed by the unfolding of events, Matiunin sent a letter to the governor of Hamgyŏng Province, complaining that "secretly dispatching government officials to another government is contrary to international norms [*mezhdunarodnye obychaia*], that we do not permit anyone to dominate in our country, and that the Koreans who live here as Russian subjects should not be disturbed by Korean officials." Threatening punishment to all "agitators," he warned the Hamgyŏng governor to put an end to such missions.[88] He deported Ni-gai and sent the letter with him.

Within tsarist circles, Matiunin interpreted the envoy's actions in the context of rapidly changing Qing-Chosŏn relations and ongoing Qing-Russia rivalries. In a letter to the military governor of the Maritime Province, he wrote that the "dispatch of this official is connected to recent events in Korea. Whether or not the European powers recognize Korea's vassalage to China . . . China has officially recognized Korea as its subordinate and lords about now like it is at home."[89] Indeed, this "sudden turn in Chinese politics" had occurred earlier in 1882, when the Qing had sent three thousand soldiers to squash the soldiers' riot in Seoul and became a quasi-imperial power on the peninsula. This change extended to the Qing's border policies in the Tumen valley. That year, Matiunin had caught wind of the Jilin banner government's efforts "to draw our Koreans across the border" by giving them money, oxen, and land in exchange for wearing Manchu clothes

---

86. Though this secret mission seems to have coincided in time with the mission conducted by Kim Kwanghun and Sin Sŏnuk, gaps in the Russian documentary record make it difficult to determine whether envoy "Kuan San Ni-gai" was part of Kim and Sin's mission or a separate mission altogether. I thus treat them as two unrelated events.

87. As reported by N. G. Matiunin in RGIADV 1/2/829, l. 48–48ob (November 18, 1882).

88. Ibid., l. 48.

89. Ibid., l. 49.

and shaving their heads in the Manchu style.[90] Given recent events, Matiunin was compelled to interpret Ni-gai's secret mission as a ploy of the Qing to extend its jurisdiction into Russian territory. He wrote, "Do not the [Qing] wish to establish themselves here by forcing the Korean government to dispatch their officials to Russia and go through pains in order that the entire settled population, which remains on our side, be recognized as Korean subjects?" In Matiunin's view, neither Chosŏn nor the Qing had a right to interfere in the affairs of naturalized Russian subjects. To forestall any future attempts by both governments to meddle in Russia's affairs, Matiunin urged that it was "absolutely necessary" to move the Koreans away from the border region and "mix them among Russian settlers." He reasoned that the Chosŏn court did not expect to have its people repatriated back to their original country.[91]

In the absence of formal relations between the two countries, Chosŏn and Russian officials were free to present their case for governing the mobility and jurisdiction of Koreans according to their own understandings of "international norms," diplomatic relations, and border policies. Yet the lack of a common language through which to agree or disagree led to an impasse on the Russo-Korean border. The continuous arrival of foreign powers in Chosŏn would soon compel the court to participate in the new language of international discourse—treaties. A newly concluded Russo-Korean agreement, however, would go further than extraterritorial treaties the court had concluded with other Western powers. Whereas the latter were confined to issues of jurisdiction and trade in specific ports, the Russo-Korean treaty would address the issue of Korean mobility across their shared boundary.

Breaking the Ban on Movement

In 1888 the Chosŏn court signed a treaty with Russia to govern movement and trade over the Tumen River boundary. The treaty was highly anticipated on both sides since they had failed to reach an agreement at the official establishment of relations in 1884 through the Treaty of Friendship and Commerce. The 1884 treaty, modeled on agreements concluded between Chosŏn and other Western powers, opened ports to Russian trade and stipulated extraterritoriality for both

---

90. RGIADV 1/1/502, l. 19 (January 26, 1882). The change in Qing policy is discussed in chapter 3.

91. RGIADV 1/2/829, l. 49–49ob (November 18, 1882).

Koreans and Russians abroad, but it did not discuss overland trade.[92] It took four years of negotiations to pass the 1888 Regulations for Land Trade on the Tumen River. The result was momentous. In a single treaty, Chosŏn pushed aside its prohibition on crossing the border and opened up the frontier region to Russia. Russians could now build houses in the border region and open a consulate in Kyŏnghŭng. Significantly, Chosŏn subjects were allowed to "travel freely in Russia for purposes of trade or pleasure" as long as they carried a passport. Once they reached the border, they were to present their passports to be endorsed by Russian authorities (art. 2, par. 3).[93] The statute de facto overturned the ban on movement that had existed for centuries and legally permitted Koreans to travel abroad.

The significance of the 1888 regulations cannot be fully appreciated without a comparison to an earlier commercial treaty. The first step in overturning the ban on movement, in fact, was the Chosŏn-Qing Regulations for Maritime and Overland Trade concluded in September 1882.[94] The agreement was unprecedented for the two countries. It repealed the ban on maritime trade (art. 1) and opened the frontier area to trade in designated towns along the Yalu and Tumen Rivers (art. 5).[95] The rules also legalized border crossings: Qing and Chosŏn subjects were now allowed to travel freely to and from these towns. The treaty reflected the Qing's newfound role in Chosŏn and was an attempt to foster commercial trade in a region that had been regulated by the ceremonial tribute system.

As groundbreaking as the 1882 treaty was, however, the Chosŏn-Qing border was still defined within the framework of the tributary system. The 1883 Twenty-Four Rules for Traffic on the Frontier between Liaodong and Korea, which clarified the earlier agreement, made the distinct point that tributary relations would continue between the two countries.[96] Local Korean authorities and customs

---

92. Li Hongzhang, Chosŏn's primary mediator vis-à-vis Western powers, helped negotiate "gentler" terms for Chosŏn after learning from China's own unfavorable experience with extraterritoriality treaties. Larsen, *Tradition, Treaties, and Trade*, 77–79.

93. *Ku Hanmal ŭi choyak*, 3:56–80; Ministerstvo Torgovli i Promyshlennosti, *Sbornik torgovykh dogovorov*, 392–404.

94. Full text can be found in *Ku Hanmal ŭi choyak*, 3:392–406. Kirk Larsen notes that Western powers used the 1882 regulations as a model for their own (revised) treaties, since the regulations stipulated lower tariffs and easier entrance of their subjects into Korea. See Kirk Larsen, *Tradition, Treaties, and Trade*, 93–94.

95. Towns included Ch'aengmun and Ŭiju on the Yalu River, and Hunchun and Hoeryŏng on the Tumen River.

96. For background on the 1882 and 1883 rules, see Larsen, *Tradition, Treaties, and Trade*, 88–91. Full text provided in *Ku Hanmal ŭi choyak*, 3:407–21.

officials were instructed to address China in the language of tribute, such as "Heavenly Court" or "Superior Country," and to avoid modern-day appellations such as "Middle Kingdom" (rule 23). Korea was supposed to uphold its part in the tributary relationship by dispatching missions to Beijing at regular intervals, as it had in the past, and by granting special trade privileges to the Qing court on the Yalu River. To confirm the particularity of the Chosŏn-Qing relationship, the 1883 agreement stated that the rules applied only to these two countries. The terms had "no connection" to foreign trade in the treaty ports (rule 10). Apart from maintaining tributary relations, the treaty also preserved the integrity of the buffer area. Permanent settlement in the zone was still prohibited. Though the rules opened specific towns for trade, they were merely a de facto recognition of the trade that was already being conducted in state-sanctioned markets, such as Hoeryŏng and Ŭiju. That the border region remained largely closed was confirmed by a clause that designated who could travel there. At the outset, the rules stated that travel privileges applied only to the "merchants of Liaodong and Chosŏn"; only "merchants" (*sangmin*) or those engaged in commerce could travel freely to the market towns, and only merchants could receive a passport (*chipjo*) to travel to the interior (*naeji*), beyond the border zone (rule 2). No commoner, slave, or person traveling for the purpose of non-government-sanctioned activity was allowed to cross the border. The historic "prohibited zone" policy thus remained in effect even as modern commerce began to make inroads into the region.

By contrast, the 1888 Russo-Korean commercial treaty broke with previous norms of travel and borders. It made no distinction between merchants, commoners, and elites and left open the purpose and destination of one's journey. The rules did not specify travelers by their status or occupation in the status system but instead defined them strictly in terms of their national association. By carrying a national passport, a Korean was designated simply as a "Korean." *Anyone* with a Korean passport could travel "freely" to Russia. The rules de facto lifted the ban on border crossing and laid the groundwork for a new system of documentation that brought Koreans into an emerging "bordered" world. Their identity and belonging to Chosŏn were no longer assumed, but put on a piece of paper to prove their identity as "Koreans" and to consent to their right to travel. The territorial border, moreover, was no longer a banned area that was off-limits to movement, but a legal place of transit. Passports, entry-exit rules, and customs fees all pointed to the making of a new kind of state border on Chosŏn's perimeter.

As for the jurisdiction of Koreans in Russia, the 1888 rules were left deliberately ambiguous. The Russian chargé d'affaires in Seoul, Karl I. Weber, had repeatedly asked the Chosŏn government to restrict further Korean migration to Russia and to recognize Koreans who had arrived before 1884—the year the two states had established official relations—as full subjects of Russia, "enjoying the same privileges as other Russian subjects." The request about regulating movement was granted by the new system of passports, but the issue of jurisdiction remained unsettled. According to Weber, commercial agent Kim Yunsik had "personally consented to the insertion of this statute in the agreement" as early as April 1887. In the same letter, Weber also claimed that the Chosŏn government had "agree[d] with me in principle about the Korean migrants [*pereselensty*]." There was no written evidence, however, that any Chosŏn official had agreed. The Chosŏn government aimed to assert its authority over Koreans by clarifying mutual extradition clauses and conducting a census of Koreans in Russia, not by accepting the Russian government's claims.[97] Even after the signing of the 1888 treaty, when Weber tried to revive the question, Cho Pyŏngjik, the new commercial agent, requested that Weber stop insisting that the Chosŏn government give him written consent. For granting such a request was, in his view, tantamount to a "renunciation of its former subjects."[98] In the end, no clause about subjecthood was included. In fact, rather than recognize a permanent change in the Koreans' legal status, the rules left open the possibility that Koreans could return to Chosŏn. At the request of Kim Yunsik, the 1888 agreement included a clause that stated, "Korean subjects residing in Russia will have the right, if they so desire, to return to their respective countries [K: *kot'o*; R: *rodina*], and the competent authorities shall grant them passports for that purpose" (art. 2, par. 5).[99] The subsequent 1891 treaty, Temporary Rules for Crossing the Tumen River, further outlined laws for cross-border movement and established a fee structure for travel, but it made no mention of jurisdiction or subjecthood.[100] The issue was off the table for negotiation as far as the Chosŏn government was concerned. Indeed, its actions in neighboring Manchuria demonstrated how far it would go to claim its people in the face of other states.

The regulations of 1888 represented not so much an end to the question of international norms, an arrival at a definitive answer, as a single piece in a tapestry

---

97. *Ku Han'guk oegyo munsŏ*, 17:62, 99–100, 60–61.

98. Cho Pyŏngjik quoted in Pak, *Rossiia i Koreia*, 68.

99. The same held true for Russian subjects residing in Korea. *Ku Hanmal ŭi choyak*, 3:70; Ministerstvo Torgovli i Promyshlennosti, *Sbornik torgovykh dogovorov*, 395; *Ku Han'guk oegyo munsŏ*, 17:62.

100. The 1891 temporary rules allowed for the direct passage of peoples and goods across the Tumen River. Previously, goods exported from Korea to Russia had to pass through two checkpoints—first in Hunchun (China) and second in Russia. Merchants had thus been forced to pay tariffs twice. The rules established customs points in Kyŏnghŭng on the Korean side and Krasnoe Selo on the Russian side. B. B. Pak, *Rossiiskaia diplomatiia i Koreia* (Irkutsk, 1998), 21, 230.

of negotiations, perspectives, and struggles that were gradually unfolding about mobile Koreans. The reinterpretation of borders and travel in 1888 was indeed significant. A culmination of previous talks, the agreement broke the policy of prohibition that hemmed subjects inside the boundaries of their respective countries and condemned those who left as traitors. In place of the long-standing prohibited zone stood a new border open to movement and a legal system that gave any Korean the right to travel as long as he carried a passport. But simultaneous to this emerging story of the making of international norms, changes inside and between Chosŏn, Russia, and the Qing set in motion antinomies of unprecedented claims that were not easily reconciled with each other. King Kojong, who looked to expatriates beyond Chosŏn's boundaries to preserve the body politic, found that his jurisdictional claims over Koreans conflicted with those lodged by the Qing and Russia. With no single hegemon in the region to force the issue, their jurisdiction remained elusive. In the decades to come, governing Koreans inside one's borders and justifying these claims to the outside world became a matter intertwined with broader concerns of the state: building sovereignty. The path each state embarked on would soon diverge.

3

CONTESTED BORDER

Multiple Sovereignties, Multiple Citizenships in Manchuria

In the late 1800s a view from the top of Mount Paektu revealed stark changes transpiring in the Tumen and Yalu valleys below. The prohibited zone, the buffer area that had been sanctioned by the Qing and Chosŏn governments to secure peace along their shared border, was gradually coming apart. Once protected by its relative remoteness and sparsity of people, the region witnessed the arrival of increasing numbers of Han Chinese and Russians who came to participate in the burgeoning frontier economy. Koreans, who had easiest access to the region, emerged as the majority population on the Qing side of the Tumen, growing to approximately 4,300 households in 1894 and to 6,000 thirteen years later.[1] The mobility and permanent settlement of people in the border region signaled to both states that the mutual policy of prohibition was no longer tenable as a border practice. New ways of governing the people and region were needed.

This chapter examines the dramatic transformation of Chosŏn and Qing officials' attempts to manage the borderland and its Korean inhabitants, from a shared policy of restraining movement and preserving an empty buffer to an

---

1. The 4,300 households were equivalent to about 21,000 people. This figure includes only Koreans who were registered by the Jilin government and incorporated into administrative institutions in an unspecified territory along the Tumen River. It was the first time that Jilin officials had conducted a survey of people in the area. The second figure, taken from Wu Luzhen's 1907 "Report on affairs in the Yanji [Yŏn'gil] border area," accounts for Koreans living in the middle and upper Tumen River region at the time of the report. Nianshen Song, "My Land, My People" (Ph.D. diss., University of Chicago, 2013), 163.

urgent project that aimed to clarify the boundaries of their respective states and peoples. Driven concomitantly by anxieties over border-crossing Koreans and threats of foreign powers on their boundaries, officials experimented with practices of exclusive jurisdiction and border control. In the early 1880s the Qing began to encourage settlement in Manchuria. Region by region, it removed the ban on the prohibited zone, with the Tumen valley one of the last to be opened. It also drastically changed its policy toward Koreans on its territory. Instead of turning Koreans away as they had in the past, Qing officials adopted a stance similar to that of their Russian counterparts in the Maritime: they accepted the Koreans as de facto settlers, gave them land, and incorporated them as Qing subjects. Chosŏn officials followed suit. They refused to accept the Qing's claims on its subjects and lodged their own claims on the expatriate population. Having accepted the presence of Koreans outside Korea, the court sent overseers to govern its subjects on the Qing side of the Tumen valley, in a region that became known as Kando.[2] The two countries also resurrected territorial disputes about the exact location of the river flows, a topic that had been left unresolved since the early eighteenth century. After the signing of the Treaty of Shimonoseki (1895), which officially ended the tributary relationship between the two powers and recognized them as equal sovereign powers, Chosŏn and Qing officials debated over Kando with renewed vigor. Incorporating the emerging global discourse of sovereignty and international law in their negotiations, each sought to defend their respective jurisdictional claims.

In the early twentieth century, the question of Kando and its Koreans became further mired in complexity as the geopolitical order of the region shifted once again. Soon after Chosŏn became a sovereign state and proclaimed itself the Empire of the Great Han in 1897, it found itself silenced on the international

---

2. The origin of "Kando" is unclear, but it seems to have come into use in Chosŏn in the 1880s, when questions about the boundary line between Chosŏn and the Qing resurfaced. Yi Chungha, a Chosŏn official who surveyed the area in the mid-1880s, noted that the Kando was not actually an island as its name suggested but the name inhabitants used to refer to an area on the Tumen River bank, between Chongsŏng and Onsŏng. He reported that people in the Six Forts area began to cultivate land in Kando in the late 1870s. "Kando" began to be more widely used in the early 1900s— first, as an irredentist movement in Chosŏn to claim this area, and second, as a Japanese imperialist maneuver. Indeed, Japanese colonial officials began to employ the transliteration of "Kantō" in territorial disputes with the Qing in the early twentieth century. In 1907 Japan established the Kantō temporary field office of the resident-general of Korea. Kantō, however, did not constitute an official administrative unit until the Japanese established the state of Manchukuo in 1932. As for the Qing, it referred to the area as "Yanji" (K: Yŏn'gil) in the late nineteenth century. It should be noted that after 1945, South Korean nationalist historians tended to use this term without recognizing its ambiguous origins or colonial appropriation by the Japanese. See "Note on Places and Terms" for more details. Yi Chungha, *Yŏkchu "Kamgyesa tŭngnok"* (Seoul, 2008), 282; Song, "Journey towards 'No Man's Land'"; Song, "My Land, My People," 158–62.

stage. In 1905, at the conclusion of the Russo-Japanese War, Korea was made a protectorate of Japan. Five years later, Korea was colonized outright. Japanese Foreign Ministry officials, seeking to build an empire on the Asian continent, took Korea's place at the negotiating table with the Qing and lodged claims over Kando and its Korean inhabitants. In 1909 Japan concluded a treaty with the Qing and acquired the right to create extraterritorial leaseholds in Kando, leaving the Qing to contend with the formation of another semicolony within its borders. China, meanwhile, splintered by the collapse of the dynasty and internal conflicts, was unable to firmly exercise its sovereignty over Manchuria. Provincial officials attempted to extend China's jurisdiction over Korean inhabitants by encouraging them to become Chinese "citizens," but even after multiple rounds of negotiations with Japanese officials, the legal status of expatriate Koreans—at once called Chinese "citizens" and Japanese "subjects"—remained contested. Japan's establishment of the state of Manchukuo in 1932 further compromised China's sovereignty over its northern territory, turning the legal status of Manchuria, including Kando, into a "question" of international concern. What emerged in Kando was an incomplete sovereignty, in which colony and empire, territorial jurisdiction and unequal extraterritorial regimes, imperial subjects and citizens uneasily coexisted in a single place.

Disintegration and Life in the Prohibited Zone

By the 1870s, protections that had safeguarded the prohibited zone were quickly fading, and the Tumen valley was opened to a larger world. As growing numbers of poachers, merchants, and farmers migrated to the region, illegal settlements sprang up everywhere. Han Chinese entered the region in search of commercial opportunity and land to cultivate, while Heje and Oroqen tribes, who were native to the Tumen, found themselves displaced from their farming and hunting grounds by the arrival of newcomers. Faced with a dwindling supply of natural resources, tribal peoples found it nearly impossible to fulfill their tribute obligations and began to move across the border to Russia.[3] A burgeoning capitalist market, precipitated in part by Russia's entrance into northeast Asia, also created new reasons for people to travel to the border area. Within this context, Koreans migrated across the Tumen and Yalu Rivers to the region of Kando.

---

3. Both native tribes and the Qing imperial court faced difficulties in meeting their respective tribute obligations. Increased military obligations, dwindling resources, banditry, and access to foreign markets all contributed to the tribute supply problem. In 1881 the Jilin general appealed to the Board of Revenue to end the tribute quota; in 1908 Beijing ordered a temporary suspension of tribute in Jilin Province. Loretta Kim, "Marginal Constituencies," 218–23.

Koreans filled a critical gap in the burgeoning frontier economy of Kando. Bordered by the Tumen and upper Yalu Rivers to the east, Russia to the north, and the rest of Jilin and Heilongjiang Provinces to the west, the fertile region of Kando found itself in the middle of economic and demographic change in the late nineteenth century. South of Mount Paektu, on the banks of the Yalu River, Koreans composed the majority of workers in barley fields and cultivated ginseng farms. Though most industries seemed to have been controlled by Han Chinese,[4] themselves relatively recent arrivals from Shandong, Liaodong, and other parts of Manchuria, Koreans outnumbered Han settlers by a ratio as large as nine to one. According to a Chosŏn envoy to the region, "there was not one place where Koreans had not been hired by Chinese as farmhands." The "countless numbers" of laborers were mostly men who "had not managed to gain families and lived lonely lives as bachelors."[5] Apart from farming, Koreans engaged in occupations that ran the gamut—cutting timber, transporting logs along waterways, reclaiming land, gathering and cultivating ginseng, hunting for deer and sable, and panning for gold.[6] North of Mount Paektu, in the Tumen valley, Koreans tilled their own land. Various geographical and environmental obstacles—mountainous terrain, harsh weather, and sheer distance—had kept Han migration to the Tumen to a minimum, hemming them into Liaodong and leaving this northern corner of the Qing empire relatively free of settlers. Koreans, by comparison, crossed the shallow Tumen River with ease and were able to claim the open fields.

Similar to compatriots who left for Russia, Koreans who migrated to Kando led cross-border lives that were guided by the seasons. Each spring, men traveled to Kando to farm, and after the harvest in autumn they returned home. In the dead of winter, the absence of people was striking. Temporary abodes built by farmers were abandoned, and the landscape looked desolate.[7] The following spring, migrants returned and the fields burst to life again. Men diligently burned, plowed, seeded, and cultivated the land. After a season or two of peripatetic living, men brought their wives, children, and extended family from Chosŏn to live permanently. Those who lived as bachelors, meanwhile, found

---

4. According to a Jilin official who conducted an inspection of the Mount Paektu/Changbai region, some of the first Han Chinese had appeared in the region in the early 1800s. Robert Lee, *Manchurian Frontier*, 108.

5. Ch'oe Chongbŏm, *Kando kaech'ŏk pisa*, ed. Ch'oe Kanghyŏn (Seoul, 2004), 39, 45.

6. Ibid., 19, 22; H. Evan M. James, *The Long White Mountain* (London, 1888), 254.

7. Kim Ch'unsŏn, "1880–1890 nyŏndae Ch'ŏngjo ŭi 'imin silbyŏn' chŏngch'aek kwa Hanin ijumin silt'ae yŏn'gu," *Han'guk kŭnhyŏndaesa yŏn'gu*, no. 8 (1998): 31.

homes among Manchus and Han Chinese, who not only sheltered and clothed them but also lent them money as needed.[8]

Koreans found themselves intermeshed in the makeshift forms of governance in the border area. By the late nineteenth century, grassroots organizations had sprung up in settlements throughout Manchuria. Founded by Han Chinese, indigenous tribes, and early Korean arrivals, the village associations (*huifang*) constituted an idiosyncratic civil government alongside the Manchu banner system, and they fulfilled the roles of tax collector, legal advisor, and police all at once. In his account of travels to Mount Paektu, H. Evan James noted that inhabitants had established guilds run by a head, deputy head, and sergeant "who legislate for the community, and exercise powers of life and death." The Jilin banner government, keenly aware of its limited capacities to rule in the region, frequently made use of the powers of the guild, calling on it to assist in catching thieves. And the association responded in turn. "On such occasions," James wrote, "the headman of the guild sends a circular round, and . . . even if a man had got a deer in every pit, he must shoulder his matchlock and go." The guilds also passed "legislation" to regulate the trade of ginseng. To James, the guilds seemed the "most efficient institutions" in the borderland.[9] His observations were corroborated by a contemporary, Cao Tingjie, who discovered similar associations in Ussuri, and, in the early 1900s, by a Jilin official, who spoke of the same guilds, albeit in a less favorable light.[10]

The loose array of governmental organizations in Kando, however, was no match for the power of bandits. As was the case in Ussuri, banditry became part of the fabric of life on the frontier, and people frequently fell victim to brigands who stormed through their villages. It seemed that the geography—encompassing dense forests, hundreds of hills sunken with caves, crisscrossing streams, and islands floating in the middle of them—and military culture that had been cultivated over centuries made Kando and broader Manchuria a fertile ground for banditry to thrive.[11] The bandits, or *honghuzi*, kidnapped the wealthy for ransom and sacked any residence where food and possessions could be found.[12] No settlement—Manchu, Chinese, Korean, or mixed—was safe. Koreans also

---

8. Ch'oe Chongbŏm, *Kando kaech'ŏk pisa*, 48.

9. James, *Long White Mountain*, 251, 252–53.

10. Robert Lee, *Manchurian Frontier*, 107–9.

11. Patrick Shan also cites the lack of an effective civilian government and high male-to-female gender ratios as factors contributing to the spread of banditry in Heilongjiang Province; the weak civilian government in particular distinguished banditry in the region from that in other parts of northern China. For a counterargument to Eric Hobsbawm's thesis that banditry was an outgrowth of agricultural society, see Shan, "Insecurity, Outlawry and Social Order," 26–31.

12. Robert Lee, *Manchurian Frontier*, 94.

attacked their fellow countrymen. In one such case, Kwŏn Sil, a native of Kang-gye who had served as the self-proclaimed leader of a gang, set out to attack his compatriots on the Qing side of the Yalu River. He was frustrated by the villagers' disobedience of his orders and charged his gang to punish them. The bandits beat the Koreans, took hostages, and set fire to a number of houses. From the villagers' point of view, there was no one more bent on harming them and their country.[13]

Perhaps the most active site of movement was the upper Tumen valley, situated at the intersection of China, Korea, and Russia. Similar to those who took advantage of the porosity of borders to commit nefarious acts, Korean migrants traveled in and out of Kando to escape bandits or to seek opportunities in Russia. Many crossed the boundaries of several states to reach their final destination simply because doing so was the most expedient travel route. Along the way, the dense communities of their compatriots allowed migrants to move from country to country without having to adjust to a foreign language or culture.

Turning a Jurisdictional Dispute on Its Side

Chosŏn officials responded to the movement of Koreans to China with the same alarm that they had shown toward Koreans in Russia. While peripatetic habits and illegal trade had been endemic to the border area, their occurrence surged in the late nineteenth century. Indeed, in 1874 the magistrate of the border town Ŭiju reported that the "vice of illegal trade" had existed in the past, but not to the present extent. He surmised that the growing use of money had facilitated the buying and selling of goods. Hwang also noted that villages had sprung up everywhere, a phenomenon that stirred worries about a region that was supposed to have been left an "empty zone."[14] The departure of Koreans to Qing territory simultaneously touched on officials' fears that subjects were losing their civilized ways. Ch'oe Chongbŏm,[15] who conducted a secret mission to the Qing side of the Yalu River bank, lamented that his countrymen appeared to have abandoned

---

13. Ch'oe Chongbŏm, *Kando kaech'ŏk pisa*, 34–36.

14. *Kojong sillok* 11/1/28 (March 16, 1874).

15. In 1872 Ch'oe Chongbŏm, along with Kim T'aehŭng and Im Sŏkkŭn, was charged with investigating the aftermath of a violent outbreak that had occurred a year earlier in the border region near Huch'ang County, Pyŏngan Province. They also surveyed the communities of Koreans on Qing territory. *Diary of the North* (*Kangbuk ilgi*) is the account of their journey—the "north" referring to the northern bank of the Yalu River, on the Qing side. Though authorship has not been confirmed, many scholars believe the writer to be Ch'oe Chongbŏm. Ch'oe Chongbŏm, *Kando kaech'ŏk pisa*, 92–94; Yi Tongjin, "1872 nyŏn 'Kangbuk' ŭi Chosŏnin sahoe," *Tongbuga yŏksa nonch'ong* 8 (2005): 289–90; Kwangmin Kim, "Korean Migration in Nineteenth-Century Manchuria," in *Mobile Subjects*, ed. Wen-hsin Yeh (Berkeley, 2013), 17–37.

their country and resigned themselves to a forlorn existence as "slaves to the barbarians." It was a sight that made him "explode with anger." How could a people
of a civilized country such as Chosŏn come into contact with barbarians? When
he asked Koreans why they had "betray[ed] their country," they gave a common
response: "I did not come to betray my country, but I was so hungry and living
such a miserable existence that I was chased here."[16] The heightened sense of
alarm, however, did not translate into action until a decade later, when Chosŏn
officials learned about the Qing's recent actions.

In the early 1880s the Qing drastically reversed its border policy. The government had already been forced to cede control of treaty ports to various foreign
powers and a vast area of its northeastern territory to Russia. It also witnessed the
decline of its own security forces. As Russian troops attacked its sentry posts and
people transgressed the border, the Qing discovered that its line of defense had
been further compromised by the growing number of Manchus who were fleeing
their banner posts. To deter Russia's advancement in the northeast, Qing officials lifted the ban on permanent settlement in Manchuria, including the Tumen
valley in 1881, and began to promote Han migration to the region. Authorities
also incorporated the Heje and Oroqen into the military system to counter the
dwindling of the ranks. They created new administrative units, reorganized
the civilian population into auxiliary military detachments, and tied the seminomadic peoples to settlements. In 1882 an official in Heilongjiang went so far as
to recommend the enlistment of the entire population of Oroqen into banners.
He reasoned that their multilingual capabilities in Chinese, Manchu, and Russian
would make them ideal soldiers, while their new full-time occupation would free
them from having to trade with Russians for a living.[17]

The Qing similarly attempted to incorporate Korean inhabitants. Rather than
commanding them to return to Chosŏn, authorities permitted the Koreans to
stay and began to claim them as Qing subjects. In 1881 Wu Dacheng, the recently
appointed minister of border affairs, and Ming'an, the Jilin garrison commander,
decided to utilize the Koreans as de facto settlers in the northeast. Koreans had
already begun to farm the most fertile land. Even Chinese who rented land from
the state ended up subleasing it to the Koreans because most Chinese, in the
words of a Qing officer, "had no skill in reclaiming and cultivating the land."[18]
After debating whether or not to allow Koreans to cultivate land in the border
area—and, if not, how to repatriate back them to Chosŏn—Ming'an gave the

---

16. Ch'oe Chongbŏm, *Kando kaech'ŏk pisa*, 41, 80, 27.
17. The Heilongjiang official referred specifically to "Pedestrian Oroqen." Loretta Kim, "Marginal
Constituencies," 207.
18. Quoted in Kim Ch'unsŏn, "1880–1890 nyŏndae Ch'ŏngjo," 17.

Koreans permission to remain and distributed land licenses, a privilege for which they had to pay taxes.[19] The next year, Qing authorities took this one step further. In addition to paying taxes, Koreans were told they should register their households with local authorities, recognize the legal jurisdiction of the Qing, shave their heads in the Manchu style, and wear Manchu clothes. They were to become Qing subjects under Qing jurisdiction.[20] If they did not comply, they would be expelled from the land.

The change in Qing policy aroused the concern of the Chosŏn court. King Kojong urged the Jilin official to remove the Koreans from the Qing registers and to repatriate all the people. The Qing agreed, even granting a grace period of one year.[21] But the repatriation of thousands of Koreans proved too unwieldy an undertaking. Little was done. In the years that followed, tensions mounted as story after story broke about acts of provocation by commanders who tried to force Koreans off the land by burning down their houses or chasing them away, even at gunpoint.[22] In 1890 a border official took it upon himself to accelerate the process of naturalization or expulsion by setting a deadline of less than three weeks within which Koreans were supposed to "change their hairstyle and clothing." On hearing the latest news, Min Chongmuk, head of the Chosŏn Office for Negotiation and Trade, promptly lodged a complaint to his diplomatic counterpart, Yuan Shikai, saying he was "deeply surprised" that this official had "dared" to set such a deadline, for no imperial edict on the matter had been passed. Such a course of action, moreover, would surely "instigate" the people to no good end. He urged Yuan to telegram the border official to stop the forced naturalization of Koreans at once. But according to the Zongli Yamen (the Qing foreign affairs office), the Chosŏn government had not owned up to its responsibility in the matter because it had delayed fulfilling its promise to repatriate the people for nine long years. Yuan added that it was too difficult for Qing officials to remove the settlers themselves, and as such, the only option left was to force the Koreans to naturalize as Qing subjects.[23]

No less vocal than officials were the settlers themselves. Since the passing of the naturalization edict, they had responded in various ways: they had acquired Qing subjecthood to remain on their farms, ignored the mandate, or simply fled. The last turned out to be the most expedient path when faced with violent

19. Ibid., 18. Ming'an was the same official who recommended the incorporation of the civilian Heje into the banner system in areas near the border. See Loretta Kim, "Marginal Constituencies," 201.

20. Schmid, *Korea between Empires*, 208; Kim Ch'unsŏn, "1880–1890 nyŏndae Ch'ŏngjo," 19.

21. As recounted by Yuan Shikai in *Ku Han'guk oegyo munsŏ*, 8:724 (August 28, 1890).

22. *Kojong sillok* 22/5/7 no. 2 (June 19, 1885); Kim Ch'unsŏn, "1880–1890 nyŏndae Ch'ŏngjo," 21.

23. *Ku Han'guk oegyo munsŏ*, 8:723, 724 (August 27, 1890).

reprisals, as an incident from 1889 revealed. That autumn, it became evident that the naturalization of Koreans was not the only aim of the Qing government: it hoped to prevent Korean migration altogether, and Qing soldiers went to extreme measures to stop them. Soldiers lined the banks of the river to form a human barrier, shot at Koreans with rifles, and continued down a destructive path by torching makeshift bridges and ferryboats, bent on eliminating modes of transportation that had apparently abetted the illegal trafficking of people and precious timber for years. One man was paralyzed in the crossfire. Koreans on the Qing side fell into a panic. Quickly weighing their odds of survival on each side of the border—reprisals in China, destitution in Korea, and potential land in Russia—many fled to Russia.[24]

This particular incident of violence occasioned a rare petition by a Korean farmer.[25] The petition illuminated the clarity with which the settlers grasped the changes in Qing policy as well as their resolve to remain on the Qing side. The petitioner, An Chŏnghyŏk, speaking to Qing authorities on behalf of his compatriots, brazenly proclaimed that the Koreans had been "deceived" by the naturalization edict. They had shaved their heads, changed their clothes, and acquired a new subjecthood—everything the Qing required them to do—but they had not received what had been promised: land. Instead, they had been forcefully expelled from their farms. An Chŏnghyŏk proposed an alternative strategy in which the Qing should abandon its attempt to change the status quo. Rather than forcing them to shave their heads and imposing a ban on farming (wŏlgan) and timber cutting, he argued, the Koreans should be allowed to grow back their hair and use the land as they had in the past. They should be able to maintain their original ways. For doing so was essential to preserving loyalty to the family as Confucian ideology dictated. Appealing to the shared customs of countries "all under Heaven," An laid out his proposal with striking aplomb:

> We beg to be treated the same as people in your domain, regardless of the boundary. . . . On the whole, in Confucian orthodoxy, though there may be differences in our rules, are we not all people under the divine Son of Heaven? Why, then, is it necessary to shave our heads and change our clothing and thus become Chinese [hwamin]? If I humbly consider it, the people have already become accustomed [to living and farming in the border region]. But once they see change, they automatically

---

24. Ibid., 9:60–61 (September 25, 1891).
25. It is highly likely that the petition of An Chŏnghyŏk, who was a commoner and probably illiterate, was written by a scrivener. Scriveners in Chosŏn employed narrative strategies to present the grievances of the petitioner in the most persuasive manner, but the content of the written document still derived from the aggrieved. Jisoo Kim, *The Emotions of Justice* (Seattle, 2015), 16–17, 46–47.

become suspicious and fearful. Those who have shaved their heads are naturally uneasy and ashamed to see the people in their homeland. They cannot endure such shame and sail back home. Alas, I pity those who have shaved their heads. Their ancestral graves and relatives are all on the other side of the river. [Because they cannot return,] there is no one to pay respect and make offerings of incense throughout the year. If the lineage of their relatives dies out, there will be no one to visit the grave to mourn. This is the normal way of man. The day the people were forced to shave their heads, the people sang a song: "thousands of families wail over the shaving of heads, [while] tens of thousands of people worry about the ban on farming."[26]

The link between sustaining the living and the dead was made particularly poignant in his letter. According to the petitioner, the recent ban on timber cutting had deprived many Koreans of their ability to properly bury the dead in the first place, for most of the wood for coffins was sourced from Qing territory. He proclaimed that the ban "forces the living to go on without firewood and the dead to have their bones exposed." Thus, "in one stroke, the means to both sustain the living and mourn the dead have been destroyed."[27]

Adding to his cries to allow the people to preserve their ways, An vehemently insisted that they should be permitted to stay on Qing soil. Since their home province of Hamgyŏng had been "completely denuded," he wrote, Koreans had come to depend on the uncultivated land on the Qing side as a lifeline. Land was not only the way they fed and clothed themselves but also the primary means for them to act out filial lives, "serving elders and raising children." It was so critical to their survival that, after the recent expulsions, even Koreans who desired to return to their homeland chose "out of necessity" to go to Russia because of its abundant land. Citing Confucian norms of propriety, An went so far as to rebuke Qing officials for driving his compatriots to the "barbarian" land of Russia:

> You have shown kindness to the people, but have not done so to the end. In one moment, ten years of nurturing have been driven away for the benefit of another [Russia]. There is friendship between the Great Country [taeguk] and the Small Country [soguk]. But losing people for the sake of [preserving your] land—isn't this due to stinginess of morality on your part?[28]

26. *Ku Han'guk oegyo munsŏ*, 9:60–61.
27. Ibid.
28. Ibid.

When Yuan Shikai saw the letter, he dismissed it and belittled An as an individual "ignorant of proper ways." An stood firmly by his position, however. If the Qing reopened the land to the Koreans, they would come.

An's petition, firmly argued on the basis of Confucian norms, turned out to be as radical as recent Qing policy. By demanding that the Koreans stay on Qing soil and remain subjects of Chosŏn, An had unwittingly proposed a new status for Korean settlers: permanent inhabitants in a foreign land who retained their original status by law. Koreans would pay rent (zu) to the Qing to use the land but would not alter their hairstyle, clothing, or records in the Chosŏn household registers. The notion that an individual would be allowed to live in a foreign land without the threat of expulsion or recrimination was novel enough, for it flew in the face of long-held governing practices. But it further contradicted the Qing's recent course of action, in which it endeavored to incorporate inhabitants around the edges of its empire as subjects. In the end, the proposal fell on deaf ears.

While officials and settlers sparred over issues of naturalization and land use on the Qing side, they simultaneously investigated a matter of equal significance: the location of the territorial border itself. Ever since the joint expedition to Mount Paektu in 1712, little had been done to verify the correct position of the border stele that had been lodged to mark the source of the Tumen River, a not-so-insignificant task when one considered the tendency of rivers, especially along mountain slopes, to shift course over time. In Chosŏn, the negligence of its envoys had given the court reason to condemn the findings of the mission—a loss of land for Chosŏn—and left future bureaucrats to dismiss it as a shameful event in the country's annals. Efforts to elucidate the border died down shortly after the expedition. The uncertainty that shrouded the stele did not matter much in practice because few people lived in the border region at the time. In the 1880s, however, the rise in number of conflicts involving border-crossing Chosŏn and Qing subjects in the Tumen valley, coupled with anxieties about external threats, incited farmers, investigators, and diplomats alike to press for a new mission to reassess the position of the border and to tie it to the question of the jurisdiction of Koreans. If the land Koreans currently occupied belonged to Chosŏn, then the basic assumption that they had crossed into Qing territory would be invalidated, and their naturalization or eviction unnecessary.

Farmers took matters into their own hands to prove that they were, in fact, still within the bounds of Chosŏn.[29] In 1882 they trekked up Mount Paektu to

---

29. The following discussion about investigations of the border stele is based on Schmid, *Korea between Empires*, 208–11.

find the famed border stele erected by Mukedeng a century and a half earlier. The stone was supposed to mark the source of the Tumen River, but what the farmers found on the surface of the stele was not the character signifying "tu" for Tumen River, meaning "diagram." Instead, "earth" had been carved into the stone. As they pointed out, even though the pronunciation was nearly identical, the different characters represented two distinct rivers. The "earth" Tumen River marked the northernmost point of Chosŏn's territory, while the "diagram" Tumen River flowed inside Chosŏn. The Qing authorities had mistakenly assumed the two rivers were one and the same, they contended.[30] In fact, their homes were *between* the two rivers, and as such, they were living inside the borders of Chosŏn. The settlers urged local officials to conduct a proper survey of the stele on Mount Paektu, because in their view, only the stele could determine the correctness of the border. Weighty questions of territory, jurisdiction, and even what one could call "home" came to rest on a piece of stone.

The discovery resurrected official efforts to investigate the source of the rivers. Ŏ Yunjung, a special inspector for the northwest, conducted two separate missions to verify the position and text of the stele. The results not only confirmed the settlers' position but also allayed any doubts the Chosŏn court may have harbored about their claim to these lands. As Ŏ reported, it was "most clear" that the lands did not belong to China. In 1885, prompted by numerous border disputes on all three sides, including a protracted Sino-Russian fight over the Korean hamlet of Savelovka, Chosŏn representatives met their Qing counterparts to conduct a joint survey of Mount Paektu. Yi Chungha, head of the Chosŏn delegation, though speaking in the humble language that the "inferior" country used to address the "superior" country, was strident in explaining his position. His claims relied on a deep historical knowledge of Mukedeng's mission of 1712 and the significance of the stele. Yi believed that the stele, the only physical remnant to mark the source of the rivers, should serve as the deciding factor in delineating the border. As such, he and his team argued that it was necessary to begin the survey from the stele and then follow the flow of water that had been demarcated as the dividing point. The Qing delegation, however, rejected the existing stele as central to the investigation. Officials went so far as to suggest that the stele, weighing about 100 *kŭn*, could have been moved from its original location by someone over the years.[31] The Qing argued that the task of clarifying

---

30. A slightly different interpretation of the location and names of the Tumen River is given in Song, "The Journey towards 'No Man's Land,'" 1035–58. Chosŏn officials, who returned to the site of the stele in 1712, found that Mukedeng had mistaken the Sungari (Songhua) River for the Tumen River.

31. Yi Chungha, *Yŏkchu "Kamgyesa tŭngnok,"* 172.

the border should not begin at the stele but rather at the mouth of the river and then be traced upstream. Doing so would not only extinguish any questions about the validity of the stele but also eliminate the need to decide which Tumen River, "earth" or "diagram," was the correct one.

The survey ended inconclusively. More questions about the corollaries of the rivers that flowed into the Sungari and Yalu Rivers emerged, as did confusion over the original Manchu pronunciations of those rivers. With each turn, Yi Chungha managed to parry Qing accusations about the stele with logic. Even if a person had successfully moved the stele, he reasoned, it would have been impossible to move the fence and stone mound next to it. He demanded to know how the Qing had come up with such an idea. In the end, the Chosŏn delegation came to believe that the Qing was attempting to take over its territory, an egregious act committed against a country that had served the "Great Country" for the past three hundred years.[32] The second mission carried out in 1887 was no more successful. Even the maps, created by the teams of geographers who accompanied the delegates to chart the various waterways on the mountain, failed to clarify the issue because the very premise on which to delineate the border remained unresolved.

With the territorial border in dispute, the question of subjecthood hung in suspense. The two issues were inextricably linked. If officials could not decide whether Koreans had crossed into Qing territory or not, neither could they decide whether Koreans should be naturalized as Qing subjects or left alone. A few years later, when tensions had died down, the Zongli Yamen pointed to the need "to verify and clarify the boundary in order to avoid doubt and contention" as well as "to repatriate [suhoe] the wandering people and assign them a place [anch'i]," whether in Korea or China.[33] But efforts were soon halted. In 1894 the eruption of the Tonghak rebellions and the outbreak of the Sino-Japanese War turned the heads of Chosŏn officials to the urgent matter of holding the country together. Discussions over the border ceased for a while.

International Dramas in Chosŏn

The dramatic events that began with the Tonghak uprising in 1894 and culminated in Chosŏn's partial colonization in 1905 open its lens to the "global" world. Diplomats and merchants from various countries arrived in Korea, officials

---

32. Ibid., 181, 259.
33. *Ku Han'guk oegyo munsŏ*, 8:724 (August 29, 1890).

experimented with foreign ideas and institutions, and new commodities made their way into the hands of villagers. The narrative of the coming of the West to Korea during the decade of high diplomacy has been well documented, as has the story of Japan's reinvention of itself as an "enlightened" advisor to Korea. Critical as it is to explaining Korea's final years as a sovereign state, however, this narrative arc, with its geographical focus on treaty ports, tends to omit pivotal events that were happening on the northern periphery, where the outcomes of diplomacy conducted in the capital were overshadowed and often overturned by the local concerns of its neighbors, China and Russia. With an eye toward capturing the links between the capital and the borderland, this section recounts the "great power" politics that forced Korea into a transnational moment.

Chosŏn's brief interlude as a modern sovereign state commenced with a regional war. In 1894 a local peasant rebellion in the province of Chŏlla instigated a far-reaching anti-establishment and anti-foreign movement that became the occasion for the first regional war since the late sixteenth century. Discontented peasants, impoverished by corrupt practices of local headmen and large-scale economic changes in the countryside, rapidly mobilized across the south. Inspired by the millenarian ideas of Tonghak, or Eastern Learning, peasant armies barraged government offices and seized control of the provincial capital. King Kojong called on Beijing to send troops to put an end to the uprising. But soon after the Qing sent troops, Japan dispatched eight thousand soldiers to the peninsula under the pretext of protecting its own residents from the violence.[34] It aimed to curtail Qing involvement in Korea and establish a base for itself. Japanese troops took over the palace, placed Kojong under house arrest, and installed the Taewŏngun, Kojong's father, as head. They then forced the Korean government to sign a "treaty" to expel the Chinese troops with the help of Japanese forces and carried out the radical Kabo reforms through a newly appointed council. In early 1895 King Kojong, who was now back in power, visited a royal ancestral shrine and promulgated a fourteen-point oath, which promised that "all thought of dependence on China shall be cut away, and a firm foundation for independence shall be secure."[35] On the battlefront, the Japanese, with its modern weaponry and military tactics, easily defeated the peasant armies; the Qing army and navy, too, were no match for Japan. It was a decisive rout. The 1895 armistice, the Treaty of Shimonoseki, formally severed Korea's tributary ties with China, stating the cessation of all ceremonial rituals that had upheld those

---

34. It should be noted that the Treaty of Tianjin, concluded by China and Japan in 1885, committed both powers to notify the other before sending troops to Korea. S. C. M. Paine, *The Sino-Japanese War of 1894–1895* (Cambridge, 2003), 59.

35. Quoted in Larsen, *Tradition, Treaties, and Trade*, 235.

ties for centuries. The "full and complete independence and autonomy of Korea" was recognized.[36] Two years later, Kojong, emulating the imperial turn around the globe, declared Chosŏn an empire.

For the next ten years, "high diplomacy" dominated Chosŏn politics as it did governments throughout East Asia. A sense of urgency to carve up what remained of land and resources in "weaker" countries such as Korea impelled foreign leaders to send an endless stream of demands to the court for a range of rights: from timber concessions in the forests of the north to fishing privileges in the bounteous southern waters; from mining gold to laying telegraph lines and railroads that would connect the peninsula to the larger region. Maneuvering through extraterritorial treaties that expressed a commitment to multilateral foreign interests in which no one power could gain the upper hand, Japan, Great Britain, Germany, France, the United States, and others pursued their interests in Korea. China, too, staked its claims. Though its political influence in Korea had diminished after 1895, the Qing aimed to benefit from concessions diplomacy. It did so with the help of the British. Seeing that Japan had already pushed the limits of treaties by chasing out Qing customs officials from Korea's port cities, Great Britain took immediate steps to aid China in reestablishing trade ties with Korea in hopes that China would counterbalance Japan. Indeed, one British consul declared outright his goal to "restore them [Chinese] to equal rights with those subjects of other Powers."[37] In 1898 the Qing renewed diplomatic relations with Chosŏn, and in 1899 the two countries concluded the Treaty of Amity and Commerce, which detailed the terms of trade and recognized Korea's political equality with China. Qing diplomats and merchants resumed their activities on the peninsula.[38]

While the Qing renewed ties with Chosŏn, intrigues at court drew Russia deeper into the orbit of Korean politics. In 1895 Miura Gorō, the Japanese minister in Seoul, ordered a band of fighters to storm the palace and kill Queen Min, who was known for her staunch anti-Japanese stance. The queen was stabbed to death and her body set on fire in the garden. In early 1896, out of concern for the king's life, officials smuggled Kojong to the Russian legation, where he remained

---

36. John Van Antwerp MacMurray, *Treaties and Agreements With and Concerning China*, vol. 1 (New York, 1921), 18.

37. Quoted in Larsen, *Tradition, Treaties, and Trade*, 243.

38. Kirk Larsen argues against a widely held assumption that the Sino-Japanese War marked the end of the Qing's presence in Chosŏn and the beginning of Japan's unrivaled ascendance on the peninsula. Though Qing political influence declined, its officials continued to benefit from privileges that they had held before the war; these privileges matched those enjoyed by Western powers and Japan in Korea. Japan's influence in Korea was undisputed only after its victory in the Russo-Japanese War. Ibid., 251–56.

for more than a year. The Russian chargé d'affaires in Seoul, Karl Weber, was initially ambivalent about sheltering Kojong in the legation. He, along with ministers in St. Petersburg, envisioned building Russia's empire in the Far East through concessions diplomacy in the form of steel railways and ice-free ports, not by becoming embroiled in political intrigues in Korea. But Weber was drawn into taking part in an imperialist game by Tokyo, which interpreted his acceptance of Kojong as an ominous sign of Russia's strategic interest in the peninsula. In 1896, to preempt a clash with Russia, Premier Ito Hirobumi urged the two sides to sign the Seoul Protocol to recognize their mutual interests in Korea. The agreement, whose language was purposely imprecise, gave Weber the latitude to send Russian instructors to train the Korean army.[39] Weber also used his new-found favored position to negotiate trade privileges for Russian merchants in ports such as Mokpo and Wŏnsan and along the rivers in the north. Particularly notable was the 1,800-square-mile timber concession on the Yalu and Tumen Rivers, which was acquired by Swiss entrepreneur Iulii Briner (Julius Bryner), grandfather of the famous Broadway actor Yul Brynner.[40]

International competition for concession rights bled through Korea's northern periphery into Manchuria, which tsarist Russia and European powers eyed with ambition. In 1895, Russia, supported by Germany and France, forced Japan to relinquish Liaodong Peninsula, its prized concession from the Sino-Japanese War. Russia quickly proceeded to negotiate treaties with China to build railroads that would link the Maritime littoral to the rest of the Siberian landmass in a seamless ride and obliterate the space from Siberia in the north to Port Arthur in the south. An opportunity arose for Russia to further advance its aims in 1900. The Boxer Rebellion, a movement that had begun as a martial arts group and transformed into organized militias that rallied against foreign powers, had spread rapidly from its original locus in Shandong northward to the capital and Jilin. That spring, Boxer forces killed four French and Belgian engineers and two British missionaries. Uprisings broke out. Using the violent outbreaks as an excuse, Western troops, including the Russians, seized the chance to advance farther into China. In July 1900, when Boxers attacked the Chinese Eastern Railway—a central piece of Russia's Far Eastern policy—tsarist officials who had initially quibbled over the pros and cons of military action fell into agreement.[41] Intervention had

39. For more information on the Seoul Protocol of May 1896 and the Moscow Protocol (Lobanov-Yamagata Agreement) of June 1896, see Andrew Malozemoff, *Russian Far Eastern Policy* (Berkeley, 1958), 86–89.

40. King Kojong granted Briner the timber concession in 1898, but the contract ended when the Japanese established a protectorate over Korea in 1905. Stephan, *Russian Far East*, 85–86.

41. War minister Aleksei Kuropatkin had advocated intervention, while finance minister Sergei Witte adopted a more cautious approach. David Schimmelpenninck van der Oye, "The Immediate

become necessary. St. Petersburg ordered the mobilization of tens of thousands of soldiers to China. By 1902 there were more than a hundred thousand Russian troops in Manchuria, a figure that exceeded the total number on the Russian side.[42] They lingered there, even when other Western powers had begun to evacuate their troops.[43] During the occupation, there was mass confusion and violence among the local population. Otherwise peaceful villagers carried out lootings, personal reprisals, and acts of vandalism in which they derailed train cars and stripped them down to the copper tubing in the boilers. In Hunchun, most likely acting out of pent-up frustration, Koreans staged bloody "pogroms" against Chinese.[44] A tense atmosphere permeated the region.

With no foreseeable end to the Russian occupation of Manchuria, the conditions for full-out war were set. Tokyo, poised for expansion on the continent, was most alarmed by St. Petersburg's aggression. It feared that Korea would be swallowed up next. Tokyo initially tried to negotiate with Russia but, after gaining the support of Great Britain and the United States, adopted a more forceful posture by 1903: it urged Russia to limit its activities in Manchuria and recognize Japan's interests in Korea. Inside Russia, an indecisive Tsar Nicholas vacillated between the widely divergent opinions of his advisors. By 1902 a coterie of officials had assembled around the figure of Alexander Bezobrazov, a retired colonel who concocted a plan to occupy northern Korea by exploiting a timber concession on the Yalu, while Finance Minister Sergei Witte, who advocated a moderate approach of forging economic ties and appeasing Japan, soon found himself ousted from power. Meanwhile, Tsar Nicholas appointed Admiral Evgenii Alekseev as viceroy of the Far East, placing all military and diplomatic policy in the Pacific in the hands of a hard-liner. By 1903 both Japan and Russia were preparing for war, but neither knew how deeply invested the other was. The last-ditch effort to negotiate failed in August, and on February 6 of the following year, a frustrated Japan cut off diplomatic relations.[45] Two days later, it acted out. Without a declaration of war, the Japanese navy staged a surprise attack on Russian warships in Port Arthur. For the next fifteen months, Japan and Russia fought a bitter war that

Origins of the War," in *The Russo-Japanese War in Global Perspective*, eds. John W. Steinberg et al. (Leiden, 2005), 34–35.

42. Stephan, *Russian Far East*, 60.

43. The April 1902 convention, in which Russia agreed to withdraw from Manchuria in stages, had limited effect. Tsarist officials remained divided over the continued occupation of Manchuria. Schimmelpenninck van der Oye, "Immediate Origins," 39.

44. Malozemoff, *Russian Far Eastern Policy*, 139.

45. Schimmelpenninck van der Oye, "Immediate Origins," 38–43; Igor V. Lukoianov, "The Bezobrazovtsy," in Steinberg et al., *Russo-Japanese War*, 65–86; Dietrich Geyer, *Russian Imperialism*, trans. Bruce Little (Leamington Spa, UK, 1987), 211–15.

consumed more battle time per soldier and more space in the public imagination than any other war in recent history. The war changed the course of geopolitics in northeast Asia. It ended in defeat for the Russians, won Japan a vaunted place among the "great powers," and marked the commencement of its empire building on the Asian continent, in which Korea became its first colony. For Korea, the war meant a partial loss of sovereignty. It was a prelude to its complete erasure five years later.

Experiments in Sovereignty

The tumultuous events that preoccupied the Chosŏn court from 1895 to 1905 by no means left it a passive onlooker to the country's demise. In fact, the events drove Chosŏn officials to act out sovereignty in discernable ways. In Kando, that meant experimenting with new and old tactics to reclaim territory and people as part of Chosŏn. It also meant borrowing from the emerging language of international law to spar with Qing counterparts about the limits of jurisdiction. With no single victor in recent military scrambles over Manchuria, Chosŏn dared to claim its own piece of the land.

In September 1899 officials of Korea and China reestablished diplomatic relations through the Treaty of Amity and Commerce.[46] The treaty not only set the terms for a new type of relationship, in which they regarded each other as equal sovereign states on par with modern states around the world; it also hinted at a new kind of citizenry in the making. The treaty annulled the earlier 1882 commercial agreement, which outlined trade rules according to historic tributary ties, and instead modeled itself on recent extraterritoriality treaties, detailing new privileges of consular representation, merchant rights, and tariffs. Further, the 1899 treaty reversed previous laws that codified Korea's inferiority; it granted "most favored nation" status to *both* countries and stated explicitly the principle of "mutual extraterritoriality," a guarantee that a Korean accused of a crime in China would be tried by the laws of Korea, and vice versa (art. 5). The eighth article, which detailed new passport rules, was the clearest indication that it was not only relations between China and Korea that had been redefined in modern terms but also the people themselves. Whereas the 1882 rules restricted the issuance of passports to individuals in the "merchant" class (*sangmin*), the new rules permitted any "subject" (*sinmin*) to travel to China or Korea "for purposes of pleasure or trade." The absence of "merchant" from the treaty was in part a consequence

---

46. *Ku Hanmal ŭi choyak*, 3:369–86.

of the Kabo reforms, a sweeping platform of social and governmental change that abolished the status system of the Chosŏn dynasty and laid the groundwork for the formation of a new citizenry.[47] Similar to the 1888 Russo-Korean overland trade agreement, the new rules suggested that a person's identity was no longer defined by his occupation within the traditional status system, whether elite or merchant, but by his national association as a "subject" of Korea. Stated another way, the rule simplified identity. The process was becoming a common practice as states everywhere attempted to "make a society legible," an object that could be known and thus governed, especially across international borders.[48]

Making people "legible" was an essential component of governing borders, but the treaty did not take the process to its logical conclusion. Fearful that regulating the border area would invite unwelcomed solicitations for trade from foreign governments, Qing officials chose to preserve its legal ambiguity: they refused to draw up any rules pertaining to the contested Qing-Chosŏn border area.[49] The treaty only mentioned that the terms of trade and travel would be concluded at a future date. Sensitivities over the region further drove officials to include a provision that prohibited people from "crossing into the border area" (wŏlbyŏn) from that point forward "in order to avoid complications" (art. 12). The question of subjecthood, moreover, remained unanswered. The treaty merely stated that "border inhabitants" who had already crossed into the area and were engaged in cultivation would be permitted "to pursue their avocations in peace and enjoy protection for their lives and property." It was an implicit promise that Koreans would not be expelled from Qing lands as they had been in the past. With the lack of an agreed-upon boundary line, the expatriate Koreans remained "illegible" and state sovereignty in Kando undetermined.

In the midst of uncertainty about the jurisdiction of Kando, the Chosŏn court acted out sovereignty in new ways. Motivated by the idea of "monarch-centered reform," Kojong, now emperor of the Great Han, undertook to extend the powers

---

47. From the mid-1890s, enlightenment thinkers conceived of a new mutual relationship between the people (inmin), later "citizenry" (kungmin), and the government: the people were to enjoy equal "rights" and fulfill their obligations to the state, while the government was to provide and protect those rights. Hwang, "Citizenship, Social Equality and Government Reform," 369–77.

48. Scott, Seeing Like a State, 2. In addition, the rule was likely a recognition of the fact that trade was no longer a monopoly of the merchant class, and that a diversifying economy had expanded the types of jobs available—and the types of people engaged in them—creating new reasons to travel abroad.

49. See Larisa Zabrovskaia, "1899 Treaty and Its Impact on the Development of the Chinese-Korean Trade," Korea Journal 31, no. 4 (Winter 1991): 30. Historian Ŭn Chŏngt'aek suggests that Chosŏn officials were too preoccupied with more pressing economic matters to push their agenda in Kando. Ŭn Chŏngt'ae, "Taehan chegukki 'Kando munje' ŭi ch'ui wa 'singminhwa'," Yŏksa munje yŏn'gu 17, no. 4 (2007): 101n17.

of the central government across all divisions of the bureaucracy and down to all levels of society in what was known as the Kwangmu reforms (1897–1910). The reforms set in motion a myriad of programs, ranging from the training of a modern army to tax revision, in which the Royal Treasury, and not local officials, collected taxes directly from the provinces to bolster sources of national revenue.[50] Most significantly, at the heart of the reform was an effort to gather detailed knowledge about the people and the land. To that end, a cadastral survey was conducted and a new household registration system mandated.[51] Though its ultimate success was unclear, the registration system was a symbolic gesture of the government's claiming of the people, the making of a "legible" body politic. Endeavors to delineate the boundaries of its inhabitants reached beyond the borders of Chosŏn. During the period of reform, Emperor Kojong appointed officials to govern the Koreans in Kando and to conduct a census with the intent to incorporate them into the household registers. In 1897 Sŏ Sangmu was installed as overseer of the Western Frontier on the Yalu River, next to northern Pyŏngan Province; in 1899, Yi Kwangha as overseer of the Northern Frontier; and in 1902, Yi Pŏmyun as overseer of Northern Kando, in the Tumen valley.[52] Kojong also called on a former Righteous Army (*ŭibyŏng*) leader, Min Yongho, to use his military savvy to advance the cause of the state across the border.

In 1900 Min Yongho traveled up and down the banks of the Yalu River to call on compatriots to return to Chosŏn.[53] By that point his duties had expanded

---

50. See Yumi Moon, *Populist Collaborators* (Ithaca, 2013), 160–70.

51. In 1896 the government had already called for censuses to be conducted more frequently and a standard registration form to be filled out. Hwang, "Citizenship, Social Equality and Government Reform," 360–64.

52. Ŭn Chŏngt'ae, "Taehan chegukki 'Kando munje' ŭi ch'ui" 107; Ryu Sŭngju, "Chosŏn hugi sŏ Kando ijumin e taehan ilgoch'al," *Asea yŏn'gu* 21, no. 1 (1978): 305. Ŭn states that Sŏ Sangmu was appointed in 1898. The exact boundaries of their jurisdictional powers are unclear. The duties of Sŏ Sangmu and Yi Kwangha in the Yalu valley area probably overlapped. There is also a debate about the existence of Chosŏn administrative districts on the northern (Qing) bank of the Yalu River. According to a 1935 Japanese colonial study, the inspector of northern Pyŏngan Province had created twenty-eight administrative districts (*myŏn*) across the Yalu as early as 1881. The study says that the inspector acted on his own volition, without the order of the court. In 1889 the districts were subsumed under the jurisdiction of existing districts on the Chosŏn side, including Kanggye, Chasŏng, Ch'osan, and Huch'ang. The study further states that Sŏ Sangmu was later appointed as overseer of the Western Frontier and that he had control over some of the twenty-eight districts, whose population had reached 8,772 households, or 37,000 individuals. The historian Yi Tongjin, however, maintains that the Japanese study is not credible because of its lack of sources. Yi Tongjin relies on Min Yongho's *Kangbuk ilgi* (*Diary of the North*), which makes no mention of Chosŏn administrative districts on the Qing side. See Yi Tongjin, "1900-nyŏn 'Kangbuk' ŭi Chosŏnin," *Manju yŏn'gu* 15, no. 6 (2013): 66–67.

53. Min Yongho's 1900 account, *Kangbuk ilgi*, is not to be confused with Ch'oe Chongbŏm's 1872 diary by the same title. Other than Min Yongho's activities in the Righteous Army, little is known about him. In 1901 he apparently sailed from Inch'ŏn to Shanghai, southern China, and Southeast

beyond his initial appointment as an officer of the commercial guild (*sangmusa*), an organization of peddler-merchants (*pobusang*) who hoped to preserve what remained of their once exclusive rights as traders in the Chosŏn economy. Fanning throughout the country to head thirty-one branches, officers such as Min were responsible for registering the peddlers and distributing licenses that served as proof of their identity as merchants and gave them the right to trade.[54] Soon, Min began to conduct a census of Koreans on the Qing side.[55] In his address to his compatriots, Min invoked ideas of filial piety and ties to the homeland:

> The north [*kangbuk*] is an empty territory between the two countries. There are tens of thousands of our people who have occupied that land. So how can we spare one envoy and abandon our children who have not received favor? If we do not take measures to subdue and encourage the people and let several years pass, then descendants will come to consider that place their hometown and think no thoughts of their fatherland. . . . If we secretly investigate the situation in the north, pass a royal edict, persuade them with propriety, and encourage them with loyalty, then after one year they will be included in the family registers, after two years they will reap favor, and after three years we will be able to govern them.[56]

His speech harkened back to language employed by envoys who had earlier gone to Kando and the Maritime Province to "encourage" the Koreans and transmit the enlightenment of the king. To bolster his authority, he brought a copy of the imperial edict as proof that the king had ordered a census and called on the people to return.

The order did not sit well with the inhabitants, however, for neither returning to Chosŏn nor being registered were agreeable options. They had grown weary of

---

Asia before returning to Korea in 1902. Min Yongho, *Kwandong ch'angŭirok: Pu Sŏjŏng ilgi, Kangbuk ilgi, Pokche simun* (Seoul, 1984).

54. The commercial guild also helped educate peddler-merchants about foreign standards of commerce and trade through schools and newspapers. The peddlers have often been seen as conservative elements who leaned on the late Chosŏn court to help preserve their privileges and even mobilized against the progressive Independence Club (*Tongnip hyŏphoe*). They became members of the Imperial Association (*Hwangguk hyŏphoe*), which brought about the demise of the Independence Club in 1898. Cho Chaegon argues that the peddlers were not entirely reactionary and acted more as free agents in the complicated politics of turn-of-the-twentieth-century Korea. See Ch'oe Chinok, "Hanmal pobusang ŭi pyŏnch'ŏn," *Chŏngsin munhwa yŏn'gu* 29 (June 1986): 158; Cho Chaegon, "Taehan cheguk ŭi kaehyŏk inyŏm kwa pobusang," *Han'guk tongnip undongsa yŏn'gu* 20 (August 2003): 127–48.

55. They were to be included in commercial registers, even though they were most likely not merchants or peddlers.

56. Quoted in Yi Tongjin, "1900-nyŏn 'Kangbuk' ŭi Chosŏnin," 57.

visits by clerks who crossed the river to the Qing side to inquire about their home district and demanded that the villagers pay the taxes that they owed. Empowered by a system that relied on local authorities for tax collection, the clerks used a free hand to pocket cash for personal profit. If registered as Chosŏn subjects, villagers pointed out, they would be subject to double taxation as subjects of both countries.[57] A census, it seemed, would not only abet the usurious practices of corrupt Chosŏn officials but also burden the Koreans with unjust demands. As for returning to Chosŏn, they explained that they could not easily pack up their things and leave with a day's notice. To be sure, their life in China was not easy. They lived in constant fear of bandit raids and, as political tensions mounted in the borderland, were reminded of their status as outsiders. But the cost of leaving China was too great. They had already lived there for generations.[58] Min Yongho decided to carry out his mission despite the lukewarm response of settlers. He gathered information for the census and looked for ways to exempt them from Qing taxes.

The Chosŏn court took similar steps to exercise jurisdiction farther upstream in the Tumen valley. In 1902 it ordered the overseer of Northern Kando, Yi Pŏmyun, to conduct a census, levy taxes, and protect the people.[59] Its action was a direct response to the violence that exploded in the wake of the Boxer uprising. The rebellion had reached the Kando area in the fall of 1900 and spilled into Chosŏn territory. Boxers crossed the Yalu, massacred Korean Christians, and hung their corpses on the riverbank. Chosŏn police forces who had assembled along the border to stop the melee became the target of attacks, too. Confused by the Western-style uniforms of the Korean police, Boxers mistook them for the foreign enemy.[60] Settlers in Kando cried out for anyone to come to their aid against the "bandits." They appealed to the Russian border commissar and the Chosŏn court, asking the latter to send an official to be stationed there.[61] When

---

57. Ibid., 56–57, 71. A Russian official confirmed that Koreans on the Qing side paid taxes to both Qing and Chosŏn authorities, depending on their proximity to the border. Larisa Zabrovskaia, "Consequences of Korean Emigration to Jiandao," *Korea Journal* 33, no. 1 (Spring 1993): 70.

58. One such example involved Qing troops returning from Pyongyang at the end of the Sino-Japanese War in 1895. Accusing Koreans of maintaining contact with Korea and Japan, the troops demanded that those who did not don Qing clothes should go back to Korea. Yi Tongjin, "1900-nyŏn 'Kangbuk' ŭi Chosŏnin," 56–57.

59. Registers compiled by Yi Pŏmyun may be found in *Pyŏn'gye hojŏk sŏngch'aek* and *Pyŏn'gye hojŏgan* (Kyujanggak Institute, Seoul National University, Korea). See also Cho Ilgwŏn, "Ku Hanmal Kando chibang chumin e kwanhan yŏn'gu" (M.A. thesis, Inha University, 1997); Yang T'aejin, ed., *1902 nyŏn pyŏn'gye hojŏgan* (Seoul, 1992).

60. Moon, *Populist Collaborators*, 69; Ŭn Chŏngt'ae, "Taehan chegukki 'Kando munje' ŭi ch'ui," 102.

61. *Chuhan Ilbon kongsagwan*, vol. 16, part 11, doc. 5 (November 21, 1901); Ŭn Chŏngt'ae, "Taehan chegukki 'Kando munje' ŭi ch'ui," 107.

a Chosŏn official arrived from Kyŏnghŭng to survey the situation, the Koreans crowded around him and asked him to "save the tens of thousands" in Kando. "Severely oppressed," the people "wait every day for [Chosŏn] to send an overseer," he reported.[62]

Conversations in the halls of the bureaucracy also revealed that irredentism, born out fears of external threats, was spurring the calls to action. Seeing the Russian occupation of Manchuria, a Kyŏnghŭng magistrate urged the government to assert its authority over the territory and people. Though the Qing had proved "feeble" and allowed its land to be "swallowed up" by foreign countries, Chosŏn should take charge of the land, clarify the border through another investigation, and pacify the people. This was the path to "prevent[ing] strong neighbors from occupying [Kando] by force again." Otherwise, if Chosŏn failed, it "would become the laughingstock of neighboring countries."[63]

Heightened awareness of international events had a telescopic effect, magnifying the Kando conflict from a localized occurrence on the border to a national problem that consumed the attention of people from all parts of the peninsula. After the Sino-Japanese War, editors of newspapers began to put Kando in their headlines next to other contemporary issues, ranging from territorial grievances—the Tokto Islands in the East Sea—to more abstract questions relating to space such as the circulation of Japanese currency on the peninsula or the problem of Japanese immigration. Though varied in nature, the stories were described as part of a national crisis and expressed in the emerging vocabulary of the sovereign nation-state. Concepts of "national rights" (kukkwŏn), "independence" (tongnip), and "international law" (man'guk chi pŏp) were used to decry the situation in Kando and were recast onto historical narratives about the 1712 mission in anachronistic ways. Authors presented the stele and fence as evidence of not only the border demarcation but an act that had established Chosŏn's sovereign jurisdiction over Kando. Newspapers also reprinted former officials' memorials about territory, additional proof that the Kando question had reached beyond the inner circle of the royal court and become an issue for a growing literate public.[64]

Widespread talk of "sovereignty" rattled Qing officials who already looked at Chosŏn's recent moves with distrust. Local commanders and diplomats lodged repeated protests against Yi Pŏmyun, in particular, who had not only conducted a census but raised a personal army, extorted money from villagers, and wreaked havoc throughout Kando. Yi's activities also threatened the viability

---

62. *Chuhan Ilbon kongsagwan*, vol. 20, part 11, doc. 10 (November 20, 1903).
63. Ibid.
64. Schmid, *Korea between Empires*, 211, 213.

of the harvest for Han farmers, who "need to be at peace to concentrate on agriculture."[65] In 1903 the Qing consul in Seoul, Xu Taishen, complained to the Korean foreign minister, saying that Yi should not cross the border and "exercise jurisdiction" over the Koreans in Kando because the territory clearly belonged to China. What was more, since the settlers had voluntarily shaved their heads and naturalized as Qing subjects, Korean officials had no business meddling in their affairs. To support his arguments, Xu cited the 1899 treaty and accused Yi of violating article 12, which guaranteed the peace of the border population and prohibited further migration to "prevent any incidents from occurring." Yi, he continued, had taken a "far-fetched interpretation of the treaty and thought that he was protecting the Koreans" when, in fact, all he had done was cause disorder.[66] Xu demanded that Yi Pŏmyun leave Kando at once, but Yi refused. Yi invoked the same treaty to make his point: the "border population" mentioned in article 12 referred to anyone living in the region, whether Chinese or Korean, and as such, officials of *both* countries had the right to protect the livelihood and property of their own subjects. He claimed that there was "no article in the treaty that states that it is the Chinese who will protect the Koreans." Yi further defended his actions by invoking "international law," saying, "It is a principle [*t'ongnye*] of the law of nations [*man'guk kongbŏp*] that our country would protect our country's people. Therefore, when Qing officials say that they will protect the Koreans, they are in direct violation of the treaty and of international law."[67] Xu Taishen, who possessed a more nuanced understanding of treaties, avowed that Qing officials had not violated the law. To be sure, a country had a right to protect its own subjects, a right guaranteed by the extraterritoriality clause of the 1899 treaty. But, he reasoned, extraterritoriality should be exercised only in treaty ports. The border region, including Kando, "is not like the commercial treaty ports." Kando was Qing land, occupied by naturalized Qing subjects, and under "our [Qing] jurisdiction."[68]

While diplomats and officials circled in and out of their respective capitals to debate legal rights in Kando, chaos in the borderland revealed that, often, sovereignty was only valid if it could be acted out by force. The overall state of confusion— lack of clear diplomatic outcomes, absence of oversight, and multiple on-the-ground contingents vying for control—enabled Chosŏn officials who had originally been dispatched by the central government to use their power for their own ends. Yi Pŏmyun and Sŏ Sangmu, overseer of the Western Frontier, had amassed

65. *Chuhan Ilbon kongsagwan*, vol. 21, part 6, doc. 8 (August 29, 1904).
66. *Chuhan Ilbon kongsagwan*, vol. 21, part 5, doc. 16 (October 14, 1903).
67. Quoted in Ŭn Chŏngt'ae, "Taehan chegukki 'Kando munje' ŭi ch'ui," 114.
68. *Chuhan Ilbon kongsagwan*, vol. 21, part 6, doc. 4 (July 16, 1903).

followers on both sides of the border, raised personal armies, and, according to a report filed by Koreans, resorted to extortion to force villagers to give money and food to their cause. Yi's efforts also took him to the Russian Far East, where he petitioned the border commissar to aid him in his mission.[69] Ordinary civilians were not immune to the allure of wielding power in the borderland. Earning notoriety alongside Qing bandits and rogue officials, one Kando Korean blurred the lines of ethnicity and national affiliation to commit criminal acts. He not only posed as a Chosŏn official, creating a seal and forging multiple documents to extort local Koreans out of money for "taxes," but also disguised himself as a Russian by wearing Russian clothes and recruited a transnational gang of robbers to carry out other crimes. He later escaped to Russia, much to the dismay of the Chosŏn government.[70]

Starting in 1904, full-scale war broke out in the border region, extracting the Kando problem from the hands of Chosŏn officials and placing it in the arms of militant groups. Korea had managed to conclude a secret agreement with the Qing in June 1904, promising to remove rebels such as Yi Pŏmyun from Qing territory,[71] but Kando and all of Manchuria had been transformed into a battleground for sovereignty between the two ascendant powers on the continent, Russia and Japan. Righteous Armies, led by Yi Pŏmyun and others, joined in the melee, allying with Russia to stop Japan's advance into Korea, while Qing bandits fought as paid irregulars for both the Russians and Japanese.[72] At the end of the war in 1905, a victorious Japan declared Korea a protectorate and took control of its foreign and economic affairs, effectively silencing Korea's voice on the international stage. Korea's fate continued to be contested in an unofficial war inside and outside Korea. Starting on the peninsula several years earlier as an anti-foreign patriotic movement and gaining strength during the Russo-Japanese War, the Righteous Army detachments, several thousands strong, waged a guerrilla war against Japan. In response, the office of the Japanese resident-general in Seoul dismantled the imperial army in 1907 and dispatched Japanese soldiers and policemen to Kando to extinguish all traces of rebel activity that could seep back

---

69. *Chuhan Ilbon kongsagwan*, vol. 21, part 6, doc. 5 (April 15, 1904), doc. 3 (January 16, 1904). During the Russo-Japanese War, Yi petitioned Russian authorities to back him in the fight against the Japanese. In 1909 a Russian officer estimated that there were about four thousand people enlisted in Yi's armies in the Maritime Province and Kando. There were reports that various contingents of Righteous Armies in the Russian Far East collected money and supplies from the expatriate community. B. D. Pak, *Koreitsy v Rossiiskoi imperii*, 2nd ed. (Irkutsk, 1994), 147, 155.

70. *Ku Han'guk oegyo munsŏ*, 18: doc. 1381, 1770, 1942.

71. Point 5 of agreement. For full text see *T'onggambu munsŏ*, vol. 3, part 14, doc. 6 (March 3, 1908).

72. Robert Lee, *Manchurian Frontier*, 94. The Japanese military also made wide use of Korean porters and supplies. Moon, *Populist Collaborators*, 111–15.

into Korea. Aiming to solidify their position not only in Korea but in Kando, the Japanese created a temporary field office on the north bank of the Tumen River; they also appointed a Korean as overseer of the expatriate community. The Qing, seeing Japan's actions as an infringement of its sovereignty, followed suit, building its own military stations and delineating administrative units to claim the people and space.[73]

In September 1909 China and Japan signed the Kando Treaty to put an end to the ongoing border dispute.[74] The treaty declared the contested area as Qing territory and de facto placed the entire expatriate Korean population on the Qing side. In return for capitulating on the territorial question, Japan won the right to extend the South Manchuria Railroad northward into Kando and Hamgyŏng Province, physically linking its informal empire in northeast Asia. It also gained the right to build consulates in Yongjŏng (Longjing), Tudogu (Toudaogou), Paekch'ogu (Baicaogou), and Kukchaga (Juzijie), part of its efforts to create "mixed jurisdictional areas" where Japanese subjects could live and trade as they did in treaty ports elsewhere.

The declaration of Japan's right to extraterritoriality in Kando precluded the establishment of full Chinese sovereignty over the territory, codifying its sovereignty as hollow and incomplete. It also created ambiguity in the jurisdiction and subjecthood of Koreans. According to the treaty, Koreans living in "mixed-resident districts" (not to be confused with "mixed jurisdictional areas" for Japanese subjects) north of the Tumen River—where Chinese, Manchus, and Koreans resided—were to be treated as "equal" to Qing subjects: Koreans would submit to the jurisdiction of local officials and abide by Qing tax, administrative, and legal codes, while the Qing government agreed to accord "equal treatment" to the Koreans (art. 4 and 8). The treaty, however, stopped short of calling them Qing subjects. The settlers were designated only as "Koreans" (*hanmin*), leaving their legal status open to interpretation. The treaty also permitted Japan to appoint consuls to attend any court case that involved Koreans, its newest colonial subjects, and thereby opened up the possibility for the Office of the Resident-General of Korea and Foreign Ministry to interfere in matters that took place on

73. Yu Pyŏngho, "Pukkando Hanin ŭi kukchŏk ŭl tullŏssan Ch'ŏng-Il yangguk ŭi kyosŏp e taehan yŏn'gu," *Chungangsaron* 21 (2005): 456–97; Ch'oe Changgŭn, "Ilche ŭi Kando 'T'onggambu imsi p'achulso' sŏlch'i kyŏngwi," *Han-Il kwan'gyesa yŏn'gu* 7 (December 1997): 86–115. In Kantō, the Japanese also stationed consular police, treating it as a distinct unit under the Foreign Ministry police. The Japanese administration of Kantō was closely tied to the Governor-General Office of Korea. Erik Esselstrom, *Crossing Empire's Edge* (Honolulu, 2009), 50–53.

74. Full texts of the treaty in various languages may be found in *Ku Hanmal ŭi choyak*, 2:262–67; MacMurray, *Treaties*, 796–97.

Chinese soil.[75] In ensuing years, as Japan and China competed for sovereignty on the Asian continent, the Kando Koreans were swept up in their debates over land rights and citizenship, becoming a persistent object of contention. As suddenly as a centuries-old border dispute had ended between Chosŏn and the Qing, then, a new grounds for conflict had emerged.

Incomplete Sovereignty and the Politics of Citizenship

From 1909 to 1931 the "Kando problem" prevailed as one of the most controversial topics of debate between China and Japan. Its agricultural potential, human capital, and geographical centrality to a triumvirate of states bestowed on Kando a political significance that transcended the relatively small area it occupied on the map and made it a target of imperial rivalry. Apart from the desirability of its resources, competition mounted due to Kando's problematic status as both a territory of China and part of the informal empire of Japan, a status that had been purposefully constructed in the Kando Treaty to appease both sides and to avert another war. Its ambiguous status was later confirmed by the contradictory conclusions of the League of Nations, which on the one hand recognized Chinese sovereignty and on the other, acknowledged the historical autonomy of Manchuria and the treaty rights of other powers there.[76] The Kando Treaty also left open the jurisdiction of the majority population of Koreans. In subsequent years, as tensions in Kando escalated, states on all three sides seized hold of this jurisdictional ambiguity. They attempted to claim Koreans, calling them "subjects" or "citizens" of China, Japan, or Russia in hopes of claiming the people first, territory second. Citizenship came to set the terms of the Kando debate,

---

75. See the annex to the Kando Treaty dated April 5, 1910. Article 2 of the 1910 agreement stated that the Ministry of Foreign Affairs had the right to order Korean criminals in Kando to be extradited to Korea by Japanese consular officers for imprisonment. MacMurray, *Treaties*, 797–98. Japanese officials invoked the principle of extraterritoriality to defend the right of their consuls to participate in court cases involving Koreans. This principle, however, did not exactly apply to the case of the Kando Koreans. In general, extraterritoriality agreements clearly delimited geographical boundaries, such as treaty ports, and guaranteed the right of a country to try its subjects in its own courts. By contrast, the Kando Treaty restricted Japanese from trying Korean criminals in their courts; criminals were to be tried in Chinese courts with Japanese participation. Further, the Japanese insisted on the right to participate in court cases involving Koreans anywhere in Kando, but their consular jurisdiction was limited to four cities in the region.

76. In 1933 Japan withdrew from the League of Nations in protest of the league's assertion that Manchuria, though historically autonomous, was still an integral part of China and should not be considered a separate entity. Duara, *Sovereignty and Authenticity*, 52–53.

becoming a tool for political control in a place where the outcome of sovereignty was still unclear.

The citizenship question rose to prominence as a contentious issue in the wake of the Twenty-One Demands of 1915. By that time, the Qing dynasty had collapsed. Multiple contingents—politicians, military officials, and local warlords and their armies—scrambled to stake pieces of the fractured Chinese Republic, battling each other in a string of civil wars that started as quickly as they ended. In the midst of the chaos, jingoistic figures in the Japanese Foreign Ministry aimed to exploit China's fragility to their advantage and capture the vast resources of Manchuria, called the "jewel in the crown." Backed by a British alliance that curtailed Russian and German influence in China, Japan imposed the Twenty-One Demands on the Chinese government and called for an extension of its lease rights in Manchuria and the transfer of German interests in Shandong. It also demanded the right for its subjects to lease land and settle in South Manchuria where they would live under extraterritorial jurisdiction. China was forced to accept all the conditions. Tensions deepened when Japan contended that the 1915 treaty had effectively abrogated the earlier 1909 Kando Treaty. Precise definitions of geography and citizenship lay at the center of the dispute. Japanese officials began to insist that "South Manchuria" included areas that lay north, in Kando. In his letter to the Republican Chinese Foreign Ministry in November 1915, Obata Yūkichi, acting minister in Beijing, stated that Japan had "never recognized that Yanji [Kando] was not part of South Manchuria."[77] Further, Japanese officials in Kando maintained that Koreans were essentially "Japanese citizens" (*sinmin*). Given that Koreans formed the majority of the population in Kando, the claims, if proven in Japan's favor, would de facto pluck the territory and people out of China's hands and place it within the bounds of Japan's consular jurisdiction. China would also be deprived of its right to try and convict any Koreans in civil and criminal cases, a right that had been guaranteed in part by the Kando Treaty.

The possibility of losing authority over the Kando Koreans unsettled officials in the Republican Foreign Ministry and Jilin administration, because it foreboded the further disintegration of China's sovereignty. Secret correspondence that passed back and forth revealed the extent of their worry. In late 1915 Wei, the Jilin police station head, reported:

> Most Koreans are settled in the Yanbian area. If the Tumen [Kando] Treaty is abrogated, then all the Korean farmers [*kaeganmin*] in Yanbian will be included in the category of Japanese citizens, and we will

---

77. *Hanin kwallyŏn charyo*, 29.

completely lose our legal rights over them. Also, there will be great danger to our national defense if Yanji, Helong, and Wangqing Counties fall under the influence of Japan.[78]

Demographic data amplified fears of Japanese influence. By 1915 Koreans composed between 70 and 90 percent of the total population of counties in Kando.[79] If Koreans were legally recognized as Japanese subjects, then a large settled population of aliens under the auspices of an enemy would exist on Chinese soil. Japanese consular officials had already begun to conduct surveillance over Koreans by arraigning and arresting those suspected of crimes regardless of their legal status as Chinese subjects. In one case, Pak Ch'anik, a naturalized Chinese subject, had been summoned by the Japanese consul to be interrogated about his debts. When Pak fled to the local Jilin administration, the consul demanded his return. From his perspective, since Pak was a Japanese subject, the harboring of a potential suspect by another government amounted to an obstruction of Japanese law. Chinese officials, in turn, condemned such actions in unambiguous terms, saying they were an affront to its "national sovereignty," a "diminish[ing] of] our legal rights," and an "extremely grave affair."[80]

Even cases involving Koreans who lived in "mixed-resident districts" north of the Tumen River, where they were explicitly designated as under the jurisdiction of China by the terms of the Kando Treaty, were highly contested. Japanese officials filled lacuna in the treaty with claims about its jurisdictional rights. In Hunchun the Japanese consul, for example, claimed that Koreans residing there were not subject to the Kando Treaty but were in fact entitled to all rights and privileges of extraterritorial status under Japanese treaties with China. Koreans had "become one [ilwǒn] with Japanese citizens."[81] To the head of Jilin Province, Japan's newest demand reeked of imperialist ambition. He asserted that Japanese consuls, who had "said nothing" since the conclusion of the 1909 agreement, were now demanding jurisdictional rights (chaep'an'gwǒn) over Koreans because "they have a different aim." Once Japan acquired rights over Koreans in Hunchun, he believed, it would expand its jurisdiction to all Koreans in South and North Manchuria. As such, China had reason to fear that "Japanese rights

78. Ibid., 47.
79. Ibid., 46.
80. Ibid., 25–26, 35, 74, 26.
81. Japanese consul quoted in letter of Jilin provincial head. Ibid., 75–76; C. Walter Young, *Korean Problems in Manchuria*, 19. Hunchun later became the site of a controversial Japanese expedition in 1920. When a "bandit" force attacked Hunchun, killing a number of Japanese, Koreans, and consular police officers, the Japanese army in Korea crossed the border and joined the Kando region consular police forces to destroy the "bandits." The event became known as the Kando/Jiandao Expedition. Esselstrom, *Crossing Empire's Edge*, 74–76.

will extend to any place where Koreans reside," an unfortunate situation that would diminish China's authority to police and govern its own territory.[82]

Faced with Japanese encroachment, Chinese officials proposed the naturalization of Koreans as the most expedient means to protect Kando. A special envoy in Jilin, appointed to investigate the region in 1915, declared that resolving the issue of Koreans' citizenship was a matter of "preserving our national sovereignty." If Koreans were legitimate Chinese subjects, then the Japanese would have no reason to interfere in their affairs. Naturalization would also allow officials to keep track of land that was owned and leased by subjects and foreigners. Concluding that it was urgent to "speed up their naturalization," the envoy began a campaign at the provincial, county, and village levels to distribute applications for citizenship and to ensure that they were processed in a timely manner.[83]

Attitudes toward the status of Koreans reflected a broader concern about forging a national community in legal terms in turn-of-the-twentieth-century China. In 1909 the Qing dynasty established internationally recognized guidelines for Chinese citizenship. Informed by an understanding of the shared ethnic and cultural identity of Chinese, the law promulgated the principle of *jus sanguinis,* or bloodline, as the basis for citizenship. It decreed that anyone who intended to acquire citizenship in another country must first relinquish his original Chinese citizenship by gaining permission from the Qing government.[84] The citizenship law was as much a proactive measure to incorporate overseas Chinese (*huaqiao*) into the nation as it was a defensive measure to protect the nation from being drained of people going abroad.[85] Indeed, seeing foreign states naturalize Chinese residents in their territories, including the Dutch in Java, the Ministry of Foreign Affairs memorialized the emperor about the need for a citizenship law, stating that such a law would "keep natural-born Chinese from falling under foreign domination."[86] In 1914 the Republican Chinese government revised the citizenship law to include rules for nonethnic Chinese residents to *become* Chinese citizens.

82. *Hanin kwallyŏn charyo*, 76.
83. Ibid., 54, 52.
84. Many European countries at this time implemented laws on the abandonment of citizenship as a reaction to political dissidents in exile. Japan, too, added an abandonment clause, which allowed second-generation Japanese to be released from their original citizenship as long as they obtained permission from the Internal Ministry. Endō Masataka, *Kindai Nihon no shokuminchi tōchi ni okeru kokuseki to koseki* (Tokyo, 2010), 46, 58.
85. For more discussion on the intervention of the Republican Chinese government in overseas Chinese communities and their liminal position in Yokohama, see Eric C. Han, *Rise of a Japanese Chinatown* (Cambridge, MA, 2014).
86. Tsai Chutung, "The Chinese Nationality Law, 1909," *American Journal of International Law* 4, no. 2 (1910): 407.

At every turn, Japanese consuls in Kando protested China's naturalization efforts on several counts. First, they appealed to citizenship laws in China. In 1916 Japanese officials pointed out that Chinese law stipulated that a person must first abandon his original citizenship to obtain another. Because Koreans in Kando had not done so, they reasoned, Koreans' naturalization as Chinese subjects could not be recognized.[87] Second, Japanese statesmen contended that Koreans, under their own nationality laws before annexation in 1910, had not been permitted to acquire another nationality; on this basis, too, their legal status as Chinese should be rejected.[88] Finally, officials stated that Koreans were considered "imperial subjects." As such, granting Chinese naturalized status to Koreans according to Chinese nationality laws was a "violation of statutes."[89]

The assertive stance of Japanese diplomats regarding Koreans' citizenship in the late 1910s reflected a gradual evolution of attitudes inside the colonial bureaucracy. As recently as 1904, when questions about the citizenship of naturalized-Russian Koreans arose, Japanese diplomats were hard-pressed to define Chosŏn's citizenship laws, and they turned to Korean officials for an explanation. The latter responded that they had never granted permission for Koreans to become subjects of other countries and, in fact, had recently sent Yi Pŏmyun to Kando to "change the citizenship of its people *back* to Korea."[90] After Japan established a protectorate in 1905, colonial bureaucrats were more assertive in claiming authority over such matters vis-à-vis Russia. In 1907 problems arose when the Russian legation discovered that the Japanese army had begun to confiscate large swaths of land in Seoul, including a plot that belonged to an ethnic Korean Russian subject who worked as an interpreter for its diplomats. Russian officials demanded the return of the land, but the acting Japanese consul general refused. He insisted that a "Korean subject naturalized in any foreign state without permission of the Korean government is not recognized by the latter as a foreigner." When the Russian consul general argued that the Korean was, in fact, a Russian subject and that his parents had naturalized as Russian subjects, his Japanese counterpart rebuffed him by appealing to the authority of the Korean government:

> A state has the perfect right of deciding whether or not its subjects shall lose their original nationality when they have acquired citizenship in a foreign country. It is true that no law or ordinance has yet been

---

87. *Hanin kwallyŏn charyo*, 66, 71.
88. C. Walter Young, *Korean Problems in Manchuria*, 22.
89. *Hanin kwallyŏn charyo*, 72–73.
90. *Kaksa tŭngnok kŭndaep'yŏn*, 1904/7/26, italics added.

established in Korea regulating naturalization of the Korean subjects in other states, but it may be observed that the inherent authority of a government can nowise be affected by nonexistence of law or ordinance governing such matters.... As his parents' government's permission has neither been applied for or [sic] given, it naturally follows that they still remain Korean subjects so far as the authority of the Korean government extends.[91]

Three years later, on the eve of the annexation treaty of 1910, Resident-General Terauchi Masatake similarly affirmed the prerogative of the state to decide who did and did not belong to its political community. In a proposal to the cabinet in Tokyo, Terauchi suggested that Koreans who already possessed de facto dual citizenship by virtue of having naturalized in a foreign country should be considered Japanese subjects, at least until a law on citizenship in Korea was promulgated.[92] If the proposal passed, all Koreans who had naturalized in Kando, Russia, and Hawaii would automatically become Japanese subjects.[93]

As Japan attempted to extend its reach over Koreans abroad, however, it became clear that the problem of naturalization was not easily resolved. Naturalization was just one of many challenges that Japanese consuls faced in Kando—lack of funds for facilities and services, problems over land rights, coordination of competing Japanese agencies, and anti-Japanese activities of Koreans. Overwhelmed, officials came to the conclusion that many of these problems could be resolved by capitulating on the issue of naturalization. In 1913 Abe Moritaro, head of the political bureau of the Foreign Ministry, submitted a plan urging moderation in its policy toward China. In a section titled "The Problems of Koreans in Manchuria," he argued that Japanese authority over Koreans should be relinquished and that they should be allowed to become Chinese subjects. Though Abe's plan was not realized—he was assassinated by a fanatical imperialist youth—others took up his cause. A decade later, Fengtian Consul General Akatsuka Shōsuke stated that "we have no reason to oppose their naturalization" since status as Chinese citizens would give Koreans various benefits, including the ability to own land. Another consul insisted that any action that prevented Koreans

91. Quoted in Barbara Brooks, "Peopling the Japanese Empire," in *Japan's Competing Modernities*, ed. Sharon Minichiello (Honolulu, 1999), 33.

92. Yamabe Kentarō, *Ilche kangjŏm ha ŭi Han'guk kŭndaesa*, trans. Yi Hyŏnhŭi (Seoul, 1998), 11.

93. About seven thousand Koreans migrated to Hawaii during a brief period in the early 1900s. Japanese consuls in Korea viewed Korean migrants to Hawaii as competition for Japanese migrants there, and they imposed a temporary ban on Korean migration to Hawaii in 1905. Wayne Patterson, *The Korean Frontier in America* (Honolulu, 1988), 68–69; see also Yŏngho Ch'oe, ed., *From the Land of Hibiscus* (Honolulu, 2007).

from renouncing their Japanese citizenship was tantamount to "discriminatory treatment." Comparing Koreans in Kando to Japanese in California, the consul stated that the Koreans' desire to naturalize had nothing to do with finding a safe haven to conduct subversive anti-Japanese activities, as many Japanese believed, but reflected their aspirations to live a better life in a new country.[94]

In spite of the voices of dissent, suspicions about subversive Korean activity pushed officials to converge on the idea of using citizenship as a tool of state surveillance. Paranoia about Koreans pervaded the Japanese empire and escalated in the wake of the Korean Independence Movement in 1919 when peaceful protests turned into horrific massacres. It was at that point that the discourse of the "unruly Korean" (*futei senjin*) emerged and quickly expanded in meaning to include all radical Korean nationalists, anarchists, and Bolsheviks who posed an imminent threat to the peace of the Japanese nation.[95] Images of Koreans as immoral and dangerous saboteurs incited widespread hysteria in Japan and led police to redouble their surveillance over Koreans within Japan and throughout its colonies.[96] Fears of Korean rebels operating in Manchuria also drove Japanese officials to deploy citizenship as a method of controlling a potentially subversive element in China. In a 1925 report the Governor-General Office of Korea stated that Japan should not approve the naturalization of Koreans in Manchuria because it would be difficult to distinguish between "real Koreans" and "naturalized Koreans," the latter of whom had used their newly acquired foreign citizenship to conduct anti-Japanese activities on Chinese territory. If they were allowed, the difficulty of surveillance would dramatically increase, for Koreans would be able to hide under the protection of Chinese law. Japanese officials continued to assert that Koreans were not allowed to abandon their Japanese citizenship, notwithstanding continuing arguments inside and outside Japan that this inadmissibility was a violation of "international principle."[97]

---

94. Brooks, "Peopling the Japanese Empire," 36–37. See also Hyun Ok Park, *Two Dreams in One Bed* (Durham, NC, 2005), 78–81.

95. Ken Kawashima, *The Proletarian Gamble* (Durham, NC, 2009), 154.

96. In the wake of the September 1923 earthquake in the Kantō region of Japan, public hysteria about Koreans spread rapidly, leading to "Korean hunts" in which at least six thousand Koreans were brutally killed in Tokyo and Kanagawa alone. Brooks, "Peopling the Japanese Empire," 31; Sonia Ryang, "The Great Kanto Earthquake and the Massacre of Koreans in 1923," *Anthropological Quarterly* 76, no. 4 (Autumn 2003): 731–48.

97. Endō Masataka, *Kindai Nihon no shokuminchi tōchi ni okeru kokuseki*, 59, 65. Japan applied different citizenship laws in Taiwan and Korea. In the former, the Japanese citizenship law of 1899 allowed Taiwanese to renounce their subjecthood; the concession was never made for Koreans. The topic was discussed at the League of Nations, which considered it a violation of human rights to prevent a citizen from renouncing one citizenship to take another.

Disputes over the naturalization of Koreans were eventually subsumed under larger crises in the region. In September 1931, after staging an explosion of the Japanese-owned South Manchuria Railway near Mukden and blaming it on Chinese forces, Japan's Kwantung Army invaded Manchuria and established the puppet state of Manchukuo the following year. China no longer had a voice in the matter of Koreans. While the army waged war on multiple fronts in the northeastern territory, the Japanese government turned to the question of settling the region with people to secure a more thorough domination of colonial society.[98] In the 1930s, amid discussions about sending Japanese farmers under the auspices of a "Millions to Manchuria" program, a debate about whether to encourage Korean migration ensued. Former Consul General Hayashi Kyūjirō, among others, argued that standards of living in Manchuria fell far beneath what was adequate for Japanese farmers and that, instead, Koreans should be the ones to settle there. That they had already shown remarkable skill as farmers, particularly in wet-rice cultivation, was proof of their capacity to thrive in an inhospitable environment. Still others asserted that Koreans should be "kicked out" to make space for Japanese migrants. While officials deliberated the future of Manchukuo, Koreans continued to migrate into and out of Kando and broader Manchuria. Those engaged in agricultural work were joined by a growing number of professionals, including employees of the vast colonial bureaucracy and soldiers in the imperial army.[99] Anti-Japanese activists, too, made the region their primary base of operations, building a clandestine network of organizations and working with various Chinese factions, both nationalist and communist, civilian and military. The flow of Koreans over the border to Kando grew at a remarkable pace, lifting the total population of Koreans from 280,000 in 1919, to 390,000 in 1930, to 620,000 in 1942.[100]

The congeries of names imposed on the northern bank of the Tumen River, on the Chinese side—"prohibited zone," "north," "border area," Yanji, Kando, Jiandao, Kantō, and various county names—illuminate the myriad contests that were

98. In 1936 the Japanese government announced a program to colonize northeast China with Japanese farmers; it aimed to send one million households to Manchukuo within twenty years. About three hundred thousand Japanese resettled there under this program. Louise Young, *Japan's Total Empire* (Berkeley, 1998), 307.

99. Brooks, "Peopling the Japanese Empire," 40–41.

100. Walter Young was charged with conducting a study of the "Korean problem" in Manchuria in 1931. He cites population figures for Koreans in the Kando/Jiandao area (defined as Yanji, Helong, Wangqing, and Hunchun districts) based on Japanese consular data from 1909 to 1931; the figures correspond to those given by the Japanese Ministry of Foreign Affairs up to 1926. C. Walter Young, *Korean Problems in Manchuria*, 27; In Teak Chung, "The Korean Minority in Manchuria, 1900–1937" (Ph.D. thesis, American University, 1966), 39; Song, "My Land, My People," 377.

waged over the territory from the 1870s to the 1930s. The most dramatic change to the Tumen in this period, however, did not concern the growing number of groups and states that vied for its control or the widening ambit of laws and names that were imposed on the region. It was that the Tumen and its people had to be actively claimed at all. From the late nineteenth century, the Chosŏn and Qing governments could no longer take for granted their jurisdictional claims to land along the boundary. The two states had governed the area through the policy of the prohibited zone, which aimed to establish empty buffers, minimize settlement, and, in the case of Chosŏn, preserve geographical ambiguity for security purposes. But the encroachment of imperialist powers, including Russia, and the rising tide of cross-border migration compelled Chosŏn and the Qing to follow the path of states elsewhere and reverse their long-held policy. They began to actively claim the territory and people through law and, when necessary, by force. Officials embarked on missions to clarify the flows of the rivers and lodged claims on the Koreans, who had become the largest settled population on the Qing side. After 1895, when the two states established relations as equal sovereign states, they began to experiment with the language of international law and signed treaties to regulate trade and movement across the border. Vowing to protect the Koreans, Chosŏn officials went so far as to appoint overseers to govern the population on Qing territory and undertook to record the people in the household registers to remove any uncertainty about their status as subjects of Korea. The Jilin government protested, but its capacity to govern the region was limited, attenuated by internal instability and external military threats. Chosŏn's own efforts to claim the area and people were short-lived.

After the conclusion of the Russo-Japanese War in 1905, the Sino-Korean dispute over the Tumen was transformed into a Sino-Japanese feud over Kando and broader Manchuria. Koreans in Kando were caught in between the claims of a weakened China and the demands of an expanding Japanese empire, which had not only colonized Korea but also advanced into Manchuria and set up extraterritorial leaseholds, consulates, a police force, and a temporary field office in Kando to protect its colonial subjects. In the 1910s and 1920s, as tensions between the two states escalated, debates over the legal status of Koreans reached new heights. Both the recently established Republican Chinese government and Japanese Foreign Ministry aimed to utilize citizenship as a tool to assert their claims over Kando and Manchuria. China held firmly to its position that Koreans be allowed to naturalize as Chinese subjects, while Japan, suspicious of anti-Japanese activists who tended to manipulate their legal status across borders, refused to acknowledge China's position. In 1931 China lost control of Manchuria and was officially silenced on the question of Koreans.

The Korean population in Kando stood as a persistent reminder to officials that claiming people was a necessary part of claiming territory. Against the backdrop of geopolitical strife in northeast Asia, contention over the sovereignty of Kando elevated the legal status of Koreans to an urgent matter. Across the border in Russia, tsarist officials grappled with parallel concerns about its Korean inhabitants. Though it retained its possession of the Maritime Province, anxieties about its powerful neighbors and their border-crossing subjects ran high. Russian officials went to great lengths to institutionalize their borders, fix the legal status of Koreans as "Russians," and exclude those who did not belong. How they did so is the subject of the next chapter.

4

CIVILIZATIONAL BORDER

Subjects, Aliens, and Illegality in the
Russian Far East

From the time that Nikolai Muraviev, governor-general of Eastern Siberia, explored the verdant Amur and Ussuri regions and helped negotiate the annexation of these territories from the Qing, it was known that a sedentary, agricultural population was necessary to develop the land. The tsarist regime envisioned the Maritime Province as a strategic outpost in East Asia, and its natural resources made it all the more attractive. Yet the littoral, thousands of miles removed from populated areas of the empire, was inaccessible for most Russians. It was also deemed too vast a territory for the native populations to farm. So when tsarist officials discovered a Korean hamlet on the left bank of the Tumen River in the 1860s, they felt they had found the requisite population. The cornucopia of buckwheat and vegetables in Koreans' gardens exhibited their ability to produce bounty from the earth, and the presence of multiple generations of families dwelling under one roof demonstrated a commitment to settle permanently. Korea's proximity to Russia was also a boon, for seasonal migrants were able to travel with relative ease into and out of the Maritime.

The very qualities that made Koreans ideal settlers, however, simultaneously rendered them a "problem" in the eyes of Russian officials. Their affiliation with not just one but a triumvirate of states was cause for concern. Unlike indigenous peoples, such as the Buryat, Koreans migrated from a centralized bureaucratic state, which lodged claims on the expatriate population and demanded that Russia recognize those claims. Chosŏn's tributary ties with the Qing and then colonial ties with Japan also drew the unwanted attention of two powers that Russia considered threats to its sovereignty at different points in the nineteenth and twentieth centuries. The possibility that outside states might use the Koreans to extend their authority into Russia's jurisdiction magnified anxieties about the transborder population. Indeed, across the empire, scares about rebellions and enemies on its perimeters drove tsarist officials to scrutinize the position of borderland peoples who had lived in Russia for generations. Poles and Germans suddenly became "other" and "foreign." In the Russian Far East, Koreans and Chinese were not only considered "foreign" but were also spurned with xenophobic epithets; they were deemed "low class," "uncivilized," and "diseased," a sharp contrast to the "civilized," "productive," and "educated" ways of Russians. From the 1880s, officials began to convene congresses about Korean migrants and formulate concrete plans about how to handle the "Korean question."

This chapter examines the ongoing debates about Korean migrants in the Maritime and larger Russian Far East, and the myriad ways in which the tsarist state attempted to govern them from the 1880s to the early decades of the 1900s, when the geopolitics of East Asia shifted dramatically. Central to the matter of governing migrants was changing how the state managed the border region and the border itself. In practice, this meant eradicating the historical practice of plural jurisdiction—a system that bestowed distinct privileges and obligations on its panoply of territories and peoples and paid little regard to one's status as a subject or foreigner. In its place, officials aimed to create a unified political community that was built on this very distinction. They began to clarify definitions of "subjects" and "foreigners" and standardized their rights and privileges accordingly. Such policies were pursued most vigorously in Russia's Far East, where anxieties about the ambitions of neighboring states were conflated with paranoia about a dark East that threatened an enlightened West. Together these imaginings transformed the border from a mere territorial line between states into a chasm between civilizations. Over the next several decades, the tsarist regime experimented with various policies to solidify the boundary, including stationing border guards, establishing customs checkpoints, and instituting passport and visa regulations. Inside the Maritime, it granted the right of subjecthood to eligible Koreans and reduced to temporary alien status those who were ineligible. By means of such bureaucratic measures of inclusion—creating subjects and distributing passports—and of exclusion—denying subjecthood and refusing entry—the tsarist state enacted institutions of modern sovereignty at its borders.

Koreans, too, were active participants in this process. The spate of laws created structures that channeled migration and defined registration practices, penetrating down to the everyday lives of Koreans. Migrants learned to structure their lives around these institutions by obeying the law or contravening it. With the passing of time, alongside the legal population, an illegal population sprang up. Koreans who crossed into Russia from the Chosŏn or Qing states daily contributed to the rising number of illegal residents. Meanwhile, the counterfeiting of passports, falsification of registration documents, and hiding of people became rampant practices. The documentary record reveals officials' frustrations about the failure of the law to achieve its goals. Yet, far from serving as evidence that the law had no effect, such illegal activities were proof that the law was being acknowledged. In place of an orderly society of subjects and aliens that neatly aligned with the boundaries of the sovereign state, the law had unintentionally occasioned the birth of an illicit population that used the law to its own advantage.

The Uncivilized Alien

Since 1860, when Russia annexed Ussuri from the Qing, representatives of the tsarist state struggled to solidify Russia's place in maritime East Asia. They arrived armed with a mission to "civilize" the easternmost edge of their empire, a preoccupation that grew with the emergence of Russian nationalism in the first half of the century. Russian nationalists, composed primarily of Pan-Slavs, aimed to carry out a program of reform and revitalization on the "pliable canvas of remotest Siberia"—Russia's New World—and to deliver salvation to Asiatic peoples who had supposedly sunk into a lethargy of moral decay.[1] The Russian peasant, who stood at the apex of the civilizational hierarchy, was to be the agent of change on the periphery, tasked with disseminating Russian culture and civilization to all peoples.[2] Yet the tsarist empire faltered in the region because it lacked the requisite population of peasants to carry out the mission of civilizing and settling the East. It also had to contend with neighboring states, which aspired to settle their own frontier areas and impose a sharply different standard of civilization, Confucian norms, on the people who lived there. Given the mandate to civilize the area, the presence of Koreans was met with both hope and ambivalence; while they fulfilled the role of de facto "colonizers," their "alien" nature cast doubt on their ability to be civilized, much less to serve as an active civilizing force.[3]

---

1. Mark Bassin, *Imperial Visions* (Cambridge, 1999), 9–10.

2. In her excellent study of the Russian nationalist movement in the southwest borderlands of the tsarist empire, Hillis notes that "Russian" was shorthand for "Orthodox East Slav." The tsarist state, its history, and its people were gradually reimagined in ethnonational terms, with "Russian" as the primary titular nationality. Faith Hillis, *Children of Rus'* (Ithaca, 2013); Chia Yin Hsu, "The Chinese Eastern Railroad and the Making of Russian Imperial Orders in the Far East" (Ph.D. diss., New York University, 2006), 180–81.

3. In tsarist officialdom, "alien," from *inorodets* (plural: *inorodtsy*), changed in meaning over time. Originally, *inorodtsy* was a distinct legal category that referred to nomadic and seminomadic Asiatic

From the first reports written by Russian explorers, it was apparent that an assumption about inherent differences between Russians and Koreans existed. In 1866 Nikolai M. Przheval'skii, a renowned explorer of the Imperial Russian Geographical Society, journeyed to the Ussuri valley to survey the newly acquired region and its Russian settlers. He also wrote about indigenous peoples he encountered, including Koreans. His description of the Koreans reflected a preoccupation with a national mission of salvation on the empire's peripheries. In contrast to Russians, the Koreans were "crude and impenitent in their ignorance." But their primitive qualities did not entirely preclude them from assimilating. In fact, he recommended that local authorities relocate them to areas farther north, to Lake Khanka and the Amur region, where ties with their homeland would be more easily broken and new ones forged with existing Russian settlements. That way they could live

> among our peasants with whom they could become better acquainted and from whom they could assimilate something new. Then gradually, the Russian language and Russian habits, together with the Orthodox religion, would begin to penetrate to them, and perhaps with time an heretofore unknown miracle would take place: the regeneration in a new life for these groups who came from tribes as stubborn and immobile as the other peoples of the Asiatic East.[4]

Otherwise, leaving the Koreans so close to the border, where ties to their homeland endured, was a "considerable mistake."[5] Przheval'skii seemed to have influenced local officials, who ended up relocating five hundred Koreans from the border region to the banks of the Amur River in 1871, when floods and bad harvests drove thousands of Koreans across the border (see chapter 2).

V. I. Vagin, who wrote about the resettlement in his 1875 work "Koreans in the Amur," condemned Przhevalskii's proposals as unsound and wasteful. Any relations that Koreans continued with their countrymen "could only serve

---

peoples; it also connoted their inferiority. Asiatic *inorodtsy* were distinguished from "cultured nationalities" (*narodnosti*), such as Baltic Germans, Poles, and Finns. After 1905 *inorodtsy* took on a broader meaning and was applied to ethnic populations who had rebelled against the state, including Jews and Poles. In regard to Koreans and Chinese, there was no consistency in how the term was used; in census data, these groups were usually classified as "Koreans" and "Chinese," respectively, but in other official records simply as *inorodtsy*. In this chapter, the term "alien" is used to convey officials' perception of Asian migrants as an inferior "other" in culture, ethnicity, and loyalty, as well as to describe the temporary and foreign legal status that was imputed to them because of this perception. For a discussion of *inorodtsy*, see John W. Slocum, "Who, and When, Were the Inorodtsy?" *Russian Review* 57 (April 1998): 173–90.

4. Quoted in Bassin, *Imperial Visions*, 196.
5. N. M. Przheval'skii, *Puteshestviie v Ussuriiskom krae* (Moscow, 1947), 231.

in our favor." Citing primarily economic reasons, he stated that Koreans who settled near the border

> could be closer to their past. Both the climate and soil here are the same as they are in their homeland. They can introduce in our country those crops that are most common (to them). Only a few have had to borrow from Russian peasants, since their farming is more developed than ours. On the contrary, our peasants should learn much from them, and learn for their own benefit—especially in growing varieties of bread and vegetables that are particular to the local area and do not exist in Russia. In South Ussuri, introducing crops that are common in Korea, a country that is nearby and similar in form, is profitable above all else. And who better than the Koreans to do this?[6]

Based on this reasoning, Vagin asserted that there should be ten Koreans for every Russian, and not the converse ratio that Przheval'skii had proposed. As it stood, the government had not only wasted money by resettling the Koreans but also deprived the region of a necessary "productive force." He was also critical of the treatment that Koreans had received. Those who had naturalized were not seen as a "free people," nor had their subjecthood put them on "equal footing" with other "citizens of the state" (*grazhdany gosudarstva*). Instead, he stated, they were treated as a mere "labor force that could be ordered about as one pleased."[7]

Whereas Vagin believed that Koreans should not be assimilated in their farming methods, there was no question in his mind that they should be "Russified" in culture. Koreans were easy to assimilate, compared to the native peoples of Siberia. He conjured a social hierarchy of peoples from the least to the most civilized, the former traveling in tribes like nomads and the latter settling on land. By this standard, he deemed Koreans more civilized than the Buryat. Koreans had also "displayed a readiness to adopt the Russian language [and] Russian customs from the very beginning."[8] His opinions resonated with those of contemporary reformers, who came to associate the tsarist state with the Great Russian culture in the 1870s and increasingly described this titular nationality in ethnic and religious terms.[9]

Varying opinions about the Koreans left local officials in a quandary about what to do about the continuous arrival of Korean migrants to the Russian Far East. For years, debates about the costs and benefits of allowing such an outside

---

6. Vagin, "Koreitsy na Amure," 24–25.
7. Ibid., 25, 26, 29.
8. Ibid., 28.
9. Hsu, "Chinese Eastern Railroad," 180–81.

force to farm the land had led to contradictory policies, as Vagin pointed out. Officials encouraged Korean migration, he said, but when it became burdensome, they suddenly took the "most energetic measures" to stop it; they allowed settlement near the border, but when it became "completely undesirable," they abruptly moved the Koreans away from the border; and while the state treasury doled out funds to feed poor Koreans, when doing so became onerous, it tightened the budget.[10] By the time the Second Khabarovsk Congress convened in 1886, officials had had enough of the frenetic changes in policy. Worried about Koreans running the frontier economy, regional governors, local representatives, and entrepreneurs recommended that Korean migration be stopped. They complained that Koreans were "useless," reversing earlier opinions about their benefits as a labor force in a region that lacked a native Russian population. Koreans were now seen as lazy: "The plight of the simpleminded Korean is hopelessly difficult, which is why he has turned into a sluggard, working only as much as is needed to feed himself and his family, and sometimes even less." Some believed that Koreans' farming methods were harmful because they had exhausted the soil. Still, a minority defended the Koreans' techniques, saying that their harmful effects had not yet been proven.[11] Proponents of Koreans touted the enormous profits they brought: they raised wheat, oats, potatoes, and livestock that ended up feeding the military personnel and saved them from importing food from the port of Odessa.[12] Koreans, both naturalized and nonnaturalized subjects, had also fulfilled their duties to the state and helped build South Ussuri into a semi-functioning region.

Apart from economic concerns, officials worried that Koreans posed a problem because of their questionable loyalty. They had settled in the strategically sensitive region of Poset, wedged between China and Korea. If a conflict ever broke out with China, the small military force of Cossacks on the border would be caught between two "enemy forces," armed Chinese troops and Korean subjects.[13] Military Governor of the Maritime Province Pavel F. Unterberger (1842–1921) echoed these concerns, saying that the district of Poset constituted a "great danger for the population who lives there in the event of war with China. It is long, narrow, and would be badly defended from the attacks of enemy troops." Russian settlers, he asserted, should take the place of Koreans.[14] Unterberger recommended

---

10. Vagin, "Koreitsy na Amure," 22–23.
11. Quoted in B. D. Pak, *Koreitsy v Rossiiskoi imperii*, 59–60.
12. RGIADV 702/1/94, l. 19–20ob (March 18, 1889) in A. A. Toropov et al., eds., *Koreitsy na Rossiiskom Dal'nem Vostoke* (Vladivostok, 2001), 57–58.
13. RGIADV 702/1/94, l. 4–17 (August 16, 1888) in Toropov et al., *Koreitsy* (2001), 44.
14. RGIADV 702/1/94, l. 41–45 (February 19, 1891) in Toropov et al., *Koreitsy* (2001), 68.

resettling Koreans from Poset to areas farther north, where they would escape "Chinese influence" and submit to Russian authorities. Unterberger's proposals, as well as those of others, were debated at length and implemented on an ad hoc basis, but systematic measures regarding Korean migration and jurisdiction were still lacking. The Korean question would soon be assessed within the broader context of laws concerning foreigners in the Russian empire.

Eradicating Plural Jurisdiction: Subjects and Aliens

Prior to the mid-nineteenth century, the tsarist empire adopted flexible measures to govern its sprawling territories and diverse peoples. According to this practice of "plural jurisdiction," the regime bestowed a distinct set of obligations and privileges—"separate deals"—to each domain or group within the empire.[15] As a principle, the regime conferred Russian subjecthood status on all new territories or people that were annexed, but the panoply of jurisdictions meant that subjecthood was hardly a unified concept or universal set of rights. Within the empire, one's religious order and estate (*sostianie*) determined the set of privileges and exemptions one received, not one's status as a subject. Foreigners who had lived for generations in the Russian empire found it more advantageous to join an estate, rather than to naturalize, since retaining the subjecthood of their original country brought privileges of diplomatic immunity. In the late 1800s, however, the tsarist state began to depart from this long-standing practice. It passed a series of legal reforms that aimed to standardize the rights and obligations of Russian subjects and foreigners, thereby eliminating plural jurisdiction. In place of the model of multiple "separate deals" to various groups and regions, the regime created a binary legal framework that divided Russian from non-Russian subjects. Under the new framework, one's subjecthood status, or political membership in the tsarist state, determined one's privileges. The reforms affected foreigners throughout the empire, but their impact was particularly visible on the fringes of the empire, in the borderlands, where foreigners mixed freely with natives. In the Maritime Province, eradicating plural jurisdiction posed a singular challenge because of the migration of Koreans and Chinese, as well as the region's unique history of annexation.

---

15. In his study of Russian subjecthood, Eric Lohr calls this practice an "embrace of exceptions" or "separate deals"; separate deals gave various combinations of rights and obligations to different immigrant groups, social orders, and national and religious minorities. Eric Lohr, *Russian Citizenship* (Cambridge, MA, 2012), 2.

Russian officials were not alone in grappling with questions that emerged due to rising mobility. In the mid-nineteenth century, states around the globe faced unprecedented numbers of foreign subjects crossing their borders at a dizzying pace. Facilitated by breaking technology in travel and brokers who organized them, people who had previously traveled only to a neighboring town now found themselves on the opposite end of the ocean.[16] Officials who were confronted with the arrival and departure of people struggled with how to govern them. Few laws existed to regulate movement across international borders, nor was there uniformity in laws that defined the jurisdiction of migrants once they arrived at their destination. The dearth of laws had as much to do with the nature and scale of migration—previously, few people had much reason or means to travel outside their countries—as it did the lack of consensus within and between states. Until then, migration had been largely regulated by local and national laws that promoted, forced, or hindered movement according a host of factors, such as vocation, class, lineage, property, and religion. Laws, moreover, had focused on mobility inside countries, not across borders. Enforcement of those laws was far from centralized, and responsibilities for overseeing them were passed to municipal and regional officials whose jurisdictional authority often overlapped. Given the lack of coordination within states, it was no surprise that laws across states conflicted with each other, too.[17]

Witnessing the millions on the move, theorists and lawyers, particularly in the Anglophone world, began to discuss migration within the broader context of intercourse and international law. Reflecting a general shift away from natural law to positivist methodology, the focus of international law changed from finding the conditions to justify the use of force between states, as in the case of war, to identifying ways to regulate interstate relations through customs and practices, especially in the area of commerce. Commerce became a significant source of codifiable international law and helped perfect the law through a myriad of customs. Migration was treated as a core component of commerce, along with goods and the transit of ships. Yet lawyers struggled to subsume migrants under the category of commerce. As it turned out, a nation could reject unwanted goods without being questioned, but it could not ban an undesirable people from its territory "without violating the spirit of the Law of Nations and endangering its very membership of [sic] the Family of Nations." The law of nations, as noted theorist Lassa Oppenheim pointed out, was fundamental to forging a community of civilized states and depended on intercourse between those states.[18]

---

16. McKeown, "Global Migration."
17. McKeown, *Melancholy Order*, 92.
18. Ibid., 94–95.

Unable to reconcile the realities of unwanted migrants with the tenets of inter-course, lawyers, politicians, and administrators left the laws governing migration deliberately ambiguous.

In the case of white settler nations around the Pacific, the key to justify-ing migration law ultimately rested on an assertion of sovereign prerogative to exclude certain countries from the Family of Nations. As historian Adam McKeown shows, settler nations—the United States, Canada, Australia, New Zealand, and others—faced the arrival of thousands of Chinese who traveled across seas to work in industries such as gold mining and railroad construction in the mid-nineteenth century. Though the Chinese filled a necessary role as labor-ers in developing frontiers, their presence was unwanted. Fueled by a belief that Chinese were an unfree, unassimilable people that opposed the Western ideal of egalitarian, self-governing societies in the Family of Nations, officials began to pass anti-Asian discriminatory laws inside their countries. They also exper-imented with various quarantine rules, taxes, and passenger laws that limited numbers of migrants by tonnage. By the turn of the twentieth century, officials moved to replace the assortment of local discriminatory laws inside states with national policies that used passports and surveillance to stop unwanted migra-tion at the first place of entry—the border itself. White settler nations justified their actions by proclaiming sovereign prerogative; no one was to question the right of the state to control entry across its borders. Their claims, to be sure, stood at odds with the idea of intercourse among equal, sovereign states. It also broke with earlier references to treaty rights. But while commerce remained a subject of intercourse, states reserved the right to subsume migration control under national law in the name of the universal right to self-protection.[19]

Parallel anxieties about uncivilized Asian migrants likewise compelled Rus-sian officials to limit the entrance of foreigners for the purpose of self-protection. But unlike their counterparts in the Anglophone world, they did not feel con-strained by the need to justify their actions through so-called liberal principles that underpinned the Family of Nations. Rather, as a landed empire that gov-erned through plural jurisdiction, the regime faced a very different challenge of forging a legal divide between foreigners and subjects in the area of privileges. In the western borderlands, where Germans, Poles, Tatars, and others had lived for centuries, disentangling the privileges of subjects from those of nonsubjects was especially difficult. During the reign of Catherine the Great (1762–96), whole communities of Germans had migrated to Russia and settled in sparsely popu-lated areas in return for various incentives. Most carried internal passports that

---

19. Ibid., 125–26, 149.

were renewable in perpetuity but remained subjects of their original country. In the second half of the nineteenth century, amid a wave of nativist sentiment and fears about aliens, officials began to pass a series of laws to distinguish aliens from subjects. The regime required foreigners to enter with "national passports" and obtain residence permits (*vid na zhitel'stvo*).[20] The more significant change was enacted in the area of land policy. Following the Polish rebellion of 1863, the tsarist government issued a secret ordinance that prohibited individuals of Polish descent from acquiring gentry properties in the western border region by any means except inheritance.[21] Two decades later, the government passed legislation regarding the Russian Far East. It declared that local tax (*zemskie povinnosti*) exemptions, both monetary and natural, and general tax waivers (*l'goti*) would not apply to foreigners who settled in the Maritime and Amur Provinces after 1881.[22] In 1886 the Council of Ministers went a step further: it prohibited all Korean and Chinese "emigrants" from settling on Russian territory that bordered Korea and China—specifically, Ussuri.[23]

To understand the significance of the 1886 settlement ban against Koreans and Chinese, it is necessary first to note the exceptional history of Ussuri's annexation to the Russian empire. Ussuri, the littoral bordering Chosŏn Korea and the East Sea, was the last piece of territory in the Maritime Province to be added to Russia in 1860. In all other annexed territories, the tsarist regime automatically granted Russian subjecthood to people living in those lands. Ussuri, however, represented the first instance in which an annexed people had been left as subjects of their original country, Qing China. As a result, there was no official provision to allow Chinese and other inhabitants there to naturalize.[24] The lack of clarity about the jurisdiction of Qing subjects in the border region created confusion among officials of both governments (see chapter 2). Alongside the unusual treaty clause, domestic Russian laws attempted to restrict the migration of additional Qing

20. M. I. Mysh, ed., *Ob inostrantsakh v Rossii* (St. Petersburg, 1911), 45–46.

21. This decree became the cornerstone of land policy in the following years, including the 1887 ban on foreign ownership and leasing of lands in the western borderlands; it was followed by a similar ban in 1892. Eric Lohr, *Nationalizing the Russian Empire* (Cambridge, MA, 2003), 87, 90.

22. The governor-general of Eastern Siberia was allowed to make exceptions as he saw fit. Mysh, *Ob inostrantsakh v Rossii*, 103.

23. The ban also applied to Koreans already living on the Russian side. Toropov et al., *Koreitsy* (2001), 42; Mysh, *Ob inostrantsakh v Rossii*, 1.

24. Some have reasoned that the Qing purposefully negotiated the Aigun treaty so that it could retain jurisdiction over its subjects in the newly annexed Russian territory. I believe that the Qing and Russian empires were acting according to their long-held practices of plural jurisdiction in the border region and decided to leave the issue ambiguous. It was the arrival of additional Chinese that incited Russia's worries. A systematic study on the Chinese in Russia is necessary to shed light on this issue. See chapter 2 in this book; Lohr, *Russian Citizenship*, 36–37.

subjects into Russian territory. In 1885 the tsarist government circumvented the ambiguous question of naturalization by passing a regulation that required "Chinese" to obtain a passport to enter the country. While all foreigners were eventually required to do so, the law was designed to place specific constraints on Chinese migration. In addition to the passport, Chinese had to obtain a special work document and, more significantly, a *bilet*, which functioned much like a modern-day visa in that it allowed them to reside in Russia for up to one year. Over time, the various fees levied on migrants rose to approximately five rubles, more than what other foreigners were required to pay.[25] Governor-General A. N. Korf expressed his hopes that such "inconvenient and even overwhelming fees" would "drive them out gradually."[26] The *bilet* system effectively limited the legal options available to Chinese on Russian territory, reducing them to the status of temporary foreign workers.[27] Russian officials had made clear their intention to restrict the migration of Chinese into the Russian Far East at the first place of entry, the border.

The 1886 ban on Korean and Chinese settlement was notable because it was the first law to prohibit a specific ethnic group from settling in a border area. Elsewhere around the empire, foreigners still had the right to enter Russia and live in most places as long as they abided by passport regulations.[28] The ban took to an extreme previous laws that aimed to distinguish Russians from non-Russians on the western frontier. It was also an extension of the regime's earlier policies toward Qing subjects, who had been limited to permanent alien status; the same status was now imposed on Korean migrants. A few years later, the tsarist empire passed a similar measure in the western borderlands, restricting non-Russians in general from settling and acquiring land.[29] Yet the 1886 law's explicit focus on Asians underscored the undesirability of this people in the eyes of the

---

25. The *bilet* (sometimes *vremennyi bilet*) is not to be confused with the "visa stamp," which Russian authorities affixed to the national passports of Chinese and later Koreans upon entering the country. The "stamp" was only valid for thirty days, after which the passport had to be exchanged for a Russian *bilet*. Since *bilet* has no English-language equivalent, usage of this Russian word has been retained. Lohr, *Russian Citizenship*, 77–78; Petrov, *Istoriia Kitaitsev v Rossii*, 250–51.

26. Quoted in Petrov, *Istoriia Kitaitsev v Rossii*, 250.

27. It seems that Chinese were given the right to naturalize only after the tsarist government had passed a general edict giving Koreans this right in 1891. See note on Statute 334 of the Siberian Establishment (1892) in Mysh, *Ob inostrantsakh v Rossii*, 30.

28. There were similar restrictions on Jews, but this group was a perennial exception to mobility laws. Ibid., xii–xiii.

29. The law, passed in 1892, banned non-ethnic Russians regardless of subjecthood status. A similar ban prohibited foreigners from acquiring land in Turkestan. Lohr, *Russian Citizenship*, 71; Mysh, *Ob inostrantsakh v Rossii*, 102.

regime. It also hinted at the extent to which the state would go to remove Asians from the border region in the future.

The tightening of borders through land policy and passport laws soon emboldened the tsarist administration to decide the question of Koreans' jurisdiction once and for all. Russian diplomats and officials had previously attempted to negotiate with the Chosŏn government to settle the issue of jurisdiction. Recognizing that Chosŏn was a tributary state of the Qing and a long-standing state in its own right, they treaded lightly on the issue to avoid any confrontation with its neighbors. As discussed in chapter 2, there was no model for determining the jurisdiction of people in the tripartite border region. Sino-Russian extraterritoriality agreements of the mid-nineteenth century overturned past mutual extradition treaties, but they neither elucidated the jurisdiction of Chinese in Russia nor discussed Koreans. After the establishment of diplomatic relations, Korea and Russia passed the 1888 trade rules to establish passport procedures for Koreans traveling to Russia. But the rules said nothing about the subjecthood of Koreans already living in Russia because the Chosŏn government had refused to relinquish its claims on Koreans abroad. Finally, in 1891, Governor Korf had come to the point where he was able to decide the jurisdiction of Koreans unilaterally, through a domestic law.

In July 1891 Korf passed a decree that classified Koreans as either subjects or foreigners.[30] He declared that Koreans in Russia should be divided into two groups: those who would receive Russian subjecthood and those who would not. The year 1884, when the two countries had established diplomatic relations, served as the dividing mark.[31] Koreans who had settled in Russia before 1884 acquired the right to become Russian subjects and had to comply with Russian law. They became part of the peasant estate, were baptized as Orthodox Christians, paid taxes, and registered in the village family records.[32] Each family of

---

30. Much debate preceded the passing of the decree, including Military Governor P. F. Unterberger's objections to the naturalization of Koreans. RGIADV 702/1/94, l. 36–38 (November 6, 1890) in Toropov et al., *Koreitsy* (2001), 66.

31. Most Russian primary and secondary sources state that it was the 1888 Russo-Korean trade rules that conferred Russian subjecthood on Koreans who had settled in Russia before 1884. There is no such clause. While it is true that Russian officials had decided in the 1880s to divide Koreans into various categories, the Korean government had not permitted Russia to include naturalization as a point in international treaties.

32. Religious conversion was an integral part of the tsarist state's policies toward new subjects, even if, until the nineteenth century, it involved only a nominal transfer of religious identity through the ritual of baptism. Conversion brought tangible benefits and social and economic mobility. In the eighteenth and nineteenth centuries, the state expanded its efforts to proselytize and teach new subjects to be Orthodox Christian. It should also be noted that "peasant" (*krest'ianin*) meant not just any peasant but, specifically, a peasant of the Russian Orthodox faith. Chapter 7 discusses Orthodox Christian missions among Koreans. See also Michael Khordarkovsky, "The Conversion of

naturalized Russians received 15 *desiatinas* of land on the condition that they not lease it to temporary Korean migrants. The edict also required naturalized Koreans to obtain a certificate (*svidetel'stvo*) with the year of their arrival and names of their family members. Finally, naturalized Koreans had to cut off their topknots so that the police could physically distinguish them from "Korean foreigners."[33] The law effectively erased Koreans' former status as an elite, merchant, or commoner and accorded them the legal status of a Russian subject.

By corollary, the 1891 edict extinguished any chance for other Koreans to become Russian subjects. They were reduced to the status of temporary dweller. All Koreans who arrived in Russia after 1884 were refused Russian subjecthood. They were divided further into two groups. The first group included those who had already settled in Russia and wished to remain. They had to obtain a Korean "national passport," procure a Russian *bilet* that allowed them to stay in Russia for up to one year, and relinquish use of state lands within two years. Koreans who failed to do so at the end of that period had to pack up their belongings and leave the country. The second group included present and future Korean laborers who had not yet "settled" on land; they were forbidden from doing so and had to pay land and quit-rent taxes that peasants were subject to. This group, too, was required to obtain a Korean national passport and *bilet*.[34] With no way to naturalize in the foreseeable future, most Korean migrants became permanent aliens. To seal their unequal status, the tsarist government subjected them to the same *bilet* fees that it had imposed on Qing subjects.

The passing of the 1891 naturalization and migration policy deepened the rift in the treatment of aliens versus subjects in the Far Eastern border region. Similar to Chinese, nonnaturalized Koreans were de facto reduced to the status of temporary dweller and excluded from accessing privileges that had previously been available to inhabitants of the empire, regardless of their subjecthood status. Required to hold "national passports," they became "Korean" in legal terms. Concomitantly, early Korean arrivals were made "Russian subjects" to put an end to Chosŏn's claims on its former subjects. The law effectively ascribed to Koreans a new identity that was defined solely by the Russian state: in the eyes of the regime, one was either an alien or a subject.

Non-Christians in Early Modern Russia," in *Of Religion and Empire*, ed. Robert P. Geraci and Michael Khordarkovsky (Ithaca, 2001), 115–43.

33. RGIADV 702/1/94, l. 22–30 (March 1860), 36–38 (November 6, 1890) in Toropov et al., *Koreitsy* (2001), 61–62, 65–66; B. D. Pak, *Koreitsy v Rossiiskoi imperii*, 66.

34. The process of obtaining passports and *bilets* was similar to that for Chinese. *Bilet* rules pertaining to both Chinese and Koreans were continuously refined because of specific worries about Koreans, who tended to settle for relatively long periods. RGIADV 1/2/1048, l. 20 in Toropov et al., *Koreitsy* (2001), 58–59.

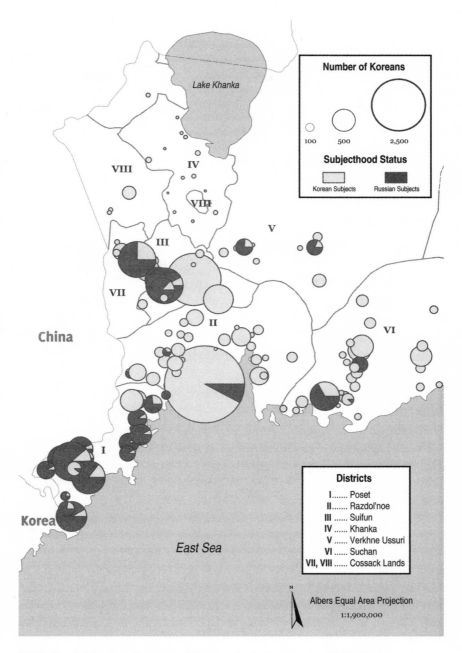

MAP 4. Subjecthood status of Koreans in South Ussuri, 1906–7. Subjecthood was part of tsarist policy to solidify the border. Early Korean arrivals, who were concentrated along the borders of Korea and China, were naturalized as Russian subjects. Later arrivals remained "Korean subjects"; they established themselves on the edges of existing villages and on church, state, and municipal lands. (Figure is a representative proportional symbol map.)

Across the empire in the late nineteenth century, the regime attempted to simplify and standardize the panoply of privileges, exemptions, and rights belonging to foreigners and subjects. In the Russian Far East, where the history of plural jurisdiction had enabled the legal growth of an alien population, there was an urgency to eradicate any ambiguity in who belonged and did not belong to the empire. Russia, similar to states around the world, had begun to exercise its right to enforce that distinction and stop unwanted people at its national borders.

Errors, Loopholes, and Missing Persons

Over the course of the next few years, Russian officials endeavored to classify the Koreans as subjects and aliens and make the law a reality. In August 1891 they charged a special commission under the leadership of Aleksandr Vasilevich Sukhanov, captain of South Ussuri, to conduct a census of Koreans. Sukhanov was meticulous from the beginning. In the preliminary stage of the investigation, he ordered Korean leaders to compose a list of names of permanent residents, their year of arrival, and financial standing in Poset and Suifun, the two districts with the largest population of Koreans. After the preliminary census was conducted, Sukhanov and an entourage that comprised the forestry warden, land surveyor, police captain, and local clergymen traveled to twenty-six villages to verify the lists over the course of three and a half months in the summer of 1892.[35] They spent two to four days in each village. By September 1892 the commission compiled what appeared to be a comprehensive and accurate list of Koreans who had the right to naturalize as Russian subjects and those who did not. By 1893 approximately 11,000 Koreans (2,900 households) had taken an oath of allegiance to the tsar and God and received certificates as proof of their subjecthood.[36] Another 4,300 Koreans were refused the right to naturalize because they had arrived after the critical 1884 cutoff year; they had to relinquish state lands within two years.[37] In subsequent years, however, as stories of careless errors and willful subterfuge surfaced, it became apparent that defining and managing a borderland population was a project inherently fraught with tension.

---

35. Members waited until October 1893 to verify lists in the five Korean villages of the Upper Ussuri and Suchan districts, where fewer Koreans lived. For an account of the 1892 investigation, see ibid., 82–85.

36. Though the term was not used in regard to documents for Koreans, the certificate was commonly known as a *prisiazhnoe svidetel'stvo*.

37. RGIADV 702/1/94, l. 81–89ob (April 29, 1894) in Toropov et al., *Koreitsy* (2001), 87.

During a reinvestigation of the Koreans in 1909–10, officials found that the 1892 effort to register the mobile population had led to many errors. In the early 1900s new concerns about the "Korean question" prompted Military Governor Vasilii E. Flug to confirm the number of naturalized Koreans by reviewing the original lists of "oaths" (*prisiazhnye listy*) signed by subjects and double-checking the lists with the physical certificates that had been given to the Koreans in the 1890s.[38] As it turned out, Sukhanov's successor, P. P. Khomiakov, had seized the certificates from the Koreans in the 1890s for some unknown reason. No one could find them.[39] So a range of officials, from peasant chiefs and police to county (*volost'*) and village heads, were tasked with delving into the local archives to retrieve unofficial oath lists and family registers.[40] Fortunately, for 11,600 people, officials managed to find oath lists with their names and issued them new certificates of subjecthood. Another 2,400 Koreans were not so fortunate. Many of these Koreans claimed to be subjects and were listed in the family registers, but there was no documentation of their oaths.

It was not enough that their names were listed in the family registers, for officials viewed them with mistrust. A gamut of errors had sprung up in the records because of confusion about Korean names. Relying on Russian scholar V. Stroshevskii's work on Korea, officials believed that Koreans had as many as six given names throughout their lifetimes—*amyŏng, pyŏlmyŏng, kwamyŏng, chaho, pyŏlho,* and *ch'ingho*.[41] Koreans had been mistakenly written into the family registers under multiple names as a result. On top of the confusion created by the vast range of first names, the relatively small number of surnames was cause for more mix-ups. In Poset district alone, there were 235 families with the surname Kim, 114 with Li, and 112 with Pak. Over time, as succeeding generations of Koreans adopted Russian names, family trees looked oddly similar; there were dozens of Ivan Kims and Vasilii Kims.[42] Changing one's name after religious conversion created other challenges. Children who were baptized into the Orthodox Church received Christian names, which were then recorded in the family registers without any mention of their given Korean names. Many parents, however, could not remember their children's new names.[43] It was for this reason that the military

---

38. 702/1/640, 14–19ob (April 3, 1909) in Toropov et al., *Koreitsy* (2001), 197.

39. Toropov et al., *Koreitsy* (2001), 203; RGIADV 702/1/640, l. 41 (April 21, 1909).

40. Toropov et al., *Koreitsy* (2001), 197–98.

41. In Stroshevskii's study, *amyŏng* was defined as a childhood name; *pyŏlmyŏng* a nickname; *kwamyŏng* a family name acquired after marriage; *chaho* a colloquial name; *pyŏlho* a nickname that noted a personal characteristic; and *ch'ingho* a posthumous title. Ibid., 200.

42. Ibid., 200, 201–2.

43. There is no mention of whether the Koreans were registered by priests in metrical books, a record of births and deaths of Orthodox children, names and estates of parents, marriages, and

governor cited the "extreme difficulty" of using the family registers to authenticate an individual's identity.[44]

Over the course of the investigation, officials encountered various ambiguities in laws concerning subjecthood. In the reforms of the 1860s, the tsarist regime attempted to unify the types of subjecthood conferred on various domains and people. But officials who traveled to the Korean villages were confronted with a number of baffling cases that were not easily resolved through the principles of jus sanguinis (right of citizenship to anyone born of a citizen) or jus soli (right of citizenship to anyone born within the territory of the state), both of which appeared in the legal code. Based on jus sanguinis, subjecthood was granted to whole families through the male head of household. As such, if a woman married a "foreign" Korean man, their children, too, would become "foreign." The death of a husband, however, could leave the children in an ambiguous position. In most cases, the widow and her children joined her father's household, and if the father was a Russian subject, his status was passed on to his daughter's children. It was unclear, however, whether this practice was lawful.[45] In other cases, tension between principles of jus sanguinis and jus soli made it difficult to arrive at a decisive answer. According to the law, the status of a naturalized Russian subject was passed down to his children at the time of naturalization. Yet what was the status of children who were born afterward? The military governor settled the question on the basis of jus soli and residence status. If the children could prove that they had been born in the Maritime Province and lived there continuously, they could become Russian subjects.[46]

As these cases revealed, ascribing a fixed legal identity on a mobile population posed a challenge from the start. An artificial divide in many ways, the cutoff year 1884 failed to account for ongoing migration and cross-border ties that had developed over decades. About twenty-five thousand Koreans traveled back and forth between Korea, Russia, and Manchuria to work, to pay visits to relatives, and to attend to the graves of ancestors, creating circular migration patterns that made it difficult to determine the exact date of arrival. Families also crossed borders. Naturalized Korean men married "foreign Koreans" (*zagranichnye koreiki*) and brought their children and extended families to Russia to live, forming

---

deaths. Charles Steinwedel maintains that metrical books were the primary register of identity in the Russian empire by the early nineteenth century. Charles Steinwedel, "Making Social Groups, One Person at a Time," in *Documenting Individual Identity*, ed. Jane Caplan and John Torpey (Princeton, 2001), 69.

44. Toropov et al., *Koreitsy* (2001), 200–201.

45. Ibid., 198.

46. RGIADV 702/1/640, l. 48ob–49 (May 31, 1909).

what the Russian border commissar called a "strongly mixed" society.[47] In 1907 the Congress on the Korean Question aptly described the mixed character of the community: "Despite the fact that the Korean population of Poset has become Russian subjects, has become like the Russian peasant population in all respects, a large portion of whom have even converted to Orthodoxy, tribal and family ties nevertheless remain between our Koreans and foreign Koreans—ties that continue to be the primary basis for persisting relations between [them]."[48] These ties sometimes compelled families to return to Korea. Local police insisted that the border commissar appeal to Chosŏn authorities to have naturalized Russian subjects sent back to Russia.[49] But it was clear that the police could not stop people from moving where they wished. Indeed, in 1910 officials discovered that almost 1,200 individuals (250 families), all supposedly Russian subjects, had disappeared. Before leaving, these families had passed on their property to other Koreans.[50]

The primary obstacle to forging a divide between subjects and aliens was the difficulty of enforcement. The 1891 edict had uneven outcomes. Many Koreans had met the qualifications to become Russian subjects but had not received the proper documents.[51] Koreans who had been categorized as foreigners and ordered to vacate their lands by 1894 were found squatting on the same lands more than ten years later. In addition, hundreds of migrants designated as aliens were resettled to areas farther north near Khabarovsk and given Russian subjecthood and land because of the absence of a farming population to develop the land.[52] At the end of the investigation in 1910, the office of the Priamur governor-general placed much of the blame on the administration itself. It concluded that because of the "negligence of authorities," oath lists had been lost and "a more or less significant number of Russian subjects [were] being deprived of their right to subjecthood."[53]

Policing migrants at the border proved as difficult as classifying subjects. The 1888 Regulations for Land Trade stipulated passport laws to control the cross-border movement of migrants. In particular, Koreans were required to arrive in Russia with a national passport that had been endorsed by a Russian consul with a "visa stamp." The lack of Russian consulates, however, hindered this process at

47. Ibid., l. 22 (February 10, 1910).
48. RGIADV 1/1/6104, l. 18ob (February 10, 1907).
49. RGIADV 1/5/1354, l. 73–73ob (April 22, 1900) in Toropov et al., *Koreitsy* (2001), 112.
50. RGIADV 702/1/640, l. 134–136ob (March 11, 1910) in Toropov et al., *Koreitsy* (2001), 213–14.
51. Toropov et al., *Koreitsy* (2001), 213.
52. The villages of Osipovka and Aleksandrovka were founded in this manner. Ibid., 150.
53. Ibid., 214.

important points of entry and exit. No consulate existed in the border town of Kyŏnghŭng until the late 1890s, and consulates were not established in the port cities of Wŏnsan and Sŏngjin until the early 1900s. The Russian border commissar in Novokievsk, 20 mi. north of the border, handled consular affairs in the meantime. Obtaining the stamp was also time-consuming, and people took up the process in various ways. Some trekked to the border, handed over their passports to the postman, and waited for him to return with the endorsed document. Others sent proxies to border points to have their passports endorsed ahead of time.[54] Still others avoided the system altogether by going to China and then to Russia. Widespread abuses arose as a result.

Acquiring a *bilet* once inside Russia was no easier. Koreans were required to obtain a *bilet* within a month of their arrival from the municipal or district police; the document allowed them to remain in Russia for up to one year, after which they had to apply for renewal.[55] Without the *bilet*, one was considered illegal. But a Korean who went to the trouble of going to the municipal police office often had to wait several days to be seen. Discouraged and afraid at the prospect of having to explain themselves in a foreign language, many gave up and left. Circumstances were worse at the district office where the police captain was usually absent.[56] In 1906 it was widely known that only 10 percent of Koreans in Russia had obtained *bilets*, resulting in a loss of 160,000 rubles to the state treasury.[57]

In addition to procedural challenges, there were loopholes in the law. In the absence of a centralized border authority, the system relied on local officials who had little incentive to comply in the first place. At the lowest governmental unit—the village—elders were responsible for keeping track of who lived, entered, and departed the village; they also minded the productive output of the entire village to calculate the collective taxes owed to the state. Elders, who were concerned with maximizing output, saw the farming capacities of permanent villagers and temporary dwellers as "absolutely the same," and for this reason they found it unnecessary to report an undocumented migrant. The law, in fact, did not require elders to conduct surveillance over the legal status of inhabitants. Thus, as the 1907 Congress on the Korean Question noted, "if Koreans living in any village in the region do not commit a criminal offense or act, then they [can] live absolutely peacefully, engaged in work without being harassed for not having Russian *bilets*." The county head, who stood one level above the village elder, did

---

54. RGIADV 1/3/1088, l. 25–25ob (November 19, 1907), l. 7 (September 5, 1907).
55. RGIADV 702/7/40, l. 91–92ob (1899) in Toropov et al., *Koreitsy* (2001), 107.
56. RGIADV 1/1/6104, l. 25–26 (February 10, 1907).
57. Ibid., l. 17–17ob (February 10, 1907).

not fare any better, since he depended on the elders for information. It was "only in isolated instances," on a trip to a village, for example, that county administrators happened to discover the illegal status of a Korean. Once a migrant's illegality was established, however, it was impossible for Russian authorities to deport him on such grounds, since deportation was allowed only if a migrant had committed a criminal act. The last recourse for surveillance was the police captain, but poor lines of communication and other burdensome duties often prevented him from taking necessary measures.[58]

Officials also lamented the difficulties of conducting surveillance over the border. Most goods and people from Korea traveled to Russia over the Sino-Russian border, especially at the towns of Savelovka and Hunchun. But in the early 1890s, only three hundred soldiers guarded the 500-km border, which was blanketed with dense forests and mountains that made surveillance even harder.[59] In spots where dozens of Russian and Chinese villages hugged the boundary, the sparse detachments of soldiers were unable to check the passports of the hundreds of people who crossed back and forth on a daily basis. Russian authorities deemed it nearly impossible to stop the "thousands upon thousands of roving Chinese and Koreans" who seemed to form a "state within a state" in the lower Maritime. Given the situation, Border Commissar E. Smirnov rejected the military governor's proposal to revamp the passport system to conform to the European system of control, saying that the latter was "absolutely unsuitable" to the Far East. If it was introduced, there would be "unceasing difficulties for local authorities, and nothing positive would come of it." In his estimation, it was "still impossible to guard the border from passport-less people."[60]

Border Commissar Smirnov's resignation about lawlessness on the border echoed what officials had expressed a few months earlier at the 1907 Congress on the Korean Question: what could be done? Border crossings occurred "freely" in spite of all the rules. The congress's report concluded, "This phenomenon has continued not just for a few years, but for dozens of years. When all is said and done, it turns out that Koreans have begun to consider all our laws . . . as completely empty words."[61] Koreans, however, did not simply ignore the law. In circumventing physical checkpoints and the law itself, Koreans proved that they understood the ins and outs of the rules and used them to their advantage.

---

58. Ibid., l. 23–24.
59. A. Ragoza, "Pos'etskii uchastok," *Sbornik geograficheskikh, topograficheskikh i statisticheskikh materialov po Azii* 45 (1891): 109.
60. RGIADV 1/3/1060, l. 20–21 (April 25, 1907).
61. RGIADV 1/1/6104, l. 21ob (February 10, 1907).

An Illicit Society

Human errors, multiplied on top of legal loopholes, resulted in what seemed like a waste of effort. And the scattershot surveillance inside the empire and along its borders seemed to render the law a dead letter. As we shall see, however, laws and policies did have clear effects on Koreans, in unexpected ways. Over time, they created structures that directed migration and defined registration practices, effecting change in the daily lives of migrants. Koreans committed themselves to these structures to fit their own purposes, either by obeying the law or contravening it.

Border crossing became a creative act, an endless proliferation of ways to circumvent customs points. Experienced guides who knew when and where checks took place led groups on foot across the Tumen River when the tide was low or crossed to Russia via the border town of Savelovka.[62] Others traveled farther north in Manchuria and then dispersed on footpaths that opened up to dozens of Korean settlements close to the border. Koreans took "exceedingly numerous" roads to Russia to bypass border posts (*pogranichnye zastavy*). Those who hailed from the central provinces of Korea—far fewer in number than their compatriots from the north—usually left Wŏnsan and ventured to the Bay of Peter the Great on their own schooners. In the Bay of the Golden Horn, where Vladivostok was situated, one could glimpse rows of Korean boats resting after multiple trips to Korean villages along the coast. After disembarking, Koreans got lost in the crowd.[63] The unlucky ones who were caught and deported by the Russian border guard eventually found a way to return.[64]

Alongside the proliferation of illicit routes, a business of counterfeit passports flourished under the shadow of the official passport system. Professional dealers in Korea and Manchuria bought the passports of thousands of Korean and Chinese laborers returning home from the Russian Far East and then resold or leased them to prospective workers. Many people, hoping to bypass such brokers, waited for boats from Vladivostok to dock at Ch'ŏngjin and bought the passports from their compatriots directly.[65] The quickest exchanges occurred on worksites themselves. There, a migrant who no longer needed his passport traded it with a coworker who needed to extend his stay.[66] Beyond the resale of

---

62. Ibid., l. 20ob; Syn Khva Kim, *Ocherki po istorii sovetskikh Koreitsev* (Almaty, Kazakhstan, 1964), 32.

63. RGIADV 1/1/6104, l. 20–21.

64. RGIADV 702/1/569, l. 193ob (March 1908).

65. *T'onggambu munsŏ*, vol. 1, part 4, no. 15 (October 15, 1909).

66. N. M., "Iz mestnoi inorodcheskoi zhizni," *Vladivostok*, October 31, 1893. The article speaks only of Manzas or Chinese, but based on other contemporary reports, one can assume that such practices were widespread among Koreans.

passports, outright forgery of documents was common. The repeated discovery of false documents compelled Russian authorities to go so far as to accuse the magistrate in Kyŏnghŭng of distributing fake passports to migrants.[67] The magistrate responded by calling this a "rumor" and suggested that a random Korean was behind the crime.[68]

Russian observers at the time believed the purchase and exchange of passports was proof that Asians neither understood nor cared about the law. According to a reporter, N. M., indigenous people (*inorodtsy*) as a whole were unable to comprehend the legal basis for the passport system because of their historic "lack of a custom of passports." For Russians, by contrast, the passport had become essential to living and being. N. M. maintained that the document had become a "constituent part" of a Russian person, along with his "body and his soul"; it was so integral that "an understanding of the passport's necessity has penetrated into the Russian's flesh and blood." It was not to be expected that a "race who [was] unfamiliar with any kind of passport" could be imbued with such understanding.[69] The 1907 congress echoed the sentiment, saying, "almost the entire population thinks it normal [to live without a passport]."[70] Yet illegal practices, ranging from simple person-to-person exchanges to larger brokering systems, demonstrated that Koreans understood the significance of this document. They just bent the rules, switching dates and names, to serve their own purposes. And it was relatively easy to do so. The passport recorded only one's name, nationality, purpose of travel, and, sometimes, a brief physical description. Luckily for Koreans, "black hair," "brown eyes," and "short stature" applied to the majority of border crossers.

Laws requiring the registration of villagers also laid the grounds for the sprouting of an illegal population. In the 1890s Border Commissar Nikolai Matiunin noted that "our Koreans would sooner hide their passport-less compatriots than turn them in. Lodging houses, of course, do not ask for documents from their guests."[71] Koreans also falsely declared people as family members.[72] What officials interpreted as mistakes in records—mix-ups due to multiple first names and a limited number of last names—thus may well have been deliberate fabrications on the part of villagers, who figured that one more lie could not make an already distorted record any worse. The ban on land acquisition by foreigners

67. RGIADV 1/3/1088, l. 18 (October 4, 1907), l. 50 (January 11, 1908).
68. Ibid., l. 18.
69. N. M., "Iz mestnoi inorodcheskoi zhizni."
70. RGIADV 1/1/6104, l. 22–22ob (February 19, 1907).
71. RGIADV 1/2/2598, l. 63–63ob (February 24, 1896) in Toropov et al., *Koreitsy* (2001), 96–97.
72. RGIADV 1/1/6104, l. 18ob (February 10, 1907).

also drove the leasing of lands underground. In 1908 Governor-General Unterberger noted that "even though no more land was distributed for ownership, [Koreans] found another outlet, that is, they rented lands from the state, peasants, Cossacks, private landlords, cities, parish lands, and officials of the forest guard."[73] In most cases, a newly arrived migrant "found refuge" in the Korean community and established himself on a plot of land.[74] When those lands grew scarce, they ventured farther north, "where there was no surveillance," and occupied state lands "without hesitation."[75] In this way, Koreans wove themselves into the productive fabric of Ussuri as a permanent second-tier population, living outside the gaze of the state.

Migrants could not have participated in such a system without the tacit consent of people who hired them, including Russian landlords and entrepreneurs. Landlords "hardly" asked a Korean worker whether he had the proper paperwork. Asking would only confirm his illegal status and the need to pay five rubles to obtain a *bilet*. Viewing such an investment for a daily wage earner as "a gamble," the landlord chose instead to hide migrants from the local administration. A large-scale industrialist, who hired entire artels (labor cooperatives) through a broker, "paid no concern at all whether the Koreans working for him have Russian *bilets* or not, of course, putting his own interests first so that work gets done without interruption." Similar to landlords, industrialists found the upfront cost of *bilets* "unprofitable" given the uncertainty of workers' performance, and so they hid undocumented workers from authorities. According to a report of the Priamur Governor-General Office, the concealment of migrants occurred in all industries where Koreans worked.[76]

Over time, illicit acts came to define the borderland population in the eyes of the tsarist government. The laws deemed "illegal" the routes and practices that already existed and abetted more illegal practices by creating new mechanisms through which migrants crossed the border and settled. Officials seemed to recognize the tensions inherent in their governing efforts, as well as the surprising outcomes. For although they lamented that the law had become "empty words," they simultaneously recognized what "view" had "taken root in all Koreans": the law had opened up space for not only circumvention but adaptation.[77]

---

73. Report of the Priamur governor-general to the Ministry of Internal Affairs (March 8, 1908) in Toropov et al., *Koreitsy* (2001), 153–54.
74. RGIADV 1/1/6104, l. 18ob (February 10, 1907).
75. Toropov et al., *Koreitsy* (2001), 153–54.
76. RGIADV 1/1/6104, l. 22–22ob (February 10, 1907).
77. Ibid., l. 21ob.

Trapped in the Homeland

While tsarist officials contended with migrants inside their borders, Korea became another testing ground where new legal categories and border laws were debated and pushed to the limits. Naturalized Russian subjects crossed back and forth across the border and were sometimes interrogated by Chosŏn officials, who tested the parameters of their jurisdictional authority over a people who spoke Korean, behaved Korean, and, most obviously, looked Korean. The case of one border crosser reveals how emerging categories of legal status, border laws, and international "norms" had become part of the vocabulary of officials on both sides of the border, and how those ideas were still subject to much interpretation.

In 1892 Han Ch'ijun caused an international stir. Han, like many other Koreans, traveled frequently between Russia and Korea. But that year his movements caught the attention of Chosŏn authorities on two occasions. According to Chosŏn reports, in January he had entered the Korean town of Onsŏng to take his mother- and sister-in-law back to Russia, his permanent country of residence. Onsŏng authorities arrested, punished, and then released him. The next month, Han returned with his wife. He was arrested again. The Onsŏng magistrate charged him with entering Korea without the proper paperwork and taking relatives who "were living peacefully" in Korea. The magistrate decided to further investigate matters and crossed the border to Krasnoe Selo to meet the Russian border commissar face to face. He was determined to confirm that Han was a Russian subject, as he claimed, and to conduct a search for Han's wife, who had disappeared. He hoped to punish her, too. The case spurred a flurry of emotional responses from diplomatic officials in the Chosŏn Commercial Office and the Russian legation in Seoul, as well as from officials stationed in border towns. Both the Russian and Korean sides accused each other of violating the law. Consul P. A. Dmitrievskii believed that Chosŏn officials had wrongfully punished Han, a Russian subject, because the 1884 Treaty of Friendship stipulated the extradition of a criminal to his original country. Chosŏn had no right to try and punish a foreign subject. Moreover, Chosŏn officials had tried to do the same to his wife. The incident, which coincided with the arrests of two other naturalized Russian subjects, was intolerable in Dmitrievskii's view.

To prove that Chosŏn officials had in fact acted lawfully, Commercial Officer Cho Pyŏngjik painstakingly cited specific rules and Han's corresponding violations. Regarding the regulations of 1888, Han had supposedly broken three points: "as a person who was born and raised in Onsŏng," he should have obtained a Korean passport (*chipjo*) to cross to Russia in the first place, but he had not; as a Russian subject, he should have obtained a passport to travel to Onsŏng because the city lay beyond the 100-*li* passport-free zone, but he had not; and, finally, as a Russian subject, he should have also obtained a seal of endorsement from Chosŏn officials on his passport the second time around, but, again, he had not. They added that Han had violated not only international law but also domestic law. He stole his family across the border, deceived local officials about his identity by not presenting proper documents, and, lastly, had worn Korean clothes (*aguk ŭigwan*). Only Koreans could wear Korean clothes. If Han had really "changed his subjecthood" (*ijŏk*) to Russia, then he should have changed his clothes to match. Cho's arguments proved that he understood the ins and outs of recent laws, both entry-exit rules and the Russian domestic law that allowed Koreans to naturalize by relinquishing their former affiliation with Chosŏn. But his approval of Han's punishment ultimately confirmed his belief that Han still belonged to Korea—that is, he remained a Korean subject. Indeed, Cho defended the Onsŏng magistrate, saying he had "punished [Han] as a Korean subject [*agukmin*] who had violated the trade rules and committed crimes." His relatively light sentence and subsequent release was "fair" and "dealt with according to the trade rules." As such, Cho concluded, there was "no reason to discuss the matter any further."[78]

Dmitrievskii assailed the magistrate, governor, and commercial agent for their apparent ignorance. He, too, appealed to the law to make his argument. According to the 1884 treaty, Chosŏn authorities should have extradited Han for improper paperwork because he was a Russian subject. Had the Onsŏng magistrate conducted an inquiry into Han's legal status, he would have learned this and responded appropriately. As it stood, the Onsŏng magistrate had "brusquely and arbitrarily punish[ed] a person without any proof of his crime." If Han had committed a crime, it was probably due to his ignorance about passport laws. But, Dmitrievskii contended, did not the magistrate "deserve greater punishment" for "not knowing the treaties"?[79] In addition to the statutes of the treaty, Dmitrievskii appealed to what he believed were universal norms of sovereign states and subjecthood to criticize Chosŏn officials:

> In Russia, there are many Englishmen, Frenchmen, Chinese, and Koreans, who though they were born in other states, have moved to Russia and become Russian subjects. They therefore exercise the rights of Russian subjects and are found under the protection of Russia. When these Russian subjects head for foreign states, in cases of need, they will

---

78. *Ku Han'guk oegyo munsŏ*, 17:231–32.
79. Ibid., 17:236.

receive the help and protection of the Russian government. The foreign state should not persecute them for having become Russian subjects. *What has been recognized by all states should be recognized by Korea.* Therefore, we cannot allow Koreans who are Russian subjects to be punished in Korea for the fact that they have become Russian subjects. Such punishment is a direct affront to our government. In addition, we do not prevent Russian subjects from changing their subjecthood. It is regrettable that the governor, who is charged specifically with enforcing treaties on the border, does not know this and has called Han Ch'ijun a Korean subject.[80]

Those universal norms extended to the issue of clothes. Dmitrievskii found it "laughable" that the donning of Korean clothes constituted a breach of law in Korea. In Russia, he explained, one's clothes did not reflect one's subjecthood. He insisted that the magistrate, who lived on the border with Russia, "should know that in Russia no form of clothing is specified for the common people. The Chinese here wear Chinese clothes, the English English clothes, and Koreans Korean clothes." There was "no prohibition" against foreigners wearing foreign dress; they could be Russian subjects regardless of how they looked.[81]

Dmitrievskii's reasoning illuminated the contradictory ways in which international "norms" were being used inside and outside Russia. In the case of Koreans on the Russian side, the "right" to subjecthood had been born out of a desire to identify and exclude unwanted Koreans from political membership in Russia. Denying this right to a particular group of Koreans had created a marginal, illegal population. By contrast, in debate with officials from a country he viewed as inferior, this "right" was touted as a liberal, universal standard that Chosŏn officials "did not know" and had failed to meet. Despite the fact that Chosŏn officials had cited international treaties, Dmitrievskii believed that they lacked a clear understanding of the law, and worse, that they had adhered to "laughable" domestic laws.

If one probes the reasoning behind the actions of Chosŏn officials, however, one sees not their ignorance of international law but rather a working out of new and old ideas about identity and political belonging. That the Onsŏng magistrate faulted Han for wearing Korean clothes was consistent with the practice of using external markers, such as apparel and hairstyle, to define and identify a person's status or country of origin. What shifted in this period was the national meaning attached to such markers. As increasing numbers of Koreans traveled

---

80. Ibid., 17:234–35, italics added.
81. Ibid., 17:235.

abroad, hairstyles in particular became one of the ways in which governments enforced their claims over Koreans. Both the Russian and Qing governments stipulated that Koreans should change their hairstyle in order to physically demonstrate that they had naturalized as subjects and submitted to the laws of their adopted countries. The magistrate's insistence on the significance of Han's appearance also suggests that nationality had become the primary form of classifying individuals. For the magistrate did not specify what kind of clothes or hat Han had donned or what status group he belonged to—elite, merchant, or commoner. In the official's thinking, Han's clothes reflected not his status within the Chosŏn social hierarchy but rather his modern identity as a Korean national subject. The official had effectively "simplified" Han's identity as a subject of Korea, an act that resonated with recent trade agreements demanding that migrants be recognized solely in terms of their national affiliations as subjects of Korea, China, or Russia.[82] Later, the magistrate was deemed "ignorant of the rules" and punished by the Chosŏn government for mishandling the case.[83] His arguments, however, demonstrated a keen understanding of the intricacies of the law, as well as the ways it was being applied to the border-crossing population.

Another Yellow Scare

In the early 1900s geopolitical strife in East Asia brought new attention to the legal status of Koreans and compelled Russian officials to reassess the population in light of a reconfiguration of power relations in the region. The threat of China, which had long existed on Russia's borders, faded momentarily, while Japan ascended as a new empire on the continent. Japan had defeated Russia in a rout in the recent war (1904–5) and forced it to evacuate Manchuria as well as surrender the southern half of Sakhalin Island. According to the terms of the Portsmouth Treaty, Russia also had to recognize a Japanese protectorate in Korea. Korea's association with an enemy—another "yellow" power—cast new suspicions on Korean inhabitants in Russia.

Within the context of defeat, officials began to consider the "Korean question" as a problem of broader international proportions. Though Korea no longer existed as a sovereign nation, Russian authorities considered Korean migrants to embody grave "dangers" because of their newfound status as imperial subjects of Japan. Concerns about the population prompted officials to convene a series

---

82. Meanwhile, what Han thought about his own identity was not disclosed in the documents.
83. *Ku Han'guk oegyo munsŏ*, 17:276–77.

of eight congresses about the "Korean question" from October 1907 to March 1908. In many ways, the back-and-forth dialogue over the benefits and costs of Korean migration echoed debates that had been taken up at the Khabarovsk Congress two decades earlier. What differed, however, was an expressed concern about Russia's national interests in East Asia and the categorization of Asians as a "yellow race" that posed a threat to those interests.[84]

Fears about national security reverberated through the halls of the imperial ministries in St. Petersburg, five thousand miles away from the Russian Far East. Officials, many of whom had never traveled to the East and thus relied on secondhand reports, imagined a danger far worse than what existed. In 1909 a member of the Ministry of Internal Affairs expressed fears about the "terrifying size" of immigration flows into the Russian Far East and secret settlements of Chinese and Koreans nestled in the deepest corners of the taiga.[85] Arbuzov, also from the ministry, believed that the continuous infiltration of "yellow subjects" from China, Korea, and the Japanese empire had brought the country into a "moment of extreme political danger." Though it was noted by objective observers that fears of a virulent peril stemmed from a shallow understanding of the region, suspicions nevertheless abounded.[86] Indeed, members of the highest echelons of government expressed similar sentiments. War minister A. N. Kuropatkin worried about a "tide of yellows" invading the Far East, while P. A. Stolypin, prime minister and chairman of the Interior Ministry (1906–11), warned of the infiltration of "aliens" from across the border.[87]

Officials in the capital believed reports about a "yellow" threat because they originated with a man deeply familiar with the region, the governor-general of the Maritime Province, Pavel Unterberger. He was a vocal opponent of Korean immigration. Described by the world traveler Isabella Bird Bishop as a "gigantic man" whose head "nearly touched the lofty ceiling," Unterberger had a formidable impact on the politics of the Russian Far East.[88] Trained as an engineer, he rose through the ranks of the imperial bureaucracy, serving in multiple positions throughout Siberia and the Far East. During his tenure as military governor of the Maritime Province (1888–97), he had considered the Korean question with

84. The phrase "yellow race" appeared in official discussions to limit Chinese migration to Russia in the 1880s and came into more frequent use after the Russo-Japanese War. Petrov, *Istoriia Kitaitsev v Rossii*, 250; Hsu, "Chinese Eastern Railroad," 218.

85. "Koreisko-kitaiskii zakonoproekt v gosudarstvennoi dume. II," *DO*, March 12, 1909, 2.

86. As reported by B. Altaiskii, "Koreisko-kitaiskii zakonoproekt v gosudarstvennoi dume. I," *DO*, March 11, 1909, 2.

87. Lewis H. Siegelbaum, "Another 'Yellow Peril,'" *Modern Asian Studies* 12, no. 2 (1978): 314; Chia Yin Hsu, "A Tale of Two Railroads," *Ab Imperio*, no. 3 (March 2006): 230.

88. Isabella Bird Bishop, *Korea and Her Neighbors* (Seoul, 1970), 217.

equanimity. But by the 1900s, having witnessed Russia's position decline vis-à-vis Japan, Unterberger, now governor-general, fervently condemned Koreans before a host of government organs, including the Ministry of Foreign Affairs, Council of Ministers, and various congresses of local and regional representatives in the Russian Far East. Unterberger pronounced Koreans as a "fundamental evil" and an obstacle to Russia's geopolitical aims in the region:

> The great danger of this phenomenon is clear. The primary goal of our politics in the Far East is the swiftest and, as far as possible, firm resettlement of Russians in the Priamur. For this reason, all of the government's concerns are connected to carrying out a settlement plan. From this perspective, every plot of land that is beneficial for Russian cultivation but is seized in significant measure by Koreans . . . is equivalent to the weakening of our position on the shores of the Pacific Ocean.[89]

Though he conceded that Koreans had reaped benefits for the Far Eastern economy, such gains came at a cost. Korean and Chinese farmhands, miners, fishermen, and carriers, numbering in the tens of thousands, had forced Russian farmers and industrialists into a perpetual cycle of dependence on foreign labor. Instead of developing an entrepreneurial spirit in industry and agriculture, he stated, Russian peasants had used foreign laborers as an excuse to nurture bad habits of "idleness and drunkenness." Still, he lay the bulk of blame on the Koreans. In a letter from 1910, he vociferously denounced their settlement, saying, "I prefer a Russian wasteland to a land cultivated by Koreans. . . . I will not have it on my conscience that I gave Russian land to any yellows for plunder."[90] Unterberger's sentiment resonated with that of Prince G. E. L'vov, a notable figure in St. Petersburg who had undertaken a four-month tour of the Russian Far East. The "entire economic life" of the region, he asserted, was "in the hands of the Chinese and Koreans." The "yellow wave" constituted a direct affront not just to Russia but to the entire continent of Europe.[91]

A minority group at the congress assessed the migrant question in its proper regional context, offering nuanced views of discussions that had largely reduced migrants to being part of one dangerous "yellow" race. F. I. Chilikin, deputy from Amur Province, pointed out that relations between China, Korea, and Russia were interwoven. As such, the Chinese and Korean migrant issue was a matter of "life and death" for the Maritime Province and "cannot be torn

---

89. B. D. Pak, *Koreitsy v Rossiiskoi imperii*, 95–96 (March 8, 1908).
90. Quoted in V. V. Grave, *Kitaitsy, Koreitsy i Iapontsy v Priamur'e* (St. Petersburg, 1912), 137.
91. Quoted in Hsu, "Tale of Two Railroads," 237–38.

from the very fabric of Manchuria and northern Korea."[92] While he asserted that more effective surveillance measures against "yellows" should be enacted, he understood that they could antagonize the Qing government, whose hold on power was "shaky and fragile but would strengthen." Demonstrating his knowledge of regional politics, Chilikin also mentioned that relations between Korea and Japan were hostile, especially in light of Japan's recent colonization of the peninsula.[93]

While delegates expressed fears about Russia's security in the Far East, they also praised Koreans for developing the region. Concrete evidence abounded that Koreans had transformed the Far Eastern territories from a no-man's-land to a bountiful network of farmsteads. A. I. Shilo, a deputy from the Maritime Province, noted that in a fickle environment where heavy rains fell on one day and sweltering heat developed on the next, Koreans provided a permanent reserve of temporary workers for farmers who had to hire workers at a moment's notice. From this pool of workers, rent income streamed into the pockets of poor Russian peasants, who had become accustomed to foreign labor. Shilo exclaimed that he did not care which foreigners worked here, even "angels from the heavens," as long as they were not lazy Russians. A general from the Ministry of War similarly supported employing Chinese and Korean laborers, saying that "cheap yellow labor is indispensable to the defense of the Priamur."[94] As conversations at the congress drew to a close, it was clear that the question of Korean migrants was no more easy to settle than it had been decades earlier. Contradictory attitudes about migrants, first noted by V. Vagin in the 1870s, had resurfaced in the wake of geopolitical strife.

Intensifying Border Control

Fears of a "yellow peril" brought tsarist officials to reassess policies toward Koreans and ultimately to pass more restrictive measures. They built on existing migration and naturalization laws that had aimed to eliminate ambiguous jurisdictions in the Russian Far East and to govern the population of Koreans as Russian subjects or as aliens. They also investigated how white settler nations in the New World battled "yellows" within their own borders. In view of international tensions, Russian officials resolved again to control the presence of foreign

---

92. "Koreisko-kitaiskii zakonoproekt v gosudarstvennoi dume. II," 2.
93. "Koreisko-kitaiskii zakonoproekt v gosudarstvennoi dume. I," 2.
94. "Koreisko-kitaiskii zakonoproekt v gosudarstvennoi dume. II," 2.

elements on Russian territory. But whereas previous laws had stopped at classify-ing Koreans as aliens, new migration laws aimed to ban them completely.

In discussions about "yellows," representatives of the First Congress in Vladi-vostok in 1907 affirmed the necessity of passport fees (*sbory*) on Koreans and Chinese. Implemented two decades earlier, the levy of five rubles allowed one to have his foreign passport endorsed by border officials and to obtain a *bilet*. From its inception, the fee had marked the unequal status of Koreans and Chinese in Russia; it was higher than what other foreigners were subject to.[95] Officials stated that Koreans must continue to be treated as a separate, less desirable category of foreigners:

> [Applying] our general passport laws for foreigners and certain rules for residence fees (*nalog na prozhivanie*) to Koreans, in particular, would put them on par with other foreigners. This is extremely undesirable to our interests. In addition, doing so would create a precedent that would demand that all our existing laws for foreigners be applied to Koreans.

Members justified categorizing Koreans as a lower class of foreigners by say-ing that "no treaty had been concluded between our government and Korea . . . that would give Korean subjects the right to all that our laws grant to foreigners in general."[96] Other officials also confirmed previous views that the uncivilized nature of Asians had made these fees necessary. In response to the Qing govern-ment's protests regarding "special fees" imposed on its subjects, the Ministry of Foreign Affairs stated that the fees covered "special sanitation measures in the dwellings of [Chinese]," who were "unskilled laborers, people of low intellectual development," and "unfamiliar with public health requirements."[97]

Officials agreed on passing more restrictive measures against Asians. In 1907 the one-month grace period to obtain a *bilet* was eliminated on the grounds that it had fostered law breaking. Officials believed that Koreans and Chinese had taken advantage of the grace period by "scatter[ing] throughout the province, evading rules for exchanging their passports for Russian *bilets* and paying the fee." They also hoped that the new measure would discourage the "absolutely poor" from migrating to Russia.[98] In 1909 officials targeted Koreans, who tended to migrate in families, by extending the fee to women and children over the age of

---

95. Lohr, *Russian Citizenship*, 77.

96. RGIADV 1/1/6104, l. 34ob (October 18, 1907).

97. RGIADV 702/7/40, l. 117–121ob in Toropov et al., *Koreitsy* (2001), 124. For more on how "yellows" were inscribed in a broader national and international discourse on public health as the emblem of a civilized nation, see Hsu, "Chinese Eastern Railroad," 231–344.

98. RGIADV 702/1/1687, l. 43–48ob (March 22, 1908) in Toropov et al., *Koreitsy* (2001), 157.

ten. They, too, were required to pay for a *bilet*. This rule, together with new laws that used health and occupational fitness as an entry test, was a direct borrowing from migration legislation in Canada and Australia. The United States provided further inspiration for immigration laws.[99]

Tsarist authorities also experimented with outright "yellow labor" bans, which eventually culminated in a single law at the federal level in 1910. Earlier, in 1907, Governor-General Unterberger had banned the employment of Korean subjects in gold mines in the Russian Far East, and in 1908 he forbade Russian subjects from leasing land to Korean and Chinese tenant farmers. Similar restrictions were extended to the railroad and fishing industries that year: a domestic law prohibited foreigners from working on the Amur Railroad, and an international agreement between Russia and Japan barred all Koreans from working in the Russian fishing industry.[100] In discussions leading up to the 1910 law, the Far East Settlement Committee debated over how to formulate a prohibition against Asian migrants without explicitly referring to their country of origin. In the Americas, the establishment of anti-Asian quotas and general immigration laws had successfully curtailed migration from Asian countries. Yet the committee acknowledged that passing such laws in Russia, even if they proved effective, would invite unwanted protests from the Chinese and Japanese governments. In order to "avoid diplomatic complications," it decided to institute a law that denied entry to "specific categories of foreigners without differentiation by subjecthood." Entry into Russia would be determined by objective factors that applied to all foreign unskilled workers, including "age, health, and a minimum of cash." These factors could be selectively used to put migrants from China, Korea, and Japan at a particular disadvantage.[101] On June 21, 1910, the Duma finally passed the federal-level prohibition against the hiring of foreign workers in state enterprises and state-subsidized construction projects in the Maritime, Amur, and Transbaikal Provinces. It also forbade the leasing of state lands to foreigners and the use of foreign contractors for state-funded work.[102] By specifying the regions in which Asian workers were concentrated, the Duma was able to target Chinese and Koreans without mentioning their nationality.

---

99. "Koreisko-kitaiskii zakonoproekt v gosudarstvennoi dume. II," 2; "Mery protiv naplyva v Priamurskii krai kitaitsev i koreitsev," *DO*, January 21, 1909, 3; Toropov et al., *Koreitsy* (2001), 156–57, 172. Also considered was the funneling of poll taxes into a special immigration fund. In 1901 examples of recent immigration legislation in Great Britain, Canada, the United States, and Australia had been compiled for the acting governor-general of the Maritime Province Benevskii. See Hsu, "Chinese Eastern Railroad," 217–18; Hsu, "Tale of Two Railroads," 231.

100. Grave, *Kitaitsy, Koreitsy i Iapontsy*, 144, 154–55.

101. Far East Settlement Committee quoted in Hsu, "Tale of Two Railroads," 238.

102. Pak, *Koreitsy v Rossiiskoi imperii*, 100; Siegelbaum, "Another 'Yellow Peril,'" 323.

In addition to the labor ban, officials revisited the intertwined question of settlement and land policy. After the passing of the 1886 prohibition on the settlement of Koreans and Chinese in the border region, officials had discussed plans to move all Koreans farther inland. But apart from forcing ad hoc groups to resettle to other locations in Ussuri and near Khabarovsk, no large-scale program had been carried out.[103] In April 1912 the Priamur Governor-General Office urged that the long-delayed plan be implemented. Citing correspondence from the chief of Ussuri, the office hoped that the local resettlement committee would "take all possible measures so that foreign subjects no longer possessed farms in the Poset region."[104] Officials proposed various incentives to encourage Koreans to leave Poset so that land would be freed up for Russian settlers. Along with the promise of 15 *desiatinas* of land per household at their new destination, Koreans were permitted to bring with them foreign tenants (and their families) who had been living on their land for decades.[105] By 1913, detailed plans had been drawn up.[106]

As a last step to intensifying control, members of committees attempted to solve the widespread problem of illegal crossings by delegating the task of surveillance to a denser, wider network of institutions. Previously, passport checks had been conducted at multiple jurisdictional levels—by police at the village, county, and district levels, by military police with municipal, *zemstvo*,[107] and maritime jurisdiction, and by customs officers at the border. In the 1900s the authority to conduct checks was widened to local leaders, including gendarmes at railroad sites, precinct captains, village elders, county heads,[108] and even Chinese and Korean societies (*obshchestva*) in cities and towns. The Russian government also proposed to increase the number of checkpoints along the Sino-Russian border.[109]

Experiments to conduct surveillance over Koreans had varying outcomes. The 1910 labor prohibition contained an exemption clause that allowed state enterprises to hire foreigners if they demonstrated an exceptional need. Russian officials overseeing frontier construction projects and private entrepreneurs contracted by the state took advantage of this clause almost as soon as the law

---

103. See, for example, RGIADV 1/1/6104, l. 37–38 (October 23, 1907).

104. RGIADV 702/5/257, l. 90–90ob (April 19, 1912) in Toropov et al., *Koreitsy* (2001), 259.

105. RGIADV 702/5/257, l. 5–7 (August 20, 1911), 22–22ob (October 19, 1911) in Toropov et al., *Koreitsy* (2001), 247–49, 251–52.

106. RGIADV 702/5/257, l. 270–285ob (May 20, 1913) in Toropov et al., *Koreitsy* (2001), 270–87.

107. *Zemstvo* denotes self-governing bodies at the provincial or district level.

108. RGIADV 702/1/569, l. 193ob (March 1908).

109. RGIADV 1/3/1160, l. 143–4 (August 29, 1908) in Toropov et al., *Koreitsy* (2001), 185.

was passed.[110] Meanwhile, the earlier 1907 ban on Korean workers resulted in an unforeseen increase in Chinese workers. Instead of the desired native Russian worker, the policies attracted Chinese and gave them a virtual monopoly in the gold mines; they began to organize strikes to negotiate higher wages, at times violently acting out against Russians when their demands were not met.[111] The 1907 ban was later amended to allow enterprises to hire Korean foreigners on a temporary basis if they intended to become Russian subjects.[112] Plans to adopt models from white settler nations also languished. Noting the successes of the U.S. Immigration Bureau, a centralized organization that conducted border surveillance, Russian officials considered establishing an organ solely dedicated to guarding its borders against Korean and Chinese migrants.[113] But because of a lack of funds, the congress opted for the "more practical and effective" method of relying on existing administrative structures.[114] Similarly, despite a push to institute an immigration law based on European, North American, and Australian models, a general immigration law about Koreans and Chinese never materialized.[115] As revolutions erupted at home and the First World War broke out on the western front, migration policy in the Far East receded from regional and national agendas. The Duma ended up repealing the 1910 ban on hiring Koreans and Chinese due to wartime exigencies. Faced with the increasing power of Japan in Manchuria and Korea, Russian officials turned to another method to shore up the border: naturalization policy.

World of Subjects

The issue of subjecthood occupied a central place in discussions about Koreans after Japan established a protectorate over Korea. Tsarist officials were well aware of the Japanese colonial government's efforts to use subjecthood—later called "citizenship"—to wield influence over Koreans in Kando and to extend its jurisdictional reach in northeast China (see chapter 3). As reported by a border

---

110. Hsu, "Tale of Two Railroads," 239.

111. By 1910, 82 percent of workers in gold and platinum mines were Chinese, while Koreans fell to less than 1 percent. See table 3 in chapter 6; RGIADV 702/1/640, l. 242–247ob (February 4, 1911) in Toropov et al., *Koreitsy* (2001), 236.

112. Ibid.; V. D. Pesotskii, *Koreiskii vopros v Priamure* (Khabarovsk, 1913), 6–7.

113. RGIADV 702/1/590, l. 2–5 (June 3, 1908) in Toropov et al., *Koreitsy* (2001), 172. Centralization of these powers of surveillance was key to modern mobility control in the Americas, British possessions, and Western Europe.

114. RGIADV 702/1/569, l. 193ob (March 1908).

115. Siegelbaum, "Another 'Yellow Peril,'" 323; Hsu, "Tale of Two Railroads," 239n109.

commissar, Kando Koreans lived "under the rule of Chinese authorities but without a precise definition of their subjecthood." The Japanese government, he continued, "considers all Koreans living there as Korean subjects."[116] Inside Korea proper, Russian diplomats had already experienced how the presence of Japan had complicated the legal status of Koreans, particularly those who had naturalized as Russian subjects. Officials grew anxious about the status of Koreans inside Russia. If Korea as a sovereign state no longer existed, what was the nationality of Korean subjects on Russian territory? Would the Japanese try to claim them as their own and use them to extend Japanese jurisdiction into Russia as they had in Kando? How was a Russian, Japanese, or Korean subject actually defined? Given Japan's ambitions on the Asian continent, answering these questions became an urgent matter that was tied to protecting Russia's sovereignty.

Around the time of Korea's annexation in 1910, tsarist officials noted Japan's efforts to claim the Koreans. The dragoman of the Russian Imperial Consulate in Tokyo, Pavel I. Vaskevich, warned of the actions of the Japanese consulate in Vladivostok in particular. He reported that Japanese officials treated Koreans in Russia with "benevolence and friendliness" and "did not miss an opportunity to remind [them] that even though they had become Russian subjects, they still remained Japanese subjects." Japanese authorities also refused to acknowledge children of naturalized subjects as Russian because they had no legal right to relinquish their original subjecthood in the first place.[117]

Fears about the spread of Japanese propaganda across national boundaries deepened suspicions about Japan's imperialist intentions. According to tsarist reports, Japan endeavored to "unite all Koreans in Kando and Ussuri on the basis of loyalty to Mikado and an aversion to Russia."[118] As evidence, the Ministry of Internal Affairs pointed to the existence of pro-Japanese organizations operating in Korean communities in the Russian Far East, including the Chōsen Kyoryūminkai (Chosŏn Resident Association) and Ilchinhoe (Advance-in-Unity Society).[119] The ministry believed that Koreans were particularly susceptible to Japanese propaganda because "in their souls they sympathized with the Japanese as a nation that was closer in kin and spirit than Russians." With the Koreans on their side, it concluded, "Russia will find it impossible to stop the Maritime Province from being annexed to Japan."[120] That threat to Russia's sovereignty was all the more real because of the large population of Koreans just across the border.

---

116. RGIADV 1/3/1088, l. 85ob (January 14, 1908).
117. AVPRI 148/487/758, l. 79 (July 5, 1911), 81ob–82 (1911).
118. Ibid., l. 79ob.
119. For more on the Ilchinhoe, see Moon, *Populist Collaborators*.
120. AVPRI 148/487/758, l. 82ob (1911), 79.

Governor Unterberger and other officials believed that the Japanese would use the Koreans to colonize the Russian Far East:

> The migration of Koreans to us is highly useful for the Japanese, who for this reason encourage it. In Korea, for example, a society was established by the Japanese government for the purpose of promoting Korean migration to South Ussuri. In addition, free passports are being distributed to Koreans headed for our territory, while passports of those heading for South Manchuria are subject to taxes.[121]

Still, not all were rattled by rumors of Japanese infiltration. An officer in the Ministry of Foreign Affairs declared that he did not see the Koreans in South Ussuri as an "evil" to Russia's foreign relations. Writing to the Ministry of War, he stated that "objections to permitting Korean immigration to our territory come not from the Ministry of Foreign Affairs." Rather, "doubts about the loyalty of the Korean element and his ability to assimilate to the Russian population arise primarily from the [Ministry of War]." Ultimately, he left it in the hands of military officials to decide whether or not Korean migration was favorable for Russia's defense.[122]

As for the practical matter of passports, Korea's new status as a colony created confusion. According to a 1907 resolution passed in Korea, Koreans who wished to travel abroad as "both imperial subjects and Korean subjects" were required to obtain a national passport issued by the Japanese resident-general.[123] But Russian border officials had no idea whether an old Korean passport or a new Japanese passport should be considered legitimate, and they allowed Koreans to enter the country with either one.[124] A black market for counterfeit "old Korean-style" passports emerged, perhaps because it was harder to obtain new Japanese-issued passports.[125] Russian officials also worried that Korean subjects had started to appeal to the Japanese commercial agent in Vladivostok to obtain paperwork to reside in Russia. The agent was granting residence permits (*vid na zhitel'stvo*), which applied only to "other foreigners," when Koreans were supposed to pay for the more expensive *bilet*. This was deemed a loss of money to the treasury.[126] Koreans, moreover, arrived from Kando, and local Russian officials did not know

---

121. Report of the Priamur Governor-General to the Ministry of Internal Affairs (March 8, 1908) in Toropov et al., *Koreitsy* (2001), 154.
122. RGIADV 702/1/640, l. 220ob–221 (June 17, 1910).
123. *Ku Hanmal ŭi choyak*, 3:524–26.
124. RGIADV 1/3/1075, l. 24 (April 9, 1907).
125. RGIADV 1/3/1088, l. 18 (October 4, 1907), l. 50 (January 11, 1908).
126. RGIADV 1/3/1075, l. 13 (March 26, 1907). See GARF 102/8 ch. 226, l. 1–11, 17 (1908) for the case of a Japanese consul issuing a "national passport" to a Korean in Perm.

whether to consider them Chinese or Japanese subjects or even how to endorse their passports.[127] Such procedural matters remained a source of contention between the Russian and Japanese governments into the 1920s.[128]

Japan's claims on Korean subjects forced the tsarist government to revisit naturalization law as a way to remove any ambiguity about the subjecthood of Koreans. More than twenty-five thousand Korean subjects resided in Russia and were probably now considered subjects of the Japanese empire. The military governor considered it imperative to grant Koreans with Russian subjecthood so that Russia could exercise full authority over them, including the authority to forcefully remove them from the border region if necessary.[129] He reasoned that if the tsarist government did not do so, it would have to "consider [the population] *de jure* Japanese subjects," a situation that would create "a series of never-ending complications" in which Japanese authorities would "continuously interfere in our affairs with Koreans."[130]

The push for subjecthood ultimately came from Korean migrants themselves. In the autumn of 1910, a few months after Korea's annexation to Japan, more than nine thousand Koreans jointly petitioned the Ministry of Internal Affairs to become Russian subjects. The petition was the culmination of a stream of requests sent over the course of the year from thirty-three thousand Koreans.[131] They affirmed their loyalty to Russia in paternalistic language that reflected the relationship between a ruler and his subjects:

> We want to become faithful subjects of Russia with the same rights as Russia's many peoples who have settled here, rights we believe the Russian government will fully establish. Like all her faithful subjects, we as Russian subjects promise to faithfully and honestly serve Russia and her Tsar, for whom we stand ready to fulfill our military obligations along with others and to serve in the ranks of Russia's military in the Far East.[132]

---

127. RGIADV 1/3/1088, l. 85ob–86ob (January 14, 1908).
128. See GARF 944/1/277, l. 2–29 (1922) for instances of the Japanese government prohibiting Korean migrants from obtaining Russian *bilets*. Officials complained that Japan was interfering in Russia's internal affairs.
129. RGIADV 702/1/640, l. 196–196ob (September 20, 1910).
130. RGIADV 1/12/94, l. 9ob (September 12, 1914).
131. The number did not include women and children. The requests had been sent to the Ministry of Internal Affairs via the Vladivostok Clerical Consistory. "Voprosy okrainnoi zhizni: Koreitsy i russkoe grazhdanstvo," *DO*, November 23, 1910, 2.
132. Grave, *Kitaitsy, Koreitsy i Iapontsy*, 423.

In a separate petition, Koreans expressed their awareness of international politics and used it to support their case for naturalization:

> Receiving us unfortunate Koreans into Russian subjecthood . . . will save us from death and the calamitous events that can befall us in our native land if we are deported. . . . All Koreans in the Maritime Province have been honored by the kindness of Your Excellency, and we presently hope to be honored by your kindness [again] by allowing us to stay as farmers and workers on the territory of the Russian empire. We should not complain about our pitiful fate—that we do not have the ability to live independently in our fatherland, which is under the oppression of the hateful enemy, the Japanese. For us, Russia is the only country that will feed and clothe us. . . . We have always hoped and will continue to hope that the Russian government will not leave us poor Koreans without charity, as children without a father or mother.[133]

The Council of Ministers considered the thousands of petitions and moved to approve the Koreans' request. On April 21, 1911, the council passed a resolution allowing the Ministry of Internal Affairs to confer Russian subjecthood on Koreans living in the Maritime Province.[134] The cutoff year for Koreans to petition for subjecthood was no longer 1884, the year that Korea and Russia had established official relations, but rather 1910, the year that Korea had ceased to exist as a sovereign state. Thousands of Koreans clamored to the offices of the local police and Orthodox church to claim their new papers, a sign of their subjecthood. Outside the Russian Far East, in distant Irkutsk and St. Petersburg, Koreans tore up their original passports to express their "national grief" at the colonization of their homeland and to protest their becoming Japanese subjects. They, too, sought to become naturalized Russians.[135]

From the 1880s to 1920s, the urgency of the border-building project in the Russian Far East had manifested itself through proclamations and policies. The tsarist regime endeavored to protect its sovereign borders from uncivilized Asians and neighboring powers in East Asia by eliminating plural jurisdiction, standardizing categories of subjects and aliens, passing migration laws and land tenure policies, and conducting surveillance. The laws, to be sure, produced uneven outcomes

---

133. RGIADV 702/1/640, l. 198–198ob (June 26, 1909).

134. B. D. Pak, *Koreitsy v Rossiiskoi imperii*, 111; Hsu, "Chinese Eastern Railroad," 224.

135. Two hundred Koreans in the Transbaikal region, who were former soldiers in the Russian army during the Russo-Japanese War, petitioned to become Russian subjects. GARF 102/8 ch. 226, l. 1 (October 7, 1911).

among the population of Koreans. But the fact that Koreans responded to these laws both by abiding and adapting them suggests that the laws carried a weight greater than officials realized. For all that officials complained about transgressions of the law, the documentary record they left behind suggests that the limits and categories created by the law had become commonsense. Classifications of identity, border institutions, and other regulations were gradually naturalized as norms, then utilized by individuals inside and across Russia's borders in legal and illegal ways to advance their own interests.

To illustrate the possibilities that the law created for individual Koreans, the chapter closes with the story of Hwang Ch'ŏlgil. In 1912 Hwang crossed the border from Russia to China and was subjected to a passport check. When asked by a Chinese policeman for his travel documents, he displayed a pair of *bilets*—a Japanese one issued in Germany to "Hwang Ubaek" and a Russian one issued in Vladivostok to "Iakov Petrovich." He confessed that he used the different *bilets* to alter his identity when it was appropriate. In Russia, Hwang explained, he showed the Russian document. He did not dare reveal the Japanese papers because it would immediately "incur the suspicion" of the Korean community, who reviled Japan for its recent colonization of Korea. In China he used his Japanese *bilet*. Here, a Russian *bilet* symbolized the "low class" of a Korean migrant, but a Japanese *bilet* granted him "more attention, honor, and respect." After receiving a Chinese *huzhao* (residence permit) from the police, Hwang threw his Japanese *bilet* into the fire and sold his Russian one to another Korean. He later appealed to the Russian border commissar to become a Russian subject.[136]

Hwang's story was both an ordinary and extraordinary tale of migration. Hwang, like many other Koreans, seemed destined to lead a transnational life: His parents were born in Kyŏngsŏng, moved to Kando in 1884, were naturalized as Qing subjects, and raised seven sons who lived nearby or abroad. Hwang left Kando and traveled to Germany, Austria, America, and throughout the Russian empire. Trained as an apothecary in America, he won fame in St. Petersburg by healing the royal princes of their various afflictions and earned a seat at the royal table. He was fluent in Korean, conversant in Russian and Chinese, and knew a little Polish from his wife of Polish descent, whom he showed off as a descendant of an "aristocratic, good family."[137] In 1912 Hwang crossed from Russia to China to start a new life. But that was where his good fortune went sideways. Two years later, he was arrested by authorities in Hunchun for suspicious practices

---

136. RGIADV 1/12/440, l. 2–2ob (February 12, 1914), l. 7 (May 17, 1914).
137. Ibid., l. 2.

in his apothecary business. Further investigation revealed that his crimes were as numerous as they were extreme: he had lied about his medical pedigree, ran an illegal, transnational drug business, inflicted suffering on his patients through dubious surgical procedures, and failed to deliver Browning rifles from Novokievsk to Koreans and Chinese who had paid an advance deposit for them. Hwang had initially enjoyed good relations with Hunchun authorities because of his network, but his many crimes undermined his credibility. He lost face with all officials.[138] Hwang was no more honest in his personal life. It turned out that Hwang had abandoned his first wife, a Korean with whom he had a ten-year-old son, but never divorced her and thus was guilty of "polygamy."

Apart from his blatant crimes of stealing and lying, Hwang had committed an offense that had become common among the borderland population. He falsified his papers, presenting a Japanese or Russian *bilet* whenever he thought it appropriate, and later sold the Russian *bilet* for money. When the Hunchun police threatened to punish him and deny him a Chinese *huzhao*, Hwang refused to give up. Recognizing that he needed a country to belong to, he appealed to the Russian border commissar to obtain Russian subjecthood. Subjecthood would give him a new legal identity and a new set of papers to travel from one place to another.

Hwang's case illuminates the possible ways in which Koreans recognized and employed laws surrounding the border and identity. The outcomes were as surprising to officials as they were useful to migrants. Korean migrants continuously crossed boundaries and settled for short and long periods of time in the Russian Far East by carrying, buying, and selling the very documents that had been created to control them. After 1905, when fears of a "yellow peril" compelled officials to redouble their surveillance efforts, Koreans adapted. They understood that a new hierarchy of states in East Asia had emerged and that political membership in a state—subjecthood—mattered. In 1910, when they faced the possibility of becoming "stateless" or imperial subjects of Japan, they used the Russian system to become Russian subjects. Migrants had gradually come to order their lives in relation to national boundaries.

---

138. Ibid., l. 3–4.

Part II
ACROSS THE TUMEN NORTH BANK

In Russia

5

TRANSFORMING USSURI
Migration and Settlement

While the Russian government undertook to shore up its sovereign borders in the east through bureaucratic policies of inclusion and exclusion vis-à-vis Koreans, inside its borders it embarked on various developmental projects to claim the recently acquired territory as its own. In the Maritime Province—especially the southernmost part called Ussuri—that meant extruding the region's natural bounty as a productive force for the state. Officials and explorers poured their energies into coal mining, gold digging, and timber cutting; invested in land reclamation and agriculture; erected new villages, ports, and cities; and laid thousands of miles of railroad tracks and telegraph lines to respectively transport people and information that were needed to unify the eastern outpost to the west. Such colonizing activities gradually transformed the north bank of the Tumen valley; its "wild" nature was "tamed" and traces of the native population were erased. Also erased were Chosŏn and Qing policies to govern the territory as a "prohibited" area that was off-limits to new settlers. Frontier industries, farms, and cities now beckoned people to live and work. Ussuri became a destination in the Russian Far East.

Within this story of state development and colonization lay multiple stories of migration, in which Koreans, alongside others, emerged as central actors. Initially pushed into Ussuri by devastating floods on the south bank of the Tumen River, natives of Hamgyŏng Province crossed the border to the Russian side and settled in large enclaves, eventually penetrating northward to the rest of Ussuri and the Maritime Province. They cultivated farms, labored on state construction projects, and worked as fishermen and loggers along the coast and deep in the interior. Aided by geographical proximity, a steady stream of Koreans filtered into Russia and helped establish ties of family and economy across the Tumen, from Hamgyŏng Province to Kando and the Maritime. By the late 1890s, they had grown to about 20,000 in the Maritime and by 1929 to 150,000. In the immediate border region of Poset, they formed 90 percent of the total population, making it look like a "continuation of Korea."[1]

This chapter explores how Ussuri (later called South Ussuri), the most populous district of the Maritime, was settled by Russians, Chinese, and Koreans.[2] It accounts for state-directed migration programs that pulled or pushed them away, as well as fortuitous but equally significant factors that shaped patterns of mobility, including the environment, geography, and cross-border networks. Bringing into view processes beyond the parameters of the tsarist state's control—indeed, beyond its borders—allows us to see the Maritime in its broader regional context, not only as a frontier outpost that was an object of colonization by the Russian empire but also as a center of an emerging frontier economy that drew in goods and people from northern Korea and Manchuria in the late nineteenth century. Each group's experience of migration and settlement was guided by a distinct set of circumstances. Russian peasants, primarily from Ukraine, received state subsidies to move from their homes on the Black Sea and settle in the Far East, but geography and local environmental conditions posed serious obstacles to the efficacy of resettlement programs. Han Chinese and Koreans were subject to a very different set of state strictures. For the Chinese, Russian land and border policies encouraged temporary visits, reinforcing cyclical patterns of movement that were characteristic of Chinese migration to other parts of the world. Carried by steamship primarily from Shandong Province in northern China, Chinese arrived in Vladivostok and moved on to other cities and large-scale enterprises throughout the Russian Far East. Korean migrants, meanwhile, turned out to be the most natural colonists in the Maritime. Hailing from locations only a river crossing away, they settled with their families in the countryside, understood the conditions of the land, and, having benefited early on from naturalization and land policies, built settled communities that formed a foundation for other Koreans to join.

Over time, the separate streams of migration and settlement became intermeshed in the economy of Ussuri. Driven by various concerns, each group traveled to different places in Ussuri and occupied distinct labor niches. Russian

---

1. Pesotskii, *Koreiskii vopros*, 66.
2. The chapter focuses on Ussuri but also includes discussion of the Maritime Province and the greater Russian Far East. See "Note on Places and Terms."

peasants became landlords and petty businessmen, Chinese temporary laborers in cities and large enterprises, and Koreans small landlords and tenant farmers, who were concentrated in the countryside of Ussuri next to Manchuria and Korea. Ussuri came to be ordered by a new spatial logic of industry and ethnicity, a logic that was often in tension with the tsarist state's vision to claim the territory and people as its own.

Geography of Ussuri

Ussuri, particularly its southern tip called Poset, was an auspicious place for settlement. It was where native peoples had made a home for centuries and where Russian explorers built ports and planted a flag to claim the area for the tsar in the late 1850s. The area was sought after for its natural resources, as well as its warmer climate and fertile land. After 1860, when the littoral of Ussuri was formally appended to the Maritime Province, it became the most densely populated territory in the Russian Far East.

Ussuri's climate was extreme, belying its comparable latitudinal position to the famed sanatoriums of the French Mediterranean and Crimea. In the winter, blistering winds from the north and northwest cooled continental Asia, lowering temperatures below the freezing point, while in the spring and early summer, humidity soaked the air. The extreme highs and lows could be attributed to two dominant water currents: a cold current that flowed south from the Sea of Okhotsk, and a warm current, the *kuroshio*, that drifted up from southeast Asia, brushed the shores of the Japanese archipelago, and continued northward along the eastern coast of the Kurile Islands and Kamchatka, where it veered toward Alaska. The cold current served to exacerbate the cooling effect of the arctic northerly winds on the landmass, and the convergence of the two currents helped congeal moisture in the atmosphere, leading to profuse rainfalls and periods of dense fog in the warm seasons. Vladivostok, which stood at a latitude of 43° north, approximately the same as that of Nice in southern France, had an average temperature of 4.6° C. In the summer, the temperature rose to about 30° C, and in winter, it often dropped to below −25° C.[3]

From a bird's-eye view, the Sikhote-Alin mountain range unified the entire Maritime territory. Connected to the Changbai and Paektu mountain chains, Sikhote-Alin began in Jilin and stretched along the coast of the East Sea, tapering at the Sea of Okhotsk. Centuries of erosion had whittled down the ancient mountain so that by the late 1800s it stood at just 3,000–4,000 feet high; Golaia,

---

3. Unterberger, *Primorskaia oblast'*, 125–27; Nansen, *Through Siberia*, 334–35.

the summit, which lay to the south, loomed just 5,000 feet above sea level. Its relatively low stature gave Sikhote-Alin the appearance of the Ural range—indeed, it is sometimes called the "Far Eastern Urals"—and lent the Maritime the character of an undulating hill region. The presence of the mountain, while unifying the region, also contributed to the development of two distinct microenvironments. Its steep slope on the eastern side blocked atmospheric moisture from the East Sea, creating a more humid climate on the coastal side and more arid climate on the western side, where its gentle slope melded into the wide river valleys of the Ussuri and Amur.[4]

The intricate system of rivers and tributaries further divided southern Ussuri into three microregions. The first comprised the valley and rivers encircling Lake Khanka, and was bounded by Manchuria to the west, the Ussuri River and Sunchaga tributary to the east, and the Suifun River to the south. Later forming part of the Khanka and Suifun administrative districts, the region had the most fertile land and was primarily settled by Russians who had arrived by sea. The second microregion extended throughout the eastern and southern slopes of the Sikhote-Alin range, from Ussuri Bay in the south to the Tatary Strait in the far north. In the late nineteenth century, land communication between the first two regions was conducted through a few paths that cut across Sikhote-Alin. Only wheeled carts, usually manned by Han Chinese, risked the journey. The third microregion, later known as Poset, was formed by the narrow littoral that lay south of the Suifun River and stretched to the border of Korea. All of its rivers flowed into the East Sea. Poset was predominantly settled by Koreans.[5]

The microregions, though different in temperature and topography, possessed favorable conditions for farming. The river valleys made of "black earth" were highly prized by farmers, who found the mineral-rich soil ideal for growing crops and vegetation. Clay soil was also common, but its unyielding texture of black earth, pebbles, and sand created conditions for swampy buildup after heavy rains and made it less valuable for agriculture. All settlers, in fact, had to contend with extreme moisture and frequent flooding. Most of the rivers in Ussuri were more like rivulets that swelled to normal size only during deluges. Because of their slight width and low-lying nature, the plains were prone to flooding and at times bore the appearance of a swamp.[6]

The delicate balance of topography, climate, and geography formed the natural environment to which new settlers had to adapt. How far one had to travel to Ussuri determined how difficult it was to adjust. Arrivals from western Russia, in

---

4. N. Przheval'skii, "Ussuriiskii krai," *Vestnik Evropy* (1870): 237; Nansen, *Through Siberia*, 334.
5. Unterberger, *Primorskaia oblast'*, 122–23, 127.
6. Ibid., 123–24.

particular, struggled. Confronted with an altogether foreign milieu, they had to rely on state support to make a home for themselves and were forced to devise strategies for survival. They were often left defeated by their new surroundings.

Challenges to Russian Migration

Eager to fulfill its mission of "civilizing the east," the tsarist state set out to populate Ussuri and the greater Russian Far East with the primary agents of its mission: Russian peasants. Officials and peasants alike were initially hopeful about this endeavor. The state invested resources into transporting families from western Russia to the east, and peasants received these resources, looking forward to adventures on the other side of the world. What both parties encountered, however, was a series of disappointing obstacles that stymied the project of colonization. For while laws, transportation technology, and money had been used toward advancing this mission, a great deal more resources were required to make colonization successful.

One of the first obstacles was a system of registration that imposed various limits on peasant mobility in particular. Similar to states elsewhere, early passport laws in Russia aimed not to encourage movement but restrain it for the purpose of enhancing the government's military and tax base.[7] In 1719 Peter the Great decreed that no one was allowed to travel from one village to another without a passport issued by his superiors.[8] Various laws, such as the 1857 "collection of statutes on passports and runaways," outlined additional requirements for travel, but they de facto applied only to members of privileged estates—noblemen, civil servants, honored citizens, and merchants—who possessed the right to choose their place of residence. While upper estates received permanent passport booklets that allowed them to travel without special permission, lower estates, including the peasantry, received temporary passports and had to pay a yearly poll tax.[9] The passing of the Emancipation Act of 1861 did not improve matters for peasants. An individual who wanted to leave his or her original place of residence had to fulfill myriad requirements: he had to obtain a certificate of discharge from

7. Limits on mobility were common prior to the mid-nineteenth century. See McKeown, *Melancholy Order*, 22–42; John C. Torpey, *The Invention of the Passport* (Cambridge, 2000).

8. Mervyn Matthews, *The Passport Society* (Boulder, CO, 1993), 2. Passports were only one of many different documents that were required for registration to reside in, move to, or leave a particular place. For a discussion of the importance of mobility documents to establishing one's membership in an estate, see Alison K. Smith, *For the Common Good and Their Own Well-Being* (Oxford, 2014), 17–18.

9. Matthews, *Passport Society*, 3–4; Steinwedel, "Making Social Groups," 74–75.

his present commune (*obshchina*), secure a certificate of admission from his new one, and possess a clean record of tax payments, military obligations, and debts in general. In practice, then, the system encouraged only a peasant of sufficient means to migrate, even though such a peasant was less likely to move in the first place.[10]

Geography and lack of resources also posed challenges to special state-sponsored programs that treated frontier regions as exceptions and encouraged migration to these destinations. A resettlement law passed in March 1861 permitted the voluntary migration (*pereselenie*) of peasants to the Amur and Maritime Provinces "on one's own funds." Peasants were promised compensation for their expenses and provided other incentives to move, such as free passage, 100 *desiatinas* of land, and exemptions from taxes and military service for up to twenty years. Few peasants, however, had the funds to travel in the first place. Those who did embark on the journey found their funds and energy depleted somewhere along the arduous journey of 5,000 miles that took two to three years to complete by land. They ended up stopping somewhere along the way in western Siberia.[11] The results of the first two decades of state-funded resettlement were abysmal. By 1883 a mere 3,800 peasants had migrated to the Maritime Province.[12]

The state also failed to use Cossacks as an effective colonizing force. A mix of Slavs and Tatars from the plains of southern Russia, Cossacks were a distinct estate that served as a military force for the tsarist state and often as de facto colonists in remote parts of the empire.[13] After the signing of the Treaty of Aigun in 1858, at the order of the governor-general of Eastern Siberia, large regiments of Cossacks from the Lake Baikal area were settled in sizable homesteads along the Amur and Ussuri Rivers. By 1861, about 14,000 Cossacks and 2,200 lower-ranking officials had gathered in the region.[14] The Cossacks had been charged with defending the border against the Qing and developing the area, but the harsh conditions were overwhelming. Having been assigned land without much care as to whether it was suitable for agriculture, they spent their early years in the Far East reclaiming land and clearing fields of trees, in addition to fulfilling their duties in the postal and transportation services. Years of toil left the population demoralized. When the Cossacks were granted permission to return to their homes in Siberia, many chose to do so notwithstanding the dangers of

---

10. A. A. Kaufman, *Pereselenie i kolonizatsiia* (St. Petersburg, 1905), 17, 25.

11. Donald W. Treadgold, *The Great Siberian Migration* (Princeton, 1957), 69–70.

12. S. P. Shlikevich, *Kolonizatsionnoe znachenie* (St. Petersburg, 1911), 98–99.

13. For origins of Ukrainian Cossacks, see Serhii Plokhy, *The Cossacks and Religion in Early Modern Ukraine* (Oxford, 2001).

14. A. V. Eliseev, "Iuzhno-Ussuriiskii krai i ego Russkaia kolonizatsiia, I–III," *Russkii vestnik* 214, no. 6 (1891): 224.

the long journey back.[15] It was only in 1879 that Cossacks reached the more distant area of the lower Ussuri valley—just north of the Tumen River—where they eventually established ten stations along the Suifun River and the Qing border. By the early 1880s, the population of South Ussuri had reached a modest six thousand people, a third of whom were Cossacks and the rest peasants and former convicts who had chosen to remain in the area after fulfilling their military duties.[16]

Migration proceeded slowly even after the advent of maritime transportation and the creation of a more robust infrastructure to assist peasants at their destination. In December 1881, the tsar passed a resolution to send peasants from the Black Sea to the Far East.[17] The carrier of choice was the Volunteer Fleet, five German merchant vessels that had been purchased during the Anglo-Russian crisis of 1878.[18] The resolution was followed by the 1882 South Ussuri Resettlement Law, which created incentives for migration, such as sizable land allotments, tax exemptions, and free food supplies and transportation.[19] In addition, authorities established a special resettlement commission to help ease peasants' transition once they arrived in Vladivostok. Working with officials, convicts, and Cossacks, the commission erected an impressive infrastructure in Vladivostok that included thirteen barracks stocked with firewood, dishes, shovels, and buckets; an infirmary with sheets and beds from Odessa and a Dutch heater; two storage facilities; and four wells to help relieve the chronic water supply problem in the city. The commission also procured food, cattle, and building materials for future arrivals and carried out the important task of surveying land for settlement.[20] Still, the outlays of capital were not enough to sustain steady migration flows to the east. Because of limited funds, the Ministry of Internal Affairs and Resettlement Commission capped the number of families who were granted free passage to 250 per year.[21] The state-sponsored programs also created a pattern

---

15. Malozemoff, *Russian Far Eastern Policy*, 2.

16. There were an additional 1,500 Russian civilians living in Vladivostok, as well as military personnel. Eliseev, "Iuzhno-Ussuriiskii krai, I–III," 230.

17. There were also changes in laws that allowed for more flexibility in leaving communes in the 1880s. See Kaufman, *Pereselenie i kolonizatsiia*, 24–25, 29–30.

18. Hostilities arose between Great Britain and Russia at the conclusion of the Russo-Turkish War of 1877–78, but when the threat of war passed, the fleet was turned to commercial purposes. Malozemoff, *Russian Far Eastern Policy*, 12–13.

19. The state offered 15 *desiatinas* of land per person, up to a maximum of 100 *desiatinas* per family. Treadgold, *Great Siberian Migration*, 70.

20. Communes sent scouts (*khodoki*) to the Russian Far East ahead of time to find suitable land. A. V. Eliseev, "Iuzhno-Ussuriiskii krai i ego Russkaia kolonizatsiia, IV–VI," *Russkii vestnik* 215, no. 8 (1891): 121–24.

21. In 1886, to lighten its burden, the state extended the right of resettlement to "self-funded" voluntary settlers, who were required to pay for their own passage and deposit to acquire land in

TABLE 1. Population of South Ussuri by ethnic designation[a]

	1898	1913	1929	1932
Korean	22,420	52,632	150,825	155,500
Chinese	26,852	47,185	42,316	31,300
Russian	110,582	385,855	428,564[b]	529,200
Other	4,041	49,980[c]		60,430
Total S. Ussuri	163,895	535,652	621,705	776,430
Total Maritime Province[d]	194,953	619,234		836,900

Source: P. F. Unterberger, *Primorskaia oblast', 1856–1898* (St. Petersburg, 1900), appendix 1; *Obzor PO za 1901–2 g*, appendix 1; *Obzor PO za 1913 g.*, appendix 1; *Itogi perepisi Koreiskogo naseleniia v 1929 g.*, iv; *K voprosu o migratsii Koreiskogo naseleniia.*

[a]Figures are given for the area that lay within South Ussuri district in 1898, plus the three cities of Vladivostok, Khabarovsk, and Nikol'sk-Ussuriisk, as well as Cossack lands. Figures for 1929 are for Vladivostok *okrug*, an area that was smaller than South Ussuri and excluded Khabarovsk.

[b]Includes "Russians" and "others."

[c]Includes 41,220 individuals settled on Cossack lands but not specified by ethnicity.

[d]Figures for the Maritime Province include South Ussuri, Udsk *okrug*, Khabarovsk *okrug*, *gornyi okrug*, and the city of Nikolaevsk. They exclude figures for Kamchatka, Okhotsk, and Sakhalin Island.

of dependence on the state. Poor peasants, who lacked sufficient means to make a living, formed the majority of applicants for resettlement, and once in the Far East they continued to rely on the state for short- and long-term loans. As such, the number of Russians transported by sea never exceeded two thousand per year. From 1883 to 1897, a period of almost fifteen years, 31,000 settlers had made it to Ussuri.[22]

The pace of migration to the Pacific accelerated only with the building of railroads in the last decade of the century. The tsarist government conceived of a grand plan to connect its vast empire by rail, the quickest mode of transportation at the time, and to collapse the physical and metaphorical space between its European and Asian empire. Surpassing the scale of contemporaneous projects such as the Canadian-Pacific, Cape-to-Cairo, and Baghdad railways, the Trans-Siberian would serve the imperial and economic interests of Russia and give it a competitive edge over other European powers in Asia.[23] It would also consolidate Russia's control over a still sparsely inhabited Siberia. In 1892 the Committee on

---

Ussuri. But the program had little effect because passage by ship was prohibitively expensive. Ibid., 133–34, 146; Malozemoff, *Russian Far Eastern Policy*, 13.

22. Malozemoff gives a lower estimate. Kaufman, *Pereselenie i kolonizatsiia*, 256; Malozemoff, *Russian Far Eastern Policy*, 13.

23. Pey-Yi Chu, "The Imperial Origins of the Baikal-Amur Mainline" (paper presented at the SSRC Russia–East Asia Dissertation Development Workshop, Princeton, 2006), 6–7.

the Siberian Railroad, an institution whose main directive was not to oversee the construction of the railway as its name suggested but to command auxiliary enterprises such as settlement, dispatched its first group of peasants eastward.[24] From that time forward, as various segments of the railroad were built and welded together, peasants traveled to Siberia and the Russian Far East with greater ease. When the Chinese Eastern Railroad (CER) was finished in 1902, a single, uninterrupted journey from western Russia to Vladivostok was at last possible.[25] Peasants who would have gone only as far as the Amur region chose the more distant Maritime Province, several hundred miles farther east, because the CER allowed them to travel entirely by rail.[26] On average, two-thirds of peasants headed for the Far East settled in the Maritime, compared to one-third in the Amur region.[27] The CER proved a boon to migration: the number of peasant arrivals in the Maritime nearly doubled from 68,200 in 1883–1902 to 134,900 in 1903–10.[28] The boost in movement was short-lived, however. Most of the people who had migrated from 1903 to 1910 had done so during the "Stolypin wave" (1907–10) when Prime Minister P. A. Stolypin renewed the state's efforts to colonize the eastern territories via the Committee for the Settlement of the Far East.[29] After 1910, migration to the Russian Far East tapered to 6,900 peasant arrivals per year.[30] With the outbreak of the First World War, the state was consumed with affairs on the western front, and resettlement programs were put on the back burner. Over time, the region did manage to witness a net increase in its Russian population, most likely due to natural population growth. Russians in the Maritime Province rose in number from 125,000 in 1898 to 450,000 in 1913.[31]

---

24. Treadgold, *Great Siberian Migration*, 109–10.

25. The Trans-Siberian Railroad was part of a system of railways that was completed in segments: the Ussuri line (Vladivostok to Khabarovsk) was opened in November 1897; the Circumbaikal section (connecting the western Siberian line to Verkhne-Udinsk near Lake Baikal) in 1900; and the Transbaikal (to Sretensk at the terminus of the Shilka-Amur waterway), CER (from Sretensk to Vladivostok via Manchuria), and South Manchurian Railroad (from Harbin to Dalian/Port Arthur) in 1902. Shlikevich, *Kolonizatsionnoe znachenie*, 98; Steven Marks, *Road to Power* (Ithaca, 1991), 172–73; Chia Yin Hsu, "Nationalizing Empire" (paper presented at the Columbia University kruzhok, New York, May 2006), 2.

26. Uninterrupted travel to Vladivostok through Russian territory was not possible until the construction of the Amur Railroad (1908–16), which connected the Transbaikal and Ussuri lines.

27. Calculated from Shlikevich, *Kolonizatsionnoe znachenie*, 98–99; A. M. Iarmosh, "Dvizhenie naseleniia Dal'nevostochnogo kraia na desiatiletie 1926–1936," *Ekonomicheskaia zhizn' Dal'nego Vostoka (Khabarovsk)*, no. 1–2 (1927): 85.

28. Iarmosh gives slightly higher figures. Shlikevich, *Kolonizatsionnoe znachenie*, 99; Iarmosh, "Dvizhenie naseleniia," 85.

29. Iarmosh, "Dvizhenie naseleniia," 85.

30. Calculated from ibid.

31. Unterberger, *Primorskaia oblast'*, appendix 1; *Obzor PO za 1913 g.*, appendix 1.

The next surge in migration and changes to the demography of the Maritime would be implemented by the Soviet regime in the late 1920s and 1930s.

From the peasants' point of view, Ussuri and the broader Russian Far East provided an opportunity for a new start. They learned of Ussuri through various means—through word of mouth, travel literature, and novels, and also by chance. The first arrivals, called "old settlers" (*starozhily*), came from the neighboring Amur region. While exploring the Ussuri and Sunchaga Rivers on barges, a few peasants floated onto Lake Khanka, the center of a verdant valley. They were astounded by the region's natural abundance and began to spread the word about Ussuri to fellow inhabitants in the Amur. Before long, they began to found villages one by one: Turii-Rog (1864), Troitskoe (1866), Astrakhanka (1868), and Kamen-Rybolov around Lake Khanka; Nikol'sk and Suifun farther south (1866); and Shkotovo, Aleksandrovka, and Vladimir, east of Vladivostok (1860s).[32] Most of the villages were small, with three to four hundred people, and remained that way through the early 1880s. Only Vladivostok, which was dominated by military personnel, boasted a larger population. The location of these early villages set the geographical boundaries for future Russian settlements; most would remain confined to the microregion circling Lake Khanka as well as the area just east of Vladivostok, near Ussuri, Askol', and America Bays. Few Russians ventured into the microregion that lay east of the Sikhote-Alin range and close to the Chinese and Korean borders—in Poset—where Koreans had already settled.

In the 1880s and 1890s, subsequent waves of peasants arrived from the Black Sea region, which was readily accessible to oceanic routes.[33] Provincial governmental bodies (*zemstvos*) targeted peasant communities in Ukraine as attractive candidates for settlement, and they coordinated with various organizations to disseminate as much information about the Far East as possible. Provincial writers and state publishing houses, often operating under the auspices of the Resettlement Commission or Committee on the Siberian Railroad, produced brochures, handbooks (*putevoditeli*), and maps to detail the benefits of resettlement and what to expect at the destination.[34] It did not matter that few peasants could read. Information traveled aurally through scribes and scouts who read aloud the contents of such brochures before whole communities, and through "failed migrants" who returned home and recounted their experiences in the Far

32. Przheval'skii, "Ussuriiskii krai," 255–60.

33. The majority of peasants came from the agricultural provinces in the central black-earth region and left-bank Ukraine, where migration to cities was less common than in other parts of European Russia. Willard Sunderland, "Peasant Pioneering," *Journal of Social History* 34, no. 4 (2001): 896.

34. Ibid., 897–98.

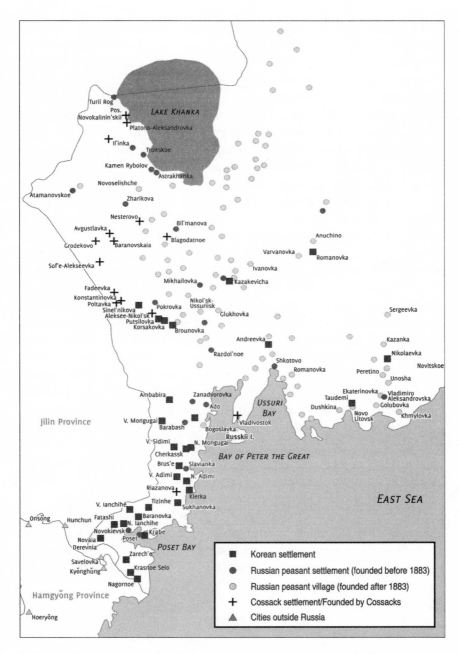

MAP 5. Settlements in South Ussuri by ethnic designation, late nineteenth century

East firsthand, even if it meant admitting failure.[35] Letters from relatives, too, offered frank advice. Opinions about the Far East were extreme, ranging from accolades—I've found a "heaven"—to utter despair. Describing South Ussuri as a "confusing and unhappy place," one peasant warned, "I don't recommend that those people [in Russia] come here."[36]

Once in Ussuri, both officials and peasants relied on bonds of family and commune to ease their transition. In Vladivostok, affiliations with specific communes in western Russia determined which barracks peasants were temporarily assigned to (experience had shown that putting peasants from different communes together led to a hostile atmosphere), and family ties guided them in their choice of permanent settlement.[37] Most sought out villages where they already knew someone. Inside the villages, peasants sought to recreate the familiar institution of the commune. Similar to western Russia, the commune in Ussuri functioned as an organ of government and community building: it had an elder, credit system, and peasant congress to air grievances and discuss matters of business.[38] It also acted as a close-knit, even hermetic, social community. In the early years, when the commune embodied the sole source of economic and emotional support, peasants prevented their daughters from marrying outside the commune because they well understood that women would bear children of the next generation. Persuading women to marry inside the commune also kept them from the lure of Vladivostok, where soldiers and former convicts roamed the streets.[39]

The commune, however, did little to help peasants adjust to local farming conditions and in some ways hindered their agricultural productivity. The environment of the Far East was much more moist and humid than that of the Black Sea region. Every spring, heavy rains clogged the narrow riverbeds and produced giant swamps of stagnant water that made it difficult to farm. The extreme humidity also ruined much of what peasants planted at first. Cereals such as rye and barley grew into weedlike straw and grains failed to ripen completely, creating a disease called "drunken bread," a parasitical growth inside grains that induced a state of dizziness or intoxication when consumed. It was only after years of experimentation and research that the phenomenon could be explained and measures were taken to eliminate it.[40] The crop rotation system that peasants

---

35. Ibid., 900. For examples of letters written by these settlers, see Poltavskaia gubernskaia zem-skaia uprava, *Pereseleniia iz Poltavskoi gubernii*, vol. 2 (Poltava, 1900), 378–94.

36. Quoted in Sunderland, "Peasant Pioneering," 905, 906.

37. Eliseev, "Iuzhno-Ussuriiskii krai, IV–VI," 135–36, 140.

38. Ibid., 130.

39. A. V. Eliseev, "Iuzhno-Ussuriiskii krai, VII–IX," *Russkii vestnik* 216, no. 10 (1891): 81.

40. Eliseev was the botanist who solved the grain pathology. Malozemoff, *Russian Far Eastern Policy*, 3; Eliseev, "Iuzhno-Ussuriiskii krai, VII–IX," 107–10.

had practiced back home also proved ineffective in the humidity.[41] Meanwhile, the architectural layout of settlements, designed with houses built side by side to reinforce close-knit ties between families and to provide a sense of security within the commune, did little to encourage peasants to tend to their farms. Living in commune-centered villages meant that a peasant had to travel several miles to his farmlands, which were usually located in river valleys, and he wasted time shuttling back and forth between his field and home.[42] Dismayed by the results of farming, A. A. Kaufman, a resettlement officer, pointed to the severity of the problem, saying, "The methods and conventions of farming, which Russian settlers brought from their homeland . . . have never suited local conditions." There was thus no "crisis of Russian farming" but plain "worthlessness of the farming methods of our new settlers [*novosely*]."[43]

Adding to peasants' troubles was a shortage of personal funds to invest in their farms. Though peasants received loans and grants from the Resettlement Commission, most had no money to buy basic materials—tools, construction materials, seed, foodstuffs, and cattle—to build and sustain farms. The results of a survey conducted in the Maritime Province were disheartening: in 1906, 20 percent of settlers had no horses, 12 percent no cultivated land, and 7 percent no homes; the figures respectively rose to 32, 44, and 25 percent two years later when thousands more arrived during the "Stolypin wave." Loopholes in the system also created abuses. After receiving a loan from the commission, peasants could easily squander the money or take the money and flee back to their home in the west.[44] Indeed, cases of flight increased when the railroad was completed in the early 1900s. Peasants who put the funds to honest use were overcome by the sheer task of managing large farms without sufficient manpower.[45] With only family and commune members to lean on, peasants ended up farming only a small portion of the land, leaving the rest fallow. Some even complained about the lack of suitable land, saying, "Why allot to us taiga, even mountains? They promised us 100 *desiatinas* of flat land, but have given us rocks and hills, which don't even amount to 10 *desiatinas* of useful land." In response, an official stated that the peasants had only themselves to blame, since they were the ones who had chosen the land and decided to settle as a commune, which required plots

41. Ragoza, "Pos'etskii uchastok," 75–77.

42. Ibid., 68. During the Stolypin reforms, officials attempted to convert commune-centered villages into homestead-style farms, similar to those of Germans and Koreans.

43. Quoted in A. N. Dem'ianenko, *Territorial'naia organizatsiia khoziaistva na Dal'nem Vostoke Rossii* (Vladivostok, 2003), 222n379.

44. Shlikevich, *Kolonizatsionnoe znachenie*, 104, 107.

45. Peasants tended much smaller farms of 3–5 *desiatinas* in their native homes in western Russia. Eliseev, "Iuzhno-Ussuriiskii krai, VII–IX," 97.

of land to be adjacent to one another. Many of the thousands of *desiatinas* of the contiguous lands allotted were bound to be unsuitable for immediate farming because of the hilly topography of Ussuri, which required intensive land reclamation.[46] Many peasants gave up and returned home, citing "insufficient means and a small family" as the primary reasons.[47]

After half a century, colonization had produced mixed results. Some officials still held hope that the Russian Far East could be successfully transformed in the model of the American West, where "virgin land" had been remade into productive farms.[48] Russian peasants, however, had not lived up to the state's expectations. Most had become landlords by renting out their lands to Korean tenants and used their land to engage in other businesses.[49] Officials looked to various sources to pinpoint the problem. It was unclear whether colonization had failed due to factors beyond the state's control—a general lack of knowledge, geography, and insufficient funds—or whether the state itself, by recruiting the wrong type of peasants and perpetuating their dependence on the state, had caused the failure. Perhaps it was a combination of all of these factors.[50] What was clear was that the situation in the eastern territories was far from what the state had initially envisioned. In place of a self-sufficient economy, the Maritime government had to import grain from western Russia and Manchuria to feed its inhabitants and military, as well as cattle from Korea, China, Mongolia, and far-off Australia.[51] And to support its frontier industries, officials had to rely on an outside "yellow labor" force, Chinese and Koreans.

Circular Chinese Migration

By the late nineteenth century, Chinese had become an integral part of Ussuri's economy. Tens of thousands of migrants arrived each year in the Russian Far East, laboring in diverse industries ranging from large-scale projects such as mining, timber, and railroad construction to petty trading and household work. Records show that between 1906 and 1910, approximately 550,000 Chinese entered the Amur and Maritime Provinces, surpassing all other newly arriving

---

46. Ibid., 97–98.
47. Shlikevich, *Kolonizatsionnoe znachenie*, 113.
48. Eliseev, "Iuzhno-Ussuriiskii krai, VII–IX," 112.
49. Dem'ianenko, *Territorial'naia organizatsiia khoziaistva*, 222–23.
50. Shlikevich, *Kolonizatsionnoe znachenie*, 118–19.
51. In 1909 wheat imports to the Maritime and Amur Provinces equaled 8,635 *pud*; beef imports 617,000 *pud*; and cattle imports 106,000 heads. Ibid., 44–45.

ethnic groups in scale of movement.[52] They also exceeded the total number of Chinese who arrived in the United States over six decades, from the early 1880s to 1940s.[53] It was not only the enormous scale of Chinese migration that was striking, but the pattern and spatial organization of their movement. Chinese tended to engage in temporary migration, or circular movement, traveling between Manchuria or China proper and Russia every season, year, or several years. Because of geographical proximity, out of the 550,000 who arrived in Russia, an estimated 400,000 left.[54] Inside Russia, Chinese were concentrated in cities and on the sites of state enterprises, their primary places of work. Thousands also labored as tenant farmers, but there were few visible signs of a permanent, settled population in the countryside (see tables 2a and 2b). For the most part, Chinese remained a temporary, mobile population in Russia, a status that had been fixed by passport and *bilet* laws from the 1880s.

Prior to the building of the Chinese Eastern Railroad, the vast majority of Chinese came to Russia from Port Chefoo in Shandong Province. Opened to trade by the 1858 Treaty of Tianjin, Port Chefoo, also known as Yantai, was a bustling city with an array of foreign settlements. The British, French, Germans, Russians, and others had appointed consuls there and established steamship lines to carry cotton, silk, and fresh fruit throughout the region. In the late 1890s, apart from Nippon Yusen Kaisha and domestic Qing lines, the Russian Steam Navigation Company was the only other company providing regular service from Chefoo. Twice a month, a steamer sailed from Shanghai to Chefoo to Chemulpo, Korea, before reaching its final destination in Vladivostok.[55] It was on this line that Chinese were transported to and from Russia. With the opening of Manchuria and the start of railroad construction in the late nineteenth century, more Chinese flocked to northern Manchuria, going as far north as Russian-occupied Harbin.[56] From there, they could travel to the Maritime Province by rail or on

52. V. V. Grave includes the number of Chinese registered by Russian authorities as well as the estimated number of Chinese departing from Port Chefoo and Manchuria for Russia. His figures are for the entire Priamur region (Maritime, Amur, Transbaikal Provinces), but the vast majority of Chinese headed for the Maritime and Amur. V. V. Grave, *Kitaitsy, Koreitsy i Iapontsy* (St. Petersburg, 1912), 16–17; T. N. Sorokina, *Khoziaistvennaia deiatel'nost' kitaiskikh poddannykh na Dal'nem Vostoke Rossii i politika administratsii Priamurskogo kraia* (Omsk, 1999), 39.

53. From 1882 to 1943, about 423,000 Chinese entered the United States. Erika Lee, *At America's Gates* (Chapel Hill, 2003), 238, 273–74n17. For works on Chinese migrants in Russia, see Sorokina, *Khoziaistvennaia deiatel'nost' kitaiskikh poddannykh*; Petrov, *Istoriia Kitaitsev v Rossii*; V. K. Arsen'ev, *Kitaitsy v Ussuriiskom krae* (Khabarovsk, 1914).

54. Grave, *Kitaitsy, Koreitsy i Iapontsy*, 16–17; Sorokina, *Khoziaistvennaia deiatel'nost' kitaiskikh poddannykh*, 39.

55. U.S. Bureau of Foreign Commerce, *Consular Reports. Commerce, Manufactures, etc.*, vol. 53, no. 196–199 (January–April 1897) (Washington, DC, 1897), 383.

56. Sorokina, *Khoziaistvennaia deiatel'nost' kitaiskikh poddannykh*, 35.

foot. The scale of Chinese migration to the Ussuri region, in particular, increased dramatically over the years. Starting from a base of 150 contracted workers from Shandong and Zhili Provinces in the 1870s, the number of yearly arrivals rose to 4,000–9,000 in the early 1890s, and to 15,000 in 1894, when construction on the Ussuri Railroad commenced.[57] In 1910, approximately 72,000 Chinese arrived in the Maritime Province. As large as the population of Chinese in Russia grew, however, most settled temporarily. Indeed, the number of migrants departing the Maritime in 1910—52,000—and the consistently high male-to-female ratios of more than 9:1 served as proof of the transitory nature of their stays.[58] Chinese typically arrived in the spring when large-scale labor projects took off and left in the autumn when cold weather and ice began to set in. It is unclear why such large numbers of Chinese left Shandong, other than the pull of work in Russia, but it is plausible that a combination of factors—environmental ruin, depletion of Qing state granaries, and dislocations caused by the international market—had created a state of unrest that pushed inhabitants to seek opportunities outside of their native towns.[59]

Migrants tended to cluster in cities and large towns where the demand for wage- and contract-based jobs was highest. Indeed, in the late nineteenth century, most Chinese in the Maritime Province lived in urban areas where they labored in household and other day jobs (29 percent of all Chinese), construction (17 percent), trading and eating establishments (11 percent), railroads (4 percent), and artisanship (4 percent).[60] Chinese workers on large-scale projects such as railroads were usually hired in prearranged artels via a contractor or mediator, an arrangement similar to that of Chinese headed for the Americas.[61] As many as 40,000 Chinese were employed each year in Vladivostok by the Russo-Chinese Bank and its subcontractors, while another 60,000 were

---

57. Ibid., 30, 37.

58. Calculated based on 550,000 Chinese arrivals and 400,000 departures during 1906–10; assumption that 65 percent headed to Maritime Province (based on estimated 65 percent of Chinese subjects living in Maritime). Grave, *Kitaitsy, Koreitsy i Iapontsy*, 16–17; Sorokina, *Khoziaistvennaia deiatel'nost' kitaiskikh poddannykh*, 40.

59. A regional study of Chinese migration that connects the local situation in northern China to that in the Russian Far East has yet to be written. In his provocative study, Davis posits that environment ruin, including the effects of the El Niño Southern Oscillation, had caused civil unrest, a situation that was exacerbated by a weak Qing state and the presence of imperial powers. Davis, citing the work of Chinese historians, sees the Boxer Rebellion as an outgrowth of this unrest. See especially chapter 11 in Mike Davis, *Late Victorian Holocausts* (London, 2001).

60. Sorokina, *Khoziaistvennaia deiatel'nost' kitaiskikh poddannykh*, 48.

61. McKeown, "Conceptualizing Chinese Diasporas."

TABLE 2A.   Demographics of South Ussuri: countryside (settlements) vs. cities[a]

	1898		1913		1929		1932	
	SETTLEMENTS	CITIES	SETTLEMENTS	CITIES	SETTLEMENTS	CITIES	SETTLEMENTS	CITIES
Korean	20,932	1,488	44,997	7,635	138,297	12,528	113,300	42,200
Chinese	13,030	13,822	9,617	37,568	17,772	24,544	14,300	17,000
Russian[b]	83,597	26,985	246,199	139,656	284,475	144,089	351,600	177,600
Other	2,069	1,972	41,843	8,137			42,930	17,500
Total S. Ussuri	119,628	44,267	342,656	192,996	440,544	181,161	522,130	254,300

[a]Cities for 1898 include Vladivostok and Khabarovsk; for 1913, Vladivostok, Khabarovsk, and Nikol'sk-Ussuriisk; for 1929, Vladivostok, Nikol'sk-Ussuriisk, Spassk, Suchan, Artem, and Ol'ga; for 1932, Vladivostok and Nikol'sk-Ussuriisk.

[b]Figures for 1929 include "Russians" and "others."

TABLE 2B.   Demographics of South Ussuri by percentage: countryside (settlements)

	1898	1913	1929	1932
Korean	93%	85%	92%	73%
Chinese	49%	20%	42%	46%
Russian	76%	64%	66%	66%
Other	51%	84%		71%
Total S. Ussuri	73%	64%	71%	67%

Source: P. F. Unterberger, *Primorskaia oblast'*, appendix 1; *Obzor PO za 1901–2 g*, appendix 1; *Obzor PO za 1913 g.*, appendix 1; *Itogi perepisi Koreiskogo naseleniia v 1929 g.*, iv; *K voprosu o migratsii Koreiskogo naseleniia*.

recruited to work on parts of the CER and South Manchuria Railway.[62] Chinese also came to dominate the trade industry in cities. In 1912 there were 1,020 Chinese trade-industrial enterprises in Vladivostok, outnumbering the 940 Russian- and foreign-owned businesses. Chinese petty traders, too, surpassed the number of Russian traders in local markets: in 1897 there were 3,500 Chinese and 1,240 Russian traders; by 1910 there were 3,200 Chinese and 3,100 Russian traders. Though their volume of trade fell far short of that of Western companies, Chinese traders supplied a cornucopia of necessary goods and services in a place where basic resources were hard to come by, including grain, farming tools, building materials, metal goods and machines, and furs, as well as services in delivery, peddling, and refurbishing.[63] Migrants also established auxiliary busi-

62. Malozemoff, *Russian Far Eastern Policy*, 189–90. In 1897 Chinese formed the largest group of non-Russians working on the Trans-Siberian Railroad (9,500 out of a total 15,700 foreign workers). Siegelbaum, "Another 'Yellow Peril,'" 312.

63. Sorokina, *Khoziaistvennaia deiatel'nost' kitaiskikh poddannykh*, 65.

nesses around long-term construction sites to support the many workers. Their numbers gradually added up. In Vladivostok alone, the population of Chinese grew from 5,600 in 1897 to more than 26,000 in 1912, or one-third of the city's total population. Over the same period, the Chinese population in Khabarovsk quadrupled to 8,000, and in Nikol'sk-Ussuriisk it rose from zero to 5,500.[64] Anecdotal evidence suggested the extent to which Asian workers as a whole had become woven into the fabric of city life. In Nikol'sk-Ussuriisk, the junction of the Chinese Eastern and Ussuri Railroads, at least two out of three shops were reportedly run by Chinese, Japanese, or Koreans. In Vladivostok, nine out of ten shipyard workers were Chinese.[65] Seeing Chinese in dense, urban areas created the impression among Russian observers that Chinese were overrunning cities with their shops, which grew quickly "on the right, left, front, and back like mushrooms after the rain."[66]

Outside cities, the Chinese became an indispensable workforce in mining, timber, and fishing operations. The gold mines of Transbaikal and Amur Provinces, in particular, attracted large numbers of Chinese. Indeed, by 1910, Chinese composed more than 80 percent of the total work force in state-owned gold and platinum mines (see table 3). Migrants hired by subcontractors endured harsh conditions and exploitation in the mines, where they earned 50 to 70 percent less than what Russians did and had to turn over as much as one-third of their wages to their brokers.[67] Thousands sought to work around the exploitative system of state mines by hiring themselves out as "free diggers" in fields that had been claimed by private merchants and entrepreneurs. Here, though they earned little for the gold they found, migrants possessed a modicum of freedom, including the possibility of pocketing a gram of gold and stealing across the border to sell it on the black market to Han merchants.[68]

A smaller, though still sizable, contingent of Chinese worked in the countryside as tenant farmers (12 percent of all Chinese).[69] Similar to Koreans, they practiced the "groove method" of cultivation (*gryadokovaya kul'tura*), in which soil was restored through fertilization and careful attention, rather than through crop rotation as Russian farmers preferred. In South Ussuri, Chinese achieved a return on sown crops of 15 to 20 fold; Russian settlers, by contrast, achieved a

64. RGIADV 702/1/840, l. 1 (October 1913).

65. Siegelbaum, "Another 'Yellow Peril,'" 316.

66. Quoted in Sorokina, *Khoziaistvennaia deiatel'nost' kitaiskikh poddannykh*, 79.

67. Chinese may have also earned less because of their lower productivity. Siegelbaum, "Another 'Yellow Peril,'" 313.

68. Ibid., 315–16.

69. Figure is for Maritime Province in 1897. Sorokina, *Khoziaistvennaia deiatel'nost' kitaiskikh poddannykh*, 48.

TABLE 3.   Number of workers in gold and platinum mines in the Russian Far East

	1906	1907	1908	1909	1910
Russians	10,484	7,664	6,160	6,046	4,136
Koreans	5,865	5,227	4,637	2,159	150
Chinese	3,871	5,754	9,674	13,682	20,022
Total	20,220	18,645	20,471	21,887	24,308

Source: V. V. Grave, *Kitaitsy, Koreitsy i Iapontsy v Priamur'e* (St. Petersburg, 1912), 422.

return of only 8 to 10 fold.[70] Taking advantage of their large numbers, Chinese subdivided plots of rented land and subleased them to other Chinese. (Koreans, by contrast, tended to work their plots themselves.) By 1913 approximately 12 percent of all rented lands in the Maritime Province were farmed by Chinese. They congregated primarily in Cossack homesteads near the Manchurian border and in the districts of Suifun, Suchan, and Ol'ga to the north. In most other areas, however, they could not compete with Korean tenant farmers who dominated the countryside. Indeed, Koreans farmed almost 70 percent of rented lands in the Maritime.[71]

Over the next few decades, Chinese migrants continued to drive the development of large-scale frontier industries. Russian officials, of course, worried about a foreign element dominating the country. Blame fell not only on the Chinese but also on Russian peasants, entrepreneurs, and merchants for perpetuating a cycle of dependence on Chinese labor. Officials criticized the settler (*novoselets*) in particular, the supposed agent of colonization, saying that as soon as he arrived in the Maritime, he "immediately becomes a large consumer of foreign products" from Manchuria and Mongolia, permitted "Russian money [to] exit across the border to China," and relied on Chinese labor.[72] In the wake of the Russo-Japanese War, when fears of a "yellow peril" escalated, officials reacted by prohibiting the employment of Chinese and Koreans on state-run enterprises. Other bans on "yellow labor" were subsequently passed. The measures remained in effect for a brief period, however, due to the practical need for workers. Officials' fears about Chinese labor were allayed only by the noticeable pattern of temporary migration. Chinese chose not to settle permanently but remained a relatively mobile population that circulated in and out of Russia's territories. And Russian laws reinforced these patterns; they discouraged Chinese from naturalizing,

---

70. Siegelbaum, "Another 'Yellow Peril,'" 314.

71. Sorokina, *Khoziaistvennaia deiatel'nost' kitaiskikh poddannykh*, 59; Petrov, *Istoriia Kitaitsev v Rossii*, 440.

72. Shlikevich, *Kolonizatsionnoe znachenie*, 104–5.

prohibited them from acquiring land, and reduced them to the status of temporary dwellers (see chapter 4). The number of "settled" Chinese in Ussuri did not change dramatically over time. Though the population grew from approximately 27,000 in 1898 to 42,000 in 1929, their numbers dropped to about 31,000 in 1932 (see table 1).

Koreans Settle North

Korean migration to Ussuri bore little similarities to the massive, temporary sojourning of Han Chinese and the state-sponsored migration of Russians. Rather, it resembled their compatriots' movement into neighboring Kando: it was spontaneous and organic, growing from a small number of settlers to an entrenched population that owned land, built farms, and filled a critical role in the local economy. The community was sustained by both a continuous flow of families into the region and temporary laborers who entered and left Ussuri in the spring and autumn seasons. This section examines the complex of geographical, environmental, economic, and political factors that pushed the first waves of Koreans to Russia.

In the 1800s successive bouts of environmental ruin and crop failure created unstable conditions for the rural population throughout the eight provinces of Korea. The nineteenth century was an unusually "wet century," characterized by heavy rainfall. Repeated flooding had a devastating impact on the land. It destroyed irrigation works, damaged paddy land, washed away topsoil, and eroded land that had already been denuded by natural processes and human actions.[73] The cycle of floods, droughts, and bad harvests was exacerbated by a lack of sufficient aid from the central government. The Chosŏn court considered it a moral imperative to care for the people by maintaining a stable food supply and lightening their load during times of crisis. The bureaucracy made sure to invest in irrigation facilities, built granaries to provide famine relief and stabilize prices, and remitted taxes with the ultimate goal of helping the large base of farmers.[74] Over the course of the nineteenth century, however, dwindling resources, corruption, and successive natural disasters had left

---

73. Environmental ruin subsequently decreased land values, fueled speculation, and accelerated the drift toward wet-rice monoculture (conversion of dry land to paddy) in the southern provinces; this had profound consequences for the general economy. Jun Seung Ho et al., "Korean Expansion and Decline from the Seventeenth to the Nineteenth Century," *Journal of Economic History* 68, no. 1 (March 2008): 269–71.

74. Ibid. Known as "ever-normal granaries," they were created to help normalize prices by buying at a high price and selling at a low price.

the court strapped for cash, and the system of relief fell into collapse. By 1862 the government had curtailed investment in irrigation facilities and watched its grain reserves drop to half their levels from 1807. When it attempted to shift the burden of relief to regional officials, even tapping into the special reserves of Pyŏngan and Hamgyŏng Provinces, local rebellions broke out.[75] Climatic shocks and political crises in the last decades of the 1800s further disquieted the peasantry.[76]

In the northern provinces, environmental and political instabilities ruined the livelihood of farmers. The overabundance of rain devastated the dry-field culti-vation of millet, barley, and hemp in the north as much as it destroyed the fragile wet-rice monoculture in the south.[77] Natural disasters also uprooted farmers. In the northern provinces, where large outlays of labor and capital were necessary for land reclamation, farmers enjoyed permanent or long-term tenure. It was in the interest of landlords to find long-term tenants who agreed to reclaim land and construct dikes along rivers in exchange for lifetime tenure as well as permis-sion to purchase the land or sell their rights at some time in the future.[78] Such contracts, however, were frequently breached by farmers who found themselves unable to pay rent because their crop had been destroyed by bad weather con-ditions. In southern Korea, farmers who fell into debt moved to a neighboring district or province to find work. In the northern provinces of Hamgyŏng and Pyŏngan, they had the option of leaving the country completely. Given the pull of employment opportunities and rumors of government aid in Russia, it was not surprising that thousands headed there.

The first record of Koreans in Russia dates to early 1864, when a group of fam-ilies settled in Poset, on the north bank of the Tumen River. They built houses and cultivated fields that yielded a crop of barley, buckwheat, corn, and vegetables by that fall.[79] Two years later, at least a thousand Koreans had settled in the villages of Tizinhe, Ianchihe, and other places in Poset, forming a population base for oth-

75. There were precedents for the court to tap into the reserves of Pyŏngan Province for fam-ine relief for other parts of the country. Pyŏngan and Hamgyŏng Provinces historically had larger reserves of granaries and a lower tax rate because of a higher burden of military service. Anders Karlsson, "Famine, Finance and Political Power," *Journal of the Economic and Social History of the Orient* 48, no. 4 (December 2005): 559; Sun Joo Kim, *Marginality and Subversion in Korea*, 71.

76. Historians have pointed to the El Niño Southern Oscillation (ENSO) as causing climate shocks, including heavy rainfalls and monsoons that resulted in drought and famine. A particularly severe ENSO event in 1876–78 resulted in flooding in Korea in 1878; droughts also struck northern China and Korea in the late 1880s and 1890s. Jun Seung Ho et al., "Korean Expansion and Decline," 274n74.

77. Ibid., 260.

78. Susan S. Shin, "Landlord-Tenant Relations," 68.

79. RGIADV 87/1/278, l. 9–10ob (September 25, 1864) in Toropov et al., *Koreitsy* (2001), 17.

ers to join.[80] They possessed land, animals, and the requisite tools to plow their fields.[81] Over the next few years, Koreans continued to cross the border.

Russian authorities, eager to develop their newest territory, not only allowed the Koreans to remain but gave them resources to settle. Officials distributed stores of seed to encourage Koreans to farm as well as supplies of grain, which had been cheaply imported from Hunchun on the Qing side.[82] In addition to basic provisions, they were given land and tax exemptions. The various incentives soon paid off. Russian officials discovered that the Koreans, being intimately familiar with local conditions and practices of land reclamation, successfully cultivated a myriad of products that could be sold to the large military population and for export to China. Koreans also developed sericulture from the abundance of silkworms in South Ussuri.[83] In addition to the growing number of families who settled permanently, many came seasonally to tend to the harvest in the late summer.[84] *Yangban* elite, too, joined the expatriate community.[85] Officials' fears that the Koreans would "create an internal enemy" were balanced by the favorable estimation of the Koreans as an "excellent" colonizing element and checked by calls to conduct systematic surveillance over the population to ensure that they did not live "enclosed in their own circle" but learned Russian language and customs.[86]

With an eye toward developing Ussuri, Russian officials also experimented with resettlement and state-funded projects to make use of Koreans. In 1865 the government sent a group of Koreans to the relatively empty region of Suchan. Later, out of concern that the group had experienced undue hardship from isolation and had grown too dependent on direct aid, Koreans were likely relocated to Suifun, an area settled by Russian peasants.[87] The state also put later arrivals to work on large-scale projects. In the late 1860s, when floods and bad harvests pushed six thousand Koreans across the Tumen River, officials initially allowed them to settle in the Korean villages of Tizinhe and Ianchihe and scrounged up food aid from the local state reserves.[88] But after the crisis died down, the

---

80. RGIADV 87/1/278, l. 61–70 (March 6, 1867) in Toropov et al., *Koreitsy* (2001), 29.

81. The Qing official's discovery of these Koreans is recounted in chapter 2. *Tongmun hwigo*, 4:515 (July 2, 1867).

82. RGIADV 87/1/278, l. 9–10ob in Toropov et al., *Koreitsy* (2001), 17.

83. RGIADV 87/1/278, l. 15–16ob (January 14, 1865); 87/1/278, l. 50–54ob (1865) in Toropov et al., *Koreitsy* (2001), 18, 23.

84. RGIADV 87/1/278, l. 50–54ob (1865) in Toropov et al., *Koreitsy* (2001), 21.

85. N. Nasekin, "Koreitsy Priamurskago kraia," *Zhurnal Ministerstva obshchestvennogo obrazovaniia* 352 (March 1904): 2.

86. RGIADV 87/1/278, l. 50–54ob in Toropov et al., *Koreitsy* (2001), 22.

87. RGIADV 87/1/278, l. 50–54ob in Toropov et al., *Koreitsy* (2001), 23.

88. Vagin, "Koreitsy na Amure," 3–4, 7.

government directed them to areas far away from the border region, to Vladi-vostok post, Nikol'sk, Razdol'noe, Astrakhanka along the Suifun River, the Bay of Ol'ga, and embankments on the Daubikhe and Lefu Rivers. In these far-flung places, Koreans were employed on numerous state-funded projects, ranging from the construction of telegraph lines, railroads, docks, roads, and edifices to indus-tries such as timber cutting, coal mining, and smelting. Many also worked as ten-ant farmers.[89] Resettlement programs, though costly to the state, were viewed as essential. As proof of their commitment, the governor of the Maritime Province, M. P. Putsillo, dipped into his personal funds to help Koreans build farms, and M. S. Korsakov, the governor-general of Eastern Siberia, committed additional money from the state treasury.[90]

The relocation programs transplanted Koreans to all parts of Ussuri and as far north as the Amur region. For Russian officials, Blagoslovennoe, or "Blessed vil-lage," on the Samara River represented a successful model of what Koreans could achieve in a remote region where ties to their compatriots were severed. Founded in 1871, the village comprised a hundred families who had initially planned to settle in Poset or the Lake Khanka region but were instead sent "against [their] will" to the area north of Blagoveshchensk. They were given provisions and state aid to build houses and farms.[91] Eventually, the settlers thrived in their new environment. Koreans' courts, governmental bodies, postal station, schools, and orderly homesteads attested to the adaptability of the population and inspired officials to plan for future projects in the Amur region. The state intended that all Korean arrivals be resettled in the Amur Province, but if that was not pos-sible, they were to be placed in Russian villages near Lake Khanka and in Suifun district.[92]

Geographical proximity made travel to Russia relatively easy for Koreans. Most migrants came from Hamgyŏng Province and crossed one or more borders to arrive at their destination, taking a direct route across the Tumen River or an indirect one through Qing territory.[93] Once in Poset, migrants settled among compatriots or moved to other parts of South Ussuri in search of land and work.[94] Koreans adeptly changed their routes across the tripartite border region according to the information they gathered. If Koreans were stopped at a Russian

89. Ibid., 3, 7–9; Nasekin, "Koreitsy Priamurskago kraia," 4–5.

90. A. I. Petrov, *Koreiskaia diaspora na Dal'nem Vostoke Rossii, 60–90-e gody XIX veka* (Vladivo-stok, 2000), 84.

91. Vagin, "Koreitsy na Amure," 13–15. For more on Blagoslovennoe, see Aleksandr Kirillov, "Koreitsy sela Blagoslovennogo," *Priamurskie Vedomosti* 58 (1895).

92. Vagin, "Koreitsy na Amure," 17.

93. Syn Khva Kim, *Ocherki po istorii sovetskikh Koreitsev*, 32.

94. Pesotskii, *Koreiskii vopros*, 31–32.

border point near Hunchun, they adjusted their path northward and crossed to Ussuri. If they heard rumors about land available on the Qing side of the Tumen River, they headed there to claim it. Others used Ussuri as a momentary stopping place en route to their final destination in Jilin. By 1911 a triangular pattern of movement had been set: for every 600–700 Koreans that left Korea and entered Russia via land every month, 150–200 in Russia departed for Kando.[95] With the advent of steamship lines, growing numbers of seasonal laborers traveled by sea to Vladivostok from the northern ports of Wŏnsan, Sŏngjin, and Ch'ŏngjin. To avoid passport checks, many sailed on schooners, docking wherever they pleased along the coast.[96]

By the early 1880s, the first waves of migrants had established a fledgling enclave of 10,100 Koreans in the Maritime Province, outnumbering the population of 8,400 Russians.[97] The district of Poset in particular continued to be dominated by Koreans even after the onset of maritime transportation. By 1891 the Russian peasant population there had risen to a mere 600, military personnel and families to 6,300, and Koreans to more than 7,000, or 90 percent of the civilian population.[98] The ratio of Koreans to non-Koreans in Poset remained constant through the 1920s and early 1930s.[99]

Cross-Border Networks

Once Poset emerged as a base for Koreans, a pattern of cyclical migration and settlement arose. In the spring, migrants arrived in parties of ten or twenty men to work on private or state farms. Some stayed through the winter, living in makeshift Korean-style houses (fanzas) and supporting themselves through day jobs. The following spring, the men found land to rent and, if they were successful, sent for their families and became permanent tenants. Others saved up enough money to build their own farms.[100] The number of seasonal workers arriving each year grew from 2,000 in Poset and 5,000 in South Ussuri in the mid-1890s, to 27,000 in 1901.[101] By 1909 the numbers had settled to around 12,000–14,000

95. Ibid., 29–30, 33, 43. Pesotskii estimated that two thousand Koreans left Korea for Kando every month in 1910–11.

96. Ibid., 70.

97. Grave, Kitaitsy, Koreitsy i Iapontsy, 129–30.

98. Ragoza, "Pos'etskii uchastok," 55–56.

99. Itogi perepisi Koreiskogo naseleniia v 1929 g., IV; K voprosu o migratsii Koreiskogo naseleniia.

100. These farms were built on rented lands belonging to the state, forest guard, and cities. Grave, Kitaitsy, Koreitsy i Iapontsy, 154.

101. Ragoza considers the Poset figure a conservative estimate. Ragoza, "Pos'etskii uchastok," 107; B. B. Pak, Rossiiskaia diplomatiia i Koreia (Irkutsk, 1998), 18. The 1901 figure is for Koreans arriving

yearly arrivals in the entire Russian Far East. Their networks stretched from various places in Ussuri and the larger Maritime to popular departure points in Hamgyŏng Province, including Sŏngjin, Kilchu, Myŏngch'ŏn, Tanch'ŏn, Kapsan, and Hamhŭng.[102]

Most of the migrants worked as tenant farmers. Russian peasants and Cossacks had grown heavily dependent on Korean and Chinese laborers, who proved they could reap bountiful harvests in the humid climate with their technique of "grooves" or "growing in beds." Peasants hired them as wage laborers or tenant farmers, accepting a percentage of the harvest as pay.[103] It was estimated that almost every household employed at least one Korean worker.[104] Cossacks, whose military and postal duties consumed most of their time, relied more heavily on foreign labor. Hundreds of Korean and Chinese households were living in the Cossack stations in Poltavka and Grodekovo near the Manchurian border.[105] By 1913 about 70 percent of rented lands in the Maritime Province was farmed by Korean laborers.[106] An official commented on the ubiquity of Koreans in the agricultural sector:

> The whole of Poset district, the mass of Cossack lands up to Khanka, peasant lands around Nikol'sk, church and forestry lands throughout South Ussuri, and even farther north toward Khabarovsk and along the Amur are all cultivated by the labor of Koreans. I estimate that the southern Maritime Province is fed almost entirely by the hands of Korean foreigners [*inostrantsy*].... Their role [in farming] is enormous, even if it is negative for the government.[107]

Hardly an agronomist could pass by the Koreans' fields without marveling at their "wonderfully cultivated and well-tended fields."[108] By the 1910s, in addition to their crops of grains and vegetables, Koreans had managed to grow rice.

Over time, Koreans' niche as farmers allowed them to fan out throughout the Ussuri countryside. And everywhere they went, they built hamlets that bore little resemblance to Russian settlements. While Russian peasants chose to live

---

in Vladivostok; officials noted that this number decreased by half immediately after 1901 because of an increase in *bilet* fees. RGIADV 28/1/234, l. 323ob (December 3, 1901).

102. N. Sen'ko-Bulanyi, "Severnye porty Korei," in *Sbornik konsul'skikh donesenii*, ed. Ministerstvo Inostrannykh Del (St. Petersburg, 1909), 26, 29.

103. Grave, *Kitaitsy, Koreitsy i Iapontsy*, 159.

104. Ragoza, "Pos'etskii uchastok," 107.

105. Grave, *Kitaitsy, Koreitsy i Iapontsy*, 160–62.

106. Petrov, *Istoriia Kitaitsev v Rossii*, 440.

107. Pesotskii, *Koreiskii vopros*, 76.

108. D. I. Shreider, *Nash Dal'nii Vostok* (St. Petersburg, 1897), 153.

together in villages, many miles from their fields, Koreans erected their homes in the middle of farms in the model of homesteads. Korean hamlets thus had no center, comprising dozens and sometimes hundreds of modest three- to four-acre homesteads that were scattered along narrow river valleys.[109] Those who had the advantage of Russian subjecthood were able to establish these homesteads legally, while those who remained foreign subjects ended up squatting on the edges of registered villages, eventually creating clusters of illegal hamlets (*vyselok* or *zaimok*).[110]

Such illegal settlements grew in tandem with the passing of Russian naturalization and residence laws, which created a mechanism for migrants to cross into Russian territory but discouraged long-term residence. New arrivals from Korea were not only banned from settling in the immediate border region (from Poset to Lake Khanka) but also denied privileges that had been granted to early Korean migrants, including the right to Russian subjecthood, land, and tax exemptions. Those who arrived in Russia after 1884 were reduced to temporary alien status; they were required to obtain a Korean national passport and Russian *bilet* every year and forbidden from settling permanently on land. Whether because of logistical difficulties involved in obtaining the proper paperwork or willful avoidance of the law, many Koreans overstayed their visits. The makeshift hamlets they established on land belonging to the forest guard, cities, state, peasants, Cossacks, and fellow Koreans de facto became permanent illegal villages.[111]

While the majority of Koreans worked in farming, many also ventured into large-scale state industries, including gold and coal mining, timber cutting, and fishing. Most of the migrants were recruited by contractors, who functioned as middlemen and organized the workers into artels, labor cooperatives consisting of ten men for the gold mining industry and 100–150 for other lines of work. Koreans also formed independent artels, known as "artels of brothers" (*hyŏngnim*) to supply labor on the docks.[112] These unions acted as surrogate family units and judicial organs for its members. The elected leader was responsible for relations with outside parties, collection of dues, caring for the ill, burying the dead, and finding work for the unemployed; he also judged and meted punishment for wrongdoings, which sometimes led to one's expulsion from the artel.[113] By 1906–7, Koreans had penetrated all industries, including state-run gold and platinum mines, where they composed about one-third of the work force (see

---

109. Pesotskii, *Koreiskii vopros*, 87.
110. Dem'ianenko, *Territorial'naia organizatsiia khoziaistva*, 230–31.
111. RGIADV 1/1/227a, l. 36ob (1890 report); Toropov et al., *Koreitsy* (2001), 153–54.
112. Sen'ko-Bulanyi, "Severnye porty Korei," 26–27.
113. Ibid., 27–28.

FIGURE 1. Korean gold miners in Lena mining district, Russia. Author's collection.

tables 2a and 2b).[114] In the mines, Koreans built up a reputation for their willingness to work in "damp, swampy places" where Russians dared not go. The mines "could not do without them," said one official.[115]

Over time, mining villages reminiscent of late nineteenth-century California boomtowns sprang up on the perimeters of work sites in Russia. Laboring in mines for several years on end, Koreans learned to build a life outside of work. To tend to their everyday needs, workers contributed a portion of their wages toward housing and clothes, and they procured their favorite foods, including *kimch'i*. Some also engaged in side businesses such as brickmaking and road repair for extra income. The more adventurous dabbled in gambling and the black market, where gold fetched a higher price.[116] The cornucopia of businesses and sources of recreation provided a momentary escape from the drudgery of work for miners and an opportunity to create a community outside their native country.

Seasonal laborers were joined by artisans, who came to Russia to meet the demands of growing villages and mining towns. Inured to a peripatetic lifestyle in Chosŏn, where they traveled from town to town to offer their services

---

114. As discussed in chapter 4, Koreans decreased in number after 1907 because of a prohibition against the employment of Korean foreigners on state enterprises, including gold mines.

115. Quoted in I. A. Sin'kevich, *Istoriia trudovoi immigratsii v prigranichnykh regionakh Dal'nego Vostoka* (Moscow, 2003), 21.

116. Sen'ko-Bulanyi, "Severnye porty Korei," 27–28; A. I. Petrov, *Koreiskaia diaspora na Dal'nem Vostoke Rossii, 1897–1917 gg.* (Vladivostok, 2001), 187.

at intermittent markets, blacksmiths, smelters, and potters expanded the geographical scope of their trade to Ussuri. During the spring and summer, they melted iron down to mold into tools and produced porcelain wares, and in the winter they drifted to logging, among other industries, to earn a living.[117] A small, homegrown population of artisans gradually arose in this manner.

Alongside workers on the Russian side, a small group of traders contributed to the growing cross-border economy between northern Korea and Ussuri. Cattle traders were particularly active. Koreans had begun to supply cattle to the Russian military in Poset Bay in the 1860s and continued to do so through the early 1900s.[118] From 1906 to 1910, 30 percent of the Maritime Province's cattle imports came from Korea.[119] Korean traders found themselves in an advantageous position to work as brokers because they were familiar with the languages, people, and terrain on both sides of the border. Agents from the Vladivostok firm Ch'oi Ch'unch'an periodically headed to Sŏngjin and other cities in Hamgyŏng Province to acquire livestock from traders who purchased thousands of heads of cattle at semiweekly bazaars. A native Korean infrastructure gradually arose to meet outside demand: buyers from the inland towns of Pukch'ŏng, Myŏngch'ŏn, and Kapsan rounded up cattle, brokers shipped them to stockyards in Kilchu and Tanch'ŏn, and from there second-level middlemen purchased the livestock and sold them to Korean agents from Russia. In the final step, most of the livestock were herded to Ussuri directly by sea from Sŏngjin.[120] Apart from cattle, traders engaged in the small-scale import of timber, which they acquired illegally from neighboring Jilin. The cultivation, transport, and sale of other contraband, including opium and the sorghum-based Chinese alcohol known as *khanshin* (*kaoliang*), provided a means of living to many Koreans in the border region.[121]

By 1913 in-migration and natural population growth had pushed the number of Koreans in South Ussuri to about 52,000, and by 1929 to 150,000, or 24 percent of the total population (see table 1).[122] Poset remained a staunch Korean enclave, with a population that was about 90 percent ethnic Korean. Other administrative districts similarly hosted large numbers of Koreans. In 1929 Koreans formed 50 percent of the population of Suifun and Suchan districts and 40 percent of Pokrovka (see table 4). Migrants had also reached the more industrial regions

---

117. Nasekin, "Koreitsy Priamurskago kraia," 17–18.

118. B. D. Pak, *Rossiia i Koreia*, 35.

119. Kajimura Hideki, "Kyūkanmatsu hokkan chiiku keizai to naigai kōeki," in *Kajimura Hideki chosakushū*, vol. 3, ed. Kajimura Hideki (Tokyo, 1990), 175.

120. Sen'ko-Bulanyi, "Severnye porty Korei," 25–26.

121. Pesotskii, *Koreiskii vopros*, 90–91.

122. In 1913 the population of Koreans in the larger Maritime Province was 57,000. *Obzor PO za 1913 g.*, appendix 1.

TABLE 4. Population of Koreans in Vladivostok *okrug* by *raion*, 1929

RAION	KOREANS	% TOTAL
Poset	35,785	88
Suifun	20,718	49
Suchan	19,698	51
Shkotovo	10,837	29
Pokrovka	10,391	39
Khanka	9,099	30
Grodekovo	7,860	32
Ol'ga	4,915	22
Spassk	4,424	13
Chernigovka	4,275	17
Ivanovka	3,380	15
Shmakova	3,166	8
Mikhailovka	2,174	7
Iakovlevka	1,575	6
Vladivostok	7,994	7
Nikol'sk-Ussuriisk	2,896	8
Other cities	1,638	6
Total Vladivostok okrug	150,825	24

Source: *Itogi perepisi Koreiskogo naseleniia v 1929 g.*, iv.

in the north, including Chernigovka, Sredne Ussuri, and Ol'ga. Ussuri had been transformed into a Korean borderland in Russia.

By the late nineteenth century, burgeoning industries and resettlement programs had pulled in Koreans, Russians, and Chinese to Ussuri and placed them in distinct yet interdependent roles within the economy. Russian peasants constituted a class of landowners, Chinese formed a large pool of temporary labor for large-scale enterprises and trade, and Koreans filled the roles of small landowner, tenant farmer, and wage laborer. The geography of settlements reflected these labor niches: Chinese congregated in cities and worksites and Koreans occupied the countryside, where they owned land or rented plots on the fringes of established settlements. From 1913 to 1929, 85 to 90 percent of Koreans and 65 percent of Russians consistently settled in the countryside, compared to 20 to 40 percent of Chinese (see tables 2a and 2b).

Koreans and Chinese were able to embed themselves into the life of the Russian Far East due to practical considerations of the frontier economy as well as state policies. Russian settlers and Cossacks, initially unable to adapt to local environmental conditions, opened up thousands of acres of their farmlands to Korean and Chinese tenants, while large-scale industrialists, faced with a perpetual lack of workers, turned to contracted laborers to aid in their resource-extraction and capital-intensive operations. The flexibility of Asian workers to penetrate various industries was facilitated and reinforced by various passport laws and decrees that created legal channels for them to enter the country but simultaneously discouraged them from settling in established villages. With some exceptions, Koreans arriving after the 1890s were also restricted from naturalizing until geopolitical circumstances necessitated a change in policy. The laws fostered the growth of a temporary labor force that moved from place to place, inside Russia and across borders. Koreans posed a particular problem for the tsarist state because of their tendency to settle. The early arrival of Koreans and their naturalization as Russian subjects had bestowed on them privileges of land acquisition and allowed them to establish a firm base in Poset. Poset became a destination for thousands more families and workers, as well as a momentary stopping point for others headed for greater Ussuri and neighboring Kando. These ties of family and labor only strengthened with time.

6

TRANSNATIONAL WORLD OF THE KOREAN SETTLEMENT

The tsarist state had learned that governing Koreans in the Maritime border region required experimentation in law and practice. International treaties and domestic laws that dated to before the 1860s offered only partial insights into how to legitimate the state's claims over the settled population of Koreans or how to regulate the continuous stream of migrants who entered and left Russia. Navigating uncharted territory, local tsarist officials improvised ways to rule over Koreans; apart from examining new treaties, they negotiated with foreign officials and instituted local laws. In the 1890s, the various measures began to converge with practices being adopted across the globe. They subsumed the ambiguous question of border-crossing migrants under the larger national project of establishing sovereignty over territory and people. In the Russian empire, this meant eradicating its flexible policy of plural jurisdiction and creating uniform practices of governance across the realm, down to the individual subject. Subjecthood, migration, and land rules directed at Koreans represented the first steps toward achieving this goal in its eastern territory.

This chapter examines the state's efforts to bring the project of jurisdiction to the local level, into the heart of Korean settlements. Motivated by practical concerns of rule and by ideas about what a civilized society should look like, officials began to incorporate Korean villages into the jurisdiction of the local Maritime government. They hoped to transform existing Korean institutions of self-rule to conform to the peasant model by transplanting governmental organizations into their settlements and by giving Koreans charge over their own counties (*volost'*), the highest level of peasant self-government. Instead of uniform Russian institutions, however, what was produced was a hodgepodge of official and unofficial methods of governance that developed alongside each other. Russian officials found themselves relying on Korean courts and elders to rule and exact justice as much as settlers depended on higher authorities for aid.

In the city of Vladivostok, officials embarked on a more radical program of change. The so-called problems engendered by Korean and Chinese workers were on full display in the compressed space of the city, where the peoples, languages, and cultures of East and West converged. As Asians grew in number, so did criticisms of their lifestyle. Municipal officials condemned Asians for their "unhygienic" habits, which were a stain on the city, both physical and moral. Deeming them unfit for self-rule, the government attempted to excise the problem at its root by removing the entire Asian population from the city's center and transplanting them to the outskirts where they would be unseen by the public eye. In this new place, the state envisioned building an orderly society from the ground up. The task, of course, was more easily said than done. The relocation plan required a radical shift in inhabitants' everyday practices as well as conscientious urban planning, both of which proved challenges. Korean and Chinese societies (*obshchestva*) flourished as the most effective organs of government instead.

Political Geography of the Village

Since their arrival in Russia in the 1860s, Koreans had exercised autonomy in their villages. According to Pak Ŭnsik's history of Koreans in Russia, "Aryŏng silgi," new arrivals governed themselves through an organization known as the *saekchungch'ŏng*. A society of itinerant merchants (*pobusang*) in its original form, the *saekchungch'ŏng* in Russia was transformed into a general governing body for migrants in markets, in gold mines, and in tiny hamlets with as few as twenty households. Officers were elected according to a ballot system and performed a host of duties: they directed the village congress, mediated disputes, punished those found guilty of misdemeanors, and excommunicated perpetrators of serious crimes. The *saekchungch'ŏng* also acted as the eyes and ears of the hamlet by circulating announcements (*t'ongmun*) throughout the region to inform fellow Koreans of recent crimes and to exhort them to collective action. Taking into account its many functions, the organization was probably most appreciated for the welfare services that it provided to its members. It cared for the sick and buried the dead using dues it had collected from members, as well as disbursed the interest that had accrued from those dues, similar to a mutual aid society.[1]

Over time, as Russian officials watched the Korean population grow, they attempted to bring it under their control by transplanting Russian methods of governance in their villages. Because early arrivals had been naturalized as subjects and made part of the peasant estate, the village society (sel'skoe obshchestvo) and county administration were logical models to adopt.[2] The society represented the lowest level of administration and typically comprised 50 to 300 households. It wielded significant authority over the social and economic life of peasants, with powers as wide-ranging as allotting communal lands, receiving and banishing members, levying state taxes, and electing and paying the salaries of officers, including the village elder, tax collectors, and police deputies who were also known as "tenners" (desiatkie). The county constituted the next level of peasant administration, with anywhere between 300 and 2,000 households under the leadership of an elder, scribe, assembly, and court. Unlike the village society, which acted as an economic body, the county served primarily as a local administrative and judicial instance.[3] The elder fulfilled his duties as an intermediary between the county and district government, primarily the district captain or police captain, and as an archivist, keeping family registers, grain supply records, tax receipts, and correspondence from the villages and higher administration that were essential to the task of governance.[4] The elder was also responsible for enforcing sentences passed by the county court, which adjudicated petty offenses and civil suits between peasants within its jurisdiction.[5]

In 1880, to bring Korean settlers under proper Russian jurisdiction, officials incorporated all Korean villages in Poset into two counties, Tizinhe and Fatashi (respectively renamed Adimi and Ianchihe in 1900). The four Korean villages in Suifun district were subsumed under Korsakovka county the following year.[6] Korean settlements located in remote regions farther north in Ussuri remained

---

1. Pak Ŭnsik, "Aryŏng silgi," in Han'guk kŭndae saryoron, ed. Yun Pyŏngsŏk (Seoul, 1979), 182n139.

2. Hereafter, sel'skoe obshchestvo will be referred to as "society" or "village society."

3. Rural observers and officials denounced the county for being a fictive administrative unit that amalgamated dispersed village societies with no economic or social ties to one another. Still, it remained the highest level of peasant self-government. Corinne Gaudin, Ruling Peasants (DeKalb, IL, 2007), 16–21.

4. Stephen Frank, Crime, Cultural Conflict, and Justice in Rural Russia (Berkeley, 1999), 37.

5. After the Emancipation Act of 1861, the county court was supposed to serve as the lowest level of justice in the countryside, but village courts continued to act as the primary judicial instance for minor infractions and civil suits. Ibid., 38.

6. RGIADV 1/1/803, l. 1 (December 20, 1880).

independent or were incorporated into Russian counties.[7] Each county had an elder, who was appointed by the Russian government and was usually bilingual. By the 1890s, there were thirty-two Korean villages in the Maritime Province, all but one of which were located in South Ussuri. Twenty-two villages fell within the boundaries of Poset district, four in Suifun, two in Verkhne Ussuri (Upper Ussuri), three in Suchan, and one in Sofia.[8]

Due to idiosyncratic settlement patterns, establishing traditional peasant societies inside Korean villages proved a more difficult task than delineating county boundaries. As discussed in chapter 5, Korean villages differed from Russian ones in structure. Russian peasants built their homes around a village, with hundreds of miles of farmlands radiating from the center. During the farming season, peasants shuttled back and forth between their centrally located homes and their farms. By contrast, Korean settlements resembled German homesteads in western Russia. The settlements had no village center but encompassed dozens and sometimes hundreds of small farms of one to one and a half *desiatinas* located along narrow river valleys. Koreans built their homes directly on their plots of land or on the farms of other Koreans and Russians so that they could tend to their crops according to their particular method of cultivation. With each season, newly arriving migrants erected more houses. Hamlets composed of a dozen or more households sprang up every few *verstas* so that it was difficult to tell where the boundaries of one village ended and another began.[9] The tsarist government could not keep up with the spontaneous growth of such hamlets. Neither could maps and records accurately depict the changing landscape. For example, Krasnoe Selo, which was designated as the customs checkpoint on the Russo-Korean border in 1888, constituted not one village as shown on Russian maps but rather eleven hamlets sprawled across the bank of the Tumen River.[10] By 1906 the population had grown to more than 133 households, or 839 individuals, most of whom had naturalized as Russian subjects.[11] Only villagers could identify the hamlets by their actual names, a curious mix of literal interpretations of place, such as Sangso for "place above" and Chungkoi for "central place," as well as

---

7. By contrast, three Russian villages (Bogoslovka, Popova Gora, and Zanadvorovka) and one Finnish hamlet (Ambabira) were located in Poset but were not made part of Korean counties; they were under the direct jurisdiction of the district or police captain. RGIADV 1/1/1227a, l. 12ob (1890).

8. A. Ragoza, "Koreitsy Priamurskago kraia," *Trudy Priamurskago otdela Imperatorskogo Russkogo Geograficheskogo Obshchestva* (1895): 4.

9. Ibid., 8.

10. Koreans referred to Krasnoe Selo as Noktundo, a disputed island at the mouth of the Tumen River. Ibid.

11. P. F. Unterberger, *Priamurskii krai, 1906–1910* (St. Petersburg, 1912), insert "Karta Primorkoi oblasti."

obscure names—Ap'sek'arimi, Sot'k'arimi, and K'ach'egi—that probably drew on the local Korean dialect.[12]

It was also a challenge to determine whether the village societies conformed to the peasant society or retained characteristics of the Korean *saekchungch'ŏng*. Similar to other societies, Koreans elected an elder, maintained a congress (*skhod*), and paid for all expenses incurred within the village—salaries of the scribe and elder, lighting and heating of the society building, postal horses, purchases of paper and ink, and road repair.[13] The elder also enforced the society's responsibilities to the tsarist state and made sure that members fulfilled all tax, military, and corvee labor requirements.[14] The Koreans relied on their own method of tax collection, however. Instead of levying taxes in kind, according to the number of working adults in a household as Russian peasants did, elders levied taxes according to the area of cultivated land and collected taxes in cash. Russian officials conceded that the Koreans' system generated more revenues than the peasant model. They were so impressed that they proposed implementing it in Russian peasant societies in Ussuri.[15]

Koreans seemed to have blended Russian practices with Korean traditions to create their own kind of self-autonomous organ in Russia. Pak Ŭnsik believed that the society (*p'ungsok*), while seemingly unique to compatriots in Russia, shared characteristics with village organizations in Korea. Both had an elder, carried out marriage and funeral ceremonies, acted as a judiciary instance, and proffered aid in troubled times.[16] Koreans in Ussuri had also replicated the grain-loan system that had existed in Korea. Apart from institutional similarities, Confucian propriety appeared to have carried across the border. Emissaries dispatched by the Chosŏn court in the 1880s observed that elders in Ussuri had successfully passed preliminary levels of the civil and military examinations in Korea or possessed hereditary privileges that allowed them to rise in the ranks of officialdom; a few had probably held minor positions in Hamgyŏng Province. Given their education and lineage, then, it was no surprise that a particular elder was commended for his keen ability to "distinguish the public [*gong*] from the private [*sa*]." The emissaries described him as a "literate, faithful, and righteous" man, who had prevented the expatriate community from losing their civilized,

12. Pan Pyŏngyul (Byung Yool Ban), "Han-Rŏ-Chung kukkyŏng chiyŏk Hanin maŭl tŭl," *Sindonga*, July 30, 2003, http://shindonga.donga.com/Library/3/05/13/102698/1. For more examples, see Pan's articles in *Sindonga* from May 25, June 25, August 25, and September 29, 2003.

13. RGIADV 1/1/1227a, l. 21ob–25ob (1890).

14. Gaudin, *Ruling Peasants*, 22.

15. RGIADV 1/1/1227a, l. 25ob–30 (1890).

16. Pak also used the term *p'ungsok* to refer to village soviets or cells that were established in the Soviet period. Pak Ŭnsik, "Aryŏng silgi," 184.

Confucian ways in this foreign land. Koreans in Russia, they believed, had not forgotten "our country's law."[17]

Whether characterized as Korean or Russian, institutions of self-rule emerged wherever Koreans settled. In mining towns and unofficial hamlets that lay beyond the boundaries of registered villages, societies embodied the sole mechanism for enforcing order and providing community. Composed of tenant farmers and contract laborers, the societies operated outside the purview of the tsarist state. And landlords had no incentive to report these activities, since farmhands assumed the landlords' natural duties, such as fixing roads and bridges, supporting coachmen, and digging paths for horse- and ox-drawn carts.[18] Some migrants caught on to the benefits of registering with the tsarist government. Registration meant the right to exist legally and potential access to land, state loans, and the right to Russian subjecthood.[19] In 1905 about 160 Koreans near Lake Khanka petitioned the superintendent of Khanka district to recognize their existing society "in order that they not be considered as temporary occupants [*vremennye*] by the Russian population." The society's present functions ran the gamut of caring for the sick, burying the dead, helping new arrivals find jobs, collecting fees, and electing officers to run their affairs. The Koreans hoped that the government would recognize their elder, Mr. Kim, with an "honorary title" and, in return, vowed to "submit to the authorities in all aspects of the Russian law."[20] Their petition, however, was rejected by a higher official. He stated that "foreign subjects cannot have an official elder, much less have him bear an [honorary] title that has been authorized by Russian law." Recognizing the elder and society would only encourage more Koreans to settle there and create a dense concentration of hamlets that "would be extremely difficult to monitor because of the lack of lower officials in the police force." Any power granted to Koreans, the official concluded, might lead to "great abuses."[21]

Still, institutions of self-rule such as the Khanka society continued to thrive in an unofficial capacity in the Ussuri countryside. Spurred by the stream of new arrivals who settled for set periods of time, societies sprang up wherever Koreans chose to work. Inside registered villages, Koreans adapted their ways of

---

17. *Kangjwa yŏjigi*, 135, 146, 162.

18. Tenant farmers who assumed natural duties and returned a percentage of the crops to the landlord paid no quit-rent taxes. In the early 1890s officials began to levy land and quit-rent taxes on temporary Korean and Chinese dwellers. RGIADV 1/1/1227a, l. 29ob–30; 702/3/302, l. 96–102 (February 26, 1907) in Toropov et al., *Koreitsy* (2001), 129.

19. The Khabarovsk Korean Society was formed through a petition to the military governor in August 1885. RGIADV 1/4/783, l. 31–32ob (August 26, 1885) in Toropov et al., *Koreitsy* (2001), 40–42.

20. RGIADV 1/2/1700, l. 31–32 (January 31, 1905).

21. RGIADV 1/2/1700, l. 30 (March 1, 1905).

governance to the Russian peasant model as they saw fit. Tsarist officials, meanwhile, persisted in their debates about transforming the physical layout of Korean
villages to conform to the peasant model. They hoped to erect Russian-style
schools and granaries, construct orderly roads, and force Koreans to build their
homes along these new roads and on registered plots of land.[22] Koreans who lived
side by side in villages instead of scattered across fields as they lived now would
make it easier for the police to conduct surveillance and for Orthodox clergy to
conduct missions among the population. But in view of the lack of manpower
and funds, ambitious projects fell by the wayside.

Circumscribing the Barbarous

Within the villages and counties, Koreans ran their own courts to administer
justice. The tsarist government allowed the courts to operate, for it conceded that
Russian courts lacked the translators and staff to handle cases involving minority
groups who could not understand or speak Russian. Koreans tried cases of homi-
cide, drunkenness, brawls, theft, illegal collection of firewood, and other crimes
and misdemeanors that arose within their jurisdiction.[23] While the majority of
the suits attracted no particular attention from Russian officials, those involving
violence, especially domestic violence, sparked a litany of responses from members of the government and press, who used the cases not only as an occasion to
decry the barbarity of Koreans but also to intervene in courts that had operated
under the sole jurisdiction of Korean villages since the 1860s.

To Russian reporters and officials, Korean courts embodied not dispassionate
institutions of justice but vehicles that propagated cruelty and inhumane practices. They compared the courts to peasant *samosud* (literally "adjudication by
oneself"), instances of popular justice that operated outside the jurisdiction of
official courts and administrative authority. In rural areas, where the presence
of the higher authorities was weak, it was the commune that acted as the moral
authority. It tried and punished the vast majority of criminal and civil cases,
which were supposed to be tried in the county courts, including thievery, arson,
sorcery, adultery, and transgression of normal conduct.[24] Enlightened jurists and
reformers condemned these unofficial courts as savagery and evidence of the

---

22. RGIADV 702/1/94, l. 22–30 (March 1890) in Toropov et al., *Koreitsy* (2001), 59–64.
23. Ragoza, "Koreitsy Priamurskago kraia," 4–6.
24. The accused rarely complained to outside authorities or sought revenge, since doing so
would challenge the decision of the assembly and authority of the community itself. Stephen Frank,
"Popular Justice, Community and Culture among the Russian Peasantry," *Russian Review* 46 (1987):
243–44; Frank, *Crime, Cultural Conflict, and Justice*, 245–47.

absence of a "legal consciousness."[25] When applied to Koreans, *samosud* likewise signified their apparent unenlightened state, but it also denoted specific
instances of violence in which Koreans (and Chinese) had taken the law into their
own hands. Local newspapers were littered with stories of Koreans and Chinese
exercising *samosud*: Korean workers, who found fault with their Korean contractor, attacked him; Chinese railroad workers, angered by wages in arrears, nearly
beat to death a Chinese contractor; and another Chinese, robbed of sixty rubles,
rounded up his friends, apprehended the thief, stripped him of his clothes, and
proceeded to torture him by lighting a candle under him.[26] Cases of *samosud*
also arose between naturalized Russian subjects and nonsubjects. One reporter
told the story of "arrogant and impudent" Russian subjects—that is, Koreans
who "had their hair cut off"—lording it over "foreign Koreans" because of their
higher economic standing in Russia. The latter endured the treatment until they
had reached the end of their rope, at which point they killed one of the agitators
and discarded his body in the bay.[27]

Specific kinds of *samosud* came under the attack of Russian officials, who
equated it with the "medieval customs" of Asiatic people. It did not help that
the media sensationalized the incidents and stoked the indignation of the public
and officials. Recounted in a newspaper article titled "Around Siberia (Brutal
samosud)," a "retribution" case involving a romance and gory death elicited harsh
criticism. A makeshift court in a Korean town in the middle of a gold mine had
recently sentenced the defendant Yi Yuna to death by being buried alive with the
man she had allegedly murdered, Cho Suin. Yi and Cho had shared a brief but
ardent love affair. After a period of time together, Cho left Yi Yuna. He eventually returned and attempted to rekindle the relationship, but Yi, who had since
married and become pregnant, ignored him and repeatedly fought off his "forceful threats to fulfill his vile intentions." At the end of her wits, Yi Yuna took a
knife and slit her ex-lover's throat, killing him instantly. Cho's family reacted by
demanding a trial and retribution. Six Korean leaders interrogated her, found her
guilty, and then sentenced her to death by being buried alive. One judge, "trying
to mitigate her suffering," struck her unconscious with a blow to the nose. When
the Russian police discovered the horrific circumstances of Yi's death five months
later, it attempted to intervene in accordance with official law. It condemned the
decision of the people's court as savage, arrested the six judges, and reopened
the trial on the grounds that the Korean court's verdict was illegitimate as it had

25. Frank, "Popular Justice, Community and Culture," 264–65.
26. "Khronika," *Vladivostok*, November 10, 1896, 8; "Khronika," *Vladivostok*, October 23, 1894, 5.
27. "Khronika," *DO*, July 7, 1911, 4.

originated according to the "medieval" custom of Asiatic culture, which had administered justice by the principle of "an eye for an eye, [a] tooth for a tooth."[28]

Also condemned was the birch method of punishment, in which the guilty was laid across a wooden bench and beaten by a birch rod.[29] In one domestic dispute, a twenty-eight-year-old woman who had refused to return to her husband had been sentenced to corporal punishment. The complainant, the woman's husband, had initially sold her to a Chinese man. But when she left the Chinese to live with a Korean man, the husband lodged a protest to the court. The court, composed of ten Koreans from the "local intelligentsia," insisted that she return to her first husband. A Russian observer noted that during the fifteen-minute interrogation, the defendant answered questions with the "deepest respect," but the judge simply shouted at her. In the end, when she refused to obey, she was condemned and ordered to be beaten with a birch rod. The Russian tried to intervene, pleading with a local priest to stop the "torture." When his efforts turned out to be futile, he commented with irony, "Yes, it is interesting to know how they discipline [in the counties]!"[30]

While sensationalist stories about the barbarity of "Asian" methods of justice spread, tsarist officials attempted to intervene. When the police chief of Nikolaevsk, for example, discovered that a Korean court had sentenced a Korean subject, Men Ta-en, to seventy blows by a birch rod for taking a betrothed woman, he condemned the court as "secret, illegal." The "judges" were taken into custody and the case transferred to the local justice of the peace.[31] In another incident, a wife, along with her son, was ordered to carry out retribution against her husband for his alleged murder of another man. A Russian official, who had learned about the incident, rushed to the village specifically to stop the "Korean *samosud*."[32] Authorities came to believe that the best way to stop the so-called barbarous acts was to imbue Koreans with a knowledge of Russian law. For "what is considered a crime in Russia is not considered a crime in [their] homeland," they said. Koreans and Chinese, "not having any understanding of our laws, frequently and quite unexpectedly end up in a hole, and from here a significant number of legal matters arise." If the most important laws were translated into their native languages and posted in public places such as a village society's office or along frequently traveled roads, officials hoped, then perhaps foreigners could learn

---

28. "Po Sibiri (zverskii samosud)," *DO*, March 18, 1911, 3.

29. Late nineteenth-century reformers condemned this practice of corporal punishment, but it was still used in county courts. Stephen Frank, "Emancipation and the Birch," *Jahrbücher für Geschichte Osteuropas, Neue Folge* 45, no. 3 (1997): 401–16.

30. "Koreiskii sud," *Vladivostok*, November 7, 1893, 9.

31. RGIADV 702/3/376, l. 27–28 (July 3, 1911).

32. Nasekin, "Koreitsy Priamurskago kraia," 42–43.

Russia's laws.[33] Newly arriving migrants, however, continued to carry out their own methods of self-rule and reinforced tsarist views of Koreans as ignorant and uncivilized.

Interethnic Conflict and Terror

While the ethnic-based economy and settlement patterns had largely confined each group to their own enclaves—Russian, Cossack, Korean, and Chinese—and helped mitigate tensions arising from competition for land and employment, petty crime was still rampant in the region. Koreans who ventured beyond the boundaries of their village came into contact with other ethnic groups and often fell victim to Russian profiteers. To resolve conflicts, Koreans employed a variety of tactics, from initiating their own manhunts to appealing to authorities at the county and regional levels to seek justice.

As migrants and settlers arrived in Ussuri in growing numbers, cases of theft and pillaging multiplied in proportion.[34] While such crimes were by no means unique, they occurred in a new environment of suspicion and alienation that emerged from rising mobility across the empire and increased contact between people who did not know each other.[35] The seasonal inflow and outflow of Asian workers in Ussuri heightened a sense of alienation among Russians who felt outnumbered in their own country. Koreans fell victim to theft at the very outset of their journeys by boat, where Russian and European ship commanders "were not content to throw together their passengers like herrings in a barrel, but encroached on their [Koreans'] paltry sums of money."[36] Koreans also became the target of attack of Russian peasants, who tracked their seasonal movements with a watchful eye. Russians "hunted" down travelers carrying packages and remittances to Korea in the fall and could pilfer as much as 700 rubles from an individual.[37] Knowing that undocumented migrants lived in fear of being discovered, peasants also exploited the liminal status of Koreans in their makeshift hamlets. In 1915 a gang of Russians, disguised as policemen and guards, stormed a Korean house on the edge of Frolovka village and commanded the

---

33. "Khronika," *Vladivostok*, April 25, 1896, 7.
34. There were various technical definitions of theft. *Grabezh* (theft) constituted the forceful and direct seizure of property, while *razboi* (armed robbery) involved individuals or gangs carrying out threats, extortion, violence, and bodily harm. Frank, *Crime, Cultural Conflict, and Justice*, 125.
35. Ibid., 147.
36. "Khronika," *Vladivostok*, April 18, 1896, 9.
37. "Prisuifunskie Koreitsy," *Vladivostok*, September 17, 1895, 12.

thirty Koreans to present their *bilets*. The group ransacked the entire house and seized the Koreans' possessions while they looked on, helpless.[38]

Korean farmers who crossed the boundaries between Korean and Russian villages to sell their fruits and vegetables were also attacked by Russians hungry for their goods and easy cash. In the summer, when produce was plentiful, signs of struggle, whether an overturned fruit cart or splattered melons, could be seen everywhere. Peasants were also known to sneak into Korean hamlets and steal prized cows and a wagon to transport them. Russian heads of village societies urged their members to stop their "occupation of hunting" against Koreans, but it seemed that petty robbery was too lucrative an activity and the consequences were minimal.[39]

As news about banditry spread, Koreans employed tactics to prevent themselves from falling prey to Russian thieves. They learned to travel in groups, because predators were more likely to pursue a lone traveler and hold him at gunpoint than attack a band of people.[40] For more serious instances of theft, they appealed to the tsarist administration.[41] In the 1915 Frolovka case of robbery, Koreans lodged a complaint to a county representative, who in turn initiated a search for the gang of robbers. The bandits were subsequently apprehended and convicted.[42] When necessary, Koreans circumvented legal means altogether and took matters into their own hands, even conducting stealth manhunts.[43]

Beyond cases of theft, villagers relied on higher district authorities to mediate land disputes that arose in or between villages and counties. Tsarist officials, recognizing the value of Koreans as colonists and tenant farmers, often ruled in favor of Koreans. When recent peasant arrivals in the Russian-dominated areas of Shkotovo and Suifun districts accused Koreans of taking land that rightfully belonged to them, officials dispatched the land surveyor to determine the original boundaries of land allotments;[44] when wealthy Russian peasants colluded to block Koreans from gaining access to a land auction, municipal authorities circulated announcements through the Korean county administration to publicize the event and took steps to give them access to the bidding.[45] The state also handled petitions from those who desired to keep Korean tenants on their lands. In 1916

---

38. "Po dalekoi okraine: s. Frolovka," *DO*, March 29, 1915, 3.
39. "Borisovka," *Vladivostok*, April 16, 1895, 10; "Bogoslovka," *Vladivostok*, November 17, 1896, 11; "Prisuifunskie Koreitsy," *Vladivostok*, September 17, 1895, 12.
40. "Shkotovo," *DO*, October 17, 1912, 3.
41. "Khronika," *Vladivostok*, October 23, 1894, 5.
42. "Po dalekoi okraine: s. Frolovka," *DO*, March 29, 1915, 3.
43. "Bogoslovka," *Vladivostok*, November 17, 1896, 11.
44. "Khronika," *Vladivostok*, July 25, 1893, 4.
45. "Nikol'sk-Ussuriiskii, Mar. 23," *Vladivostok*, March 28, 1899, 3.

regional officials in Ol'ga passed a resolution that required Koreans living temporarily on peasant lands to join an official settlement. When the tenants opted to leave, the wives of landowners appealed to the county administration to delay the order, explaining that because all able-bodied men had gone to war, only the Koreans were left to farm the land. They further asserted that the county's proposal to hire convicts from a neighboring town would leave them in a vulnerable position. Having the Koreans as farmers was safer. Their petitions, along with letters from churches and industrialists in the mining business who were equally dependent on Korean labor, traveled from the county administration and through the higher bureaucracy, until they were finally read by the Maritime governor and Priamur governor-general themselves.[46]

Banditry and the "Manzas"

While instances of interethnic conflict were a regular occurrence that could be dealt with through the police or community defense forces, protecting oneself against the "Manza" bandits posed a more significant challenge. Since the late 1860s, the Manzas, also called *honghuzi*, had become a symbol of lawlessness in the border region.[47] Similar to those on the Qing side, they pillaged settlements, pursuing food, oxen, money, and people wherever they could. Though theft and violence were not uncommon in rural areas, crimes perpetrated by Manzas posed a thorny issue for Russian officials because they were considered to be under the jurisdiction of the Qing. When inhabitants saw that their individual efforts to counter the waves of Manzas were futile, they banded together, uniting with local and regional officials to fight against a common enemy.

While Manzas conducted their attacks around Ussuri throughout the year, they were particularly active along the Manchurian boundary during the harvest season. The forested border area was an ideal place to hide and organize. It was reported that Manzas would "go from house to house, devouring everything [the Koreans] had like hungry wolves, merrymaking at the expense of the host and violating women and girls, even carrying them off."[48] Brigands also targeted Chinese. They stole from wealthy Chinese and kidnapped employees

---

46. RGIADV 702/5/462, l. 12, 20, 42, 46, 53 (1915–16).

47. I use "Manza" to discuss the *honghuzi* on the Russian side as this was commonly used in Russian-language sources; I also replace the Russian transliteration *khunkhuzy* with "Manza" for readability. For information on the interethnic violence caused by a disagreement over mining rights near Vladivostok in 1867–68, called the Manza wars, see I. P. Iuvachev, "Bor'ba s khunkhuzami na Manchzhurskoi granitse," *Istoricheskii vestnik* 82 (October 1900): 177–206.

48. "Khronika," *Vladivostok*, September 22, 1896, 9.

of medium-sized Chinese companies in hopes of collecting ransom.[49] Often ignorant of the Russian language and subject to the whim of their contractors or Russian landlords, Chinese generally had little recourse when attacked. The change of seasons, too, affected the frequency of incidents. During the harvest period, when food and money changed multiple hands, cases of petty crime perpetrated by Manzas surged. They stole from Koreans who had just been paid by the commissariat for their foodstuffs and from opium cultivators in the environs of Shkotovo.[50] Various gangs of Manzas forced their way onto the poppy farms of Koreans and Chinese, demanding a percentage of the crop. In late summer of 1912, fears had escalated to the point where entire households of Koreans daily moved to a neighboring village, two *verstas* away, to pass the night, while those who remained stood guard.[51] When autumn arrived, Koreans exulted, for attacks on their opium farms dwindled, the need for community policing died down, and nightly shootings ceased.[52]

Victims of the "Manza terror" and the Russian administration sought justice by a number of means. People appealed to higher authorities, such as the Cossack chief and South Ussuri captain, who sent detachments of soldiers to locate and arrest the bandits and then deported them to Manchuria.[53] Officials also prohibited Manzas from living inside Korean villages.[54] Increased surveillance over Manzas affected the Chinese population as both groups became associated with crime, whether a crime of violence or that of missing papers. In the name of protecting Koreans, soldiers deported *bilet*-less "Chinese," only to face the complaints of Russian contractors who were left with a smaller pool of able-bodied workers to hire.[55] In addition to petitioning authorities, villagers also resorted to organizing grassroots self-defense groups to protect themselves and even hired local hunters to apprehend bandits.[56]

Where Russian authorities were powerless to stop the plundering of Manzas, they accepted the help of Chosŏn and Qing border officials who had similarly endured a barrage of attacks. Manzas had not only victimized subjects on all sides of the border but had repeatedly disrupted the growing import-export business in the region. Cossack chiefs cooperated with Qing commanders to conduct passport checks and arrests, and Chosŏn border officials distributed matchlock

49. "Khronika," *DO*, June 21, 1909, 4; "Nashestvie khunkhuzov," *Vladivostok*, September 19, 1893, 4.
50. "Nikol'skoe," *Vladivostok*, January 25, 1898, 7.
51. "Shkotovo," *DO*, August 12, 1912, 3–4.
52. "Shkotovo," *DO*, October 17, 1912, 3.
53. "S Ussuri," *Vladivostok*, August 25, 1896, 10; "Nikol'skoe," *Vladivostok*, January 25, 1898, 7–8.
54. RGIADV 1/2/1011, l. 2 (February 11, 1887); Ragoza, "Pos'etskii uchastok," 61.
55. "Nikol'skoe," *Vladivostok*, January 25, 1898, 7–8.
56. "Khronika," *DO*, June 21, 1909, 4.

guns to Koreans to protect themselves.[57] Help also came with the expansion of the powers of Korean and Chinese societies in Russian cities. In 1911 Chinese in Vladivostok petitioned to organize a merchant society under the auspices of the Qing consul general to hunt down bandits. Their familiarity with the language and culture of the bandits gave them the ability to size up the problem that had consistently confounded Russian authorities:

> In view of the mass arrival in Vladivostok of *honghuzi* [*khunkhunzy*], who do not at all fear the Russian authorities and day and night engage in plundering, the victims, out of fear of the *honghuzi*, do not report them to the police. Because of the superior organization of the *honghuzi*, the police can arrest only the less dangerous elements, while the more daring *honghuzi* slip away and are not deported.[58]

The Chinese society proposed to aid the Russian police on several fronts: it would track the whereabouts of the bandits and conduct interviews to ascertain whether the "bandits" were, in fact, guilty of the crimes of which they had been accused and not innocent people who had been mistakenly arrested. It would also identify innkeepers who housed bandits in their guesthouses. Displaying their knowledge of travel routes into and out of Russia, society members urged authorities to deport the Manzas not by land, as was customary, but by sea in order to deter their quick return to Ussuri. On hearing the proposals of the society, the military governor of the Maritime Province, Vasilii Flug, agreed.[59] Similar proposals were submitted by Chinese in Khabarovsk and Nikol'sk-Ussuriisk and presumably by Koreans in Vladivostok.

While authorities worked together on all sides of the border and inside Ussuri, Manzas continued to wreak havoc in the region. Political instability and poverty pushed dispirited men to join gangs of bandits, while the lack of a large police force allowed them to act with relative impunity. Newspapers, meanwhile, fed the public's fascination and fears of the roving bands. Translating romantic descriptions of cowboys in the American "Wild West" to the local context of the "Wild East," they evoked images of the strong Russian soldier and Cossack chief while portraying Manzas, Chinese, and Koreans as roving criminals or hapless victims, both descriptions that reinforced perceptions of these groups as "other."[60]

---

57. Qing authorities were also criticized for not taking enough measures. "S Ussuri," *Vladivostok*, August 25, 1896, 10; RGIADV 1/2/1262, l. 10–10ob (February 3, 1897).

58. RGIADV 1/3/1181, l. 82a (February 25, 1911).

59. Ibid., l. 80–83.

60. The capture of Manzas was given wide media coverage. See "Sudebnaia khronika: Pokhishchenie Viktora Medvedeva," *DO*, April 16, 1909, 3–4; "Pokhishchenie Kima," *DO*, July 5, 1909, 2.

Korean-Chinese Ghetto

Similar to the countryside, Vladivostok offered Koreans a space to live and rule. By the late nineteenth century, Koreans had gathered by the thousands in the city and, along with Chinese, Russians, Europeans, and indigenous populations, helped transform it into a meeting place between East and West. They ran kiosks in the bustling bazaar on Semenovskii Boulevard and carried goods to and from the bustling port on the Bay of the Golden Horn. In the heart of the city, nestled in between the houses of Russian and European settlers, they also built their own enclaves. Yet as Koreans and other Asians grew in number, they stood out as an "alien" presence in the eyes of the Russian public. The more Asians arrived, the more officials, journalists, and ordinary inhabitants denigrated the foreign population as "uncivilized" and "unhygienic," a moral and physical stain on the city. Drastic measures were proposed to deal with the so-called problem, including a relocation program, but it was not so easy to remove Koreans and Chinese from the places that they lived and worked.

The first glimpse of Vladivostok from the Bay of the Golden Horn belied its Asian cosmopolitanism. The edifices that rose out of the landscape suggested the presence of European and American denizens. As her ship turned into the harbor, the globe-trotting Englishwoman Isabella Bird Bishop recorded her initial impressions:

> There is nothing Asiatic about the aspect of this Pacific capital, and indeed it is rather Transatlantic than European. Seated on a deeply embayed and apparently landlocked harbor, along the shore of which it straggles for about 3 miles—lofty buildings with bold fronts, Government House, "Kuntz and Albers," the glittering domes of a Greek cathedral, a Lutheran Church, Government Administrative Offices, the Admiralty, the Arsenal, the Cadet School, the Naval Club, an Emigrant Home, and the grand and solid terminus and offices of the Siberian Railway, rising out of an irregularity which is not picturesque, attract and hold the voyager's attention.[61]

Bishop glimpsed but a small part of the city's international character. Vladivostok had become the adopted home of a handful of illustrious Westerners who instilled in the city a European or "Transatlantic" flair. One had only to walk down the main street and glance at the names and flags affixed to European-style buildings to know who the elite were and where they had come from. James Cornelius de Vries, an American entrepreneur, had acquired land on the waterfront

---

61. Bishop, *Korea and Her Neighbors*, 214–15.

of Svetlanskii thoroughfare for his future business as early as 1865. A Swede, Otto Linholm, built the district's biggest grain mills. George Denbigh, a Scot, teamed up with the local "seaweed king," Iakov Semenov, and organized Vladivostok's largest food wholesaler, Semenov & Denbigh Co. A French flag flew over the De Louvre Hotel. Scandinavians, Germans, and Japanese held a monopoly over cabotage and international shipping. Gustav Kunst and Adolf Albers, two merchants who hailed from Hamburg, Germany, brought the most recent gadgets and fashions from Paris and Savile Row to their eponymous department store, which was decked with marble interiors and electric lights. Beyond retail, Kunst and Albers had diversified into heavy agricultural machinery, shipping, and insurance and expanded to thirty branches throughout the Maritime Province and western Russia. Also among the roster of entrepreneurs was the Swiss Iulii Briner of Briner & Co., a conglomerate that sourced timber from the Amur, coal from Sakhalin, and lead from Tetiukhe. Briner also managed a timber concession in northern Korea. Alongside the world of business, diplomats contributed to the cosmopolitanism of the city. Great Britain, France, the Ottoman Empire, Greece, the Netherlands, Norway, and the United States had all stationed representatives in the Russian Far East. From their perch in the hills of the bay, where most consulates were located, they could see steamships arrive from faraway places and sailors alight on the wharf below.[62]

Located between the motley array of European and Russian trade houses, a lively Korean and Chinese world thrived. A stroll down *millionka* (present-day Fontanka Street), one of their centers of business, revealed a line of shops selling all manner of produce, fish, meat, furs, and trinkets, as well as restaurants and inns. Everywhere, Korean and Chinese porters could be seen delivering packages that were hoisted on their backs or driving carts. Their bazaar on Semenovskii, "four large wooden buildings" by the late 1890s, had provided a lifeline for the city since its early days, when there were hardly any Russian civilians to speak of.[63] Indeed, through the 1900s Koreans and Chinese supplied most of the unskilled labor, ran most of the small businesses, and controlled the inventory of drinking water, food, firewood, and animal feed in the city. Census data confirmed their widespread presence: in 1877 four out of every five civilians in Vladivostok was Chinese or Korean, and in 1906 the ratio was one out of every two. The Chinese were the most populous non-Russian group, with 3,400 in 1880; 10,100 in 1898; and 24,000 in 1906. The Koreans followed in size, with 1,300 in 1898 and 3,800 in 1906. In the 1920s, though the number of Asians

---

62. Stephan, *Russian Far East*, 84–86.
63. Bishop, *Korea and Her Neighbors*, 219.

FIGURE 2.   Market on wharf of Vladivostok, early twentieth century. Author's collection.

relative to the rest of the city's population decreased, the proportion was still significant at one out of every five.[64]

Inside their enclaves, Koreans and Chinese built self-governing bodies that served multiple functions. Officially recognized in 1890, the Vladivostok Korean Society (Hanin kŏryu minhoe), along with its larger Chinese counterpart, assumed police, judicial, and administrative duties, as village and county administrations did in the countryside.[65] They operated under the jurisdiction of the Vladivostok police chief. The societies elected elders and representatives, appointed judges to their own courts, and hired policemen, supplementing the force with additional guards during the summer months when the population grew. In the absence of bilingual Russian officials, members also acted as intermediaries. The Chinese society had concluded large-scale contracts with famous trading houses such as Shevelev and Co., governed the transport of freight into the city, and aided tsarist authorities in conducting passport checks, distributing residence permits, and

64. In the 1920s and early 1930s, the Chinese population decreased while the Korean population increased. Stephan, *Russian Far East*, 84; Unterberger, *Primorskaia oblast'*, appendix 1; *Obzor PO za 1906 g.*, appendix 1; *Obzor PO za 1913 g.*, appendix 1; *Itogi perepisi Koreiskogo naseleniia v 1929 g.*, IV; *K voprosu o migratsii Koreiskogo naseleniia.*

65. Ethnic-based societies existed in all larger cities, including Nikol'sk-Ussuriisk (same organization for Chinese and Koreans), Khabarovsk, and Blagoveshchensk.

FIGURE 3. Semenovskii market, Vladivostok, 1918–22. Courtesy of the Arsen'ev State Museum of the Primorskii Region.

Владивостокъ. Свѣтланская ул. уголъ Китайской ул.
Wladiwostock. Swetlanska-Str. Ecke der Chinesischen Str.

FIGURE 4. Central location at the corner of Svetlanskii and Kitaiskii Streets (Okeanskii Prospekt), Vladivostok, early twentieth century. Publication of Gustav A. Tsorn. Courtesy of the Arsen'ev State Museum of the Primorskii Region.

apprehending bandits.[66] Enforcement of city codes was equally important. The Vladivostok police chief depended on these self-governing bodies to carry out basic administrative and police tasks at the municipal level. The societies not only explained recent changes in Russian laws but also collected taxes on land allotments and enforced sanitation and building codes. In the case of the Korean society, taxes collected from residents and temporary workers were funneled directly into public health programs,[67] which ranged from sanitation checks and inoculations to the building of cholera barracks and infirmaries. The money also paid for the sick and dead to be transported back to Korea.[68] After 1907 new Korean societies, supported in part by nationalist émigré groups, ran campaigns to fight opium and gambling addiction and to promote sober lifestyles in general.[69] It was hard to imagine the city government functioning without these organizations.

As was common in cities elsewhere, the growth of a diverse population in Vladivostok's compressed quarters triggered paranoia about disease and corruption in the mind of the public. Perennial talk of "dirty" and "immoral" foreigners reinforced racialized stereotypes that undercut the reputation of Asians as diligent workers and alienated Asians as an uncivilized "other." They were blamed in particular for spreading deadly disease. Early outbreaks of cholera and the plague in the 1880s were traced to migrants and cattle from China and Korea. The diseases never reached pandemic levels—influenza was often cited as the most widespread illness[70]—but they nevertheless generated a stream of commentary from officials and inhabitants, who tended to conflate disease with the apparent squalor and laziness of Asians. When "Asian cholera" broke out in 1886, a tsarist official attributed the illness to the Koreans' inherent shortcomings, saying:

> Koreans in Vladivostok live in terrible poverty and are an overwhelming evil for the whole city in these hard times. . . . Koreans are very lazy, dull-witted pilferers and for that reason receive a pittance for their labor.

66. "O Kitaiskom obshchestvennom upravlenii," *Vladivostok,* January 24, 1893, 7, 8.

67. *Taedong kongbo,* August 25, 1909, 3. Koreans complained about the tax and threatened to leave the enclave. *Kwŏnŏp sinmun,* October 3, 1913, 3.

68. Toropov et al., *Koreitsy* (2001), 81 (April 28, 1893); RGIADV 28/1/391, l. 64 (March 1897); "Khronika," *Vladivostok,* May 4, 1897, 7; "Khronika," *Vladivostok,* June 29, 1897, 7.

69. There was significant overlap between members and leaders of nationalist organizations, such as the Workers' Promotion Association (Kwŏnŏphoe), Korean society, youth leagues, and educational societies that arose in the late 1800s to early 1910s. The Workers' Promotion Association and the original Korean society, in fact, merged in March 1914. Discussion of morality campaigns is further discussed in chapter 7. *Kwŏnŏp sinmun,* March 22, 1914, 2.

70. In 1906 there were 3,351 cases of influenza, 1,107 cases of measles, and 154 cases of smallpox or typhus, the two diseases commonly associated with Chinese and Koreans. *Obzor PO za 1906 g.,* 43–45.

They are more often without work. If a Korean manages to earn a pittance, then he indulges himself in stillness until hunger comes upon him. Only then does he creep out of his stinking lair to find work.[71]

Chinese and Korean dwellings were also deemed culprits. Large numbers of laborers crammed together in close quarters, a situation that created unsanitary living conditions. In describing the habitats, the media suggested that filth was characteristic of their ways of being. "Rotting canals, musty culinary waste, smelly rubbish—these are the belongings and adornments of a Chinese home," a newspaper reported. "There is the smell of ammonia, known to all, that emanates from the lanes and alleys, but also the corners of homes and fences."[72] Officials also pointed to the pernicious effects of careless burials. Karl Weber, the Russian chargé d'affaires in Seoul, reported that the "corpses are carefully hidden and are either secretly carried outside the city limits or shipped out to sea at night. [Local authorities] often found bodies of Koreans that were barely covered with dirt in areas outside cemeteries." The list of Koreans' apparent faults led Weber to conclude that Koreans were a "source of various kinds of diseases and contagions for Vladivostok."[73] Similar outcries against Asians arose in the cities of Nikol'sk-Ussuriisk and Khabarovsk.

As much as complaints about Asians reflected worries about matters of public health in a growing city, they also expressed larger national anxieties about Russia's level of civilization. Indeed, discussions about Asians grew in tandem with a broader discourse that made public health a barometer for the country's progress. In his 1905 dissertation for the Imperial Medical-Military Academy, F. A. Derbek, an expert on bubonic plague, proposed that the "cultural level of a people" could be "judged from its attitude to epidemics." The lower the cultural level, the "more it [sic] is helpless with regard to various types of harmful external influences"; the same correlation could be seen on a larger scale when comparing the "effect of epidemic diseases among various contemporary peoples that stand at different stages of civilization." Reformers and activists in Russia lamented that their country had not followed the example of Europe, which had implemented laws to nurture people who were less oppressed, "almost fully literate," and thus seldom fearful of plague and cholera. Still, they continued to lay the bulk of the blame on the "terrible Asian guest."[74]

71. RGIADV 1/1/1026, l. 325 (October 2, 1886).
72. "Nash sanitarnyi vopros," *Vladivostok*, July 26, 1892, 3–4.
73. *Ku Han'guk oegyo munsŏ*, 17:19.
74. Quoted in Chia Yin Hsu, "Chinese Eastern Railroad," 238, 275, 265.

On top of complaints about sanitation, there were a multitude of reports about illicit practices of opium smoking and gambling. Chinese and Koreans grew opium in the city's fields and sold it in their shops, where they hung gold lacquered signs with advertisements such as "Smoke Premium Aromatic Opium."[75] They also ran opium parlors for smokers. Consumption of the drug invited the criticism of ethnographers and reporters who believed that migrant workers were particularly susceptible to falling into addiction. D. I. Shreider, who traveled to Chinatowns and Koreatowns throughout the Maritime Province, described the haunting effects of the drug while relying on familiar tropes of the lethargic, sickly Asian male:

> A certain weird, almost unearthly calm reigns over everything. It is quiet in the *fanza*—so quiet that one can hear the buzzing of a fly, aroused by the faintly flickering light of the single fire illuminating the interior of the *fanza*. Along the entire length of one of its walls are wooden plankbeds not covered by anything. Across them, human figures lie without stirring. Emaciated, gaunt, pale, and shrouded in the sweetish, stupefying aroma of opium, they look like skeletons prepared, or rather dried out, for an anatomy class.[76]

Such images of Asians as weak extended to their practices of gambling.[77] "Gambling halls" (*igornye doma*) had been established in cities and villages as early as the 1860s and attracted Chinese, Koreans, Russians, merchants and blue-collar workers, young and old alike. By 1902, approximately two hundred gambling houses had sprung up in Vladivostok alone. Gambling activities reached their peak in the fall, after the harvest season, and continued through the festivities of the Lunar New Year. Losses from the popular game *yabao*, similar to the European game of faro, could cost a migrant worker a significant percentage of his wage earnings, much to the dismay of his family and broker.[78] Some racked up enough losses to cost them their entire savings and home. The games were certainly addictive. During his visit to Shkotovo in the late 1860s, the Russian explorer N. Przheval'skii observed that a game often began at around ten o'clock

75. "Nash sanitarnyi vopros," *Vladivostok*, July 26, 1892, 3. For a discussion of the opium trade in East Asia, see John Mark Jennings, "The Opium Empire" (Ph.D. diss., University of Hawai'i, 1995).

76. Quoted in David Eugene Habecker, "Russian Urban Administration and the Chinese, Koreans, and Japanese in Vladivostok" (Ph.D. thesis, University of Maryland, College Park, 2003), 288–89.

77. Chinese opium dens in nineteenth-century California were similarly criticized for becoming "corrupt community centers" that encouraged gambling, prostitution, and the like. Martin Booth, *Opium* (New York, 1998), 193.

78. In Korean, it was known *yahwi*; in Russian *bankovka*. Habecker, "Russian Urban Administration," 293, 295.

in the morning and continued until midnight and "sometimes all night if the gamblers are especially daring."[79] While gambling and opium use had victimized all ethnic groups, Chinese, who ran many of the "dens," were vilified for drawing others into these vices. If an indigenous Heje or Gilyak was found drinking, he must be drinking the illegal Chinese alcohol *khanshin*; if a Korean was gambling, he must have fallen under the "evil influence" of the "Manzas."[80] Still, the media portrayed Koreans as bearing equal responsibility for their moral failings because of their feeble character. They had "acquired a taste for gambling and quickly blew their money to the last half-kopeck," becoming the "new victims" of this unsavory activity.[81]

Creating a Hygienic Place

As anxieties about the well-being of the city deepened, tsarist officials attempted to carry out in Vladivostok what they had done at the international border: separating uncivilized foreigners from the civilized denizens of Russia. In Vladivostok this meant physically removing Korean and Chinese migrants from their central location on Semenovskii meadow to the outskirts of the city. Officials hoped to contain the Asian population in a single space to allow for stricter surveillance over registration, sanitation, and other activities. According to a proposal passed in 1892, a new Chinese-Korean quarter would be built in Kuperov valley at First Creek, at the time a sparsely settled area on the city's perimeter. All Koreans and Chinese had to vacate their present homes and relocate to First Creek by 1893. In the new quarter, everything was supposed to be built to specification: land allotments were to be surrounded by fences and canals to facilitate waste disposal; houses had to be erected of stone and wood, with steel roofs, and built about a hundred meters from the Ussuri Railroad; and streets were to be planned in an orderly grid.[82] The new quarter was to be called "Korean Outskirts" (Koreiskaia Slobodka), though it was later referred to as "New Koreatown" (Sinhanch'on) by Koreans.

The municipal administration successfully transplanted the Asian population to the city perimeters, but New Koreatown hardly embodied the hygienic space that officials had envisioned. Though the city defrayed some of the costs of relocating, Koreans and Chinese had little time to prepare for the move and lacked sufficient funds to build their new homes and plots of land according

---

79. Quoted ibid., 292.
80. RGIADV 702/2/414, l. 29–29ob (August 26, 1889).
81. "Temnye piatna na mestnoi inorodcheskoi zhizni," *Vladivostok*, August 15, 1893, 11; "Sinelovka," *Vladivostok*, October 9, 1894; Letter, *Vladivostok*, April 6, 1897, 4.
82. RGIADV 28/1/176, l. 56 (April 30, 1893); 28/1/234, l. 126ob (July 16, 1907).

FIGURE 5.   Boats docked in Amur Bay, Vladivostok, 1920s. Courtesy of the Arsen'ev State Museum of the Primorskii Region.

to specification. Constructing durable wooden or brick homes would have guaranteed them a minimum ten-year lease, but they instead found themselves scrambling to gather scraps of wood and thatch to erect makeshift huts and "tents" that ended up looking much like their homes downtown.[83] It was only several years later that the population managed to build proper houses. Centrally located Semenovskii meadow, meanwhile, remained a base for Asian workers. New Korean and Chinese arrivals quickly filled whatever vacancies had been created by the eviction. An estimated 3,000 Koreans disembarked in the port each month, except in winter, for a total of 27,000 in 1901;[84] Chinese exceeded that number. One journalist reported that the thousands of migrant Chinese workers had never left their original place on Semenovskii.[85]

In the late 1890s and early 1900s, officials attempted to carry out another relocation program, from First Creek to the new outer boundary of the city at

83. RGIADV 28/1/176, l. 58–58ob (June 26, 1898); RGIADV 28/1/234, l. 322–322ob (December 3, 1901).

84. RGIADV 28/1/234, l. 323ob (December 3, 1901).

85. "Na Semenovskom pokose," *Vladivostok*, July 28, 1896, 13.

Second Creek. The city hoped to make room for new waves of Russian and European settlers who were arriving by rail and deemed First Creek an ideal place for them to live. By then it was considered "the best of the central part of our city, located along the railway line, on a beautiful, level spot of the Amur Sound, with convenient connections." Officials estimated that it would "undoubtedly" become "one of the most expensive parts of the city in the future."[86] That Koreans and Chinese had already established their new quarter there did not matter. City officials decided that the entire population should be relocated to the area north of Second Creek, where Koreans and Chinese had already established farms.[87] In 1906 the city Duma prohibited the majority of Asians from living in the city center, including First Creek; only those who possessed Russian subjecthood, owned property, and worked in trade were allowed to live within city limits.[88]

The complete relocation of Asians was never fulfilled. Officials found that earmarked lands at Second Creek were already so full of Chinese and Koreans that there was no space for an additional twenty thousand Asians to be relocated from the "European part" of the city.[89] More significantly, municipal authorities expressed ambivalence about evicting Koreans. Koreans had protested the imminent move, saying that they had not yet harvested their crops and had no time or money to pack up their things and build new abodes for themselves. Korean subjects, who could not purchase land, also petitioned the city council for new leases or extensions on existing land leases in New Koreatown.[90] Officials listened to their petitions. They delayed the deadline for relocation several times and came up with alternative recommendations, including building multistoried houses in New Koreatown to accommodate more people.[91] Efforts to evict the Asian population were temporarily halted under Governor-General Nikolai L. Gondatti, who, though anti-Korean in other policy matters, argued that the lives of Russians and Asian workers had become intertwined to the point where it was impossible to disentangle:

> [The Russians'] needs are, for the most part, provided for by the Chinese and Koreans. It is, unfortunately, impossible to do without their services in the dacha region for the time being, since even in government

86. Quoted in Habecker, "Russian Urban Administration," 228–29.
87. Ibid., 229–30.
88. RGIADV 28/1/234, l. 306–306ob (March 22, 1906).
89. Habecker assumes that the officials were discussing conditions at First Creek, not Second. RGIADV 28/1/391, l. 3–3ob (May 24, 1912); Habecker, "Russian Urban Administration," 237–38.
90. Petrov, *Koreiskaia diaspora, 1897–1917*, 133; A. A. Toropov et al., eds., *Koreitsy na Rossiiskom Dal'nem Vostoke (1917–1923)* (Vladivostok, 2004), 242–43.
91. Habecker, "Russian Urban Administration," 238–39.

installations [*na kazennykh sooruzheniiakh*] the shortage of Russian workers makes itself felt, and depriving the residents of their right to use yellow labor—especially without being properly forewarned—would place them in an extremely difficult spot.[92]

Well-to-do denizens also profited from the presence of Asian workers. Doctors, pedagogues, and even members of the city Duma and council rented their property to Asians and had little incentive to get rid of them.[93] In 1914 the Duma came to a similar conclusion, stating that the removal of Asians "could not improve the sanitary conditions of the city nor could it improve the material position of the mass of working Russian people," who included petty traders and industrialists.[94] With the outbreak of the First World War that year, relocation plans were dismissed, and Asian migrants remained planted in the city center for several more years.[95]

The tsarist state had brought its governing experiments from the international border to the countryside and cities in the Maritime, establishing institutions of rule and law. Owing to its size and history of plural jurisdiction, the system of government was flexible, and peasants governed themselves through the village commune and through organs of self-rule, frequently ignoring mandates to abide by official law. This flexible system of rule was starkly visible in the Maritime border region. Koreans exercised wide latitude in government, using a deliberate mix of institutions, including Korean and Russian peasant models, to impose order, collect taxes, and punish offenders. They carried out basic tasks of governance and conducted surveillance, and tsarist officials relied on them to do so. In the close quarters of Vladivostok, too, where they lived and worked among Russians and Europeans, Korean and Chinese societies provided one of the primary means by which municipal authorities imposed order. Tsarist officials continued to decry the "barbaric" practices and mindset of the population, but they could not deny that Koreans, their labor, and their forms of rule had become indispensable.

---

92. Quoted ibid., 235.
93. "Na Semenovskom pokose," *Vladivostok*, July 28, 1896, 14.
94. RGIADV 28/1/391, l. 91 (January 8, 1914).
95. Other relocation programs took place outside of Vladivostok. The tsarist government built an agricultural complex, called Lavriu, for newly naturalized Koreans in Iman district in the north. Koreans who wanted to move from Vladivostok submitted applications through the Workers' Promotion Association. Ban, "Korean Emigration to the Russian Far East," 199; *Kwŏnŏp sinmun*, April 20, 1913, 2.

7

MAKING THEM ONE OF US

While Koreans were incorporated into the Russian empire through subjecthood laws and administrative life, they also became the object of two competing nationalist agendas, "Russian" and "Korean." In the nineteenth century, neighboring countries in Europe and East Asia began to assert common history, language, and religion—what can be considered "culture"—as foundational to solidifying the boundaries of the sovereign nation and undertook to mold their peoples into unique "nationalities."[1] Russia and Korea embarked on a similar path. Though beset by a different set of challenges, both tsarist officials and Korean nationalists instituted various cultural programs to respectively transform the expatriate population into loyal "Russians" and "Koreans." For tsarist officials, doing so meant grappling with the long-standing practice of maintaining difference between multiple ethnic and confessional groups and instead instilling in all subjects a unitary definition of what it meant to be a loyal Russian. Paramount were knowledge of Russian language and membership in the Orthodox Church.[2] Koreans, who ostensibly persisted in their "backward," "uncivilized" ways in administrative life as well as in language and thinking, stood as reminders to the tsarist regime that much needed to be done in the Maritime border region. Officials and clergymen from the Orthodox

---

1. Robert Crews, *For Prophet and Tsar* (Cambridge, MA, 2006), 294.
2. Crews shows that the criteria of religion and language competed with loyalty to the dynasty as measures of allegiance to the imperial order in the nineteenth century. Ibid., 302.

Church traveled far and wide to Korean villages to make loyal, "enlightened" Russians out of the population.

The integration of Koreans into the cultural life of the empire was carried out in fits and starts, stymied both by a lack of capable Russian missionaries to implement policies on the ground and by the participation of Korean intermediaries in these programs. The task of Russification fell largely on the shoulders of Korean leaders whose goals did not necessarily align with those of the church. Bilingual teachers and administrators seemed more intent on expanding the stature of their villages through new school buildings and ceremonies than instilling Russian ways in the people. Inspections of classrooms, infrequently carried out, revealed a dim understanding of elementary texts and a lack of knowledge of basic Russian language among school-age children.

After 1905 the arrival of Korean nationalist émigrés into the Maritime added a new "Korean" dimension to the cultural landscape. That year, Japan imposed a protectorate over Korea and began to crack down on political dissenters, who collectively formed the Korean nationalist movement. Hundreds of activists were driven abroad, primarily to Russia and China, where they set out to free Korea from its colonizer through methods as diverse as guerrilla warfare, diplomacy, and cultural programs. The activists believed that Korea's independence lay in the hands of political forces both internal and external to the peninsula, and they saw expatriate communities in the border regions as a logical base to stage their programs. For intellectuals, the expatriate community became a site of experimentation to create a nation outside Korea. Inspired by the idea that the colonized nation was not bounded by territorial borders but transcended them, émigrés hoped to mold their compatriots into loyal subjects of the nation by teaching them Korean language, culture, and history. Yet Korean reformers, like their tsarist counterparts, found expatriates "traditional" and "primitive" in their behavior, an obvious hindrance to the making of enlightened subjects.

While Korean and Russian nationalists attempted to transform the population into their respective ideals of a national people, local Koreans threw into question the assumption that being Russian and Korean were mutually exclusive identities. In their religious practices, daily customs, and homes, Koreans demonstrated that they were not ignorant of what it meant to be Russian or Korean, but that they understood the differences between the two seemingly disparate cultures and used them for their own ends. The same Korean who paid visits to her local shaman, a "native" practice that was criticized by both Russian and Korean intellectuals, also petitioned to be baptized into the Orthodox Church and recited the contents of a textbook on Korean history. To local Koreans, one's national identity—similar to one's legal status as a subject of a particular state—had become an interchangeable set of practices that they could selectively adopt to live and work.

This chapter examines the endeavors of tsarist agents to transform the Korean border population, the active accommodation of cultural practices by the population, and, after 1905, the imposition of a new Korean identity on the people. It shows that while the respective agendas of Russian and Korean nationalists were ostensibly at odds with each other, both subscribed to the idea that to be civilized, a subject needed to exhibit devotion to a single nation and adhere to specific types of moral behavior. By the early 1900s, ideas of "civilization" had become inseparable from the ideology of the nation. Instead of adopting a single country's customs and thinking, Koreans proved as adaptable in their customs and behavior as they did in methods of rule and governance.

Making Russians

By the early twentieth century, opinions about the assimilability of Koreans had changed little since the 1860s when the first Russian explorer Przheval'skii visited their villages in Ussuri. Many observers saw Koreans as pliant and docile. In his report of the Amur Expedition of 1910, Lieutenant V. D. Pesotskii expressed that Koreans were "good-hearted, honest, and trusting." Their character, he believed, had both positive and negative consequences. Their innocent, childlike spirit made them susceptible to trickery by fortune tellers, jesters, and vagabonds who arrived at their doorsteps in search of room and board and to the temptations of gluttony, which led them to consume massive quantities of food and wine "as if they had not eaten anything for several days." Yet this same quality also made them open to outside influence. Pesotskii believed that Koreans were adaptable compared to Chinese, who were deemed "incapable of assimilating." For while Chinese were "more intellectually advanced, more energetic, enterprising, proud of their centuries-old national civilization," they were, as a result, "ill disposed to adapting to the laws and rights of a country that is foreign to them."[3] Koreans, however, were "not stubborn in their national character [national'nost']." There was hope that the community would be a fertile ground for Orthodox Christianity and Russian ways to flourish; they had already proven themselves "soft" and "indifferent towards religion, ready to submit to any demand on our part," said an official in the 1880s.[4]

---

3. Pesotskii, *Koreiskii vopros*, 71, 72, 74, 95.
4. RGIADV 702/1/69a, l. 2–5ob (November 25, 1881) in Toropov et al., *Koreitsy* (2001), 38.

Estimations about their pliancy coexisted with doubts about their ability to assimilate. In the late nineteenth century world, a hierarchy of nations measured by a universal (Western) standard of civilization had been drawn up, and Korea sat near the bottom. According to one writer, Koreans had been born into a country with few traces of European civilization; it also idled on the lowest rung of East Asian civilization itself, rendering Koreans "inferior in many ways to their Chinese and Japanese neighbors from whom they still had much to learn."[5] Inside Korea, it was perceived, the people had no good models to emulate. The government was run by factions who "perpetually schemed against each other" and "dreamed about the profits they could extract from relations with European powers." According to Border Commissar N. G. Matiunin, such rulers had cultivated a corrupt system of "ceaseless stealing among officials, absence of any justice in the courts, abuse and punishment that are more cruel than in China, polygamy, slavery, and extreme despotism" that had, in turn, "spawned massive evils in the people." Korea, he concluded, needed "a most radical revolution," with an "overhaul" of the government and "reeducation" (*perevospitanie*) of the people. But he considered that neither Korea nor their neighbors China and Japan possessed the necessary "element" to instigate such a revolution.[6]

Russian nationalists believed that Russia should play its part in this corner of the world by bringing enlightenment to Koreans on its own territory. Similar to European imperial agents who brought salvation to their overseas colonies, Russian intellectuals imagined Siberia and the Russian Far East as spaces to be civilized. Officials took their earlier experience among the indigenous Gilyak, Buryat, Gold' (Heje), and other "primitive" peoples and attempted to apply it to Koreans. The people would be inculcated with "Russian principles, life, and education."[7]

The tsarist regime began to carry out a mission of Russification among Koreans as early as 1865, when Orthodox priests conducted baptisms of Koreans to complete their oaths as Russian subjects. The regime dispatched the same mission that had worked among the indigenous peoples of the Amur, Amgun, and Zeia regions. In the 1880s the Holy Synod established the Kamchatka Diocese and, in 1899, the Vladivostok Diocese to directly oversee the Far Eastern region. It soon founded an independent missionary station to oversee all Korean settlements in

---

5. M. A. Podzhio, "Koreitsy," in *Po Dal'nemu Vostoku*, ed. V. L'vovich (Moscow, 1905), 76.

6. N. G. Matiunin, "Nashi sosedi na krainem vostoke," *Vestnik Evropy* 126, no. 22 (July 1887): 77, 78.

7. Pesotskii, *Koreiskii vopros*, 97.

South Ussuri as well as four villages of mixed ethnicity.[8] By the 1890s, that number had expanded to six stations, and by the 1910s to twelve.[9]

The tsarist regime worked with the local elite to accomplish the task. A homegrown elite had taken charge of county and village administration and took it upon itself to bring the two "powerful lamps of Christian culture"—churches and schools—to fellow Koreans. From the 1890s to 1910s, the county administrations of Ianchihe and Adimi built a network of parish schools and churches, which were often housed in the same buildings. Benefiting from an idiosyncratic tax structure in which they were able to collect six times as much revenue as Russian districts, they paid for all or part of the new edifices as well as teachers' salaries and training and set themselves apart from poorer Russian villages, which depended on funds from the impecunious Holy Synod and Ministry of Education. Independent fund drives provided additional resources. When the building of a church in the Poset missionary station was delayed, Nikolai Nikolaevich Tsoi rallied villagers to donate timber, bricks, and money. Everywhere he went, he "pulled out an accounting book from his bag, asking [people] to donate as much as they could." Villagers from far and wide gave to the cause.[10] The two county headmen, Petr Kim and Petr Semenovich Tsoi (Ch'oi Chaehyŏng), a graduate of the first Korean parish school in Tizinhe in 1872, were so diligent in their efforts that the tsar and Holy Synod awarded them with gold medals engraved with the inscription "for zeal." By 1902 they had helped build twenty-nine primary schools in Ussuri with a total of 1,010 students. Half of the schools were Orthodox parish schools and half informal "literacy" schools; two additional schools were run by the Ministry of People's Education.[11] By 1923 the number of schools increased to thirty-five or forty.[12] In 1907 Poset district, which was densely settled by Koreans, had the most schools per school-age children (one for every seventy-four children) in all of Ussuri and one of the highest penetration rates with 86 percent of villages having at least one school.[13]

---

8. These four villages included Zanadvorovka, Bogoslovka, Popova Gora, and Ovchinnikov.

9. The six stations included Ianchihe, Mongugai (1888), Tizinhe, Adimi, Zarech'e, and Poset (1891). RGIADV 702/3/579, l. 4.

10. "Otchet Vladivostokskogo eparkhial'nogo komiteta pravoslavnogo missionerskogo obshchestva za 1902 g. (prodolzhenie)," VEV, no. 8 (1903): 166; RGIADV 702/3/579, l. 8.

11. "Otchet Vladivostokskogo eparkhial'nogo komiteta 1902 g. (okonchanie)," VEV, no. 9 (1903): 193–94. The 1864 education reforms confirmed tsarist ministries, including the Ministry of Education, as sponsors of primary schools. There were also Orthodox parish schools and those that were financed by peasant communities, including informal "literacy" schools. Ben Eklof, Russian Peasant Schools (Berkeley, 1986), 52–53.

12. RGIADV R2422/1/1492, l. 7–7ob.

13. The ratio of schools per school-age children was 1:87 in Suchan district, 1:132 in Suifun, and 1:147 in Khanka. In Khanka, 83 percent of villages had schools; for all of South Ussuri, 50 percent

FIGURE 6. Classroom in an Orthodox Christian church-school, 1904. Courtesy of the Arsen'ev State Museum of the Primorskii Region.

The growth of church-schools in Ussuri was accompanied by the building of impressive, lasting structures. As counties and individuals accrued revenue from land taxes and businesses, they poured money into constructing solid edifices made of brick and stone. The new buildings, which cost as much as twelve times the yearly salary of a teacher, could accommodate up to three hundred students. The most ambitious project was perhaps the church-school in Adimi, where Koreans erected a two-floor structure with four spacious classrooms, three rooms outfitted with stoves and beds, a dormitory, storage rooms, and a library.[14] Other schools were erected in Zarech'e, Mongugai, Tizinhe, and Ianchihe in the early 1900s.[15]

There was abundant evidence that church-schools were reaching their desired audience, the souls of young children. Matriculation rates attested to this. In 1908, 76 percent of male school-age children in Poset had enrolled in schools,

---

of villages did. "Otchet eparkhial'nogo nabliudatelia tserkovnykh shkol Vladivostokskoi eparkhii za 1906–7 uch. g. (prodolzhenie)," *VEV*, no. 19 (1908): 470–71.

14. RGIADV 702/3/579, l. 5–7.

15. "Otchet Vladivostokskogo eparkhial'nogo komiteta 1902 g.," *VEV*, no. 7 (1903): 143.

compared to 68 percent in the Russian-dominated Khanka district and 50 percent in Suifun.[16] Anecdotal evidence suggested that families went to great lengths to send their children to school. In one case, when no appropriate school existed in Tizinhe, concerned parents sent their children to the one in Ianchihe, located twenty *verstas* away.[17] Those who lived in Nikolaevka traveled even farther, forty *verstas* to Vladimiro-Aleksandrovka in Suchan, only to be turned away because there was no room.[18] Koreans in Vladivostok's Koreatown also gave their children to the Orthodox authorities to be baptized so that they could matriculate in the new parish school.[19]

Children and adults alike displayed their devotion to the church and Russia at public ceremonies held on school grounds. The celebration of a Zarech'e school opening in 1903 drew students and teachers from all over Ianchihe county, along with four missionaries from the Poset station and the diocesan inspector himself. After the inspector recounted the history of Koreans in Poset in an introductory speech, one person delivered his version of the community's past. In impassioned language, he described the tragic years of 1863 to 1867 when a famine had forced Koreans to leave their homeland, and he cited the growing number of schools, churches, and teachers as proof that his compatriots had committed to their new country. When he finished, the entire audience, who had sat in silence until the end of his monologue, shouted a resounding "Hurrah!"[20] At Christmas celebrations children displayed their faith by reciting prayers and singing carols.[21] For missionaries who visited their schools they sang well-known hymns, including "Many years, Master," which commemorated the historical arrival of the bishop from Constantinople.[22]

Orthodox education had also laid the grounds for the creation of a new generation who facilely straddled the worlds of the Korean and Russian village. By 1907 almost every household had at least one or two speakers of Russian. Graduates of parish schools also seemed to change both their "internal" and "external" way of life: they attended church services, learned the Orthodox liturgy, obeyed the laws of the Holy Confession, and in general led their

---

16. "Otchet eparkhial'nogo nabliudatelia tserkovnykh shkol 1906–7 uch. g. (prodolzhenie)," 471.
17. "Shkol'noe delo v Ianchikhinskoi i Adiminskoi volostiakh," *Nikol'sk-Ussuriiskii listok*, April 22, 1901, 2–3.
18. Nasekin, "Koreitsy Priamurskago Kraia," 29.
19. "Iz eparkhial'noi khroniki," *VEV*, no. 3 (1903): 60.
20. "Osviashchenie tserkovno-prikhodskoi shkoly v koreiskom s. Zarech'e, Pos'etskogo uchastka (okonchanie)," *VEV*, no. 2 (1903): 32–33.
21. "Khronika eparkhial'noi zhizni," *VEV*, no. 3 (1908): 81.
22. "Poezdka ego Preosviashchenstva v s. Zarech'e, Pos'etskogo uchastka dlia osviashcheniia tserkvi-shkoly," *VEV*, no. 5 (1903): 107.

lives according to the Christian faith.[23] Some chose to further their studies by attending seminary and "brotherhoods" whose mission was to disciple Orthodox Koreans and convert existing "Korean pagans." Members of such brotherhoods expressed their appreciation for new learning. "We strive for civilization, for progress," they stated. "This is our only goal which we strive for with all our heart—to renounce our old traditional superstitions, which frightfully prey on our intellect, and to follow the path of truth."[24] The new elite pursued careers in the church as Orthodox priests, teachers, and psalmists; in government as county and village secretaries and telegraphers; and in business as clerks in large trading houses, agents in small and large industrial enterprises, and suppliers to the Russian military.

Many tsarist officials and missionaries extolled the Koreans for their dedication. G. V. Podstavin, professor of Korean studies at the Far Eastern Institute in Vladivostok, believed that the proliferation of churches, schools, and brotherhoods proved that the "activity of missionaries found for itself completely auspicious soil."[25] In his report on the first five years of activity of the Vladivostok Diocese, former secretary A. Razumovskii agreed with this positive assessment, saying that "all the blessed results of the activity of the [diocesan] leadership . . . have met with the response of the Koreans themselves, and everything accomplished in this direction has been done with their participation." He also tolerated the tepid faith of recent converts: "If, internally, they still have been insufficiently inculcated with the spiritual principles of Orthodox Russian culture, then their external engagement with this culture—expressed in their attitude toward the church and school (donations for construction, interest in missionaries, teachers)—is extremely significant and evident, and merits all favor and praise." Such outward accomplishments contented church leaders because they still held hope that youth who had been "raised under the shadow of the church and church-schools" would be changed "internally" sometime in the future.[26]

At the same time, evidence showed that education had produced uneven results in the classroom. In Krounovka and Putsilovka, students could speak Russian, read Russian texts, and demonstrate knowledge of poetry and history,[27] but those in other villages had difficulty comprehending texts. Though they could recite the main events in the New Testament and short liturgical prayers in

---

23. "Otchet Vladivostokskogo eparkhial'nogo komiteta 1908 g.," *VEV*, no. 13–14 (1909): 390.

24. RGIADV 702/3/579, l. 9–10.

25. Ibid., l. 10.

26. A. Razumovskii (1906) quoted ibid.

27. N. Nasekin, "Koreiskii vopros v Priamur'e," *Russkii vestnik* 269 (1900): 27–28.

Russian, they could not explain their meaning. The inspector who evaluated the schools concluded that the children must have learned everything by memory.[28] Such difficulties followed students after they graduated from primary school. On completion of their education, Koreans hardly attended church and "[fell] into their own milieu—their former family life."[29]

There were multiple reasons for the ostensible shortcomings of schools. The first was a lack of personnel. The Orthodox mission suffered from a dearth of clergymen, who doubled as priests and teachers in parish schools. The Vladivostok Diocese, which oversaw all activities in Ussuri, struggled to attract Russian clergymen to Poset from among its own ranks, much less those from other dioceses. It seemed that rumors about Poset as a "backwoods," a place populated by people who were "inhospitable and foreign to the Russian person," had spread among church officials. Married clergymen, who were ideally suited for work among the settled Korean population, refused to bring their family to a place they imagined as "remote and backwater," while monks who did serve quit soon after their arrival. One monk renounced his clergy status entirely. The high turnover rate of priests, who selected and trained clergymen, did not help matters. In 1912 thirteen out of seventeen priests in the Korean missionary stations had served three years or less; three priests did not even live in the stations. After they had served the minimum required period, they sought posts in Russian parishes or preferred to remain without a post. The constant coming and going of priests forced those who stayed to oversee several stations simultaneously. Missions languished as a result.[30]

Lack of attention to teaching was cited as another reason for the lukewarm faith of Koreans. Clergymen were so overwhelmed with performing standard duties such as baptisms, church services, discipleship, and visitations, all of which demanded travel over long distances and rough terrain, that they were hard-pressed to find any quality time for teaching. Church officials discussed the possibility of creating an institute to train itinerant Russian teachers and to organize student field trips to the missionary station to facilitate closer relations with instructors, but nothing materialized. Apart from busy schedules, clergymen invested little time in teaching because they did not consider it a priority. Teaching sat at the bottom of missionaries' to-do list, as the diocesan inspector noted: "The missionaries themselves are hardly without guilt in this matter because few have been struck to a sufficient degree by the idea of missionary

---

28. "Kratkosrochnye pedagogicheskie kursy dlia uchashchikh v tserkovnykh shkolakh Vladivostokskoi eparkhii, byvshie v mae-iune 1902 g. (prodolzhenie)," *VEV*, no. 9 (1903): 208.

29. "Otchet Vladivostokskogo eparkhial'nogo komiteta 1904 g.," *VEV*, no. 15 (1905): 328.

30. RGIADV 702/3/579, l. 23–4.

work. Many of them, accustomed to a purely formal notion of schools, apparently do not agree that here—that is, in the educational-pedagogical part of school life—lies one of the most important elements of the success and entire future of their ministry."[31] This lackadaisical attitude pervaded the ranks of the clergy. They showed "no leadership whatsoever nor even a basic interest in teaching."[32]

Inadequate training was a third reason for the floundering of education. Korean schools followed the basic curriculum found in all four-year primary schools: Russian and Church Slavonic, grammar, penmanship, arithmetic, geography, Russian history, ecclesiastical history, New Testament and Old Testament history, and hymns and prayers. Teaching these subjects to native speakers of Russian and second- and third-generation Koreans was hard enough, especially since many of the textbooks used antiquated language from the 1830s,[33] but it was even more challenging when instructing newly arrived Koreans. Until the early 1900s, when textbooks were published for Koreans, Russian clergymen, most of whom did not speak Korean, used perfunctory memorization of Bible verses and prayers as the primary method of teaching.[34] It was no surprise, then, that children who were questioned about the meaning of a text could not explain it.

Despite their own shortcomings, church authorities still laid the harshest blame on the Koreans themselves. Over time, native Koreans had ascended to the majority of teaching positions in Korean villages. By 1902 thirteen out of nineteen schools in Poset had Korean teachers. Even in villages where Russian clergy resided permanently, Koreans played indispensable roles as translators and coteachers. Their Russian language skills, pedigrees, and commitment to Bible instruction made them sought-after instructors in Orthodox circles. Yet they were still deemed unnatural agents of Russification because they "always travel[ed] only among Koreans" and were "naturally imbued with a sympathy toward an intrinsic Korean way of life."[35]

Stories about ill-run schools stirred officials' doubts about Korean teachers, too. Instructor Petr Kim was one such example. Kim was featured in a piece

---

31. Ibid., l. 29–30.

32. "Otchet o sostoianii tserkovnykh shkol Vladivostokskoi eparkhii za 1902–3 uch. g. v uchebno-vospitatel'nom otnoshenii," VEV, no. 19 (1905): 437–38.

33. "Prisuifunskie Koreitsy," Vladivostok, September 3, 1895, 11.

34. These textbooks included First Russian Language Textbook for Koreans, Russian Speech, and the Volper reader. "Kratkosrochnye pedagogicheskie kursy . . . byvshie v mae-iune 1902 g. (prodol-zhenie)," 207–8.

35. "Otchet Vladivostokskogo eparkhial'nogo nabliudatelia o sostoianii tserkovnykh shkol Vladi-vostokskoi eparkhii za 1901–2 uch. g. po uchebno-vospitatel'noi chasti," VEV, no. 14 (1903): 312.

in *Vladivostok* by a reporter who visited his two-room school in Poset. The reporter expressed confusion at what he saw and heard. Though Kim claimed to teach Russian language using standard textbooks, his language skills fell short of the proficiency required for a teacher. Unable to form complete sentences, Kim resorted to speaking to the journalist in "Kor-Russian," a hodgepodge of chopped-up words that was commonly used by Russians and Koreans to communicate with each other. As for the students, they appeared to have made little headway in their lessons. Some had memorized the Russian alphabet and others could recite texts from memory, but no one could read farther than the third page of the alphabet book even though they had been studying it for more than a year.[36] Such accounts, though extreme, deflated any sense of achievement officials may have felt.

Apart from the faults of educators, the Orthodox mission believed it had conceded its sway over the project of Russification by relying too heavily on Korean county and village administrations to accomplish the task. Village societies had control over budgets, including educational funds that paid for school maintenance and teachers' salaries. Not having access to village ledgers, the diocese came to believe that Korean leaders had poured exorbitant amounts of money into building new schools and renovating existing ones, instead of paying for what it believed were more pressing needs, among them training. Officials also blamed teachers who used their bilingual skills to work in village administration as secretaries, translators, and recordkeepers. In their eyes, multitasking had not simply diverted teachers' attention away from the important job of instruction but, worse, had further subjected schools to the authority of village leaders, figures who symbolized "traditional Korean ways."[37]

At the end of several decades, on-the-ground observations revealed that Christian education and proselytizing had produced mixed results. Church-schools had become permanent fixtures in Korean villages and permanent expenditures in village budgets, but inside classrooms, understanding of ecclesiastical history and Russian grammar was dim. In 1881 Military Governor Baranov had pointed to the lack of Russian ways in Koreans' everyday lives. They avoided the chapels and schools that had been built in the 1860s, prayed to their ancestors, and learned from Korean textbooks. Baranov proclaimed that "not in religion, nor domestic ways, nor societal structures, nowhere and in nothing can you see our

---

36. "Korrespondentsiia: Iz Pos'etskogo uchastka," *Vladivostok*, July 7, 1896, 12–13.
37. "Otchet Vladivostokskogo eparkhial'nogo nabliudatelia . . . 1901–2 uch. g. po uchebno-vospitatel'noi chasti," 314–15.

influence."[38] Thirty years later, little seemed to have changed. In 1914 Border Commissar Smirnov summed up his views on Russification efforts:

> Koreans hide [traces] of Russian influence in their lives. For us they put on outward appearances, but among themselves, they—in soul, in religion, and everything we dislike—mix rituals of Christianity with Buddhism and shamanism in the same family. In most cases, Orthodox Christian rituals are simply ignored or merely fulfilled out of obligation, giving the advantage to shamans. In most cases, not only do the baptized not have crosses, but their homes lack icons, or they lie idle somewhere in a box.[39]

Comments about the "mixed" nature of the Koreans' lives revealed an underlying assumption that being Russian meant living out Russian customs to the exclusion of others. By this definition, Russification programs appeared to be a failure. Further investigation into Koreans' daily lives, however, revealed that a careful process of selection had taken root.

Negotiating Everyday Life

While tsarist officials and priests struggled to assess the outcomes of Russification, their comments suggested a subtle truth. The myriad reports that detailed an array of contradictory practices—the persistence of "traditional Korean" customs and the denial of "Russian" ones or the successful adoption of "Russian" ways and departure from "backward" ones—reveal that Koreans did, in fact, understand what it meant to be "Russian." As Smirnov notes, Koreans "mix[ed]," willfully "ignored," and "fulfilled out of obligation" the various religions for their own purposes. Through their actions and inactions, Koreans demonstrated that they understood the differences between the two seemingly disparate cultures and negotiated the boundary in between. In other words, to Koreans, being "Russian" meant knowing a set of practices and electing to exchange it for another. Where sources are silent on what Koreans thought, their maneuvers in everyday life—in performing rites, on their bodies, and in the space of their homes—illuminate these practices.

In celebrating and commemorating events in a lifecycle, Koreans appropriated "Russian" and "Korean" customs. Marriage was one example. Missionaries

---

38. RGIADV 702/1/69a, l. 2–5ob (November 25, 1881) in Toropov et al., *Koreitsy* (2001), 39.
39. RGIADV 1/12/574, l. 17–17ob (June 6, 1914).

complained that Korean marriages were on the whole "illegal" and barbaric practices. Officials deemed the matchmaking process authoritarian and unjust; parents decided who their children married without a thought to their children's "tastes," gave their teenage daughters to middle-aged men, and yoked young boys to women who were old enough to be their mothers. Further, despite their numerous pleas for Koreans to marry within the Orthodox Church, the majority of Koreans ignored them and chose to marry by "Korean" tradition.[40] The reality of Koreans' actions was more complex. Many Koreans married twice. They first lived in "Korean marriage," sometimes having two or three children, and after several years tied the knot for a second time in the church. Village societies also abided by the church's regulations in their own ways. County elders issued marriage certificates as required and ordered parents to prohibit their children from marrying young. At the same time, they altered the status of women who had already borne children to "single" or "maiden" on their newly issued certificates so their marriages would be legitimate in the eyes of the church.[41]

Similar decisions could be seen in infant baptisms. Koreans tended not to give their children to the Orthodox Church to be baptized right after birth, much to the dismay of missionaries who believed that their reluctance unnecessarily risked the security of their children's souls. "None of the Koreans speak about the birth of their children," a missionary noted. But their inactions were only temporary. They elected to follow "Russian" and "Korean" traditions whenever they deemed appropriate. Koreans hid their children until they were ready to have them baptized so that they would not have to answer to authorities who believed that they married too early. Gender also played a part in their avoidance of baptisms. Women, the primary caretakers of babies, would "run away" from missionaries when they visited their homes because the women deemed it unsuitable to interact with men outside the family.[42]

In death, too, Koreans adapted "Russian" and "Korean" burial rites to their own purposes. While no longer refusing Christian burials as they had in the past, Koreans usually waited three to five days before reporting a family member's death to the missionaries. In the interim, they performed their own "Korean" ceremony, itself a mix of Confucian ancestral and Buddhist practices. Entire families and villages gathered at the home of the deceased to pay their respects, pray, and

---

40. Nasekin, "Koreitsy Priamurskago kraia," 50–51; "Neskol'ko slov Koreiskogo missionera po povodu nekotorykh narekanii," *VEV*, no. 4–5 (1904): 89–90; "Chislo missionerskikh stanov v missii, nalichnyi sostav missionerov i deiatel'nost' ikh (prodolzhenie)," *VEV*, no. 14 (1905): 308.

41. County authorities had received orders from the superintendent to do so. "Neskol'ko slov Koreiskogo missionera," 90; "Otchet Vladivostokskogo eparkhial'nogo komiteta 1907 g.," *VEV*, no. 12–13 (1908): 328.

42. "Neskol'ko slov Koreiskogo missionera," 88–89.

eat. After the fifth day, Koreans allowed Orthodox priests to perform a funeral service in the church and bury the dead.[43] Still, Koreans did not leave the bodies to rest in the graves of Christian cemeteries. It was common for Koreans to consult shamans about the most auspicious places for burial, disinter the corpses, and then move them to suggested locations, sometimes across the border in Korea. In 1914 Koreans in Ianchihe confessed that they had disinterred and moved half of the corpses in the cemetery, leaving a smattering of crosses atop empty graves.[44]

Visitations to churches, temples, and shamans, in particular, demonstrated that Koreans crossed back and forth from "Russian" to "Korean" customs for different purposes. The same individuals who sought out Orthodox missionaries to heal the sick, pray for the dead, and prognosticate the weather also consulted with shamans and monks. Throughout the year and on holidays such as Lunar New Year and the Autumn Harvest Festival, Koreans visited Buddhist temples and traveled to remote valleys where shamans had built altars, totem poles, and idols to perform their rituals. Koreans also employed animistic methods to protect their villages. To ward off evil spirits, they hung an enormous idol with a Janus face, one side positioned toward the village and the other toward the outside world.[45] Those who could not travel benefited from the services of itinerant shamans. Traveling from house to house, these shamans performed routine prayers, divinations, and miraculous healings for the price of fifty kopecks or a ruble.[46] In one case, a villager threatened an Orthodox clergyman, a fellow Korean, for attempting to shut down the activities of a shaman he had employed.[47]

Adults also appropriated the rite of baptism to adopt a new country. During the project to register Koreans as Russian subjects in the 1890s, thousands of Koreans were baptized into the Orthodox faith, since pledging allegiance to the tsar and church went hand in hand. Few Koreans exhibited any understanding of the actual vows, yet their consent to be baptized signaled that they comprehended that a profession of faith was necessary to receive the benefits of subjecthood, including land and the right to remain in Russia. As seen in chapter 4, the fall of Korea to Japan in 1910 compelled more Koreans to seek an affiliation with the tsarist state. They flocked "in droves" to the Orthodox Church to be baptized, saying, "We have lost our fatherland, lost everything. We are left now only with one comfort—faith. But our own faith does not give us contentment. We are fond of the Orthodox Christian faith. We recognize it as the true religion

43. Ibid., 90.
44. RGIADV 1/12/574, l. 48ob–49 (June 23, 1914).
45. "Otchet Vladivostokskogo eparkhial'nogo komiteta 1905 g.," VEV, no. 10 (1906): 200–201.
46. Nasekin, "Koreitsy Priamurskago kraia," 47.
47. RGIADV 1/12/574, l. 6 (June 3, 1914).

and for this reason ask to be received into Orthodoxy."[48] Whole communities in Vladivostok, Poset, Suchan, and the villages of Ekaterinovka, Nikolaevka, and Taudemi inundated churches with petitions to be baptized. Even Christians who had belonged to the Rimsky-Catholic Church and Presbyterian denomination expressed their desire to be affiliated with the Orthodox Church.[49] Priests traveled throughout Ussuri to conduct individual and mass baptisms in the streams of the rivers.

Similar to ceremonies and rites, the space of the home and the bodies of Koreans displayed the interplay between "Russian" and "Korean" elements in their lives. Koreans chose not to build their homes along streets, as Russian officials ordered, but in courtyards enclosed by whitewashed walls or tall fences made of woven reeds. Their dwellings featured characteristic Korean-style thatched roofs, clay walls, underground flues (*ondol*), and papered sliding doors.[50] Inside their homes, objects representing the Russian state and church rested next to Korean objects. On the walls, portraits of the tsar and tsaritsa, crucifixes, icons of Christ and of various saints, framed cards of twelve Christian prayers, paintings of "Ecce Homo," and illustrated publications were hung next to pieces of homemade embroidery, braided strands of soybean, and plaits of hair that were used as "adornments."[51] Koreans also mixed Western-style tables and chairs procured from Russian villages with Korean furniture and utensils imported from Korea by merchants or made in Ussuri by local artisans. During her visit to Krasnoe Selo and Novokievsk, Isabella Bird Bishop described their neat homes and plethora of furnishings, which she took as signs of prosperity:

> Most of the dwellings have four, five, and even six rooms, with papered walls and ceilings, fretwork doors and windows, "glazed" with white translucent paper, finely matted floors, and an amount of plenishings rarely to be found even in a mandarin's house in Korea. Cabinets, bureaus, and rice chests of ornamental wood with handsome brass decorations, low tables, stools, cushions, brass samovars, dressers displaying brass dinner services, brass bowls, china, tea-glasses, brass candlesticks, brass kerosene lamps, and a host of other things, illustrate the capacity to secure comfort.[52]

---

48. "Otchet Vladivostokskogo eparkhial'nogo komiteta 1910 g.," *VEV*, no. 10 (1911): 320.
49. Ibid., 321–23.
50. "Prisuifunskie Koreitsy," *Vladivostok*, June 25, 1895, 9–10; Bishop, *Korea and Her Neighbors*, 226–27.
51. "Prisuifunskie Koreitsy," 9–10; Bishop, *Korea and Her Neighbors*, 229, 235.
52. Bishop, *Korea and Her Neighbors*, 235.

Such "plenishings" of comfort, while they may have represented Koreans' accumulation of wealth, were most likely gifts. Koreans often received candelabras and candles during baptismal ceremonies and home visitations by priests and missionaries. Others may have collected such luxury items to imitate the lifestyle of *yangban* elite in Korea.

Similar to their choice of furnishings, Koreans' style of hair and dress revealed a purposeful selection process. In Russia, Koreans' clothes had shed much of their traditional function of marking one's status in society and had become a symbol of one's national affiliation. Koreans easily changed their "native" (*rodnoi*) outfits to suit particular occasions, a practice that a Russian journalist called "mixed" dressing. For example, men continued to wear different hats to signify their commoner or elite status among Koreans, but when doing business with Russians, they wore "Russian" clothes on top of their native dress, an action that subordinated class distinctions to national identity. Others chose to mix and match native costumes: they donned an all-Russian outfit with Korean pants or an all-Korean outfit with Russian pants on the bottom or a peaked cap on top. Many Koreans, poor and rich, could afford to wear Russian clothes since they had received hats, shirts, and other clothing items as gifts at their baptisms.[53] Hairstyle, too, was easily adjusted to display one's national affiliation. Adults who had been baptized into the Orthodox faith cut off their topknots to show their new status as Russian subjects. During baptismal ceremonies, children, too, had their hair cut off.[54] These visual markers of national identity gained particular importance as geopolitical rivalries intensified at the turn of the twentieth century. One's clothes, whether "Russian clothes" (*russkii kostium*) or "Korean national clothes" (*natsional'nyi koreiskii kostium*) became a way for Koreans themselves to differentiate between "local" Koreans and those who were "foreign."[55] Additionally, when the Russo-Japanese War broke out, many Koreans took it on themselves to cut their own hair out of fear of being attacked by the Japanese. Short hair would signal to both Japanese and tsarist troops that they were baptized Russian subjects and thus deserved the protection of the Russian government.[56]

---

53. "Prisuifunskie Koreitsy," 10.
54. "Iz eparkhial'noi khroniki," 60.
55. "Otchet Vladivostokskogo eparkhial'nogo komiteta 1902 g. (prodolzhenie)," 167.
56. "Otchet Vladivostokskogo eparkhial'nogo komiteta 1905 g.," 199. In Korea, short hair did not symbolize national affiliation but a rejection of the traditional hierarchy. In 1895 the Chosŏn government passed a haircutting decree as part of the Kabo reforms. In 1905 the Ilchinhoe (Advance-in-Unity Society) also embarked on a haircutting campaign to embrace a "new look" for a "new civilization." See Yumi Moon, *Populist Collaborators*, 121–30.

Making New Koreans

Alongside tsarist efforts to Russify the Korean population, a new contingent of reformers hoped to mold the people in their own likeness: Korean émigrés. After 1905, self-avowed nationalists—a diverse group of guerrilla fighters, monarchists, Confucian scholars, and liberal intellectuals—fled the peninsula in increasing numbers to escape the violent strikes of the Japanese army and censorship controls imposed by Japanese authorities who had begun to encroach on all areas of political and economic life. The nationalists traveled to far-flung places, establishing bases in cities and rural areas that dotted the Pacific Rim and capitals of the world—San Francisco, Hawaii, Washington, D.C., the Netherlands, Kando, and the Russian Far East—to restore sovereignty to their country. From their bases abroad, they pursued multiple avenues of action. They took up diplomacy, petitioning foreign powers to chastise Japan for its takeover of Korea, and engaged in armed violence, raising Righteous Army detachments to battle Japanese troops in the border region. They also turned to cultural campaigns to raise awareness about Korea. Neither diplomatic nor violent in their approach, such campaigns aimed to create a "nation outside a nation" by instilling in expatriates knowledge about their country. This knowledge, nationalists hoped, would inspire a patriotic spirit and preserve the "national essence" (*kuksu*) of a country whose territorial sovereignty had been eclipsed by a colonial force. Inspired by anticolonial activists in India and Siam and the plight of oppressed peoples around the world, they charted a new path for reclaiming national sovereignty.

The key to realizing this vision was to identify a diasporic community that had already proven itself to be patriotic. Koreans in Russia were a logical choice. By 1905 they formed the second-largest population of Koreans outside Korea and had fought against the Japanese in the recent war, either as soldiers in the tsarist army or as fighters in guerrilla detachments led by Yi Pŏmyun. Those who did not fight donated funds to the cause. The community also belonged to a Western power that had helped the Chosŏn monarch during the tumult of the late nineteenth century when Japanese broke into the royal palace and killed the queen. After the revolution of 1917, the Soviet Union captivated the minds of Korean nationalists who were drawn to its socialist principles and promises to help emancipate colonized peoples. Perhaps the most compelling reason to choose Koreans in Russia was the practical consideration of geography. Ussuri was close enough to Korea that one could travel there in a day.

From 1905 to 1920, the Russian Far East bloomed as a vibrant center of nationalist activities. Many patriots who had studied in Japan and the United States endeavored to implement in Russia the democratic ideals they had learned and practiced abroad. They published newspapers for a local and transnational audience, formed mutual aid societies, and established cultural organizations with religious and educational goals. The first branch of the United Korean Association (Kongnip Hyŏphoe), a San Francisco–based organization, was established in Ussuri's Suchan district in 1908, followed by openings in Vladivostok, Khabarovsk, and Harbin. In a series of reorganizations, it was renamed the National People's Association (Kungminhoe) in 1909 and the Workers' Promotion Association (K: Kwŏnŏphoe; R: Razvitiia Truda) in 1911. It flourished even after the conclusion of the 1911 Russo-Japanese Treaty of Extradition in which the Russian government agreed to extradite to Japanese colonial officials any Koreans who were suspected of engaging in anti-Japanese activity on Russian soil.[57] Newspapers published in Vladivostok, including the *Hanin sinbo*, *Taedong kongbo*, *Kwŏnŏp sinmun*, and *Ch'ŏnggu sinbo*, became the voice of the nationalist movement after all forms of public expression were suppressed inside Korea by the Office of the Governor-General in 1910.

In promoting their nationalist agenda, activists were ostensibly at odds with the tsarist government, which aimed to imbue Koreans with its own national thinking. But their commonalities were striking. In language and in tactics, both groups employed a universal ideal of civilization that made hygiene, morality, and love of the nation the foundation not just of a loyal subject but of a modern, enlightened individual. Korean nationalists determined that the expatriate community should shun their primitive ways, adopt the habits and thinking of the modern person, and thereby preserve the nation.

Vanguard of the Nation?

Nationalists believed that Koreans who had left the peninsula for wealthier, more civilized countries such as the United States and Russia possessed the political and financial clout to liberate their country from the Japanese and elevate the backward thinking of their compatriots in Korea. The San Francisco newspaper *Sinhan minbo* boasted that Koreans in America had "breathed this new air" and "immediately developed a new way of thinking, discarding more than five-thousand years of corrupt thinking and, in one morning, broke stubborn customs."[58] That Russia may have lagged behind the United States in democratic

---

57. Hara Teruyuki, "The Korean Movement in the Russian Maritime Province," in *Koreans in the Soviet Union*, ed. Dae-Sook Suh (Honolulu, 1987), 4.

58. Quoted in Schmid, *Korea between Empires*, 249. The *Sinhan minbo* was previously named *Kongnip sinbo*.

institutions mattered little. For the tsarist regime had extended practical aid to compatriots by feeding poor migrants and proffering shelter, land, and the right to naturalize. As the Vladivostok-based paper pointed out, such generosity had provided the conditions for the growth of upwardly mobile Koreans who worked as secretaries, teachers, missionaries, and soldiers and attained the status of "heartfelt friends" with Russians.[59] Just as writers in America and China imagined their own expatriate communities as the best place for preserving the nation, so did those in Russia:

> If you look at the multitude of places where our compatriots live, there is America, there is China, and there is Japan. It is not our private opinion that these places all fall into second and third place and that Russia's Vladivostok stands in first place—it is a publicly acknowledged fact. First, our Great Han [Taehan] people are most numerous here. Second, the heart of the Russian empire toward the Great Han people is truly generous. Third, the economic situation [of compatriots] is better than that of Koreans elsewhere. Fourth, there is no particular hindrance as long as we do our best.[60]

With those in Vladivostok as the vanguard, Koreans abroad would "lead the twenty million compatriots, together proceed to a state of civilization, and thus recover our nation's rights."[61]

The workers' revolution of 1917 offered another source of inspiration to nationalist émigrés in the border region. Russia, which had already offered compatriots a place to live and work, now advocated a grand vision of liberation for all oppressed people and the birth of a classless society. Deeming Lenin's principle of self-determination as a radical alternative to Woodrow Wilson's own doctrine of self-determination, a group of Korean nationalists who were sympathetic to the communist cause cast their lot with Soviet Russia to aid Korea in its fight against the Japanese. They hoped Russia would provide material support through the funding of arms and military campaigns as well as through education by teaching that the enlightened were those who endeavored to overturn the existing social hierarchy. In the new world, the proletariat would be elevated to the position of the elite (*yangban*), while the elite reduced to the level of the commoner (*sangnom*). Enlightened Koreans in Russia would, in turn, lead their compatriots in

---

59. *Taedong kongbo*, July 29, 1909, 2, *nonsŏl*.
60. "Kwŏnophoe ch'angnip ilchunyŏn kinyŏm," *Taedong kongbo*, March 19, 1913, 1.
61. *Taedong kongbo*, March 10, 1909, 3, *kisŏ*.

this topsy-turvy world.[62] The nationalist intellectual Pak Ŭnsik expounded on this hope in his "History on Russian Territory":

> Because these compatriots have directly studied and observed the new education of the Russian Revolution, they are more prepared for their weighty responsibility to remake the fatherland than their compatriots in northern and southern Kando and America are, and have adopted action in the most circumspect and enlightened manner. In addition, they have the potential to supervise the new-thinking education [*sinsasangjŏk kyoyuk*] of our entire people [*minjok*] in the future. It is my sincere hope that this potential is realized.

Considering the multitude of benefits, Pak declared it "Heaven's will" that Koreans had crossed the border to Russia; they had prepared the path for the future of the Korean people.[63] Vladivostok Koreans beamed such hope that nationalist thinkers exhorted all Koreans to move to Russia.[64]

Though émigrés offered up unbridled praise about the benefits of living on Russian territory, they simultaneously expressed ambivalence about the material preparedness of their compatriots to lead the nation. Their discussions mirrored the contradictory comments made by tsarist officials, who at once extolled Koreans' ability to assimilate to Russian traditions and denigrated them for clinging to their backward, "national" Korean customs. While Korean émigrés admired the preservation of "national" customs, they, too, criticized the community for clinging to their primitive ways and for falling short in their knowledge of the nation.

In praise of Koreans in Russia, Pak Ŭnsik cited numerous ways they had preserved Korean practices. In language that resonated with that of secret envoys who had traveled to Russia in the 1880s, Pak wrote that many customs seemed to have "simply crossed over the river" to Russia: his compatriots had built villages of Koreans, respected their elders, and given and taken children in marriage. They had also been unwavering in their endeavors to become scholar-officials. He reserved his highest adulation for the autonomous system of village governance, which he called the "most satisfactory and beautiful" custom. Koreans had implemented the motherland's (*moguk*) system of village administration in which the elected head oversaw farms and markets, officiated marriages and funerals, and

---

62. *Hanin sinbo*, September 24, 1917, 1, *kisŏ*; Iv. Gozhenskii, "Uchastie koreiskoi emigratsii v revoliutsionnom dvizhenii na Dal'nem Vostoke," in *Revoliutsiia na Dal'nem Vostoke* (Moscow, 1923), 363.

63. Pak Ŭnsik, "Aryŏng silgi," 198, 159.

64. "Kwŏnophoe ch'angnip ilchunyŏn kinyŏm," *Taedong kongbo*, March 19, 1913, 1; August 1, 1909, 1, *nonsŏl*.

distributed welfare to the needy.[65] Finally, Pak highlighted how his compatriots had preserved the Korean language despite slight changes to everyday words. In Russia, pure Korean words had replaced words composed of Chinese characters: "*hwach'a*," fire wagon, had become "*pulsulgi*," and "*chŏnbo*," telegram, had become "*soijulgŭl.*"[66] "Even though fifty long years have passed under the powerful Russian policy of assimilating ethnic groups," he declared, "the thinking of their native country has not dissipated."[67]

The same attributes that embodied positive, nativist traditions, however, also elicited criticism, for they had impeded the development of modern, civilized habits. According to Pak, by preserving marriage traditions Koreans had committed a myriad of "inhumane marital vices of the past," in which eighteen-year-old brides were given in marriage to twelve-year-old boys, close relatives intermarried, men took second wives, poor families adopted future sons-in-law to marry their infant girls, and men consummated their marriages by force.[68] In addition, by striving to become scholar-officials, Koreans had not departed from the traditional "fever" for upward mobility and outward displays of prestige. They had acquired titles without the slightest understanding of what it meant to be a scholar-official and bought physical adornments to flaunt their newfound status. Pak complained, "If an official conspicuously displayed a mere jade insignia in his plait of hair, today, even the descendants of the basest classes [*ch'onmin*] are able to receive the treatment and title of a *yangban*."[69] He attributed their deficiencies to a low level of education. Though he understood that his compatriots had faced hardships and had been too "busy filling their mouths and stomachs" in their new land to devote themselves to education, he considered it inexcusable that they had failed to progress beyond the simple proverbs of Mencius and Confucius, produced no intellectuals to speak of, and refused to send their children to Russian schools because "traditional customs are so deeply ingrained."[70]

While Pak focused on Koreans in the countryside, other nationalist thinkers turned their attention to the uncivilized ways of migrants in cities. Echoing the complaints of Russian reformers, Korean intellectuals grumbled about the visibility of their uncivilized habits in the city of Vladivostok. They contrasted the filth of the Korean quarters to the spacious streets, tidy gardens, and colorful

---

65. Pak Ŭnsik, "Aryŏng silgi," 167–69, 184.

66. He also noted that Korean, Chinese, and Russian words were used together in a "mixed" manner. Ibid., 168.

67. Ibid.

68. Ibid., 169–70.

69. Such practices were not particular to the Koreans in Russia, but were prevalent in late Chosŏn. Ibid., 179–80.

70. Ibid., 192–3.

houses of Westerners' quarters, a difference as vast as that between "heaven and earth." Quoting the proverb "laziness is the root of all hardship," an editorialist claimed that such squalid living conditions proved that Koreans had simply reaped what they had sown. It was because of their laziness, he wrote, that adults allowed young boys who were no older than seven or eight to roam the streets of Vladivostok looking for goods to transport on their A-frames and permitted girls to cook and serve food in the markets, all while adults sat idly with tobacco pipes hanging from their mouths. He urged that the "poisonous disease" of laziness should be replaced with diligence.[71]

Émigrés reserved the harshest criticism for young migrant workers who had flocked to mining towns in Siberia and even Alaska. They deemed the migrants guilty of moral dissolution. Workers who had left Korea to earn money were reported to be squandering their wages in gambling houses and opium dens. Korean newspapers were littered with stories of wayward workers. Migrants who barely had ten *wŏn* in their pockets had wagered hundreds of *wŏn* in countless games of *yabao*, while others wandered in and out of inns in search of sexual pleasures with prostitutes and fell victim to opium addiction and occasional overdoses. In one case, a worker had died from consuming an opium-filled rice cake.[72] Editors and individuals, in response, exhorted migrants to pursue virtuous lives. In a poignant letter, one mother expressed her concern for her "unworthy son" who was pouring his earnings into gambling matches instead of sending money home. As she fell into arrears with her elder son's tuition payments and creditors demanded payment for various loans, she confessed she had lost countless nights of sleep.[73] Such reports left nationalist émigrés worried about the preparedness of their compatriots in Russia: "Why are they going to such a dirty place [gambling houses]? How can they be the future leaders of the nation [*kukka*]?"[74]

Added to their deficiencies in morality was an apparent lack of national consciousness. Intellectuals bemoaned that, similar to Koreans inside the peninsula, those outside had only a shallow understanding of their homeland and had forgotten their duties to the nation. An editor at *Kwŏnŏp sinmun* worried in particular that ignorance about national history had led to empty celebrations of holidays. He cited various examples, saying,

> Our compatriots have a feeble understanding of history [*yŏksa sasang*]. They know that the swallow comes on the third day of the third month,

71. *Taedong kongbo*, May 12, 1909, 1, *nonsŏl*.
72. *Kwŏnŏp sinmun*, March 8, 1912, 1, *nonsŏl*.
73. *Kwŏnŏp sinmun*, October 12, 1912, 2.
74. *Taedong kongbo*, October 8, 1909, 3.

but do not know that it is a celebration of Koguryŏ in the heavens. . . .
They know that the moon becomes full in the eighth month, but do not
know that it is the mid-autumn festival of the Silla period. They know
that they eat rice cakes on the third day of the tenth month, but do not
know that it is a celebration of Tan'gun.[75]

This lack of knowledge was accompanied by questionable patriotism. Both
Koreans who spoke Russian fluently and those who spoke it poorly were
deemed unpatriotic, the former for utilizing their skills for private profit and
the latter for neglecting to develop language skills that would be useful for
fostering diplomatic relations between their countries.[76] Similarly, émigrés
criticized Koreans for squandering the wealth of economic opportunities available in Russia. Instead of expanding trade ties with other Western countries or
donating money for the cause of the nation, Koreans had been lazy, stagnating
at the level of miners and farmers. They fared no better in the realm of politics.
According to intellectuals, Koreans, though having benefited from the protection of Russia and living in peace for decades, had failed to rally the tsarist
government to lend a "benevolent hand to Korea so that there would be a place
for all compatriots to return to."[77] Though the Koreans had resided in Russia
for nearly fifty years, observers concluded, they had not "managed anything
nor gained anything."[78]

What was to be done to ensure that Koreans were prepared to lead the nation?
As with the self-designated roles of the Russian Orthodox Church and government leaders, nationalist émigrés took it on themselves to reverse the backward
ways of their Russian compatriots. Fervent in their calls for civilization and
enlightenment (*munmyŏng kaehwa*), activists aimed to transform Koreans into
a new people, a people who would shed their selfish ambitions and traditional
thinking and cultivate a national essence by knowing "our country's language . . .
our country's history, and our country's beautiful customs and habits."[79] With
this agenda in mind, émigrés set out for Korean villages.

75. Koguryŏ and Silla were states that existed during the Three Kingdoms period (fourth to
seventh centuries). The former occupied territory in present-day North Korea, northeast China,
and Russia, and the latter the southeastern part of the Korean peninsula. Unified Silla existed from
668 to 935 CE. Tan'gun was known as the mythical founder of the Korean people. *Kwŏnŏp sinmun*,
June 8, 1913, 1, *nonsŏl*.
76. Pak Ŭnsik, "Aryŏng silgi," 178.
77. *Taedong kongbo*, March 17, 1909, 1, *nonsŏl*.
78. *Haejo sinmun*, February 26, 1909, 1, *nonsŏl*.
79. *Kwŏnŏp sinmun*, June 23, 1912, 1, *nonsŏl*.

New Schools, New Knowledge

Émigrés, local Korean leaders, youths, migrant workers, and Protestant missionaries from northern Korea and Kando experimented with promoting "new learning" among the expatriate community through schools and civic associations. The first three nationalist schools—Kyedong, Syedong, and Sindong (merged with Hanmin school in 1910)—were established in Vladivostok's New Koreatown after 1905 with the financial backing of wealthy members of the local Korean community and managed by activists who held leadership roles in organizations such as the United Korean Association and National People's Association.[80] To run these schools, the Korean society of Vladivostok collected donations from individual members, fees from parents and the three thousand inhabitants, and yearly soul taxes on migrant workers who passed through the city.[81] It was not only children who became the first students in newly organized schools, but workers themselves. Night schools in urban areas, including Vladivostok and Khabarovsk, educated laborers and petty merchants in ethics, history, and Korean language, as well as Russian and English.

With Vladivostok as a launching point, dozens of Korean-language schools sprang up throughout the countryside. These "unofficial" schools, which were self-funded, thrived in areas where large populations of "foreign" migrants lived, at the edge of legal settlements. In Nikolsk-Ussuriisk and Suchan district, for example, such schools constituted 84 to 94 percent of the total number of schools in 1923. By contrast, in Poset, where longtime expatriates had naturalized and established a system of self-governance and Orthodox schools in the 1880s and 1890s, self-funded schools represented just 48 percent of the total.[82] Most of these schools were established during the Civil War in the Russian Far East (1918–22), growing from a base of 45 to 50 schools before the war to well over 200 by the war's end.[83]

---

80. The Korean community decided to merge the schools after learning that all foreign schools were required to obtain an official permit. *Taedong kongbo*, August 5, 1909, 3; August 15, 1909, 3; September 5, 1909, 3; Yi Sanggŭn, "Noryŏng chiyŏk e ijuhan hanin e taehan kyoyuk," *Sahakchi* 28 (April 1995): 473.

81. *Taedong kongbo*, August 15, 1909, 3.

82. B. D. Pak, *Koreitsy v Sovetskoi Rossii* (Moscow, 1995), 137.

83. Schools were categorized as state-funded (35–40 schools) or privately funded. Private schools included those established by religious organizations, such as Lutheran and Methodist churches (45–50 schools); "Korean national" schools (*natsshkol*; 145–50 schools); and "Japanophile" schools, which existed only during the Siberian Intervention of 1918–22 (20–30 schools). The establishment of schools appears to have been the result of grassroots activity among local Koreans, but nationalist émigrés most likely participated too. Regardless of their origins, émigrés were quick to claim the schools as expressions of Korean patriotism. RGIADV R-2422/1/1492, l. 7–7ob (1923).

While it is difficult to know the range of Koreans' responses to the spread of schools, they were portrayed by nationalist émigrés as enthusiastic participants. Parents who had previously paid to send their children to Russian Orthodox schools as far as forty kilometers away, or did not send them at all, were reported to have sent their children to the new schools. In the village of Krounovka, parents pulled their children out of the local parish school so that they could attend a "secret school" run by a newly arrived émigré, who wished to teach children not only the basics of arithmetic but also Korean language, because he believed that Korean children should never forget their native tongue.[84]

Nationalist-affiliated schools quickly became places for children and adults to solidify their national "foundation" (*pon*) because there they learned Korean national language and history. They departed from the traditional curriculum of Confucian academies (*sŏdang*), which taught students in the "old language" of classical Chinese script, and instead guided them to read and write in the "new language" (*sinhangmun*) of han'gŭl, the vernacular writing system. By day, one could observe elementary students reciting the Korean alphabet "*ka na da ra*" using books imported from Korea or poring over the contents of nationalist newspapers published in Vladivostok.[85] At night, adults filed into schools after a day's work, commenting that their time there was far from a chore, but rather "quite fun." To prove that knowledge had the power to create true Koreans, *Kwŏnŏp sinmun* published a letter written by a worker who attended night school. Described as brimming with joy about his newfound knowledge, he wrote that it was only after he learned "my country's letters and venerated the language that the country fell" and that he became a full-fledged Korean (*Taehan saram*).[86]

National histories also constituted a fundamental part of the curriculum. Children learned the significant events marking the history of Korea, such as Pak Hyŏkkŏse's birth from an egg, an event that marked the beginning of the Silla dynasty,[87] and the genealogy of Tan'gun, the mythical founder of the Korean people. To deepen students' knowledge of the vernacular language and exhort them "not to forget their fatherland," émigrés translated histories from classical Chinese to modern Korean. Further demonstrating their devotion to education, émigrés and members of the local Korean community founded the publishing company Pomunsa in Khabarovsk and made plans to publish an official history of Tan'gun. They also hoped to complete a two-volume work *Patriotic Soul* (*Aegukhon*) about the fifty-year history of Koreans in Russia, not

---

84. RGIADV 702/3/515, l. 24–25ob (August 6, 1914).
85. *Hanin sinbo*, September 10, 1917, 1, *nonsŏl*; November 4, 1917, 3.
86. *Kwŏnŏp sinmun*, May 5, 1914, 2.
87. *Hanin sinbo*, November 4, 1917, 3.

only to inscribe these events into the larger history of Korea but to teach the expatriate community their collective history.[88] Such histories would substitute the Confucian classical works, which had been taught in underground academies for decades.[89]

Schools offered students the opportunity not only to learn the national language and history but also to perform it. Following the tradition of poetry competitions for Chosŏn literati, teachers organized poetry and speech contests for students and leaders of the community to display their knowledge about Korea. Hundreds and at times thousands of spectators gathered to witness students writing poems about Tan'gun on his birthday or the president of the nationalist association reciting a speech on a more contemporary topic, such as the colonization of the fatherland.[90] The Workers' Promotion Association and United Korean Association also sponsored weeklong speech competitions for literati, assigning topics ranging from elements of the existence of the Korean people (*minjok*), Confucian classics, Korean history, art history, principles of economic society, philosophy, and cultivation of the minds of youth.[91] People from inside and outside the country were invited to attend such events.[92]

National knowledge was also performed through plays and songs to celebrate holidays. During a New Year's celebration, teachers and students staged a reenactment of the Japanese occupation of Korea in the theater of the school in New Koreatown. In the play, the peaceful life of Koreans on the peninsula was interrupted by a militant foreign power, which trampled on them and turned the "land of the morning calm" into a country filled with "disorder, oppression, and violence."[93] Members of nationalist organizations themselves staged productions that commemorated heroes of the independence movement. At the Workers' Promotion Association theater, Koreans reenacted the suicide of Min Yŏnghwan, a late Chosŏn diplomat who had petitioned the Russian government to come to the aid of Korea; the life and death of the patriot Yi Chaemyŏng who had been killed by the Japanese; and the patriotic decision of a student named Choi, who had divorced his wife in order to study the Korean language.[94] The productions drew several hundred Koreans as well as Russian spectators for whom

88. *Hanin sinbo*, October 15, 1913, 3; November 4, 1917, 2; January 6, 1918, 2.
89. Not all Koreans were enthusiastic about learning modern history. A teacher by the name Yi, who had come to Russia "early on," attempted to stop schools from teaching in the neighborhood. Yi insisted on preserving classical learning. *Kwŏnŏp sinmun*, February 8, 1914, 1.
90. *Hanin sinbo*, November 4, 1917, 3; *Kwŏnŏp sinmun*, June 12, 1914, 2.
91. *Kwŏnŏp sinmun*, February 24, 1912, 3.
92. *Taedong kongbo*, March 17, 1909, 3.
93. "Teatr: Vecher v Koreiskoi slobodke," *DO*, January 9, 1911, 3.
94. *Kwŏnŏp sinmun*, January 11, 1910, 2; January 18, 1910, 3.

"Russian-style" and Russian-language acts were performed. Money from ticket sales was usually donated to schools that lacked funds for day-to-day expenses or to individuals who had fallen on hard times.[95]

Celebrations of the birth of Tan'gun, in particular, became occasions for the community to gather and participate in a national affair. Lasting through the morning, opening ceremonies began with speeches explaining the significance of Tan'gun's birth, continued with performances of songs that extolled Tan'gun and the nation and children marching with their fists clutched around national flags. A full banquet and theater performances were held at night. Hundreds of inhabitants of Vladivostok and its environs attended.[96] Commemorations also extended beyond the span of the day and outside the space of the theater through photographic technology. Choi, a native of Pyongyang, was reported to have obtained a copy of Tan'gun's portrait, reproduced it by the hundreds at a copy shop, and distributed the images to compatriots so that they could hang them in their homes and be reminded daily of the nation's forefather.[97]

Protestant missionaries, too, affiliated themselves with the nationalist movement and traveled abroad to raise the civilizational level of expatriate communities. They established churches, organized prayer meetings, and created "Jesus" schools where they mixed elements of the nationalist curriculum with teachings of Mencius, Confucius, and Jesus. To demonstrate what they had learned about the nation, children sang patriotic songs such as "The East Sea Waves and Mount Paektu" ("Tonghaemul kwa Paektusan") and recited the history of Korea at Christmas productions and other holidays.[98] Koreans also learned "civilized" practices from various associations that had been created for this purpose. Mutual aid clubs, youth education leagues, elderly societies, women's societies, and other organizations aimed to teach the importance of diligence and virtue in every area of life. Workers' "circles" encouraged thrifty habits; youth leagues promoted education and the development of "customs" as well as collected funds for the construction of new schools; women's associations taught rules of public etiquette and raised money for schooling; and opium-addicts-anonymous societies targeted addicts to help them kick their habit. Protestant missionaries participated in these moral campaigns, helping their compatriots turn from their "foolish ways, repent for these [habits], and nurture new ways."[99]

---

95. *Kwŏnŏp sinmun*, February 23, 1913, 3; March 27, 1913, 3; *Hanin sinbo*, December 31, 1917, 2.

96. *Kwŏnŏp sinmun*, February 10, 1912, 3; *Kwŏnŏp sinmun*, February 2, 1913, 2; *Hanin sinbo*, November 4, 1917, 2; November 12, 1917.

97. *Kwŏnŏp sinmun*, March 15, 1912, 2.

98. *Hanin sinbo*, December 31, 1917, 2.

99. *Taedong kongbo*, July 29, 1909, 1, *nonsŏl*.

The campaigns also spread to gold and coal miners in the depths of the Maritime, Amur, and Siberia. News about the homeland spread quickly in these tight-knit communities, especially each spring when a fresh crop of workers from Korea and Manchuria arrived with the latest news. As they passed through Vladivostok, a transit hub, workers also established contacts with émigrés and became familiar with the nationalist movement on Russian soil. Miners paid an audience to famous activists, including Yi Tonghwi, who traveled throughout Siberia to mobilize Koreans and establish chapters of the Workers' Promotion Association.[100] Newspapers reported on the enthusiastic response of workers. They started night schools, circulated newspapers, and joined societies to help remedy their various addictions. By 1914 ten thousand workers had joined the Workers' Promotion Association.[101] After visiting the gold mines of Alaska, a writer for *Kwŏnŏp sinmun* offered a glowing report: "I was very happy to see that our compatriots in the gold mines think about our country [*choguk*] night and day and help compatriots who are destitute or lost through their acts of benevolence and generosity. They have an abundance of patriotic spirit [*aeguk chŏngsin*]."[102]

Expressions of Korean patriotism culminated in Russia in the aftermath of the March First Movement in 1919. On that day, masses, young and old, gathered in Pagoda Park in the heart of Seoul to stage a peaceful demonstration against their Japanese colonizers. Recitations of the "Declaration of Independence," an assertion of Korea's natural right to nationhood, alternated with resounding shouts of "Mansei" (Ten thousand years) by the people. Protests sprang up in public areas throughout the peninsula and eventually spilled across national borders. On March 17, 1919, members of the National People's Association in Russia helped organize a demonstration in Vladivostok, which then spread to all corners of Ussuri, to Nikol'sk-Ussuriisk, Suifun, Suchan, and Spassk.[103] The patriotic mood of Koreans in New Koreatown was vividly captured by a Russian onlooker:

> The Korean settlement in Vladivostok is decorated with national flags and red flags: today is the Koreans' holiday—the demonstration of the independence of Korea. Meetings are held. A Korean demonstration moves from the Korean settlement throughout the city. Leaflets titled the "Declaration of Independence of Korea" are scattered on moving vehicles, racing throughout the city. Korean children and youth dominate the demonstration: this is the "Red flower of an awakening Korea."

100. *Kwŏnŏp sinmun*, June 15, 1913, 2.

101. Byung Yool Ban, "Korean Nationalist Activities in the Russian Far East and North Chientao" (Ph.D. diss., University of Hawai'i, 1996), 197–98; *Kwŏnŏp sinmun*, July 26, 1914, 1–2.

102. *Kwŏnŏp sinmun*, June 8, 1913, 3.

103. Pak Ŭnsik, "Aryŏng silgi," 198.

The Russian proletariat joins the demonstration. A special Korean delegation delivers to all consuls the "Declarations," which are printed in English, Russian, Chinese, and Korean. A Japanese gendarme looks on, scurries through the Korean *fanzas*, and tears up the leaflets. . . . The single-heartedness of the Koreans is manifested with great strength. Korean demonstrations also occurred in other cities of the Maritime.[104]

For a brief period from 1905 to the 1920s, Korean nationalist organizations carried out a flurry of campaigns to disseminate knowledge about the nation among their compatriots in the Maritime. Significant to their plan were local Korean leaders who crossed the boundaries between local and national, secular and religious institutions. Their efforts mirrored those of tsarist officials, who relied on the same transnational leaders to implement their Russification programs and subscribed to a similar ideology of civilization—that all people should be loyal to a single state and exhibit enlightened thinking and practices. Koreans were exposed to both sets of national practices, pursuing opportunities when they suited their needs, educational, moral, and financial. In the 1910s war and revolution precipitated an end to the tsarist regime's cultural policies. Korean émigrés, meanwhile, inspired by the promise of a communist revolution, renewed their campaigns. And naturalized Korean-Russians, who had fought in the Russian army against Germany on the western front, set out to mobilize their compatriots in the Maritime toward revolution. With communism as the new ideal, however, they strove not to make "Russians" or "Koreans," but new socialist citizens.

104. A. N. Iaremenko, "Dnevnik kommunista," in *Revoliutsiia na Dal'nem Vostoke* (Moscow, 1923), 216–17; Hara Teruyuki, "Korean Movement," 13.

Epilogue

DENOUEMENT OF BORDERS

In the 1920s the project of border making passed to the Soviet Union and Japan. Japan had incorporated the Korean peninsula into its empire and expanded beyond Korea's borders, deepening its administrative and military infrastructure in Manchuria. In the Soviet Union the Bolsheviks took power on the heels of a far-reaching revolution and civil war, which flung open the eastern border region to multiple domestic and international contingents. The Bolsheviks found themselves vying for sovereignty in the Russian Far East against an array of Reds, Whites, and partisans, while eleven foreign expeditionary forces, including 73,000 Japanese, plunged into the war, adding to the chaos.[1] Thousands of Korean partisans took up arms as well. Driven out of their native land, they staked out positions in Russian factions to fight a proxy war against a common enemy.[2]

---

1. The partisan movement comprised heterogeneous contingents of peasants, miners, Cossacks, Chinese, and Koreans who pledged allegiance to Whites, Reds, and various Russian leaders. Among expeditionary forces, the Japanese were the largest, followed by 55,000 Czechs, 12,000 Poles, and 9,000 Americans. For the Japanese army, the goal was the creation of an anti-Bolshevik buffer state east of Lake Baikal; it also hoped to gain concessions that it had failed to obtain in the aftermath of the Russo-Japanese War of 1904–5. Stephan, *Russian Far East*, 131–37; Edward Drea, *Japan's Imperial Army* (Lawrence, KS, 2009), 141–43.

2. Figures for the number of Korean participants in the civil war vary widely. Boris Pak gives a figure of 10,000–15,000 but offers no source, while Anosov gives a more conservative estimate of 3,000. B. D. Pak, *Koreitsy v Sovetskoi Rossii*, 108; S. D. Anosov, *Koreitsy v Ussuriiskom krae* (Khabarovsk, 1928), 8.

Gradually, one by one, each contingent fell, and in November 1922, a month after Japanese soldiers left Vladivostok, the Bolsheviks claimed victory in the east.

The war had ended, but suspicions of enemies, both internal and external, continued to shape how the new Soviet regime governed its border region and border populations, including Koreans. The Maritime remained a geopolitically sensitive region in the face of an aggressive Japan, which, notwithstanding its retreat from Russian territory, had shown by its recent actions in Siberia and Manchuria that it had not yet finished its imperialist run in the region. Its claims over Koreans as subjects of the Japanese empire also rankled Soviet authorities, who watched Japanese soldiers overstep international boundaries in order to track down and arrest guerrillas and other émigré leaders involved in the Korean nationalist movement. Indeed, Japanese armies, fearful that such "unruly Koreans" would infiltrate Korean communities in the border region and spread subversive "Bolshevik" ideas, conducted periodic raids on villages in the Maritime and Kando. During the civil war, the Japanese command issued a warning to the local Maritime government, saying that it would take steps to control "our subjects in the region, including Koreans." In April 1920 it stormed Vladivostok and ordered the dissolution of Korean socialist organizations, claiming the lives of three hundred Koreans and arresting another one hundred in the process.[3] Japanese consular police and army forces also staged "search and destroy" campaigns in Kando later that year, killing three thousand Koreans.[4] The Soviet regime responded to Japanese reprisals by withdrawing its support of Korean nationalist groups in the region. It could not tolerate the possibility that Japan would use its authority over colonial subjects as a pretense to infringe on Soviet territory.[5]

Subsequent reports revealed that Soviet leaders continued to believe that Japan would use the Korean population to extend its jurisdiction into the Maritime. They considered that Koreans, "long-term enemies of the Japanese, who were

---

3. Later known as the April Disaster, the incident also involved Japanese attacks on Russian revolutionaries and Koreans in Ol'ga, Nikol'sk-Ussuriisk, Khabarovsk, and Shkotovo. Wada Haruki, "Koreans in the Soviet Far East," in *Koreans in the Soviet Union*, ed. Dae-Sook Suh (Honolulu, 1987), 17–18; Ban, "Korean Nationalist Activities," 452–53.

4. This was known as the Kando/Jiandao Incident. It should be noted that ordinary Korean villagers entreated Japanese consular police in Kando to protect them from the depredations of criminal gangs and Korean anti-Japanese resistance groups. Ban, "Korean Nationalist Activities," 465; Esselstrom, *Crossing Empire's Edge*, 72–78.

5. The Soviet Union formally agreed to discourage anti-Japanese movements on its territory in the 1925 Soviet-Japanese Treaty. The Chinese government lodged similar protests against Japan's interference in the affairs of Koreans in Manchuria; the two powers signed the Mitsuya Agreement in 1925 in which the Chinese agreed to help clamp down on anti-Japanese activities on its territory. Ban, "Korean Nationalist Activities," 453–54; Esselstrom, *Crossing Empire's Edge*, 87–88; Hyun-Gwi Park, *The Displacement of Borders among Russian Koreans in Northeast Asia* (Amsterdam, 2018), 73.

forcing them out of their own land, can some day turn into a tool of intrigue for some imperialist state against the USSR."[6] These fears were reiterated in a 1929 report, which stated that Japan viewed Korean migration to the Soviet Union "as the natural expansion of the boundaries of Korea, which at the proper moment could be claimed formally."[7] Concerns about Koreans' ties to an external power exacerbated internal anxieties about land possession among ethnic groups in the Maritime Province. The socioeconomic gap between Koreans and Russians had widened over the years. In the early 1920s, approximately 84 percent of Korean households were landless. In 1925, 69 percent of Koreans cultivated exclusively rented lands (versus 8 percent of Russians), and the average Korean household possessed plots of land that were one-third the size of those of Russians. Under the Soviet policy of transferring land to the tiller, the government would have to expropriate Russian-held land and redistribute it among Korean tenants. Russian peasants, however, were reluctant to give up land and responded by refusing even to rent land to Koreans. They demanded the resettlement of Koreans to a different region.[8] Ethnic tensions over the land question rumbled on through the 1920s.

To solidify the boundaries of its political community, the Soviet regime pursued a familiar strategy toward Koreans, one that centered on citizenship, migration, and cultural policies. The regime had more Koreans to manage than the tsarist state. The population had continued to grow over the years: in 1923 there were 107,000 Koreans in the former South Ussuri region; 123,000 in 1926; and 150,000 in 1929.[9] According to the 1926 All-Union Census, the Korean population in the entire Russian Far East stood at 168,000.[10] Since the early 1910s, about one-third of Koreans possessed Russian subjecthood or Soviet citizenship. The rest were de facto considered Japanese subjects. For the socialist state, ensuring that territory along the eastern border was held by bona fide Soviet citizens was not only an ideological necessity but also a safeguard, and it decided to accept petitions from the population to naturalize. Officials gave priority to Koreans who were able to demonstrate that they had worked on their present land

---

6. Quoted in German N. Kim, "The Deportation of 1937 as a Logical Continuation of Tsarist and Soviet Nationality Policy in the Russian Far East," *Korean and Korean American Studies Bulletin* 12, no. 2–3 (2001): R26.

7. Quoted in Terry Martin, *Affirmative Action Empire* (Ithaca, 2001), 317–18.

8. Ibid., 317.

9. The 1923 figure is for Primorskaia *guberniia* and the 1929 figure for Vladivostok *okrug*. Though their boundaries differed from those of former South Ussuri, Koreans remained concentrated in the southernmost part of all of these districts. RGIADV R-2422/1/1503, l. 70; Anosov, *Koreitsy v Ussuriiskom krae*, 8, 28–29, 30; *Itogi perepisi Koreiskogo naseleniia v 1929 g.*, IV.

10. Wada Haruki, "Koreans in the Soviet Far East," 34.

allotments for at least two years, as well as to those who could prove that they had lived in the Far Eastern territory (Dal'krai) since late 1922, when the region was formally appended to the USSR.[11] From 1923 to 1926, the government received 18,000 petitions for citizenship; it approved 10,500 of them. An estimated 40 percent of Koreans in former South Ussuri had become naturalized citizens by the end of that period.[12]

Though imputing a legal status onto the existing Korean community was, in theory, a manageable task, it became decidedly more difficult when considering the elasticity of the population, a result of the continuous inflow, outflow, and internal mobility of migrants. By the early 1920s, Kando's Korean population had outpaced the Maritime's by a ratio of at least two to one, but the latter remained a choice destination. In addition to large-scale construction, farming, and mining enterprises, more recent innovations in rice paddy cultivation beckoned seasonal laborers to the region.[13] Korean laborers held a virtual monopoly in this sector, leasing land from individual farmers as well as collective (*kolkhozy*) and state farms (*sovkhozy*).[14] In January 1926, hoping to break the pattern of back-and-forth movement, the Commissariat of Foreign Affairs demanded emergency measures to stop Korean migration. In December the Council of Labor and Defense mandated "decisive action" to restrict Koreans from entering the USSR, and it brought to the attention of authorities that future migration must be regulated according to laws that were already in place.[15] Further, in a move that harkened back to one of the first "ethnic bans" enacted by the tsarist regime exactly four decades earlier, the central government issued a secret decree to resettle Koreans to the area north of Khabarovsk—far removed from the border region. Those who had not yet received land would be resettled. The Koreans would be replaced by Slavic peasants from the central regions of Russia.[16]

---

11. The legal code demanded the eviction of noncitizen squatters from state lands. The law was intended to help prevent white landowners from reoccupying their former estates. Jonathan Bone, "Asia Stops Here" (paper presented at the American Association for the Advancement of Slavic Studies Conference, St. Louis, November 1999), 18n66.

12. Wada Haruki estimates that the number of naturalized Koreans in the entire Maritime Province was higher. Anosov, *Koreitsy v Ussuriiskom krae*, 29; Wada Haruki, "Koreans in the Soviet Far East," 34.

13. From 1923 to 1929, rice fields grew to more than 20,000 hectares in total area. GAPK 1125/1/51, l. 10.

14. Koreans cultivated 85 percent of rice paddy fields in the Three Eastern Provinces of Manchuria and eastern Mongolia in 1931. Wada Haruki, "Koreans in the Soviet Far East," 35; Ki-hoon Kim, "Japanese Policy for Rural Korean Immigration to Manchukuo, 1943–1945" (Ph.D. thesis, University of Hawaii, 1992), 54.

15. Martin, *Affirmative Action Empire*, 318; Jonathan Bone, "Socialism in a Far Country" (Ph.D. diss., University of Chicago, 2003), 253.

16. The resettlement plan was put on hold. Martin, *Affirmative Action Empire*, 318–19.

While the regime attempted to align the legal and land status of Koreans to conform to its borders, it simultaneously sought to transform the ideological thinking of Koreans and exhort them to participate in the great socialist experiment. Recent scholarship has recognized that the Bolsheviks set for themselves the task of building socialism in a large multiethnic state and that, in part to accelerate the Marxist historical process and in part to garner the support of the people, they undertook to create titular "nationalities" from the many ethnic groups.[17] To that end, they encouraged Koreans to study Korean language and engage in Korean culture. By 1926 Korean had been approved as the official language of administration in Poset district. A host of new establishments sprang up to raise the "national" consciousness of Koreans and spread knowledge of Marxist-Leninist teachings, including pedagogical institutes, schools, publishing houses, newspapers, and half a dozen journals.[18] All activities were conducted under the leadership of Korean members of the Communist Party, regional administration, and heads of village soviets.[19]

The march to "Sovietize" people and territory accelerated during the collectivization campaigns of the late 1920s and precipitated a wave of violence and a swift reversal in migration. In December 1927 the Fifteenth Party Congress declared the collectivization of agriculture to be the main task of the Communist Party. Proclaiming a "revolution from above," Stalin decreed the expropriation of land from so-called kulaks, the tethering of peasants to collective farms, and the seizing of their land and livestock. Massive killings, protests, and a famine ensued. A year later, the "revolution" came to the Russian Far East, and landless Koreans turned out to be some of the most avid proponents of collectivization. Exploited as tenant farmers by Russian and Korean landowners, many jockeyed to gain their share of land and to find a shortcut to citizenship status. By the start of 1930, about 90 percent of land in Poset and Suifun districts had been collectivized.[20] Collectivization, however, deepened social and ethnic cleavages.

17. Hirsch shows that the Bolsheviks' long-term goal was to move the entire population through the Marxist trajectory of historical development, in which feudal-era clans and tribes became nationalities, nationalities became socialist-era nations, and nations were eventually merged under communism. The Bolsheviks saw themselves as the sponsors of this evolutionary process. Francine Hirsch, *Empire of Nations* (Ithaca, 2005), 1–20.

18. The main Korean newspaper was *Sŏnbong* (*Avangard*), an organ of the Korean Bureau of the Far Eastern Regional Committee of the Communist Party of the Soviet Union. O Sŏngmuk became editor in chief in 1929. For a collection of other Korean-language newspapers published in the Russian Far East during the Soviet period, see publications by Hallim Taehakkyo Asea Munhwa Yŏn'guso.

19. Michael Gelb, "An Early Soviet Ethnic Deportation," *Russian Review* 54, no. 3 (1995): 395–96; Wada Haruki, "Koreans in the Soviet Far East," 37–38.

20. Wada Haruki, "Koreans in the Soviet Far East," 40.

Confronted by a sharp turn in their fortunes, landowning Slavic peasants lashed out at the Korean and Chinese population. Peasants and party members carried out violent beatings against Koreans.[21] Whether in reaction to violent encounters or to collectivization itself, Chinese left in droves. Approximately 50,000 Koreans fled across the border to Manchuria from October 1929 to March 1930, taking their horses, cows, and other belongings with them.[22] The consistent growth of the Korean population was halted for the first time since the beginning of their migration to the Maritime. Between 1929 and 1932, the Korean rural population fell by almost 25,000, while the urban population increased by 30,000, figures that yielded a net increase of only 5,000 Koreans (see table 1).[23] The loss of a significant labor force left the region with a crisis in the coal-mining industry and severe grain shortages, which subsequently led to hunger riots in the spring of 1930.[24] The revolution that was intended to invigorate the economy had instead depleted the region of its workers.

In the 1930s suspicions surrounding enemies of the state that had rumbled for a decade widened amid international pressures, social tensions, and an intensification of class war throughout the country. The consequences were grave for all, including the most loyal and hardworking of party members and toilers, who found themselves accused of conspiring against the people and state and were subsequently arrested and killed. Those who lived in sensitive border regions, where internal threats converged with external ones—notably, the German and Japanese threat—were categorically condemned as "enemies" and "unreliable elements." The regime reevaluated its support of "national" cultures and, in the mid-1930s, began to remove Germans, Poles, Finns, and other "diasporic" groups, who might foster ties with their original countries, away from border areas and resettle them in the interior of the country. Most were moved to Siberia and Central Asia.[25] In the east, Soviet leaders adopted similar measures toward Koreans. Koreans came under increasing suspicion in the wake of Japan's military ventures in Manchuria. In 1931 Japan's Kwantung Army staged an explosion near Mukden and used it as a pretext to establish its own regime in Manchuria the following year. By 1936 relations between Japan and the Soviet Union had soured to the point that the Japanese government reinstated the Soviet Union as its first enemy,

---

21. Ibid., 42; Martin, *Affirmative Action Empire*, 323.

22. Still, as reported by Korean soviets, some families who had left in 1929 returned the following year, raising questions about how to issue identification papers. GAPK 48/4/50b, l. 66–70; Wada Haruki, "Koreans in the Soviet Far East," 40; Martin, *Affirmative Action Empire*, 323.

23. *Itogi perepisi Koreiskogo naseleniia v 1929 g.*, IV; *K voprosu o migratsii Koreiskogo naseleniia.*

24. Wada Haruki, "Koreans in the Soviet Far East," 40.

25. Martin, *Affirmative Action Empire*, 328–33.

along with the United States.[26] In this tense atmosphere, Koreans, who were associated with the Japanese empire, were stigmatized as a disloyal people. Many were arrested. In July 1936 the Far Eastern Regional Committee decided to take concrete action and petitioned the Council of People's Commissars (Sovnarkom) to change the status quo on the eastern border. The committee stated that it wished to frustrate "the aggressive tactics of the local authorities in Manchuria and the Japanese, who exploit every border crossing from our side, either to recruit spies and saboteurs or to make various accusations against the Soviet Union."[27] Recognizing the need to protect the country's sovereign borders, it planned to remove Koreans from the Maritime and thereby extinguish any opportunity for Japanese influence to seep across the border and into the communities.

The proposed resettlement was a deportation, a removal of all Koreans from the Russian Far East. The deportation was unprecedented, differing from the resettlements of Germans, Poles, and Finns from the border areas of Ukraine and Leningrad in 1935–36 because it targeted *only* ethnic Koreans and aimed to resettle the *entire* population from the region. The plan, though initially conceived by Joseph Stalin and Viacheslav Molotov in August 1937 to cover just a handful of administrative districts close to the border, quickly expanded in scope to encompass all Koreans, regardless of whether they lived near or far from the actual boundary. It seems that V. V. Chernyshev, assistant head of the People's Commissariat of Internal Affairs (NKVD), had requested permission from his superior, Nikolai Ezhov, to carry out the plan to the fullest. His reasoning was strikingly similar to that of officials who had earlier argued for the resettlement of Koreans. He stated that "to leave these few thousand Koreans in the Far Eastern region (Dal'krai), when the majority have been deported will be dangerous, since the family ties of all Koreans are very strong. The territorial restrictions on those remaining in the Far East will undoubtedly affect their mood and these groups will become rich soil for the Japanese to work with."[28] Ezhov agreed with the assessment and, at Stalin's request, personally oversaw the operation.[29]

The forced migration of Koreans was the first instance of a deportation of an entire ethnic group by the Soviet regime. The operation was executed swiftly, most likely because it occurred at the onset of the mass operations of the Great Terror. In the short span of six weeks in autumn 1937, more than 170,000 Koreans were transported by train from their homes in the Far East to Kazakhstan

---

26. Wada Haruki, "Koreans in the Soviet Far East," 47.
27. Quoted in Martin, *Affirmative Action Empire*, 333–34.
28. Ibid., 334.
29. Bone, "Socialism in a Far Country," 258.

and Uzbekistan.[30] The 2,500 Koreans who protested were pronounced guilty of "counter-revolutionary agitation" and shot to death.[31] The 170,000 Koreans represented nearly a quarter of the 800,000 individuals who were arrested, killed, or deported in mass operations that targeted ethnic groups between 1935 and 1938. And victims of such ethnonational operations constituted one-third of the total number of political victims of the Great Terror.[32] Immediately following the deportation, the NKVD's Resettlement Section collaborated with the Red Army and local governmental organs to transport demobilized Red Army soldiers to the Maritime border region. From 1938 to 1946, tens of thousands of Slavic troops and their families settled in the region.[33] They occupied the land, gardens, and homes that Koreans had left behind.

When Japanese officials learned about the deportation, they protested. In November 1937 the Japanese embassy in Moscow wrote to the Soviet government, reminding officials about citizenship laws. Similar to earlier debates, the Japanese stated that Korean law—and by extension Japanese law—did not allow Koreans to abandon their nationality; Koreans abroad retained their status as Korean (now Japanese) subjects even if they had naturalized as subjects of a different state. As such, the Soviet government was not allowed to do as it wished in regard to the population. The NKVD, however, rejected Japan's claims, saying that it had no right to intervene in Koreans' affairs because they were already Soviet citizens.[34] There was little that Japan could do. By deporting Koreans to a remote region of Central Asia, out of the sight of foreign authorities, and by replacing the "disloyal" Koreans with a Slavic military population, the Soviet regime had brought all disputes about this borderland people to an end.

The deportation of Koreans was the conclusion of a sovereignty project that figured around the state's attempt to attain its ideal form: the alignment of state

---

30. The figure of 171,781 individuals was equivalent to 36,442 families. About 11,000 Chinese were deported with the Koreans. Koreans from Kamchatka and other remote regions in the Far East were resettled later that year. Recent studies show that Koreans were also deported to Astrakhan and Rostov *oblasts*. Martin, *Affirmative Action Empire*, 335–36; Bone, "Socialism in a Far Country," 258; German N. Kim, "Deportation of 1937," R34–R35.

31. Bone, "Socialism in a Far Country," 262–63.

32. Martin, *Affirmative Action Empire*, 340. For an interpretation of the terror (1936–38), see Stephen Kotkin, *Magnetic Mountain* (Berkeley, 1995), 280–354.

33. An estimated 19,700 households were resettled. The program was temporarily suspended in 1941 due to the war and resumed in 1946. Bone, "Socialism in a Far Country," 182–83.

34. The Soviet government claimed that Koreans were citizens, but their status was unclear. The 1930 citizenship law declared that any resident of the USSR would be deemed a Soviet citizen as long as he "has not [already] proven his belonging to the citizenship of a foreign government." Koreans, however, were rarely able to prove this. Wada Haruki, "Koreans in the Soviet Far East," 52; Bone, "Socialism in a Far Country," 256.

authority with territorial borders and people. Resettlement, a common practice of managing the population in a vast state, had been proposed regarding Koreans many times in the past by tsarist officials who endeavored to deflect the claims of neighboring countries on the population and their potential claims on territory. Moving Koreans from the border area, it was also hoped, would weaken their affinities of kinship, culture, and loyalty to their original country and strengthen their attachment to Russia or the Soviet Union in equal measure. Yet these bonds persisted. Koreans continuously crossed borders and moved within states, while states reacted to the movement by trying to control it. The tension that arose out of these two contending currents—mobility across borders on the one hand, and efforts to regulate it on the other—was never resolved. It was a defining characteristic of the Tumen border region and a conundrum for statesmen on all three sides. At the height of scares of foreign enemies and internal spies, the Soviet regime was driven to attend to the "problem" through a drastic measure: removing the borderland Koreans and, save for demobilized soldiers and their families, leaving the banks of the Tumen empty.

There is no doubt that the Soviet regime was a dictatorial one that all too often employed force, including forced migration, to achieve its ends. But one should not dismiss altogether its plans and decrees, as well as those undertaken by the tsarist state, as peculiar or blunt methods that were intrinsic to an illiberal regime and are thus beyond the scope of proper comparison. The same holds true for Korea and China, both of which were seen by contemporary Russian and Western officials as despotic states that prohibited their people from leaving or, conversely, weak states that failed to contain their people within borders. Japan, too, deployed this rhetoric of weakness, using it as justification for colonizing Korea and Manchuria. When the actions and conversations of officials in these various states are viewed together, it becomes clear that their methods for handling migrants and settlers were not unlike those used by other states in the late nineteenth century. In the Tumen, officials considered seriously the Korean migrant "problem," drew connections between "immigrants" and "emigrants" and matters of national and international concern, and experimented with multiple ways to govern the population—negotiating through old and newly established diplomatic channels, interpreting treaties, retooling subjecthood and land policies, implementing "guest" status for undesirable Asian workers, resettling people as part of colonizing projects, and incorporating them into the administrative and cultural life of their states. To be sure, language about the necessity to govern frequently overshadowed states' capacity to do so, but the former nevertheless illuminates the impulses and aspirations of administrators that were of central concern. Officials expressed and acted on these impulses with particular intensity in the Tumen region because it was there that they encountered local, national, and global agendas that competed with their own. To them, Koreans embodied all of these conflicting agendas.

The migration of Koreans did not stop in 1937, nor did questions about their citizenship and belonging. Laborers traveled to the Soviet Union to work in mining, fishing, and logging industries, often in remote places in the Far Eastern territory. Families also continued to cross back and forth across the borders of northern Korea, the Soviet Union, and Manchukuo, though news of the deportation likely compelled Koreans to direct their movement farther north in the Maritime, away from the sensitive border zone. With the official start of war between China and Japan in 1937, Koreans were also swept up in massive population movements in the region that carried soldiers, officials, farmers, and profiteers throughout East Asia. By 1942 the official number of Koreans in Kando had grown to 620,000; the figure doubles when including other areas of Manchuria. At the end of the war in 1945, the direction of movement was suddenly reversed, as the Allied powers began a large-scale repatriation program to return people to their original countries, a key component of their plan to dismantle the Japanese empire.[35] It was a remarkable feat that more than a million Koreans returned home, but the division of the peninsula posed a new conundrum for returnees: it was not clear where Koreans belonged, the Russian-occupied North or the U.S.-occupied South. The presence of two regimes on the peninsula also complicated the citizenship status for many Koreans who were either unable to repatriate or chose to remain in their adopted countries. Since Japan had renounced its claims over colonial subjects after the war, hundreds of thousands of Koreans in Japan, Manchuria, Sakhalin, and other places were rendered "stateless."[36] With little diplomatic contact across northeast Asia in the post-1945 period, they remained so until their adopted states took action. To settle their legal status, they would have to wait for the formation of new sovereign states—North and South Korea in 1948 and the People's Republic of China in 1949—as well as the recovery of the Soviet Union from the devastating war and thawing of relations between South Korea and Japan.

Whereas citizenship was disputed, the borders of North Korea, Russia, and China remained fixed. Traces of the once-extreme border-making project are still visible across the Tumen valley today. Its prominent feature is the empty space

---

35. Lori Watt, *When Empire Comes Home* (Cambridge, MA, 2009), esp. 26; Matthew Augustine, "From Empire to Nation."

36. In Japan the Diet passed the 1947 Alien Registration Law, which identified Koreans as belonging to Chōsen based on their family registers. But because the ROK and DPRK did not yet exist as sovereign states, Koreans in Japan became stateless. With the signing of the San Francisco Peace Treaty in 1952, they were formally declared "aliens." Erin Chung, "Politics of Contingent Citizenship," in *Diaspora without Homeland*, ed. Sonia Ryang and John Lie (Berkeley, 2009), 155.

along the river. On the Russian side, in the southernmost part of Khasan district (formerly Poset), the rules have changed little since the 1940s, when the government restricted residence in the region. This piece of Khasan remains a special protected zone where visitors, both citizens and foreigners, must travel with a pass.[37] China, notwithstanding its encouragement of tourism and trade with Russia, has similarly left its side of the river empty. The significant numbers of Chinese and Korean-Chinese traders enter the Maritime through a point farther north, in Suifunhe-Grodekovo. The only legal journeys across the Russia–North Korea border today involve state officials and North Koreans headed to Russia for work. On the China–North Korea border, limited trade brings brokers and merchants to cross the bridges that link the two countries. There is, of course, far more illegal movement in the region. Like those who preceded them, North Koreans have turned to clandestine methods to cross the border to Russia, China, and beyond, hoping for a new beginning. Yet, in these countries, their futures remain uncertain.

---

37. In 1923 the Soviet government created an administrative-territorial unit called *pogranichnyi raion* ("border region"). A string of such *raiony* ran along the entire land and sea border of the Soviet Union. The *raiony* were designated as high-security areas and placed under the supervision of a special border police. It is unclear when this designation was applied to Khasan district, or when it was removed. Vladivostok, as the base of the Soviet Pacific fleet, was designated a "closed city" after World War II but reopened after the collapse of the Soviet Union. Martin, *Affirmative Action Empire*, 314.

Glossary

anmusa A royal commissioner in Chosŏn. 按撫使

artel In Russia, a cooperative of workers.

banner Manchu system of social, administrative, and military organization.

bilet A permit that allowed a nonsubject to reside in Russia for a set period of time.

Chosŏn The state that ruled Korea from 1392 to 1910.

desiatina A Russian unit of area equal to approximately 1 hectare or 2.7 acres.

fanza The Russian name for a house or hut built by Koreans, Manchus, or Chinese. Also the Russian unit for a household of Koreans, Manchus, or Chinese.

Four Counties Counties established along the Yalu River by early Chosŏn rulers to defend against Jurchens. Later abolished, they became the Four Abolished Counties. 廢四郡

fudutong A lieutenant garrison commander in a Qing banner. 副都統

han'gŭl The vernacular Korean script.

hojŏk The household registration system in Chosŏn. 戶籍

honghuzi The Chinese term for bandits in the northeastern region; originally known for the red color of their masks.

Jurchen Seminomadic peoples in Manchuria, one tribe of whom established the Qing Dynasty.

kamsa A governor of a province in Chosŏn. 監司

khanshin The Russian name for the sorghum-based alcohol known as *kaoliang jiu* to Chinese. Also called *gaolian* and *sul'*.

khunkhuzy The Russian transliteration of *honghuzi* (plural).

krai An administrative unit or territory in an outlying area of Russia.

kŭn A Korean and Japanese measure of weight equal to 600 grams. 斤

li A unit of distance equal to 0.449 km or about one-third of a mile. 里

Manza The Russian word variously applied to bandits, Manchus, and indigenous peoples in the Ussuri region and Manchuria.

novosely In Russia, newly arrived settlers in a frontier area.

nyang A measure of weight equal to approximately 40 grams. Also a denomination of money, including silver coins. 兩

oblast' A province. In Russia, an administrative unit larger than an *uezd*.

obshchestvo (-a) A society, sometimes called *sel'skoe obshchestvo*. In Russia, the lowest level of rural administration.

obshchina A commune. In Russia, it was sometimes equated with a village.

okrug A region. In the Soviet Union, an administrative unit larger than a *raion*.

pereselenie In Russia, resettlement or migration.

pereselentsy In Russia, people who resettled from one location to another, often through state-run programs.

pobusang A peddler-merchant in Chosŏn.

poddannyi (-ye) In Russia, a subject of the empire.

pŏmwŏl A term for border transgression. 犯越

ponggŭm chidae Prohibited zone. A buffer area between the Qing and Chosŏn. 封禁地帶

prisiazhnye listy Oaths of allegiance taken by people who became Russian subjects.

pud A Russian measure of weight equal to 16 kg.

pusa A magistrate of undefined rank in Chosŏn. 府使

Qing The dynasty that ruled China from 1644 to 1912.

raion A district. In the Soviet Union, an administrative unit smaller than an *okrug*.

selo A village.

Shengjing The auxiliary capital of the Qing in Manchuria. Also known as Mukden and Shenyang. 盛京

Shengjing Board of Rites A branch of the Beijing Board of Rites, which was one of six top-level divisions in the Qing bureaucracy with a broad range of duties. 盛京禮部

sinmin A subject or citizen. 臣民

Six Forts Fortresses built along the Tumen River by early Chosŏn rulers for protection against Jurchens. 六鎮

soslovie A social estate category in imperial Russia.

svidetel'stvo (-a) A certificate given to Koreans as proof of Russian subjecthood, usually identifying the year of their arrival in Russia and names of family members. Also known as a *prisiazhnoe svidetel'stvo*.

starozhily In Russia, people who moved to a frontier area and have long been settled there.

Ŭijŏngbu State Council. The highest executive organ in the Chosŏn bureaucracy. 議政府

uchastok A district. In Russia, an administrative unit smaller than a *volost'*.

uezd A region. In Russia, an administrative unit larger than a *volost'* and smaller than a province.

ŭibyŏng Righteous Army. Civilian volunteer armies in Chosŏn that arose during the Japanese invasions of 1592–98 and engaged in the anti-Japanese movement in the early twentieth century. 義兵

versta A Russian unit of distance equal to approximately 1 km or two-thirds of a mile.

volost' A county. In Russia, an administrative unit smaller than an *uezd*, and the highest level of peasant self-government.

vyselok A hamlet.

yangban The elite ruling class, also known as scholar-officials, in Chosŏn.

zuoling A captain in a Qing banner garrison. 佐領

Note on Sources

This transnational history brings together materials from multiple geographies that have previously not been considered as a whole. For Korean and Chinese perspectives, the book uses primary materials from published compilations.[1] These include *Tongmun hwigo* (Compendium of diplomatic documents) and the Chosŏn royal annals, which offer important details about cross-border conflicts and discussions between Seoul, Shengjing (Mukden), and local officials stationed in the border region. Other diplomatic sources include *Ku Han'guk oegyo munsŏ* (Diplomatic documents of Old Korea) and Russian archival documents. Travelogues written by Korean envoys and émigrés and vernacular Korean newspapers published in Russia are invaluable in shedding light on the aspirations of officials and activists vis-à-vis the Korean community in Russia and China. The book further makes wide use of secondary literature in South Korea, where interest in borderlands has led to a burst of scholarship on northern Korea and Manchuria in the past two decades.

The book also draws on published and unpublished Russian materials. Most of the unpublished sources derive from the Russian State Historical Archive of the Far East, a central repository for documents generated by the administration of the Russian Far East. The archive's vast collections continue to be declassified and made available to researchers.[2] Sources employed include reports, resolutions, and statistical data on population levels, migration, economy, trade, and geography; petitions and meeting memoranda; and correspondence between officials within the tsarist government and between officials and their counterparts in China and Korea. These materials were supplemented by local newspapers, journals, ethnographies, travelogues, and published geographical surveys, the majority of which were written by members of the Imperial Russian Geographical Society. The tendency of Koreans to settle, the continuous arrival of new Koreans, and their ties to neighboring

---

1. Translations of these literary Chinese sources are based on annotated Korean versions, which are available as published compilations or were commissioned by the author.

2. For more about the history and details of working in this archive, see Alyssa Park, "Navigating Northeast Asia in Vladivostok," http://dissertationreviews.org/archives/5447.

states made them one of the most studied groups in official and academic circles in the region.

Sources for maps include P. F. Unterberger's *Primorskaia oblast', 1856–1898 gg.* and *Priamurskii krai, 1906–1910 gg.*; *CHGIS, Version: 6* (c) Fairbank Center for Chinese Studies of Harvard University and the Center for Historical Geographical Studies at Fudan University, 2016; and data in the public domain.

Selected Bibliography

Archival Sources

Arkhiv vneshnei politiki Rossiiskoi imperii, Moscow

Fond 148: Tikhookeanskii stol

Gosudarstvennyi arkhiv Rossiiskoi Federatsii, Moscow

Fond 102: Departament Politsii Ministerstvo Vnutrennikh Del
Fond R-944: Upravlenie vnutrennimi delami Priamurskogo zemskogo
kraia

Gosudarstvennyi arkhiv Primorskogo Kraia, Vladivostok

Fond 48: Khasanskii raiispolkom
Fond 1125: Ussuriiskaia oblastnaia planovaia komissiia

Rossiiskii gosudarstvennyi istoricheskii arkhiv Dal'nego Vostoka, Vladivostok

Fond 1: Primorskoe oblastnoe pravlenie
Fond 28: Vladivostokskaia gorodskaia uprava
Fond 87: Kantseliariia voennogo gubernatora Primorskoi oblasti
Fond 702: Kantseliariia Priamurskogo general-gubernatora
Fond R-2422: Dal'nevostochnyi revoliutsionnyi komitet

Newspapers and Periodicals

Russian

Dalekaia okraina
Nikol'sk-Ussuriiskii listok
Vladivostokskie eparkhial'nye vedomosti
Vladivostok

Korean

Haejo sinmun
Hanin sinbo
Kwŏnŏp sinmun
Taedong kongbo

Contemporary Sources

Anosov, S. D. *Koreitsy v Ussuriiskom krae* [Koreans in Ussuri krai]. Khabarovsk: Khnizhnoe Delo, 1928.

Arsen'ev, V. K. *Kitaitsy v Ussuriiskom krae.* Zapiski Priamurskogo otdela Imperatorskogo Russkogo Geograficheskogo Obshchestva 10, no. 1. Khabarovsk: Tip. Kantseliarii Priamurskago general-gubernatora, 1914.

Bishop, Isabella Bird. *Korea and Her Neighbors: A Narrative of Travel, with an Account of the Recent Vicissitudes and Present Position of the Country.* Seoul: Yonsei University Press, 1970. First published 1905 by John Murray (London).

Ch'oe Chongbŏm. *Kando kaech'ŏk pisa: Kangbuk ilgi* [Undisclosed history of the development of Kando: Diary of the north]. Edited by Ch'oe Kanghyŏn. Seoul: Sinsŏng Ch'ulp'ansa, 2004.

Delotkevich, P. M. "Dnevnik Pavla Mikhailovicha Delotkevicha na puti peshkom iz Seula v Pos'et cherez severnuiu Koreiu (s 6 dekabria 1885 g. po 29 fevralia 1886 g.)" [Journal of Pavel Mikhailovich Delotkevich on his travels from Seoul to Pos'et through northern Korea]. *Sbornik geograficheskikh, topograficheskikh i statisticheskikh materialov po Azii* 38 (1887): 128–97.

Eliseev, A. V. "Iuzhno-Ussuriiskii krai i ego Russkaia kolonizatsiia, I–III" [South Ussuri krai and its Russian colonization]. *Russkii vestnik* 214, no. 6 (1891): 199–231.

——. "Iuzhno-Ussuriiskii krai i ego Russkaia kolonizatsiia, IV–VI" [South Ussuri krai and its Russian colonization]. *Russkii vestnik* 215, no. 8 (1891): 118–58.

——. "Iuzhno-Ussuriiskii krai i ego Russkaia kolonizatsiia, VII–IX" [South Ussuri krai and its Russian colonization]. *Russkii vestnik* 216, no. 10 (1891): 78–113.

——. *Po belu-svetu (Ocherki i kartiny iz puteshestvii po trem chastiam starogo sveta)* [Across the world (Essays and drawings from travels across three parts of the old world)]. Vol. 4. St. Petersburg: Izdaniie P. P. Soikina, 1898.

Garin, N. G. *Iz dnevnikov krugosvetnogo puteshestviia (po Koree, Man'chzhurii i Liaodunskomu poluostrovu)* [From the journals of my travels around the world (through Korea, Manchuria, and Liaodong peninsula)]. Moscow: Gos. Izd-vo Geog. Lit-ry, 1950.

Gozhenskii, Iv. "Uchastie koreiskoi emigratsii v revoliutsionnom dvizhenii na Dal'nem Vostoke" [Participation of Korean emigration in the revolutionary movement in the Far East]. In *Revoliutsiia na Dal'nem Vostoke,* 357–74. Moscow: Gos. Izd-vo, 1923.

Grave, V. V. *Kitaitsy, Koreitsy i Iapontsy v Priamur'e* [Chinese, Koreans, and Japanese in the Priamur]. Trudy Amurskoi ekspeditsii. St. Petersburg: V. F. Kirshbaum, 1912.

Great Britain. Naval Intelligence Division. *A Handbook of Siberia and Arctic Russia.* London: H.M. Stationery Office, 1920.

Hallim Taehakkyo Asea Munhwa Yŏn'guso, ed. *Kwŏnŏp sinmun. Taehanin Chŏnggyobo. Ch'ŏnggu sinbo. Hanin sinbo.* 2 vols. Ch'unch'ŏn: Hallim Taehakkyo Asea Munhwa Yŏn'guso, 1995.

——, ed. *Yŏnhae-ju ŏbu. Kwangbu. Tangkyoyuk. Tongbang kkommuna. Konggyŏk taewŏn. Ssŏttallinnyech'ŭ. Lenin kwangsŏn. Nodongja.* 3 vols. Ch'unch'ŏn: Hallim Taehakkyo Ch'ulp'anbu, 1997.

Iaremenko, A. N. "Dnevnik kommunista" [Diary of a communist]. In *Revoliutsiia na Dal'nem Vostoke,* 131–279. Moscow: Gos. Izd-vo, 1923.

Iarmosh, A. M. "Dvizhenie naseleniia Dal'nevostochnogo kraia na desiatiletie 1926–1936" [Population movement in the Far Eastern krai during the decade 1926–1936]. *Ekonomicheskaia zhizn' Dal'nego Vostoka (Khabarovsk),* no. 1–2 (1927): 83–101.

Iuvachev, I. P. "Bor'ba s khunkhuzami na Manchzhurskoi granitse" [Struggle with khunkhuzy on the Manchurian border]. *Istoricheskii vestnik* 82 (October 1900): 177–206.

James, H. Evan M. *The Long White Mountain, or, A Journey in Manchuria: With Some Account of the History, People, Administration and Religion of that Country.* London: Longmans Green & Co., 1888.

Kaufman, A. A. *Pereselenie i kolonizatsiia* [Resettlement and colonization]. St. Petersburg: Biblioteka "Obshchestvennoi Pol'zy," 1905.

Koryŏ Taehakkyo Asea Munje Yŏn'guso, ed. *Ku Han'guk oegyo munsŏ* [Diplomatic documents of Old Korea]. 22 vols. Seoul: Koryŏ Taehakkyo Ch'ulp'anbu, 1965–73.

Ku Sŏnhŭi and Cho Myŏnghŭi, eds. *Chungguk tongbuk chiyŏk Hanin kwallyŏn charyo* [Documents on Koreans in China's northeastern region]. Haeoe saryo ch'ongsŏ. Kwach'ŏn, Kyŏnggi-do: Kuksa P'yŏnch'an Wiwŏnhoe, 2008.

Kukhak Chinhŭng Yŏn'gu Saŏp Unyŏng Wiwŏnhoe, ed. *Kangbuk ilgi; Kangjwa yŏjigi; Aguk yŏjido* [Journal about the north; Diary on the left bank of the river; Map of Russia]. Sŏngnam, Kyŏnggi-do: Han'guk Chŏngsin Munhwa Yŏn'guwŏn, 1994.

Kukhoe Tosŏgwan Ippŏp Chosaguk, ed. *Ku Hanmal ŭi choyak* [Treaties of Old Korea]. 3 vols. Seoul: Sinsŏwŏn, 1989.

Kuksa P'yŏnch'an Wiwŏnhoe, ed. *Chuhan Ilbon kongsagwan kirok* [Records of the Japanese legation in Korea]. http://db.history.go.kr.

———, ed. *Kaksa tungnŏk kŭndaep'yŏn* [Records of administrative bureaus].

———, ed. *Kojong sillok* [Veritable annals of Kojong].

———, ed. *Pibyŏnsa tŭngnok* [Records of the Border Defense Command].

———, ed. *T'onggambu munsŏ* [Documents of the resident-general].

Matiunin, N. G. "Nashi sosedi na krainem vostoke" [Our neighbors in the far east]. *Vestnik Evropy* 126, no. 22 (July 1887): 64–88.

Ministerstvo Torgovli i Promyshlennosti. *Sbornik torgovykh dogovorov i drugikh vytekaiushchikh iz nikh soglashenii, zakliuchennykh mezhdu Rossiei i inostrannymi gosudarstvami* [Collection of commercial treaties and subsequent agreements concluded between Russia and foreign governments]. Petrograd, 1915.

Mysh, M. I. *Ob inostrantsakh v Rossii: sbornik uzakonenii, traktatov i konventsii s otnosiashchimisia k nim pravitel'stvennymi i sudebnymi raz"iasneniiami* [On foreigners in Russia: Collection of decrees, treaties, and conventions with administrative and legal explanations]. 2nd ed. St. Petersburg, 1911.

Nadarov, I. P. "Iuzhno-Ussuriiskii krai v sovremennom ego sostoianii" [South Ussuri krai in its present situation]. *Izvestiia Imperatorskago Russkogo Geograficheskogo Obshchestva* 25 (1889): 197–227.

———. "Materialy k izucheniiu Ussuriiskogo kraia" [Materials for the investigation of Ussuri krai]. *Sbornik geograficheskikh, topograficheskikh i statisticheskikh materialov po Azii* 26 (1887): 91–150.

Nansen, Fridtjof. *Through Siberia, the Land of the Future.* Translated by Arthur G. Chater. London: W. Heinemann, 1914.

Nasekin, N. "Koreiskii vopros v Priamur'e" [Korean question in the Priamur]. *Russkii vestnik* 269 (1900): 296–303.

———. "Koreitsy Priamurskago kraia" [Koreans of Priamur krai]. *Zhurnal Ministerstva obshchestvennogo obrazovaniia* 352 (March 1904): 1–61.

Obzor Primorskoi oblasti za 1901–2 g. [Survey of the Maritime oblast' in 1901–2]. Vladivostok: Tip. Primorskago oblastnogo pravleniia, 1902.

Obzor Primorskoi oblasti za 1906. Vladivostok: Tip. Primorskago oblastnogo pravleniia, 1907.

Obzor Primorskoi oblasti za 1910. Vladivostok: Tip. Primorskago oblastnogo pravleniia, 1911.

Obzor Primorskoi oblasti za 1913. Vladivostok: Tip. Primorskago oblastnogo pravleniia, 1915.

Pae Usŏng and Ku Pŏmjin, eds. *Kugyŏk 'Tongmun hwigo' pŏmwŏl saryo* [Compendium of diplomatic documents on border crossings in Korean]. Vol. 4, Tongbuga yŏksa charyo ch'ongsŏ; 20. Seoul: Tongbuga Yŏksa Chaedan, 2012.

Pak Ŭnsik. "Aryŏng silgi." In *Han'guk kŭndae saryoron*, edited by Yun Pyŏngsŏk, 152–200. Seoul: Ilchogak, 1979.

Pesotskii, V. D. *Koreiskii vopros v Priamur'e* [Korean question in the Priamur]. Trudy Amurskoi ekspeditsii 11. Khabarovsk, 1913.

Podzhio, M. A. "Koreitsy" [Koreans]. In *Po Dal'nemu Vostoku: Sakhalin, Ussuriiskaia oblast', Man'chzhuriia, Koreia i Iaponiia. Sbornik pisatel'nykh statei dlia domashniago i shkol'nago chteniia*, edited by V. L'vovich, 74–78. Moscow: M. V. Kliukin, 1905.

Poltavskaia gubernskaia zemskaia uprava. *Pereseleniia iz Poltavskoi gubernii s 1861 po 1900 g.* [Resettlement from Poltavka guberniia from 1861 to 1900]. Vol. 2. Poltava, 1900.

Przheval'skii, N. *Puteshestviie v Ussuriiskom krae, 1867–1869 gg.* [Journey in Ussuri krai]. Moscow: OGIZ Gos. Izd-vo Geog. Lit-ry, 1947.

——. "Ussuriiskii krai. Novaia territoriia Rossii" [Ussuri krai. New territory of Russia]. *Vestnik Evropy* 5 (1870): 236–67.

Ragoza, A. "Pos'etskii uchastok" [Pos'et uchastok]. *Sbornik geograficheskikh, topograficheskikh i statisticheskikh materialov po Azii* 45 (1891): 47–135.

——. "Koreitsy Priamurskago kraia. I. Kratkii istoricheskii ocherk pereseleniia Koreitsev v Iuzhno-Ussuriiskii krai" [Koreans of Priamur krai. I. A short historical survey of the migration of Koreans to South Ussuri]. *Trudy Priamurskago otdela Imperatorskogo Russkogo Geograficheskogo Obshchestva* (1895): 1–36.

Sen'ko-Bulanyi, N. "Severnye porty Korei. Koreiskiie rabochiie v Rossii" [Northern ports of Korea. Korean workers in Russia]. In *Sbornik konsul'skikh donesenii*, edited by Ministerstvo Inostrannykh Del, 23–29. St. Petersburg, 1909.

Shlikevich, S. P. *Kolonizatsionnoe znachenie. Zemledeliia v Priamur'e* [Significance of colonization. Agriculture in the Priamur]. Trudy Amurskoi ekspeditsii 5. St. Petersburg: V. F. Kirshbaum, 1911.

Shreider, D. I. *Nash Dal'nii Vostok (tri goda v Ussuriiskom krae)* [Our Far East (Three years in Ussuri krai)]. St. Petersburg: Izdanie A. F. Devriena, 1897.

Toropov, A. A., et al., eds. *Koreitsy na Rossiiskom Dal'nem Vostoke: Dokumenty i materialy (vt. pol. XIX–nach. XX vv.)* [Koreans in the Russian Far East (late nineteenth century to early twentieth century): Documents and materials]. Vladivostok: Izd-vo DVU, 2001.

——, ed. *Koreitsy na Rossiiskom Dal'nem Vostoke (1917–1923 gg.): Dokumenty i materialy* [Koreans in the Russian Far East (1917–1923): Documents and materials]. Vladivostok: Izd-vo DVU, 2004.

Unterberger, P. F. *Priamurskii krai, 1906–1910* [Priamur krai, 1906–1910]. St. Petersburg: V. F. Kirshbaum, 1912.

——. *Primorskaia oblast', 1856–1898 gg.* [Maritime oblast', 1856–1898]. St. Petersburg: V. F. Kirshbaum, 1900.

Vagin, V. I. "Koreitsy na Amure" [Koreans in the Amur]. *Sbornik istoriko-statisticheskikh svedenii o Sibiri i sopredel'nykh ei stranakh* 1 (1875): 1–29.

Vladivostokskii okruzhnoi statisticheskii otdel. *Itogi perepisi Koreiskogo naseleniia Vladivostokskogo okruga v 1929 goda* [Summary of the census of the Korean population of Vladivostok okrug in 1929]. Khabarovsk: Dal'nevostochnoe kraevoe zemel'noe upravlenie, 1932.

Yi Chungha. *Yŏkchu "Kamgyesa tŭngnok."* Tongbuga yŏksa charyo ch'ongsŏ; 14. Seoul: Tongbuga Yŏksa Chaedan, 2008.

Yu Ŭiyang. *Pukkwan nojŏngnok* [Travelogue on the North]. Edited by Ch'oi Kanghyŏn. Seoul: Ilchisa, 1976.

Secondary Sources

Amrith, Sunil S. *Crossing the Bay of Bengal: The Furies of Nature and the Fortunes of Migrants.* Cambridge, MA: Harvard University Press, 2013.

——. "Tamil Diasporas across the Bay of Bengal." *American Historical Review* 114, no. 3 (2009): 547–72.

Anderson, Benedict. *Imagined Communities: Reflections on the Origin and Spread of Nationalism.* Revised ed. London: Verso, 1991.

Arrighi, Giovanni, Takeshi Hamashita, and Mark Selden, eds. *The Resurgence of East Asia: 500, 150 and 50 Year Perspectives.* London: Routledge, 2003.

Augustine, Matthew. "From Empire to Nation: Repatriation, Immigration, and Citizenship in Occupied Japan, 1945–1952." Ph.D. diss., Columbia University, 2009.

Azuma, Eiichiro. *Between Two Empires: Race, History, and Transnationalism in Japanese America.* Oxford: Oxford University Press, 2005.

Ban, Byung Yool. "Korean Nationalist Activities in the Russian Far East and North Chientao (1905–1921)." Ph.D. diss., University of Hawai'i, 1996.

Barth, Fredrik, ed. *Ethnic Groups and Boundaries: The Social Organization of Culture Difference.* Boston: Little, Brown, 1969.

Bassin, Mark. *Imperial Visions: Nationalist Imagination and Geographical Expansion in the Russian Far East, 1840–1865.* Cambridge: Cambridge University Press, 1999.

Bello, David. "The Cultured Nature of Imperial Foraging in Manchuria." *Late Imperial China* 31, no. 2 (December 2010): 1–33.

Benton, Lauren. *A Search for Sovereignty: Law and Geography in European Empires, 1400–1900.* Cambridge: Cambridge University Press, 2010.

Benton, Lauren, and Adam Clulow. "Legal Encounters and the Origins of Global Law." In *The Cambridge World History,* vol. 6, *The Construction of a Global World, 1400–1800 CE, Part 2: Patterns of Change,* edited by Jerry H. Bentley, Sanjay Subrahmanyam, and Merry E. Wiesner-Hanks, 80–100. Cambridge: Cambridge University Press, 2015.

Bohnet, Adam. "Migrant and Border Subjects in Late Chosŏn Korea." Ph.D. diss., University of Toronto, 2008.

Bone, Jonathan. "Asia Stops Here: Border-Zone Slavicization and the Fate of the Far Eastern Koreans, 1925–1937." Paper presented at the American Association for the Advancement of Slavic Studies Conference, St. Louis, Missouri, November 1999.

——. "Socialism in a Far Country: Stalinist Population Politics and the Making of the Soviet Far East, 1929–1939." Ph.D. diss., University of Chicago, 2003.

Booth, Martin. *Opium: A History.* New York: St. Martin's Press, 1998.

Breyfogle, Nicholas, Abby Schrader, and Willard Sunderland, eds. *Peopling the Russian Periphery: Borderland Colonization in Eurasian History.* London: Routledge, 2007.

Brooks, Barbara. *Japan's Imperial Diplomacy: Consuls, Treaty Ports, and War in China, 1895–1938.* Honolulu: University of Hawai'i Press, 2000.

——. "Peopling the Japanese Empire: The Koreans in Manchuria and the Rhetoric of Inclusion." In *Japan's Competing Modernities: Issues in Culture and Democracy, 1900–1930,* edited by Sharon Minichiello. Honolulu: University of Hawai'i Press, 1999.

Brophy, David. *Uyghur Nation: Reform and Revolution on the Russia-China Frontier.* Cambridge, MA: Harvard University Press, 2016.

Brower, Daniel, and Edward Lazzerini, eds. *Russia's Orient: Imperial Borderlands and Peoples, 1700–1917.* Bloomington: Indiana University Press, 1997.

Brown, Kate. *A Biography of No Place: From Ethnic Borderland to Soviet Heartland.* Cambridge, MA: Harvard University Press, 2004.

Burbank, Jane, and Frederick Cooper. *Empires in World History: Power and the Politics of Difference.* Princeton: Princeton University Press, 2010.

Burbank, Jane, Mark von Hagen, and Anatolyi Remnev, eds. *Russian Empire: Space, People, Power, 1700–1930.* Bloomington: Indiana University Press, 2007.

Cassel, Pär Kristoffer. *Grounds of Judgment: Extraterritoriality and Imperial Power in Nineteenth-Century China and Japan.* Oxford: Oxford University Press, 2012.

Chan, Shelly. "The Case for Diaspora: A Temporal Approach to the Chinese Experience." *Journal of Asian Studies* 74, no. 1 (2014): 107–28.

Chang, Kornel. *Pacific Connections: The Making of the U.S.-Canadian Borderlands.* Berkeley: University of California Press, 2012.

Chen, Shuang. *State-Sponsored Inequality: The Banner System and Social Stratification in Northeast China.* Stanford: Stanford University Press, 2017.

Cho Chaegon. "Taehan cheguk ŭi kaehyŏk inyŏm kwa pobusang" [Reform ideology of the Great Han Empire and pobusang]. *Han'guk tongnip undongsa yŏn'gu* 20 (August 2003): 127–48.

Cho Ilgwŏn. "Ku Hanmal Kando chibang chumin e kwanhan yŏn'gu: 1902-nyŏndo pyŏn'gye hojŏk e punsŏk" [Study on residents of Kando in Old Korea: Analysis of 1902 household registers of the border area]. M.A. thesis, Inha University, 1997.

Ch'oe Changgŭn. "Ilche ŭi Kando 'T'onggambu imsi p'achulso' sŏlch'i kyŏngwi" [Account of the Japanese establishment of the "resident-general temporary field office" in Kando]. *Han-Il kwan'gyesa yŏn'gu* 7 (December 1997): 86–115.

Ch'oe Ching Young. *The Rule of the Taewŏngun, 1864–1873: Restoration in Yi Korea.* Cambridge, MA: Harvard University Press, 1972.

Ch'oe Chinok. "Hanmal pobusang ŭi pyŏnch'ŏn" [Changes in the pobusang in late Korea]. *Chŏngsin munhwa yŏn'gu* 29 (June 1986): 143–60.

Ch'oe, Yŏngho, ed. *From the Land of Hibiscus: Koreans in Hawaii, 1903–1950.* Honolulu: University of Hawai'i Press, 2007.

Chu, Pey-Yi. "The Imperial Origins of the Baikal-Amur Mainline: Siberian Development in the Context of World History." Paper presented at the SSRC Russia–East Asia Dissertation Development Workshop, Princeton, New Jersey, 2006.

Chung, Erin. "Politics of Contingent Citizenship: Korean Political Engagement in Japan and the United States." In *Diaspora without Homeland: Being Korean in Japan,* edited by Sonia Ryang and John Lie, 147–67. Berkeley: University of California Press, 2009.

Chung, In Teak. "The Korean Minority in Manchuria, 1900–1937." Ph.D. thesis, American University, 1966.

Chutung, Tsai. "The Chinese Nationality Law, 1909." *American Journal of International Law* 4, no. 2 (1910): 404–11.

Clark, Donald N. *Living Dangerously in Korea: The Western Experience, 1900–1950.* Norwalk, CT: EastBridge, 2003.

Crews, Robert. *For Prophet and Tsar: Islam and Empire in Russia and Central Asia.* Cambridge, MA: Harvard University Press, 2006.

Crossley, Pamela Kyle, Helen Siu, and Donald Sutton, eds. *Empire at the Margins: Culture, Ethnicity, and Frontier in Early Modern China.* Berkeley: University of California Press, 2006.

Davis, Mike. *Late Victorian Holocausts: El Niño Famines and the Making of the Third World*. London: Verso, 2001.

Dem'ianenko, A. N. *Territorial'naia organizatsiia khoziaistva na Dal'nem Vostoke Rossii* [Territorial organization of the economy in the Russian Far East]. Vladivostok: Dal'nauka, 2003.

Drea, Edward. *Japan's Imperial Army: Its Rise and Fall, 1853–1945*. Lawrence: University of Kansas Press, 2009.

Duara, Prasenjit. *Sovereignty and Authenticity: Manchukuo and the East Asian Modern*. Lanham, MD: Rowman & Littlefield, 2003.

Duncan, John B. "*Hwanghwain*: Migration and Assimilation in Chosŏn Korea." *Acta Koreana* 3 (2000): 99–113.

Dvorenko, I. M., V. S. Novikova, and I. V. Chernova, eds. *Primorskii krai: Rekomendatel'nyi ukazatel' literatury* [Maritime krai: Recommended guide to literature]. Vladivostok: Primorskoe knizhnoe izd-vo, 1962.

Eklof, Ben. *Russian Peasant Schools: Officialdom, Village Culture, and Popular Pedagogy, 1861–1914*. Berkeley: University of California Press, 1986.

Elliott, Mark C. *The Manchu Way: The Eight Banners and Ethnic Identity in Late Imperial China*. Stanford: Stanford University Press, 2001.

Endō Masataka. *Kindai Nihon no shokuminchi tōchi ni okeru kokuseki to koseki* [Nationality and household registers under colonial rule in modern Japan]. Tokyo: Akashi Shoten, 2010.

Esselstrom, Erik. *Crossing Empire's Edge: Foreign Ministry Police and Japanese Expansionism in Northeast Asia*. Honolulu: University of Hawai'i Press, 2009.

Fairbank, John K. "A Preliminary Framework." In *The Chinese World Order*, edited by John K. Fairbank, 1–20. Cambridge, MA: Harvard University Press, 1968.

Ford, Lisa. *Settler Sovereignty: Jurisdiction and Indigenous People in America and Australia, 1788–1836*. Harvard Historical Studies. Cambridge, MA: Harvard University Press, 2010.

Frank, Stephen. *Crime, Cultural Conflict, and Justice in Rural Russia, 1856–1914*. Berkeley: University of California Press, 1999.

——. "Emancipation and the Birch: The Perpetuation of Corporal Punishment in Rural Russia, 1861–1907." *Jahrbücher für Geschichte Osteuropas, Neue Folge* 45, no. 3 (1997): 401–16.

——. "Popular Justice, Community and Culture among the Russian Peasantry, 1870–1900." *Russian Review* 46 (1987): 239–65.

Gaudin, Corinne. *Ruling Peasants: Village and State in Late Imperial Russia*. DeKalb: Northern Illinois University Press, 2007.

Gelb, Michael. "An Early Soviet Ethnic Deportation: The Far-Eastern Koreans." *Russian Review* 54, no. 3 (1995): 389–412.

——. "'Karelian Fever': The Finnish Immigrant Community during Stalin's Purges." *Europe-Asia Studies* 45, no. 6 (1993): 1091–116.

Geraci, Robert P., and Michael Khodarkovsky, eds. *Of Religion and Empire: Missions, Conversion, and Tolerance in Tsarist Russia*. Ithaca: Cornell University Press, 2001.

Geyer, Dietrich. *Russian Imperialism: The Interaction of Domestic and Foreign Policy, 1860–1914*. Translated by Bruce Little. Leamington Spa, UK: Berg, 1987.

Goswami, Manu. *Producing India: From Colonial Economy to National Space*. Chicago: University of Chicago Press, 2004.

Habecker, David Eugene. "Russian Urban Administration and the Chinese, Koreans, and Japanese in Vladivostok, 1884–1922." Ph.D. thesis, University of Maryland, College Park, 2003.

Haboush, JaHyun Kim. "Constructing the Center: The Ritual Controversy and the Search for a New Identity in Seventeenth-Century Korea." In *Culture and the State in Late Chosŏn Korea*, edited by JaHyun Kim Haboush and Martina Deuchler, 46–90. Cambridge, MA: Harvard University Asia Center, 1999.

Hämäläinen, Pekka, and Samuel Truett. "On Borderlands." *Journal of American History* 98, no. 2 (2011): 338–61.

Han, Eric C. *Rise of a Japanese Chinatown: Yokohama, 1894–1972.* Cambridge, MA: Harvard University Asia Center, 2014.

Han Young-woo (Han Yŏngu), Ahn Hwi-Joon (An Hwijun), and Bae Woo Sung (Pae Usŏng). *The Artistry of Early Korean Cartography.* Translated by Choi Byonghyon. Larkspur, CA: Tamal Vista, 2008.

Hara Teruyuki. "The Korean Movement in the Russian Maritime Province, 1905–1922." In *Koreans in the Soviet Union*, edited by Dae-Sook Suh, 1–23. Honolulu: Center for Korean Studies, University of Hawai'i, 1987.

Harvey, David. *The Condition of Postmodernity.* Cambridge, MA: Blackwell, 1990.

Heffern, Richard. *The Complete Book of Ginseng.* Millbrae, CA: Celestial Arts, 1976.

Hevia, James. *Cherishing Men from Afar: Qing Guest Ritual and the Macartney Embassy of 1793.* Durham, NC: Duke University Press, 1995.

Hillis, Faith. *Children of Rus': Right-bank Ukraine and the Invention of a Russian Nation.* Ithaca: Cornell University Press, 2013.

Hirsch, Francine. *Empire of Nations: Ethnographic Knowledge and the Making of the Soviet Union.* Ithaca: Cornell University Press, 2005.

Howell, David L. "Ainu Ethnicity and the Boundaries of the Early Modern Japanese State." *Past and Present* 142 (February 1994): 69–93.

———. *Geographies of Identity in Nineteenth-Century Japan.* Berkeley: University of California Press, 2005.

———. "Territoriality and Collective Identity in Tokugawa Japan." *Daedalus* 127, no. 3 (Summer 1998): 105–32.

Hsu, Chia Yin. "The Chinese Eastern Railroad and the Making of Russian Imperial Orders in the Far East." Ph.D. diss., New York University, 2006.

———. "Nationalizing Empire: 'Yellow Labor,' Agrarian Colonization, and the Making of Russianness at the Far Eastern Frontier." Paper presented at the Columbia University kruzhok, New York, May 2006.

———. "A Tale of Two Railroads: 'Yellow Labor,' Agrarian Colonization, and the Making of Russianness at the Far Eastern Frontier, 1890s–1910s." *Ab Imperio* 3 (March 2006): 217–53.

Hwang, Kyung Moon. "Citizenship, Social Equality and Government Reform: Changes in the Household Registration System in Korea, 1894–1910." *Modern Asian Studies* 38, no. 2 (2004): 355–87.

———. "Country or State? Reconceptualizing *Kukka* in the Korean Enlightenment Period, 1896–1910." *Korean Studies* 24 (2000): 1–24.

———. "From the Dirt to Heaven: Northern Koreans in the Chosŏn and Early Modern Eras." *Harvard Journal of Asiatic Studies* 62, no. 1 (June 2002): 135–76.

Iankovskii, Valerii. *From the Crusades to Gulag and Beyond.* St. Petersburg: M. Gorky Scientific Library, 2007.

Ispolnitel'nyi komitet Primorskogo kraevogo Soveta narodnykh deputatov. Arkhivnyi otdel. *K voprosu o migratsii Koreiskogo naseleniia na iuge Dal'nego Vostoka (1864–1932 gg.)* [Question of Korean migration in the south of the Far East]. Vladivostok, 1991.

Jennings, John Mark. "The Opium Empire: Japan and the East Asian Drug Trade, 1895–1945." Ph.D. diss., University of Hawai'i, 1995.

Jun Seung Ho, James B. Lewis, and Kang Han-Rog. "Korean Expansion and Decline from the Seventeenth to the Nineteenth Century: A View Suggested by Adam Smith." *Journal of Economic History* 68, no. 1 (March 2008): 244–82.

Kajimura Hideki. "Kyūkanmatsu hokkan chiiku keizai to naigai kōeki" [Economy of the northern region and internal and external trade in Old Korea]. In *Kajimura Hideki chosakushū*, vol. 3, edited by Kajimura Hideki, 159–85. Tokyo: Akashi Shoten, 1990.

Kane, Eileen. *Russian Hajj: Empire and the Pilgrimage to Mecca*. Ithaca: Cornell University Press, 2015.

Kang Sŏkhwa. "1712-nyŏn ŭi Cho-Ch'ŏng chŏnggye wa 18-segi Chosŏn ŭi pukpang kyŏngyŏng" [The Chosŏn-Qing border in 1712 and Chosŏn management of the north in the eighteenth century]. *Chŏngbo chindan hakpo* 79, no. 1 (1995): 135–65.

——. "Chosŏn hugi Hamgyŏng-do yukchin chiyŏk ŭi pangŏ ch'egye" [Defense system of the Six Fort region of Hamgyŏng province in late Chosŏn]. *Han'guk munhwa* 36 (2005): 297–337.

——. *Chosŏn hugi Hamgyŏng-do wa pukpang yŏngt'o ŭisik* [Hamgyŏng province and consciousness about the northern territories in late Chosŏn]. Seoul: Kyŏngsewŏn, 2000.

Karlsson, Anders. "Famine, Finance and Political Power: Crop Failure and Land-Tax Exemptions in Late Eighteenth-Century Chosŏn Korea." *Journal of the Economic and Social History of the Orient* 48, no. 4 (December 2005): 552–92.

Kawashima, Ken. *The Proletarian Gamble: Korean Workers in Interwar Japan*. Durham, NC: Duke University Press, 2009.

Khodarkovsky, Michael. *Russia's Steppe Frontier: The Making of a Colonial Empire, 1500–1800*. Bloomington: Indiana University Press, 2002.

Kim Ch'unsŏn. "1880–1890 nyŏndae Ch'ŏngjo ŭi 'imin silbyŏn' chŏngch'aek kwa Hanin ijumin silt'ae yŏn'gu" [The Qing policy of 'populating the border regions' in the 1880s–1890s and the situation of Korean migrants]. *Han'guk kŭnhyŏndaesa yŏn'gu* 8 (1998): 5–36.

Kim Dongchul. "The Waegwan Open Market Trade and Tongnae Merchants in the Late Chosŏn Period." Translated by Han Seokyung and J. B. Lewis. *Acta Koreana* 7, no. 1 (January 2004): 9–46.

Kim, German N. "The Deportation of 1937 as a Logical Continuation of Tsarist and Soviet Nationality Policy in the Russian Far East." *Korean and Korean American Studies Bulletin* 12, no. 2–3 (2001): R19–R44.

——. *Istoriia immigratsii Koreitsev: Vtoraia polovina XIX v.–1945* [Korean immigration history: Second half of nineteenth century to 1945]. Almaty, Kazakhstan: Daik-Press, 1999.

Kim, Jaeeun. *Contested Embrace: Transborder Membership Politics in Twentieth-Century Korea*. Stanford: Stanford University Press, 2016.

Kim, Jisoo. *The Emotions of Justice: Gender, Status, and Legal Performance in Chosŏn Korea*. Seattle: University of Washington Press, 2015.

Kim, Key-Hiuk. *The Last Phase of the East Asian World Order: Korea, Japan, and the Chinese Empire, 1860–1882*. Berkeley: University of California Press, 1980.

Kim, Ki-hoon. "Japanese Policy for Rural Korean Immigration to Manchukuo, 1943–1945." Ph.D. thesis, University of Hawai'i, 1992.

Kim, Kwangmin. "Korean Migration in Nineteenth-Century Manchuria: A Global Theme in Modern Asian History." In *Mobile Subjects: Boundaries and Identities in Modern Korean Diaspora*, edited by Wen-hsin Yeh, 17–37. Berkeley: Institute of East Asian Studies, University of California, 2013.

Kim, Loretta. "Marginal Constituencies: Qing Borderland Policies and Vernacular Histories of Five Tribes on the Sino-Russian Frontier." Ph.D. diss., Harvard University, 2009.

Kim, Seonmin. "Borders and Crossings: Trade, Diplomacy, and Ginseng between Qing China and Chosŏn Korea." Ph.D. thesis, Duke University, 2006.

———. Ginseng and Borderland: Territorial Boundaries and Political Relations between Qing China and Chosŏn Korea, 1636–1912. Berkeley: University of California Press, 2017.

Kim, Sun Joo. Marginality and Subversion in Korea: The Hong Kyŏngnae Rebellion of 1812. Seattle: University of Washington Press, 2007.

———, ed. Northern Region of Korea: History, Identity, and Culture. Seattle: University of Washington Press, 2011.

Kim, Sun Joo, and Jungwon Kim. Wrongful Deaths: Selected Inquest Records from Nineteenth-Century Korea. Seattle: University of Washington Press, 2014.

Kim, Syn Khva. Ocherki po istorii Sovetskikh Koreitsev [A study of the history of the Soviet Koreans]. Alma-Ata, Kazakhstan: Nauka, 1964.

King, Ross, and German N. Kim. Kul'tura, istoriia i iazyk Sovetskikh Koreitsev: Istoriografiia i bibliografiia [Culture, history and language of the Soviet Koreans: Historiography and bibliography]. Alma-Ata, Kazakhstan, 1993.

Kinzley, Judd. "Staking Claims to China's Borderland: Oil, Ores and State-building in Xinjiang Province, 1893–1964." Ph.D. diss., University of California San Diego, 2012.

Ko Sŭnghŭi. "19 segi huban Hamgyŏng-do yukchin kwa Manju chiyŏk kyoyŏk ŭi sŏnggyŏk" [Six Forts in Hamgyŏng province and characteristics of trade in Manchuria in the latter half of the nineteenth century]. Chosŏn sidaesa hakpo 25 (2003): 173–99.

———. Chosŏn hugi Hamgyŏng-do sangŏp yŏn'gu [Study of the economy of Hamgyŏng province in late Chosŏn]. Seoul: Kukhak Charyowŏn, 2003.

———. "Chosŏn hugi Hamgyŏng-do ŭi kyojech'ang unyŏng kwa chinja konggŭpch'aek ŭi pyŏnhwa" [Changes in the mutual relief granary and famine food supply operation in Hamgyŏng province in late Chosŏn]. Ihwa sahak yŏn'guso 27 (2000): 237–60.

Ko Tonghwan. "Chosŏn hugi Kaesŏng ŭi tosi kujo wa sangŏp" [The structure of Kaesŏng and its economy in late Chosŏn]. Yŏksa munhwa hakhoe 12, no. 1 (May 2005): 327–80.

"Koreans in Manchuria." Contemporary Manchuria 4, no. 2 (April 1940): 49–69.

Kotkin, Stephen. Magnetic Mountain: Stalinism as a Civilization. Berkeley: University of California Press, 1995.

Kotkin, Stephen, and David Wolff, eds. Rediscovering Russia in Asia: Siberia and the Russian Far East. Armonk, NY: M. E. Sharpe, 1995.

Kotsonis, Yanni. "'Face to Face': The State, the Individual, and the Citizen in Russian Taxation, 1863–1917." Slavic Review 63, no. 2 (Summer 2004): 221–46.

———. States of Obligation: Taxes and Citizenship in the Russian Empire and Early Soviet Republic. Toronto: University of Toronto Press, 2014.

Krushanova, A. I., ed. Administrativno-territorial'noe delenie Primorskogo kraia, 1856–1980 gg. Spravochnik [Administrative-territorial delineation of the Maritime krai, 1856–1980. A reference]. Vladivostok, 1984.

Kwon, June Hee. "Mobile Ethnicity: The Formation of the Korean Chinese Transnational Migrant Class." Ph.D. diss., Duke University, 2013.

Larsen, Kirk. "Trade, Dependency, and Colonialism: Foreign Trade and Korea's Regional Integration, 1876–1910." In Korea at the Center: Dynamics of Regionalism in

Northeast Asia, edited by Charles K. Armstrong, Gilbert Rozman, Samuel S. Kim, and Stephen Kotkin, 51–69. Armonk, NY: M. E. Sharpe, 2006.

——. *Tradition, Treaties, and Trade: Qing Imperialism and Chosŏn Korea, 1850–1910.* Cambridge, MA: Harvard University Asia Center, 2008.

Ledyard, Gari K. "Cartography in Korea." In *Cartography in the Traditional East and Southeast Asian Societies*, edited by J. B. Harley and David Woodward, 235–344. Vol. 2, bk. 2, of *The History of Cartography*. Chicago: University of Chicago Press, 1994.

Lee, Erika. *At America's Gates: Chinese Immigration during the Exclusion Era, 1882–1943.* Chapel Hill: University of North Carolina Press, 2003.

Lee, Hoon K. "Korean Migrants in Manchuria." *Geographical Review* 22, no. 2 (April 1932): 196–204.

Lee, Peter H., and William Theodore De Bary, eds. *Sources of Korean Tradition.* Vol. 2. New York: Columbia University Press, 2000.

Lee, Robert. *The Manchurian Frontier in Ch'ing History.* Cambridge, MA: Harvard University Press, 1970.

Lefebvre, Henri. *The Production of Space.* Translated by Donald Nicholson-Smith. Cambridge, MA: Blackwell, 1991.

Lewis, James Bryant. *Frontier Contact between Chosŏn Korea and Tokugawa Japan.* London: RoutledgeCurzon, 2003.

Lewis, Martin W., and Kären Wigen. *The Myth of Continents: A Critique of Metageography.* Berkeley: University of California Press, 1997.

Lie, John. *Zainichi (Koreans in Japan): Diasporic Nationalism and Postcolonial Identity.* Berkeley: University of California Press, 2008.

Lohr, Eric. *Nationalizing the Russian Empire: The Campaign against Enemy Aliens during World War I.* Cambridge, MA: Harvard University Press, 2003.

——. *Russian Citizenship: From Empire to Soviet Union.* Cambridge, MA: Harvard University Press, 2012.

Lucassen, Jan, and Leo Lucassen. *Migration, Migration History, History: Old Paradigms and New Perspectives.* Bern: P. Lang, 1999.

Lukin, Alexander. "Russian Views of China, Korea, and the Regional Order in Northeast Asia." In *Korea at the Center: Dynamics of Regionalism in Northeast Asia*, edited by Charles K. Armstrong, Gilbert Rozman, Samuel S. Kim, and Stephen Kotkin, 15–34. Armonk, NY: M. E. Sharpe, 2006.

Lukoianov, Igor V. "The Bezobrazovtsy." In *The Russo-Japanese War in Global Perspective: World War Zero*, edited by John Steinberg, Bruce W. Menning, David Schimmelpenninck van der Oye, David Wolff, and Shinji Yokote, 65–86. Leiden: Brill, 2005.

MacMurray, John Van Antwerp. *Treaties and Agreements With and Concerning China, 1894–1919.* Vol. 1. New York: Oxford University Press, 1921.

Malozemoff, Andrew. *Russian Far Eastern Policy, 1881–1904.* Berkeley: University of California Press, 1958.

Marks, Steven. *Road to Power: The Trans-Siberian Railroad and the Colonization of Asian Russia, 1850–1917.* Ithaca: Cornell University Press, 1991.

Martin, Terry. *The Affirmative Action Empire: Nations and Nationalism in the Soviet Union, 1923–1939.* Ithaca: Cornell University Press, 2001.

Matthews, Mervyn. *The Passport Society: Controlling Movement in Russia and the USSR.* Boulder, CO: Westview, 1993.

McKeown, Adam. *Chinese Migrant Networks and Cultural Change: Peru, Chicago, Hawaii, 1900–1936.* Chicago: University of Chicago Press, 2001.

——. "Conceptualizing Chinese Diasporas, 1842–1949." *Journal of Asian Studies* 58, no. 2 (May 1999): 306–37.

——. "Global Migration, 1846–1940." *Journal of World History* 15, no. 2 (June 2004): 155–89.

——. *Melancholy Order: Asian Migration and the Globalization of Borders, 1834–1939.* New York: Columbia University Press, 2008.

Moon, Yumi. *Populist Collaborators: The Ilchinhoe and the Japanese Colonization of Korea, 1896–1910.* Ithaca: Cornell University Press, 2013.

Morris-Suzuki, Tessa. *To the Diamond Mountains: A Hundred-Year Journey through China and Korea.* Lanham, MD: Rowman & Littlefield, 2010.

Ngai, Mae. *Impossible Subjects: Illegal Aliens and the Making of Modern America.* Princeton: Princeton University Press, 2004.

O Sŏng. "Insam sangin kwa kŭmsam chŏngch'aek" [Ginseng merchants and restrictions on ginseng trade]. In *Chosŏn hugi sangin yŏn'gu,* 8–58. Seoul: Ilchogak, 1989.

Ong, Aihwa. *Flexible Citizenship: The Cultural Logics of Transnationality.* Durham, NC: Duke University Press, 1999.

Paasi, Anssi. *Territories, Boundaries, and Consciousness: The Changing Geographies of the Finnish-Russian Boundary.* Chichester, UK: J. Wiley & Sons, 1996.

Paichadze, Svetlana, and Philip Seaton, eds. *Voices from the Shifting Russo-Japanese Border: Karafuto/Sakhalin.* Abingdon, UK: Routledge, 2015.

Paine, S. C. M. *Imperial Rivals: China, Russia, and Their Disputed Frontier.* Armonk, NY: M. E. Sharpe, 1996.

——. *The Sino-Japanese War of 1894–1895: Perceptions, Power, and Primacy.* Cambridge: Cambridge University Press, 2003.

Pak, B. B. *Rossiiskaia diplomatiia i Koreia. Kniga vtoraia. 1888–1897* [Russian diplomacy and Korea. Book 2]. Irkutsk: Irkutskii GPU, 1998.

Pak, B. D. *Bor'ba Rossiiskikh Koreitsev za nezavisimost' Korei, 1905–1919* [Struggle of Russian Koreans for the independence of Korea]. Moscow: IV RAN, 2009.

——. *Koreitsy v Rossiiskoi imperii* [Koreans in the Russian Empire]. 2nd ed. Irkutsk: Mezhdunarodnyi tsentr koreevedeniia MGU, 1994.

——. *Koreitsy v Sovetskoi Rossii: 1917-konets 30-kh godov* [Koreans in Soviet Russia: 1917–late 1930s]. Irkutsk: Irkutskii GPU, 1995.

——. *Rossiia i Koreia* [Russia and Korea]. Moscow: Nauka, 1979.

Pak, Hwan. *Chaeso Hanin minjok undongsa: yŏngu hyŏnhwang kwa charyo haesŏl* [History of the Korean nationalist movement in the Soviet Union: The current state of research and examination of materials]. Seoul: Kukhak Charyowŏn, 1998.

Pak Kyŏngsuk. "Singminji sigi (1910–1945) Chosŏn ŭi in'gu tongt'ae wa kujo" [Situation and structure of the population of Chosŏn during the colonial period]. *Han'guk in'guhak* 32, no. 2 (August 2009): 29–58.

Palais, James B. *Politics and Policy in Traditional Korea.* Cambridge, MA: Harvard University Press, 1975.

Pang, Kijung, Michael Shin, and Yongsŏp Kim. *Landlords, Peasants, and Intellectuals in Modern Korea.* Ithaca: East Asia Program, Cornell University, 2005.

Park, Hyun-Gwi. *The Displacement of Borders among Russian Koreans in Northeast Asia.* Amsterdam: Amsterdam University Press, 2018.

Park, Hyun Ok. *Two Dreams in One Bed: Empire, Social Life, and the Origins of the North Korean Revolution in Manchuria.* Durham, NC: Duke University Press, 2005.

Patterson, Wayne. *The Korean Frontier in America: Immigration to Hawaii, 1896–1910.* Honolulu: University of Hawai'i Press, 1988.

Perdue, Peter C. "Boundaries, Maps, and Movement: Chinese, Russian, and Mongolian Empires in Early Modern Central Eurasia." *International History Review* 20, no. 2 (1998): 263–86.

———. *China Marches West: The Qing Conquest of Central Eurasia*. Cambridge, MA: Belknap Press of Harvard University Press, 2005.

Petrov, A. I. *Istoriia Kitaitsev v Rossii. 1856–1917 gody* [History of Chinese in Russia. 1856–1917]. St. Petersburg: OOO "Beresta," 2003.

———. *Koreiskaia diaspora na Dal'nem Vostoke Rossii, 60–90-e gody XIX veka* [Korean diaspora in the Russian Far East, 1860–1890s]. Vladivostok: DVO RAN, 2000.

———. *Koreiskaia diaspora na Dal'nem Vostoke Rossii, 1897–1917 gg.* [Korean diaspora in the Russian Far East, 1897–1917]. Vladivostok: DVO RAN, 2001.

Piao, Changyu. "The History of Koreans in China and the Yanbian Korean Autonomous Prefecture." In *Koreans in China*, edited by Dae-Sook Suh and Edward Schultz, 44–77. Honolulu: Center for Korean Studies, University of Hawai'i, 1990.

Plokhy, Serhii. *The Cossacks and Religion in Early Modern Ukraine*. Oxford: Oxford University Press, 2001.

Pyŏn Chusŭng. "Chosŏn hugi yumin ŭi pukpang pyŏn'gyŏng yuip kwa kŭ silt'ae" [Situation of the flow of migrants into the northern border region in late Chosŏn]. *Kukhak yŏn'gu* 13 (December 2008): 195–223.

Reardon-Anderson, James. *Reluctant Pioneers: China's Expansion Northward, 1644–1937*. Stanford: Stanford University Press, 2005.

Remnev, Anatolyi. "Siberia and the Russian Far East in the Imperial Geography of Power." In *Russian Empire: Space, People, Power, 1700–1930*, edited by Jane Burbank, Mark von Hagen, and Anatolyi Remnev, 425–54. Bloomington: Indiana University Press, 2007.

Rieber, Alfred. *The Struggle for the Eurasian Borderlands: From the Rise of Early Modern Empires to the End of the First World War*. Cambridge: Cambridge University Press, 2014.

Robinson, Kenneth R. "Centering the King of Chosŏn: Aspects of Korean Maritime Diplomacy, 1392–1592." *Journal of Asian Studies* 59, no. 1 (February 2000): 109–25.

———. "From Raiders to Traders: Border Security and Border Control in Early Chosŏn, 1392–1450." *Korean Studies* 16 (1992): 94–115.

Rouse, Roger. "Mexican Migration and the Social Space of Postmodernism." *Diaspora* 1 (1991): 8–23.

Ruggie, John. "Territoriality and Beyond: Problematizing Modernity in International Relations." *International Organization* 47 (1992): 139–74.

Ryang, Sonia. "The Great Kanto Earthquake and the Massacre of Koreans in 1923: Notes on Japan's Modern National Sovereignty." *Anthropological Quarterly* 76, no. 4 (Autumn 2003): 731–48.

Ryang, Sonia, and John Lie, eds. *Diaspora without Homeland: Being Korean in Japan*. Berkeley: University of California Press, 2009.

Ryu Sŭngju. "Chosŏn hugi sŏ Kando ijumin e taehan ilgoch'al: 'Kangbuk ilgi' ŭi haeje e put'yŏ" [Study of migrants in west Kando in late Chosŏn: Annotating "Diary of the North"]. *Asea yŏn'gu* 21, no. 1 (1978): 297–317.

Safran, William. "Diasporas in Modern Societies: Myths of Homeland and Return." *Diaspora* 1 (1991): 83–99.

Sahlins, Peter. *Boundaries: The Making of France and Spain in the Pyrenees*. Berkeley: University of California Press, 1989.

———. *Unnaturally French: Foreign Citizens in the Old Regime and After*. Ithaca: Cornell University Press, 2004.

Saveliev, Igor, and Yuri Pestushko. "Dangerous Rapprochement: Russia and Japan in the First World War, 1914–1916." *Acta Slavica Iaponica* 18 (2001): 19–41.

Schimmelpenninck van der Oye, David. "The Immediate Origins of the War." In *The Russo-Japanese War in Global Perspective: World War Zero*, edited by John W. Steinberg, Bruce W. Menning, David Schimmelpenninck van der Oye, David Wolff, and Shinji Yokote, 23–44. Leiden: Brill, 2005.

Schlesinger, Jonathan. *A World Trimmed with Fur: Wild Things, Pristine Places, and the Natural Fringes of Qing Rule*. Stanford: Stanford University Press, 2017.

Schmid, Andre. *Korea between Empires: 1895–1919*. New York: Columbia University Press, 2003.

———. "Tributary Relations and the Qing-Chosŏn Frontier on Mount Paektu." In *Chinese State at the Borders*, edited by Diana Lary, 128–50. Vancouver: University of British Columbia Press, 2008.

Scott, James C. *The Art of Not Being Governed: An Anarchist History of Upland Southeast Asia*. New Haven: Yale University Press, 2009.

———. *Seeing Like a State: How Certain Schemes to Improve the Human Condition Have Failed*. New Haven: Yale University Press, 1998.

Scully, Eileen P. *Bargaining with the State from Afar: American Citizenship in Treaty Port China, 1844–1942*. New York: Columbia University Press, 2001.

Shan, Patrick Fuliang. "Insecurity, Outlawry and Social Order: Banditry in China's Heilongjiang Frontier Region, 1900–1931." *Journal of Social History* 40, no. 1 (2006): 25–54.

Shin, Susan S. "Some Aspects of Landlord-Tenant Relations in Yi Dynasty Korea." *Occasional Papers on Korea* no. 3 (June 1975): 49–88.

Shin Yŏng-ha. "Landlordism in the Late Yi Dynasty (I)." *Korea Journal* 18, no. 6 (June 1978): 25–32.

———. "Landlordism in the Late Yi Dynasty (II)." *Korea Journal* 18, no. 7 (July 1978): 22–29.

Siegelbaum, Lewis H. "Another 'Yellow Peril': Chinese Migrants in the Russian Far East and the Russian Reaction before 1917." *Modern Asian Studies* 12, no. 2 (1978): 307–30.

Sin Kisŏk. "Kando kwisok munje" [The Kando jurisdiction question]. In *Chungang taehakkyo nonmunjip*, 1–51. Seoul: Chungang Taehakkyo, 1955.

Sin'kevich, I. A. *Istoriia trudovoi immigratsii v prigranichnykh regionakh Dal'nego Vostoka* [History of labor immigration in the border regions of the Far East]. Moscow: RITS ISPI RAN, 2003.

Slezkine, Yuri. "The USSR as a Communal Apartment, or How a Socialist State Promoted Ethnic Particularism." *Slavic Review* 53, no. 2 (Summer 1994): 414–52.

Slocum, John W. "Who, and When, Were the Inorodtsy? The Evolution of the Category of 'Aliens' in Imperial Russia." *Russian Review* 57 (April 1998): 173–90.

Smith, Alison K. *For the Common Good and Their Own Well-Being: Social Estates in Imperial Russia*. Oxford: Oxford University Press, 2014.

Song, Nianshen. "The Journey towards 'No Man's Land': Interpreting the China-Korea Borderland within Imperial and Colonial Contexts." *Journal of Asian Studies* 76, no. 4 (2017): 1035–58.

———. "My Land, My People: Discourses and Practices in the Tumen River Demarcation, 1860s-1910s." Ph.D. diss., University of Chicago, 2013.

Sorokina, T. N. *Khoziaistvennaia deiatel'nost' kitaiskikh poddannykh na Dal'nem Vostoke Rossii i politika administratsii Priamurskogo kraia (konets XIX–nachalo XX vv.)* [Economic activity of Chinese subjects in the Russian Far East and political administration of the Priamur krai (end of nineteenth to beginning of twentieth century)]. Omsk: Izdanie OmGU, 1999.

St. John, Rachel. *Line in the Sand: A History of the Western U.S.-Mexico Border*. Princeton: Princeton University Press, 2011.

Steinwedel, Charles. "Making Social Groups, One Person at a Time: The Identification of Individuals by Estate, Religious Confession, and Ethnicity in Late Imperial Russia." In *Documenting Individual Identity: The Development of State Practices in the Modern World*, edited by Jane Caplan and John Torpey, 67–82. Princeton: Princeton University Press, 2001.

Stephan, John J. *The Russian Far East: A History*. Stanford: Stanford University Press, 1994.

Sunderland, Willard. "Peasant Pioneering: Russian Peasant Settlers Describe Colonization and the Eastern Frontier, 1880s–1910s." *Journal of Social History* 34, no. 4 (2001): 895–922.

——. *Taming the Wild Field: Colonization and Empire on the Russian Steppe*. Ithaca: Cornell University Press, 2004.

Suny, Ronald Grigor. *The Revenge of the Past: Nationalism, Revolution, and the Collapse of the Soviet Union*. Stanford: Stanford University Press, 1993.

Taeuber, Irene. "The Population Potential of Postwar Korea." *Far Eastern Quarterly* 5, no. 3 (May 1946): 289–307.

Taeuber, Irene, and George Barclay. "Korea and the Koreans in the Northeast Asian Region." *Population Index* 16, no. 4 (October 1950): 278–97.

Thomson, Janice E. *Mercenaries, Pirates, and Sovereigns: State-Building and Extraterritorial Violence in Early Modern Europe*. Princeton: Princeton University Press, 1994.

Thongchai, Winichakul. *Siam Mapped: A History of the Geo-Body of a Nation*. Honolulu: University of Hawai'i Press, 1994.

Tilly, Charles. "Transplanted Networks." In *Immigration Reconsidered: History, Sociology, and Politics*, edited by Virginia Yans-McLaughlin, 79–95. New York: Oxford University Press, 1990.

Torpey, John C. *The Invention of the Passport: Surveillance, Citizenship, and the State*. Cambridge: Cambridge University Press, 2000.

Treadgold, Donald W. *The Great Siberian Migration: Government and Peasant in Resettlement from Emancipation to the First World War*. Princeton: Princeton University Press, 1957.

——. "Russian Expansion in the Light of Turner's Study of the American Frontier." *Agricultural History* 26, no. 4 (October 1952): 147–52.

Trewartha, Glenn, and Wilbur Zelinsky. "Population Distribution and Change in Korea, 1925–1949." *Geographical Review* 45, no. 1 (January 1955): 1–26.

Troitskaia, N. A., K. B. Abramova, and O. V. Ustalova, eds. *Ukazatel' dokumentov po istorii goroda Vladivostoka* [Guide to documents on the history of Vladivostok]. Vladivostok: RGIA DV, 2000.

Troitskaia, N. A., et al., eds. *Bibliograficheskii ukazatel' gazet i zhurnalov, vykhodivshikh na Russkom Dal'nem Vostoke do 1922 g. i khraniashchikhsia v bibliotekakh i arkhivakh regiona* [Bibliographical guide to newspapers and journals published in the Russian Far East until 1922 and preserved in the libraries and archives of the region]. Vladivostok: RGIA DV, 2000.

Ǔn Chŏngt'ae. "Taehan chegukki 'Kando munje' ǔi ch'ui wa 'singminhwa'" [The "Kando question" under the empire of the Great Han and issue of "colonization"]. *Yŏksa munje yŏn'gu* 17, no. 4 (2007): 93–122.

Von Hagen, Mark. "Empires, Borderlands, and Diasporas: Eurasia as Anti-Paradigm for the Post-Soviet Era." *American Historical Review* 109, no. 2 (April 2004): 445–68.

Vradiy, Sergey Yu. "Primorskii Borderland on the 'Map of Russia' *Aguk-yeojido*." *Eurasia Border Review* 3, no. 2 (Fall 2012): 103–18.

Wada Haruki. "Koreans in the Soviet Far East, 1917–1937." In *Koreans in the Soviet Union*, edited by Dae-Sook Suh, 24–59. Honolulu: Center for Korean Studies, University of Hawai'i, 1987.

Walker, Brett L. *The Conquest of Ainu Lands: Ecology and Culture in Japanese Expansion, 1590–1800.* Berkeley: University of California Press, 2001.

Wang, Gungwu. "A Note on the Origins of Hua-Ch'iao." In *Community and Nation: Essays on Southeast Asia and the Chinese,* edited by Gungwu Wang and Anthony Reid, 118–27. Singapore: Published for the Asian Studies Association of Australia by Heinemann Educational Books (Asia), 1981.

Watt, Lori. *When Empire Comes Home: Repatriation and Reintegration in Postwar Japan.* Cambridge, MA: Harvard University Asia Center, 2009.

White, Richard. *The Middle Ground: Indians, Empires, and Republics in the Great Lakes Region, 1650–1815.* Cambridge: Cambridge University Press, 1991.

Wigen, Kären. "Culture, Power, and Place: The New Landscapes of East Asian Regionalism." *American Historical Review* 104, no. 4 (October 1999): 1183–1201.

Wilson, Thomas M., and Hastings Donnan. *Border Identities: Nation and State at International Frontiers.* Cambridge: Cambridge University Press, 1998.

Woodruff, Phillip. "Status and Lineage among the Jurchens of the Korean Northeast in the Mid-Fifteenth Century." *Central and Inner Asian Studies* 1 (1987): 117–54.

Yamabe Kentarō. *Ilche kangjŏm ha ŭi Han'guk kŭndaesa* [Modern Korean history during the Japanese occupation]. Translated by Yi Hyŏnhŭi. Seoul: Samgwang Ch'ulp'ansa, 1998.

Yang T'aejin. *1902 nyŏn pyŏn'gye hojŏgan* [Household registers of the border area in 1902]. Seoul: Pŏpkyŏng Ch'ulp'ansa, 1992.

Yi Sanghyŏp. "Chosŏn chŏn'gi pukpang samin kwa min ŭi tonghyang" [Resettled people in the northern region and their character in the early Chosŏn period]. *Kangwŏn sahak* 17–18 (2002): 177–95.

Yi T'aejin. *Kojong sidae ŭi chae chomyŏng* [Reassessment of the Kojong era]. Seoul: T'aehaksa, 2000.

Yi Tongjin. "1872 nyŏn 'Kangbuk' ŭi Chosŏnin sahoe" [Chosŏn society in the "north" in 1872]. *Tongbuga yŏksa nonch'ong* 8 (2005): 285–332.

———. "1900-nyŏn 'Kangbuk' ŭi Chosŏnin: 'Kangbuk ilgi' e nat'ananŭn pyŏn'gyŏng kwa pyŏn'gyŏngmin" [Koreans in the "north" in 1900: Border and border people in "Diary of the North"]. *Manju yŏn'gu* 15, no. 6 (2013): 47–100.

Yi Uk. "17–18 segi pŏmwŏl sagŏn ŭl t'onghae pon Hamgyŏng-do chumin ŭi kyŏngje saenghwal" [Economic activities of residents of Hamgyŏng province seen through the lens of illegal border crossings in the seventeenth to eighteenth centuries]. *Han'guk kukhak chinhŭng yŏn'guwŏn* (2005): 139–64.

Yoon, Sharon. "Re-Conceptualizing the Enclave in an Era of Transnationalism: Ethnic Solidarity and Upward Mobility in the Korean Enclave in Beijing." Ph.D. diss., Princeton University, 2013.

Young, C. Walter. *Korean Problems in Manchuria as Factors in the Sino-Japanese Dispute: An Analytical and Interpretative Study.* Geneva, 1932.

Young, Louise. *Japan's Total Empire: Manchuria and the Culture of Wartime Imperialism.* Berkeley: University of California Press, 1998.

Yu Pyŏngho. "Pukkando Hanin ŭi kukchŏk ŭl tullŏssan Ch'ŏng-Il yangguk ŭi kyosŏp e taehan yŏn'gu—t'onggambu pa'ch'ulso sigi rŭl chungsim ŭro" [Research on Sino-Japanese talks about the citizenship of Koreans in northern Kando during the time of the field office of the resident-general]. *Chungangsaron* 21 (2005): 456–97.

Zabrovskaia, Larisa. "1899 Treaty and Its Impact on the Development of the Chinese-Korean Trade (1896–1905)." *Korea Journal* 31, no. 4 (Winter 1991): 29–39.

———. "Consequences of Korean Emigration to Jiandao." *Korea Journal* 33, no. 1 (Spring 1993): 69–78.

Zatsepine, Victor. *Beyond the Amur: Frontier Encounters between China and Russia, 1850–1930*. Vancouver: University of British Columbia Press, 2017.

——. "Remembering the Blagoveshchensk Massacre: The Sino-Russian War and Global Imperialism." In *Beyond Suffering: Recounting War in Modern China*, edited by James Flath and Norman Smith, 107–29. Vancouver: University of British Columbia Press, 2011.

Index

Page numbers followed by letters *f*, *m*, and *t* refer to figures, maps, and tables, respectively.

western borderlands, in Russian empire, 111, 118–19, 120

West/Western powers: Chosŏn Korea's opening to, 56, 86–87; and extraterritoriality treaties in East Asia, 50–51, 69; and "high diplomacy" in East Asia, 3, 56, 88; Korean migrants' knowledge of, as asset, 63

Wilson, Woodrow, 226

Witte, Sergei, 89n41, 90

Workers' Promotion Association (Kwŏnŏphoe), 225, 233, 235

World War II: Japan's defeat in, 12, 246; Korean diaspora at end of, 13; repatriation program following, 246; and resettlement programs, interruption in, 161; Vladivostok as "closed city" after, 247n37

Wu Dacheng, 80

Xu Taishen, 97

Yalu River: area along, 23; as Chosŏn-Qing boundary, 25, 25m, 39, 40; source of, missions to find, 39, 40–41, 84–86; timber concession on, 89

yellow race, categorization of Asians as, 137–39, 171

Yi Chungha, 75n2, 85, 86

Yi Kwangha, 93

Yi Pŏmyun, 93, 95, 96–98, 104, 224

Yi Sŏnggye, 26, 30

Yi T'aejin, 64n77

Yi Tonghwi, 235

Yuan Shikai, 81, 84

Yun Hyŏp, 45, 46

Yu Ŭiyang, 23–24, 29–30, 35

Studies of the Weatherhead East Asian Institute
Columbia University

Selected Titles

(Complete list at: http://weai.columbia.edu/publications/studies-weai/)

Statebuilding by Imposition: Resistance and Control in Colonial Taiwan and the Philippines, by Reo Matsuzaki. Cornell University Press, 2019.

Nation-Empire: Ideology and Rural Youth Mobilization in Japan and Its Colonies, by Sayaka Chatani. Cornell University Press, 2019.

The Invention of Madness: State, Society, and the Insane in Modern China, by Emily Baum. University of Chicago Press, 2018.

Fixing Landscape: A Techno-Poetic History of China's Three Gorges, by Corey Byrnes. Columbia University Press, 2018.

Japan's Imperial Underworlds: Intimate Encounters at the Borders of Empire, by David Ambaras. Cambridge University Press, 2018.

Heroes and Toilers: Work as Life in Postwar North Korea, 1953–1961, by Cheehyung Harrison Kim. Columbia University Press, 2018.

Electrified Voices: How the Telephone, Phonograph, and Radio Shaped Modern Japan, 1868–1945, by Kerim Yasar. Columbia University Press, 2018.

Making Two Vietnams: War and Youth Identities, 1965–1975, by Olga Dror. Cambridge University Press, 2018.

A Misunderstood Friendship: Mao Zedong, Kim Il-sung, and Sino–North Korean Relations, 1949–1976, by Zhihua Shen and Yafeng Xia. Columbia University Press, 2018.

Raising China's Revolutionaries: Modernizing Childhood for Cosmopolitan Nationalists and Liberated Comrades, by Margaret Mih Tillman. Columbia University Press, 2018.

Buddhas and Ancestors: Religion and Wealth in Fourteenth-Century Korea, by Juhn Y. Ahn. University of Washington Press, 2018.

Idly Scribbling Rhymers: Poetry, Print, and Community in Nineteenth Century Japan, by Robert Tuck. Columbia University Press, 2018.

China's War on Smuggling: Law, Economic Life, and the Making of the Modern State, 1842–1965, by Philip Thai. Columbia University Press, 2018.

Forging the Golden Urn: The Qing Empire and the Politics of Reincarnation in Tibet, by Max Oidtmann. Columbia University Press, 2018.

The Battle for Fortune: State-Led Development, Personhood, and Power among Tibetans in China, by Charlene Makley. Cornell University Press, 2018.

Aesthetic Life: Beauty and Art in Modern Japan, by Miya Elise Mizuta Lippit. Harvard University Asia Center, 2018.

Where the Party Rules: The Rank and File of China's Communist State, by Daniel Koss. Cambridge University Press, 2018.

Resurrecting Nagasaki: Reconstruction and the Formation of Atomic Narratives, by Chad R. Diehl. Cornell University Press, 2018.

China's Philological Turn: Scholars, Textualism, and the Dao in the Eighteenth Century, by Ori Sela. Columbia University Press, 2018.

Making Time: Astronomical Time Measurement in Tokugawa Japan, by Yulia Frumer. University of Chicago Press, 2018.

Mobilizing Without the Masses: Control and Contention in China, by Diana Fu. Cambridge University Press, 2018.

Post-Fascist Japan: Political Culture in Kamakura after the Second World War, by Laura Hein. Bloomsbury, 2018.

China's Conservative Revolution: The Quest for a New Order, 1927–1949, by Brian Tsui. Cambridge University Press, 2018.

Promiscuous Media: Film and Visual Culture in Imperial Japan, 1926–1945, by Hikari Hori. Cornell University Press, 2018.

The End of Japanese Cinema: Industrial Genres, National Times, and Media Ecologies, by Alexander Zahlten. Duke University Press, 2017.

The Chinese Typewriter: A History, by Thomas S. Mullaney. The MIT Press, 2017.

Forgotten Disease: Illnesses Transformed in Chinese Medicine, by Hilary A. Smith. Stanford University Press, 2017.

Borrowing Together: Microfinance and Cultivating Social Ties, by Becky Yang Hsu. Cambridge University Press, 2017.

Food of Sinful Demons: Meat, Vegetarianism, and the Limits of Buddhism in Tibet, by Geoffrey Barstow. Columbia University Press, 2017.

Youth For Nation: Culture and Protest in Cold War South Korea, by Charles R. Kim. University of Hawaii Press, 2017.

Socialist Cosmopolitanism: The Chinese Literary Universe, 1945–1965, by Nicolai Volland. Columbia University Press, 2017.

The Social Life of Inkstones: Artisans and Scholars in Early Qing China, by Dorothy Ko. University of Washington Press, 2017.

Darwin, Dharma, and the Divine: Evolutionary Theory and Religion in Modern Japan, by G. Clinton Godart. University of Hawaii Press, 2017.

Dictators and Their Secret Police: Coercive Institutions and State Violence, by Sheena Chestnut Greitens. Cambridge University Press, 2016.

The Cultural Revolution on Trial: Mao and the Gang of Four, by Alexander C. Cook. Cambridge University Press, 2016.

Inheritance of Loss: China, Japan, and the Political Economy of Redemption After Empire, by Yukiko Koga. University of Chicago Press, 2016.

Homecomings: The Belated Return of Japan's Lost Soldiers, by Yoshikuni Igarashi. Columbia University Press, 2016.

Samurai to Soldier: Remaking Military Service in Nineteenth-Century Japan, by D. Colin Jaundrill. Cornell University Press, 2016.

The Red Guard Generation and Political Activism in China, by Guobin Yang. Columbia University Press, 2016.

Accidental Activists: Victim Movements and Government Accountability in Japan and South Korea, by Celeste L. Arrington. Cornell University Press, 2016.

Ming China and Vietnam: Negotiating Borders in Early Modern Asia, by Kathlene Baldanza. Cambridge University Press, 2016.